T0113451

VIRTUAL EQUALITY

THE
MAINSTREAMING
OF GAY AND LESBIAN
LIBERATION

VIRTUAL EQUALITY

URVASHI VAID

ANCHOR BOOKS
A DIVISION OF RANDOM HOUSE, INC.
NEW YORK

ANCHOR BOOKS TRADE PAPERBACK EDITION

The Library of Congress has cataloged the Anchor hardcover edition as follows:
Vaid, Urvashi.
Virtual equality : the mainstreaming of gay and lesbian liberation / Urvashi Vaid.
p.   cm.
Includes index.
1. Gay liberation movement—United States.   2. Homosexuality—United States.
3. Gay rights—United States.   I. Title.
HQ76.8.U5V35   1995   305.9′0664—dc20
95-16869   CIP

ISBN-10: 0-385-47299-4

ISBN-13: 978-0-385-47299-9

Book design by Terry Karydes

www.anchorbooks.com

Printed in the United States of America

144915995

FOR KATE—

lover and soulmate

ACKNOWLEDGMENTS

My deepest debt is to the activists whose determination created, and still sustains, the gay, lesbian, bisexual, and transgender movement. I thank friends at *Gay Community News*, NGLTF, Roadwork and Sisterfire, LIPS, LMF, ACT UP, Lambda Legal Defense and Education Fund, the Blue Mountain Groups, Provincetown Positive/People With AIDS Coalition, the South Asian Lesbian and Gay Association, Trikone, and all my punk-rock friends in Boston.

For assistance with research, documents and facts, thanks go to: Chip Berlet and Jean Hardisty at Political Research Associates; the Data Center; Chai Feldblum and the Federal Legislative Clinic at Georgetown Law Center; Suzanne Goldberg at Lambda Legal Defense and Education Fund; Robin Kane and the staff of the National Gay and Lesbian Task Force; Greg Herek; Cathy Woolard at the Human Rights Campaign Fund; the National Museum and Archive of Lesbian and Gay History at New York City Lesbian and Gay Community Services Center; Brenda Marsten at the Human Sexuality Archives, Cornell University; countless friends on the Internet, in particular at GayNet, Soc.motts, the Gay and Lesbian Community Forum at America Online; and the Queer Resources Directory.

Nearly sixty movement activists generously gave me hours of time for formal interviews, which helped shape the context of this book. Thank you to: Diane Abbitt, Virginia Apuzzo, David Barr, Vic Basile, Leslie Belzberg, Roberta Bennett, Joan Biren, Susie Bright, Charlotte Bunch, Richard Burns, Larry Bush, Leslie Cagan, the late Michael Callen, Kevin Cathcart, Angela Davis, Marty Delaney, Chai Feldblum, Ruth Finkelstein, Nanette Gartrell, Gilberto Gerald, Rebecca Hensler, Alan Hergott, Amber Hollibaugh, Marjorie Hill, Sue Hyde, Rev. Jesse Jackson, June Jordan, Larry Kramer, Jeff Levi, Steve Lew, Mary Matalin, Rodger McFarlane, Tim McFeeley, Dee Mosbacher, Ralph Neas, Stanley Newman, Ann Northrop, Torie Osborn, Melinda Paras, Suzanne Pharr, Betty Powell, Eric Rofes, Richard Rouillard, Michael Seltzer, Ben Schatz, Jeff Soref, Peter Staley, Charles Stewart, Tom Stoddard, Tim Sweeney, Hank Tavera, Carmen Vazquez, Reggie Williams, Phill Wilson, and Maxine Wolfe.

Several other writers and friends contributed insights and support in countless informal conversations: Terry Anderson, Maggie Barrett, Nancy Bereano, Kevin Berrill, Robert Bray, Claudia Brenner, Margaret Cerullo, Marla Erlien, Ruth Eisenberg, Liz Galst, Richard Goldstein, Mark Harrington, Barbara Herbert, Holly Hughes, Nan Hunter, Lisa Keen, Michael Klein, Frances Kunreuther, Sandy Lowe, Michael Marco, Eric Marcus, Armistead Maupin, Jean McGuire, Joel Meyerowitz, Tim Miller, the late Paul Monette, Phranc, Nancy Polikoff, Minnie Bruce Pratt, Peri Jude Radecic, Cindy Rizzo, Doug Sadownick, Sarah Schulman, Curtis Shepard, Michelangelo Signorile, John Silberman, Barbara Smith, Victoria Starr, Andrew Sullivan, Ann Viitala, Linda Villarosa.

My sincere gratitude goes to my overworked friends who took the time to read countless drafts of chapters or the entire manuscript, and whose comments helped make this a better book: Susan Allee, Michael Bronski, Richard Burns, Kevin Cathcart, John D'Emilio, Chai Feldblum, Amy Hoffman, Sue Hyde, Eric Rofes, and Ivy Young.

Heartfelt thanks go to the wonderful Donald Huppert, confidant, transcriber, and computer consultant, who gave me hundreds of hours of time, advice, and loving support throughout the gestation of this book. Thanks are also due to my lecture agents George Greenfield, Lee and Jefferson at Lecture Literary Management for their patience with how little I could do!

My gay and lesbian family in Provincetown and around the country gave me the emotional and political foundation from which everything else followed. In particular, thank you to Susan Allee, Nancy Asch, Leslie Belzberg, Eileen Bindell and Susan Goldberg, Sandra Bolin, Mark Bulman, Richard Burns, Kevin Cathcart, Ruth Eisenberg and Binnie Miller, Melissa Etheridge and Julie Cypher, Mary Farmer and Laura Flegel, Roslyn Garfield and Phyllis Temple, Roz Gruber, Jade McGleughlin, Alan Hergott and Curt Shepard, Amy Hoffman and Roberta Stone, Tom Huth, Wendy Johnson, Barry Krost and John DeShane, Sue Metro and Debbie Nadolney, the gang at Mussel Beach Gym, Betsy Ringel and Kirk Kolodner, Katina Rodis, Anne Lewis, Pasquale Natale, Jim Rann, Eric Rofes and Crispin Hollings, Greg Russo and Ken Russo, Will Seng, Tim Stein, Stanley Tiploff, Tom Walsh and Don Richards, Trudy Wood and Jesse Miguel Wood, Thalia Zedek and Julie Hardin, and the many friends in Provincetown who heard my doubts and encouraged me to keep going, no matter what.

Thanks are also due to my other families for their strong support throughout these two years. My parents, Krishna B. Vaid and Champa R. Vaid, inspire me with their example as writers and their willingness to change. My sisters, Rachna Vaid and Jyotsna Vaid, have been unfailing in their good humor and love. My brothers-in-law, Ramesh Jagannathan and Ram Menon, offered wonderful support and great e-mail. Thanks to my niece Kaveri for her interest in politics, to my nephew Shantanu for his great sense of fun, to Alka for being so smart, and to Alok for being so sweet! On the other side of my family, I want to thank all the Clintons (from Syracuse, not Little Rock), thanks especially to 'Dad,' or, as I still call him, Mr. Clinton; Bill and Mary; Jim and Eileen; and all the Concannons (Mary, Michael, Grace and Paul)!

Copy editor Frances Apt did an extraordinary job cleaning up messy prose and pushing me to write more precisely.

This book is in memory of a number of friends, lost to AIDS or other illness, whose work and love I remember, and whose loss I still mourn: Bob Adams, Paul Anderson, Steve Ansolabahere, Bob Andrews, Bill Bailey, Walta Borawski, Mark Bulman, Kevin Caligeri, Michael Callen, Sioung Huat Chua, Craig Davidson, Ken Dawson, Steve Endean, Mike Gamache, George Gewirtz, Craig Harris, Byron Harris, Raymond Hopkins, Greg Howe, Bill Hunt, Ian Johnson, Lew Katoff, John Kelley, Nathan Kolodner, Andy Kopkind, Mark Kostopolous, Gabe Kruks, Carlton Lee, Chris Locke, Peter Medoff, Paul Monette, Brandy Moore, John Preston, Mike Riegle, Marlon Riggs, Jim Ryan, Assoto Saint, Phillip Shehadi, Michael Shower, Drew Siegel, Steve Smith, Michael Weltmann, and so many others.

More than any others, four people made this book possible.

I am indebted to my literary agent, Jed Mattes, for his wise and steadying advice and for his keen political insights. Jed saw this as a book from a shaky outline, and pushed me to imagine a much larger project.

Anchor Books' publisher Martha Levin's commitment to presenting feminist politics afforded me the chance to make this real.

My anchor at Anchor Books, editor Charles Flowers, infused this book with a care and passion that shows up on every single page. For his kindness, calm, and intelligence, all of which saw me through many bleak moments, I will always be grateful.

Finally, I thank the person whose contribution also appears on each page, my love, Kate Clinton, for her kind spirit, her wit, and her endless patience. Our life together makes everything seem possible, especially liberation.

PREFACE

On June 28, 1969, as gay people took to the streets outside the Stonewall Inn, I was ten years old. Three years earlier, my family had emigrated to America, and I still remember the drive from Kennedy Airport to upstate New York, where I grew up, not only for its twelve-hour length, but for my excitement at seeing snow. My father, an accomplished novelist, taught English literature and writing at the State University of New York at Potsdam, while my mother, an equally accomplished teacher and poet, tried for many years to get a job in that little town. We were part of the second large wave of Indian migration to the United States. Questions of assimilation, of crossing cultural borders, and developing an authentic identity marked my coming of age.

My first overtly political act was to write a letter, when I was ten years old, to Richard Nixon, urging him to sign the ABM missile treaty. I never got an answer. In the spring of 1972, when I was thirteen, I gave my first political speech—a pro-McGovern valedictory talk at my junior high school graduation. As the San Francisco gay leader Jim Foster became the first openly gay person to address the Democratic Convention, that same summer, I got ready for high school. I had not heard about gay liberation, but I was already pro–civil rights, antiwar, and a women's libber. Still, my passion was rock-and-roll more than politics, and my first true love was Mick Jagger of the Rolling Stones.

In the summer of 1975, as the Washington gay activist Frank Kameny battled the U.S. Civil Service commission to allow gay federal employment, I graduated from high school and got ready for Vassar. College taught me, without intending to, how to organize. In protests over admissions and financial aid, through the women's group on campus, and through the anti-apartheid group that I helped establish there, I learned all the tools of activism. As I organized, I studied and fell in love—with the Romantic poets, Patti Smith, the Frankfurt School, the Situationist Movement, Shulamith Firestone, a number of my women professors, and all my best girlfriends.

The most formative influences of my college life were the four feminist conferences I helped organize on campus. In 1977, my friends Susan Allee and Betsy Ringel met Amy Horowitz of Roadwork and decided to produce a women's music concert. The result was Olivia Records' Varied Voices of Black Women Tour, which we brought to Poughkeepsie in 1978. The encounter with the women on the tour—notably the late poet Pat Parker and musicians Linda Tillery, Mary Watkins, and Gwen Avery—changed us in profound ways; we had discovered a lesbian culture. Producing Holly Near in 1979, and going to the Michigan Womyn's Music Festival that same year, further exposed me to the national community of lesbians and feminists.

By the end of college, I was sure that I was a lesbian. For me, coming out happened when I first fell in love with a woman. I should have known when my rock-and-roll idol changed from Mick to Patti Smith. I told my sisters immediately, and we worried about breaking the news to our parents. Despite my hesitation about dealing with their reaction, I kept up my political work.

At the time of the first National March on Washington for Lesbian and Gay Rights, on October 14, 1979, I had just turned twenty-one. I had moved to Boston that same month with my best friend, to "join the women's movement." I opted to look for work instead of taking a bus to the march, and I am still mad at myself for not going. Working as a part-time secretary for two lawyers, I threw myself into Boston's feminist, lesbian, and gay communities. In my lesbian group, Lesbians United in Non-Nuclear Action (LUNA), I worked on a civil disobedience action at the Seabrook nuclear plant in New Hampshire. I joined the most important political group in my life in 1980—the nonprofit newspaper *Gay Community News*. Volunteering every Friday night to stuff and mail papers, I formed friendships that would last me a lifetime.

As I moved through law school at Northeastern University in the early 1980s, I realized that the lifetime of many of my friends was to be shorter than we had imagined. AIDS entered my life through my closest gay male friends. Today, as AIDS overwhelms so many men and women I love with its relentless horror, I remember the incredulity and paranoia we felt in those early years as the epidemic emerged. We had no idea then what devastation awaited us. And we still do not have adequate ways to explain to unaffected straight people the terror turned into anger, the anger become numbness, the numbness turned into an unrelenting despair, as the traumatic experience of mass death unfolds and shrouds our lives.

In 1980, I went home to Potsdam to come out. I wanted my parents to hear it from me, not read about my activism in the paper. But I could not get the words out of my mouth. The night I returned to Boston, my sister called with the news that as soon as I left my father had asked her if I was gay; she had said yes. My dread of this disclosure proved worse than their reaction. Over the years, my parents moved from disapproval to incomprehension to acceptance to tremendous support. In some ways, my choice to leave mainstream work for full-time gay political activism was harder for them to accept than my sexual orientation.

By the time HIV was identified in 1983, I was living in Washington, D.C., working as an attorney for the National Prison Project of the American Civil Liberties Union. I still worked with Roadwork to produce women's culture, and when Reagan was re-elected, in 1984, I cofounded a lesbian direct-action group, called LIPS. In 1985, with the encouragement of Mike Riegle, who founded *GCN*'s Prisoners' Project and who died with AIDS in 1991, I began the National Prison Project's work to bring more attention to the treatment of prisoners with HIV and AIDS. Living in Washington led me to meet National Gay Task Force's lobbyist Jeff Levi and its exciting director, Ginny Apuzzo, and I began to consider gay rights work as something to do full time.

When the Second National March on Washington was held, on October 11, 1987, I had quit my legal job at the ACLU and had been working at NGLTF as its public information director for more than a year. Over the next several years, I threw myself into media organizing, developing relationships with grassroots activists, organizing direct actions, devising strategy and policy positions, and eventually, when I became NGLTF's director, trying to raise the money to do all this work. By the time of the Third National March on Washington, on April 25, 1993, I had left NGLTF after six and a half years on its staff, and had begun to work on this book.

I left NGLTF for personal and political reasons. Personally, I grew tired of juggling the pressure of national work with my desire for a personal life. I loved the movement, yet I wanted a fuller life. I wanted time to develop my relationship with Kate, with whom I had maintained a long-distance relationship for five years; and I wanted the time to think and feel, something that the pace of national organizing precluded. On a political level, I left NGLTF because I was not sure that it could do what I felt needed to be done by the movement. At the time I made the decision to leave, in early 1992, I was clear about the importance of the mainstream civil rights work done by the organization—and others like it. Yet I was not clear that this was the work I wanted to do, or that I had the ability to steer the group further in the progressive direction I believed was necessary. A national organization is a cumbersome load; the demands for it to represent a wide array of people are real and well-made. I felt increasingly stifled in acting on the politics of social justice and liberation that I hold dear. Leaving to write was a decision that respected my needs as well as the realities of the organization.

My reasons for writing this book have not been literary or scholarly, but activist and also personal: to gain a better understanding of the problems the gay political movement faces and, in part, to figure out how best to use my own energies. This time of reflection became a chance to assess my political work over the past fifteen years of involvement in gay communities.

In its first incarnation, the book was a consideration of what happened in 1992, why it was such an unusual year for gay politics, and what Bill Clinton's election meant. I vividly recall the night Clinton won, because I walked around in such shock. The candidate we had supported, who had openly embraced us, had won! At the national level, I had seen the gay movement move from the margin of political life during the Reagan and Bush years to the center of the policy-development process. I had seen gay men, in particular, live with the complete destruction and reconstruction of their communities and gay families as a result of AIDS. After my involvement in crafting the national gay and lesbian movement's strategies for several years, I wanted to understand and explain how it happened.

By early 1993, the book had come to be a document of self-criticism more than a history of the movement's accomplishments. I saw the shattering of my own illusions of change, as Clinton did to gay people what most politicians have done, and as our movement experienced the paradox of unprecedented cultural possibility accompanied by the persistence of prejudice and the same stigmatization gay people have challenged for decades.

Out of these observations came the idea of virtual equality—a state of conditional equality based more on the appearance of acceptance by straight America than on genuine civic parity. New leaps in gay access, visibility, and power have not transformed the second-class status of gay, lesbian, bisexual, and transgender people. The political access some have gained has translated poorly to genuine clout, and the lack of an organized grassroots base remains the gay movement's Achilles' heel.

This book begins with an examination of where we stand and ends with a series of specific tasks to be tackled by those interested in doing more. My hope is to bring about a rethinking of our approach to the dilemmas gay people face. As Allen Ginsberg wrote, "America, I'm putting my queer shoulder to the wheel." Let us do just that.

Urvashi Vaid
May 1995

VIRTUAL EQUALITY

CHAPTER ONE

VIRTUAL EQUALITY

A solitude ten thousand fathoms deep
Sustains the bed on which we lie, my dear:
Although I love you, you will have to leap;
Our dream of safety has to disappear.

—*W. H. Auden*

Basically, [Virtual Reality] makes the artificial as realistic as the real.

—*Nicholas Negroponte,* Wired

As the American gay and lesbian movement approaches its sixth decade of political activism, it finds itself at a contradictory juncture: what Dickens would call the best of times and the worst of times. On one level, our movement has been a staggering, if controversial, success; yet on another level, gay and lesbian people remain profoundly stigmatized, struggling against the same crises—in health, violence, discrimination, and social services—that have plagued us for decades. Hundreds of thousands of gay and lesbian Americans are openly integrated into our communities, families, and workplaces. Yet the vast majority of our people remain closeted, still unwilling to openly acknowledge their sexual orientation. A backlash against gay rights swells at the same instant we witness the widest cultural opening gay people have ever experienced; public opinion is deeply divided about how to respond to our emergence from the shadows. Gay and lesbian participation in the cultural, commercial, political, religious, and civic arenas of our society is evident everywhere, and occasionally even celebrated. But in the eyes of most of our straight peers, gay people are still seen as immoral, unnatural, and unhealthy.

Perhaps this state of affairs is merely the inevitable consequence of civil rights progress; as any movement succeeds, vestiges of the old ways persist. Like the civil rights movements that preceded us and on which we model our goals and strategies, we have reached the moment of partial fulfillment. The system has adapted to our existence, but it has still not changed in fundamental ways. We are freer than we were in the 1940s and 1960s, but we have failed to realize true equality or win full acceptance as moral human beings. The modern black civil rights movement began to face this dilemma in the early 1960s, soon after the passage of major federal civil rights legislation, like the Civil Rights Act of 1964 and the Voting Rights Act. Laws were changed, people's lives improved, but the economic condition of large numbers of African Americans remained the same or, indeed, deteriorated over the next thirty years. Racial prejudice stayed in place even as its age-old legal operation was dismantled. The women's liberation movement faced this moment in the late 1970s, as its national leadership targeted the Equal Rights Amendment (ERA). By the mid-1980s, the effort to pass the ERA had failed, the radical and grassroots women's movement was splintered into warring, single-issue factions, and the term *postfeminism* was more popular than *feminist*. Gender-based discrimination, sexism, and violence persisted, even as women's participation in all aspects of cultural life increased.

Today, the gay and lesbian movement is at a similarly decisive moment, in which we face progress and defeat, opportunity and seemingly insurmountable barriers. We can choose in this moment to follow the path our predecessors paved—of pursuing incremental legal and legislative reform, increasing gay and lesbian visibility, pressing for fair treatment in all aspects of life. This work, of securing and broadening civil equality, is in itself a lifetime's work, in which there is indeed very little choice; all of us who support gay rights must engage in it. But we do have the choice of reaching beyond the civil rights framework of mainstream integration, and beyond the partial equality that it delivers, to imagine and create a different movement whose goal is genuine social change. At this contradictory juncture, it behooves the gay and lesbian movement to re-examine long-held assumptions about our politics, our sexual identities, our political strategies, and our social agenda. We must begin to debate and define our particular moral vision: What do we stand for as a gay and lesbian people? Instead of asking the old

questions we have chanted at gay demonstrations for fifty years—
"What do we want and when do we want it?"—the time has come for
us to ask and answer "What do we represent?" For what vision of
society do we fight? How does a freedom-based movement differ from a
rights-based movement? What will it mean for each of us, our nation,
and the world to accept homosexuality as morally, politically, and socially equal to heterosexuality?

Answering these questions requires us to examine what has been the
guiding principle of our movement and the most widely shared ideal we
have: that of integration into the status quo, or mainstreaming. From its
inception in the fifties, the gay and lesbian movement has sought mainstream social acceptance for homosexual people through the strategies
of legislative and legal reform, public education, and community organizing. Mainstreaming has been at once the goal and the logical
consequence of our successes. By reframing the meaning of homosexuality in order to mainstream gay, lesbian, bisexual, and, more recently,
transgender people into all aspects of American political and cultural
life, we have improved the lives of our people dramatically. Greater
social tolerance has yielded us a wider space in which to participate in
our society, and mainstream legal and political reform has allowed millions of gay and lesbian Americans to work, raise families, and contribute to our communities. But the limits of mainstreaming are equally
evident today. The liberty we have won is incomplete, conditional, and
ultimately revocable. All gay and lesbian people remain stigmatized and
subject to violence; certain gay and lesbian people are freer than others
(for example, those who live in urban centers). Even the advances we
have made—like passage of local civil rights ordinances—have proved
as vulnerable, revocable, and limited as the advances made by other,
nongay civil rights movements.

A mainstream civil rights strategy cannot deliver genuine freedom
or full equality for one fundamental reason: the goal of winning mainstream tolerance, or "toleration," as Representative Newt Gingrich calls
it, differs from the goal of winning liberation or changing social institutions in lasting, long-term ways. The latter was once the goal of the gay
and lesbian movement; we explicitly identified ourselves as a liberation
movement. History may conclude that this naming was merely an affect
of the 1960s, but I believe that our movement's roots in the values
represented by liberation run deep. How the pursuit of fundamental
change mutates (and is muted) into the more limited goal of tolerance
or mainstream integration is a story common to many historic move-

ments that have threatened the status quo. In many ways, the triumph of mainstream civil rights over liberation is the victory of pragmatic politics over moral politics: instead of doing the right thing, movements like ours do the expedient thing. As the tale of short-term goals overshadowing long-term vision, it is a story I attempt to tell in the hope that understanding the civil rights strategy from this vantage point will allow us to build the road not yet taken.

VIRTUAL EQUALITY

In the high-technology world of computers, the simulation of events and situations produced through computer and video technology is called *virtual reality*. Most often used to train airline pilots in flight simulation, or by the Defense Department to play "war games," virtual reality has, till now, been mostly the fascination of cyberjunkies. But the technology of virtual reality may one day be as common as earplugs, headphones, and portable television. In virtual reality, the "virtual" or simulated reality can be made to seem as believable as the "real" experience. In virtual reality, nothing is real, but we experience it as if it were. So, too, with virtual equality.

The irony of gay and lesbian mainstreaming is that more than fifty years of active effort to challenge homophobia and heterosexism have yielded us not freedom but "virtual equality," which simulates genuine civic equality but cannot transcend the simulation. In this state, gay and lesbian people possess some of the trappings of full equality but are denied all of its benefits. We proceed as if we enjoy real freedom, real acceptance, as if we have won lasting changes in the laws and mores of our nation. Some of us even believe that the simulation of equality we have won represents the real thing. But the actual facts and conditions that define gay and lesbian life demonstrate that we have won "virtual" freedom and "virtual" equal treatment under "virtually" the same laws as straight people.

In the state of virtual equality, gay and lesbian people are at once insiders, involved openly in government and public affairs to a degree never before achieved, and outsiders, shunned by our elected officials unless they need our money or votes in close elections. We are at once marginal and mainstream, at once assimilated and irreconcilably queer. We are at once members of the traditional family—as its children, as siblings, parents, and grandparents—but are treated as if we are aliens to the family as an institution. We participate daily in every community, culture, profession, and corner of the earth—but we are forced to deny that we exist, to keep silent about our sexual orientation, and to be ashamed of loving members of the same sex. Gay men and lesbians work alongside their heterosexual counterparts in every job and type of employment in the world, but the condition for keeping these jobs is pretending not to be gay or lesbian. We pay taxes, yet our government denies gay people its public embrace, access to its programs, and its protection. Government leaders either ignore us (as President Clinton has since he encountered an antigay opposition), sell us out (as dozens of congressional liberals did in the military vote, AIDS votes, votes on the National Endowment for the Arts, votes on antigay amendments to education bills in 1994) or sanction bias that deliberately tries to exclude us from full participation in our nation's political and cultural life (as blatant homophobes like Senators Jesse Helms and Phil Gramm, and less blatant homophobes like Newt Gingrich, Bob Dole, and Dick Armey have successfully done for more than a decade).

Despite the recent burst of media attention, the mainstreaming of homosexuals has not resulted in the marginalization of the prejudice we face. Instead, antigay prejudice, rooted in religious and moral principles, has been reincarnated in each decade since the forties: from sin to criminality to sickness to psychopathology to sexual immorality and back to sin again. Homophobia is embedded in the major institutions of our society—in the church, the schools, the government, and the military. Antigay prejudice is broadcast every day on hundreds of Christian radio and television stations and is openly endorsed by the Catholic Church, by Orthodox Judaism, and by Islamic fundamentalism. It fuels the aggression of sports and the violence of those who are threatened by our emergence. More insidiously, homophobia remains, as the writer Suzanne Pharr recounts, the principal "weapon of sexism," intimately linked to the second-class status of women and used to maintain the status quo of heterosexual male authority.

I believe that the notion that homosexuality has been mainstreamed is an illusion we yearn to believe because we are so tired of being vilified, loathed, and marginalized. We want to be accepted and loved. We deserve to be safe, to be treated as fully equal, to enjoy every human right to be free and ourselves. But all the progress we have unquestionably made has not yet won us the respect, acceptance, and support of the heterosexual majority. The persistence of discrimination and the prejudicial attitudes reflected in most public opinion polls quantifies how much farther we have to go before we join the mainstream. Meanwhile, inside our own communities, the persistence of the closet—and our continued tolerance of the large numbers of us who pass—illustrate other ways in which we are far from mainstreamed. An examination of the rampant discrimination, fickle public opinion, and the closeted nature of the gay and lesbian community provides ample evidence of our virtual equality. Each of these realities challenges the gay and lesbian movement to question whether mainstream civil rights alone will deliver our people genuine freedom and full human dignity.

VIRTUAL NONDISCRIMINATION

Discrimination is the hallmark of our virtual equality, the pervasive condition we face each time we enter the world as openly gay people. Few states and cities outlaw antigay discrimination; violence against us is widespread; and the active opposition we encounter from the right politicizes every aspect of our lives—from our relationships to our children to the curricula they learn in schools, from laws and court decisions to art, from images on television to our moral integrity as human beings.

In a speech delivered at the annual fundraising dinner for the Human Rights Campaign Fund in Boston on November 5, 1994, Tim McFeeley, the former executive director of HRCF, argued that "there are two gay and lesbian Americas: the one in which people at this dinner live, and the other, in which nothing has changed." The first gay and lesbian America consists of those people whose lives have been touched by the movement. This activist gay and lesbian America is found in Boston, New York, San Francisco, Chicago, Madison, Washington, D.C., Seattle, Dallas, and Atlanta, to name a few places. These communities are ones in which gay and lesbian people have mobilized to assert political power, pass gay rights laws, build openly gay and lesbian businesses and subcultures, and assert a presence in the life of their city. Populated by individuals who are out of the closet, this gay America is filled with people holding jobs with businesses that ban discrimination, students at colleges and universities that ban sexual-orientation discrimination, liberal families in which acceptance of their children's homosexuality is a matter of principle.

The other gay America is much larger; it is the one in which most of our people live, dominated by fear, permeated by discrimination, violence, and shame. A place where people are still governed primarily by the fear of disclosure of their sexual orientation, this other gay America has been only tangentially reached by our movement. It is filled with people of every age, color, and background, who struggle in actual or virtual isolation to acknowledge their sexual orientation to themselves and to others. It's the gay America where poor people live, or where rural and suburban gay people live quiet lives far removed from the much-analyzed spectacle of urban gay communities. Conventional wisdom holds that gay people in the coastal cities enjoy "better" lives than their peers in the heartland or in rural America. Yet sometimes the converse is true. And while the national movement has done little to speak to the needs and concerns of rural lesbian and gay Americans, of those of us living in the Bible Belt or the heartland, of those in the suburbs or in small towns, conditions in the best gay and lesbian ghettos themselves are far from ideal. Even in large cities, prejudice, discrimination in employment, housing, and equal opportunity, and the threat of violence are daily realities for the majority of gay, lesbian, and bisexual people. But it is important to remember just what has been won and how much more remains unchanged. If gay and lesbian life is examined through the four lenses of work, community life, family, and faith, the discrimination we face becomes readily apparent.

Discrimination in employment, housing, public accommodations, credit, educational access, and many other aspects of life is the norm for people who are openly lesbian or gay. In most parts of the country, such discrimination remains legal. No federal law yet exists to render antigay discrimination illegal. The Federal Gay and Lesbian Civil Rights Bill, a comprehensive revision of the 1964 Civil Rights Act, was originally introduced in Congress by former New York Representative Bella Abzug in 1975. By 1994, the prospects of its passage had dimmed so dramatically that lesbian and gay lobbyists focused on the more narrow (and, they argued, winnable) Employment Non-Discrimination Act (ENDA), which would ban sexual-orientation discrimination in employment as a matter of federal law. ENDA is currently pending in Congress. Only five Republicans cosponsored the bill in 1994, and its prospects of passage were made even bleaker by the congressional elections in the fall of 1994. The fact is that, like congressional Democrats, most Republican political leaders have been unwilling to press the unpopular cause of gay equality. Because the margin of victory in 1994 was likely given to Republicans by the support of religious conservatives (like members of the Christian Coalition), it is less likely that the current Republican majority will press an agenda so strongly opposed by its base.

Only nine states have passed some form of gay and lesbian rights legislation: Wisconsin (1982), Massachusetts (1989), Hawaii (1990), New Jersey (1990), Connecticut (1991), Vermont (1991), California (1992), Minnesota (1992), and Rhode Island (1995). A number of statewide gay rights bills are introduced annually and generally fail to proceed beyond committee review. According to the *Washington Blade*, in the first three months of 1995 thirty-eight pro-gay rights bills were introduced in state legislatures; as of April only thirteen had survived committee review, and only five were given any chance of passing. Among the pro-gay rights bills pending in state legislatures today are those in Maine, Illinois, and Maryland. Approximately 150 cities and counties nationwide have passed local gay rights ordinances.

But a new legislative trend seems to have grown in the 1990s: affirmatively antigay legislation. According to a *Washington Blade* survey, in 1984 only five antigay measures were introduced in state legislatures. By comparison, in 1994 there were twenty-four antigay bills pending in state bodies. In the early months of 1995, eleven antigay bills had been introduced. Utah and South Dakota debated antigay marriage bills; the Utah law was passed. Montana, South Carolina, Oklahoma, and Washington sought to place restrictions on gay adoption and foster parenting. Montana even passed and shortly repealed a law that would have required all persons convicted under the state sodomy law to register their whereabouts with the state for the rest of their lives. Although the *Blade* suggested that there may be a slowing down, the fact is that an ever-more specific and sophisticated legislative backlash to gay rights is under way at the state and local level.

In addition, more than three dozen antigay ballot measures have passed since 1991, when the Christian Coalition and the religious right began aggressively to pursue such hostile measures. Antigay referenda continue to be introduced and planned, even though they have been declared unconstitutional by every court that has so far considered them. The gay movement's effort to defeat such referenda was dealt a potential blow when the U.S. Supreme Court agreed to review a Colorado Supreme Court decision declaring that the antigay Amendment 2, passed by voters in 1992, was unconstitutional. The U.S. Supreme Court will hear the case in the fall of 1995.

Gay rights laws are widely misunderstood even by those who support fair treatment of gay and lesbian people. None of the laws mandate special treatment or unusual rights. They merely declare that discriminatory practices based on a person's sexual orientation are illegal. The allegation of illegal policies or actions must still be proved in court, with the burden of proof falling on the person alleging discrimination. None of the existing gay and lesbian rights laws requires affirmative action or other kinds of gay and lesbian outreach. Instead of ordering compliance by all entities, many of the statutes are riddled with exemptions for religious organizations or contain other limits on their reach. For example, exemptions that allow discrimination by religious organizations exist in Wisconsin, Massachusetts, Connecticut, and New Jersey. The California law covers only public sector employment, while the Minnesota law exempts all youth organizations from its coverage—a bow to the most persistent and untrue myth about gay and lesbian people: that we are bad role models for children and are sexually predatory toward them. Ironically, in Minnesota the Girl Scouts actively lobbied against this limitation, while the exemption was supported by the openly gay members of the state legislature.

Invisibility remains a major barrier to addressing the discrimination gay people face. Politicians and the general public often greet claims of discrimination with disbelief: gay rights advocates are asked to "prove" that such prejudice exists. But because most gayness remains closeted and stigmatized, widespread data on employment, housing, and other types of discrimination are difficult to obtain. For one, gay people who experience such treatment do not always report it, because they know they lack recourse or because they fear further stigmatization if they disclose their sexual orientation. For another, researchers studying discrimination have not asked the gay question and have therefore uncovered little data. Finally, legislative hearings on antigay and antilesbian discrimination are rare. Only two such hearings have been held at the congressional level, most recently in May 1994, and previously in the late 1970s, when the first gay and lesbian rights bill was introduced.

Existing data on employment discrimination come from three sources: individual complaints brought in court or before state human rights agencies; surveys done by civil rights organizations on employment discrimination; and the widely documented incidence of violence and harassment directed at people because of their sexual orientation. Individual cases abound, but the people suffering discrimination are rarely able to bring them to trial, because most states and municipalities do not recognize sexual orientation as a category against which discrimination is banned. A widely publicized example of this is the situation at Cracker Barrel Corporation, a chain of fast-food restaurants headquartered in Tennessee. In 1991, Cracker Barrel fired at least eleven employees for being lesbian or gay under a new corporate policy that held "homosexual employees are incompatible with traditional family values." The case drew national news attention, calls for a boycott, several shareholder actions protesting the policy, and even resulted in a threat by one municipal pension fund—the New York City Pension Fund—to divest itself of all involvement with Cracker Barrel stock. In response to the uproar, the company remained intractable, and in a coup de grâce, former Vice President Dan Quayle patronized a Cracker Barrel restaurant during the 1992 presidential campaign. But the fired employees had no recourse under state or federal law.

Surveys done by nearly a dozen organizations reveal that gay and lesbian employees report high levels of workplace discrimination. Data indicate that gay people reported being fired when their sexual orientation was disclosed, reported sexual and violent harassment, and reported a number of unfair work practices, including the denial of promotion, job upgrades, and pay raises.

Data such as these have led a few gay and lesbian employees to form very effective employee associations. The focusing of national attention on the workplace as a vital site of gay rights organizing was the brainchild of the late George Kronenberger, a San Francisco–based activist, who died of AIDS in late 1994. Kronenberger argued that the next wave of progress for gay and lesbian nondiscrimination in the workplace would come not from legislative activism, but from the efforts of gay and lesbian employee groups. Through his efforts, the National Gay and Lesbian Task Force (NGLTF) founded its Workplace Organizing Project, and convened several conferences on gay and lesbian organizing in the workplace. Some of the biggest successes of the gay rights movement came in the 1990s through changes in corporate policies that covered thousands of employees. So, for example, Apple Computers, Lotus, and Microsoft recognized domestic partnership, allowing their unmarried and gay employees to qualify for the same benefits as nongay employees. Notwithstanding the pioneering efforts of the high-tech-nology industries, most American corporations and small businesses still do not ban antigay and antilesbian discrimination. Indeed, if business response to the AIDS health crisis can be cited as a barometer of policy changes that could benefit gay employees, as recently as December 1994 the business- and labor-led National Leadership Coalition on AIDS released a report concluding that only a small percentage of American businesses had adopted policies, initiated education, or attempted to plan for the occurrence of AIDS among their employees.

The one area in which extensive, if still incomplete, data on discrimination exist is the incidence of violence against people because of their sexual orientation or their perceived homosexuality. However, even these data did not exist until 1982, when Virginia Apuzzo, then the executive director of NGLTF, established its Anti-Violence Project and hired Kevin Berrill to run it. For over ten years, Berrill conducted research, lobbied law enforcement and legislative bodies, and helped start antiviolence groups and campaigns in cities and schools across the country. In the early years, Berrill and NGLTF established a national toll-free crisis line to collect data on antigay and antilesbian violence. In 1984, NGLTF published the first national survey of violence and victimization experienced by gay men and lesbians. The survey found that one in seven gay men and one in ten lesbians had been subjected to violence because of their sexual orientation. In annual surveys since 1984, the NGLTF Anti-Violence Project documented literally thousands of incidents of bias-motivated violence—incidents ranging from violent assault, murder, and battery, to arson, threats, and harassing behavior. The accumulating evidence was carefully marshaled by Berrill and NGLTF to secure the first congressional hearings on antigay violence, in September of 1986. These data led the Reagan administration's Justice Department to commission a report on bias violence in 1987; it concluded that "homosexuals are probably the most frequent victims."

Berrill's work at the federal level culminated in the passage of the Hate Crime Statistics Act in 1990. On its own, the Hate Crimes legislation did little more than require the FBI to gather statistics on crime motivated by prejudice. Yet what made this simple data-collection act controversial was its inclusion of antigay violence as a bias crime. It was the first measure to put the federal government on the record as opposing violence against gay men and lesbians in any way.

Despite gay and lesbian progress in the nineties, we have not seen a decrease in the prevalence or severity of violence against us. Indeed, overwhelming evidence suggests that antigay violence is escalating. In 1991, the FBI intercepted two members of the Aryan Nation on their way to bomb a popular gay disco in Seattle. In 1992, the antigay ballot campaigns in Oregon and Colorado were marked by death threats,

vandalism, and, in Oregon, the robbery of mailing lists and at least one
incident of arson that resulted in the murder of a white gay man and a
black lesbian in Salem, the capital. In its 1993 report, NGLTF cited the
trend toward more severe crimes, even as it noted a slight decrease in
overall reports of violence and victimization. Each year, the gay-supportive Metropolitan Community Church, an evangelical denomination with more than 250 churches nationwide, reports arson, death
threats, and assaults on its facilities and pastors. In October 1994,
reports of the brutal murders of two gay men in Laurel, Mississippi,
brought national attention to the persisting terror of violence in gay and
lesbian lives. In the nation's capital in 1994, some 206 incidents of
antigay violence and harassment, including eleven murders of gay men,
were documented by Gays and Lesbians Opposing Violence.

According to FBI statistics released in June 1994, antigay bias
crimes made up 12 percent of the more than 7600 hate crimes reported
to law enforcement agencies in forty-six states and the District of Columbia. Since the FBI statistics were based on reporting by participating agencies, which covered 56 percent of the United States population,
the actual level of antigay hate violence is probably even higher. Data
released early in 1995 by local antiviolence projects in Washington,
D.C., Texas, New York, Minnesota, and Pennsylvania reveal that violence against gay and lesbian people remains high and brutal. A number
of prevalence studies, which measure the experience of violence over a
lifetime, have also been conducted by academic researchers, government
agencies, and gay organizations. These studies uniformly reiterate the
high levels of violence found in the 1984 study done by NGLTF. A
1991 study of four hundred people conducted in New Orleans by the
Mayor's Advisory Committee on Lesbian and Gay Issues, for example,
found that 28 percent of gay men surveyed and 10 percent of lesbians
surveyed had been beaten because of their sexual orientation; 26 percent
had experienced threats of violence; and 64 percent had been subjected
to verbal harassment. Cruelly, our increased visibility has not changed
people's hostility or actions, but has given homophobes more opportunities to express the violence they feel.

Curiously, even though nearly everyone from law enforcement officials to the Catholic Church has condemned antigay and antilesbian
violence, the inclusion of sexual orientation in laws and policies aimed
at stopping hate crimes remains controversial. Despite the passage of
the federal bill, lawmakers in many states have refused to pass state
versions. In New York State, for example, former Governor Mario

Cuomo failed for more than seven years to secure passage of a state bias-crime bill that would have required data collection, training, and bias penalty enhancement for crimes motivated by prejudice. In addition, federal law enforcement officials still claim to lack authority to intervene in antigay-bias crime situations. Thus, in 1994, the Justice Department told gay rights groups that it could not investigate a pattern of hate crimes in the state of Mississippi, even when asked by gay residents to do so and despite suggestions of possible antigay bias on the part of local police officials. The justification: a claim that the Justice Department lacked the jurisdiction because the Hate Crimes Act granted no such authority, but merely authorized the collection of bias-crime data.

Government-sanctioned discrimination has long been a target of gay rights organizers. At the federal level, the repeal of antigay employment laws, immigration policies, and the military ban on gay and lesbian service are the chief projects our movement undertook. We were successful in the first two, and failed dramatically in 1993 on the last. Antigay employment laws were instituted in the post–World War II era as the Cold War began. Their baseless rationale was to prevent federal civil servants from being blackmailed. In large part due to the work of Mattachine Society activists like Dr. Franklin Kameny, these restrictions were mostly eliminated by the U.S. Civil Service Commission in 1975. Immigration reform too was successful, with tremendous credit for this victory going to Representative Barney Frank (D-MA), who urged Congress to steadily dilute and eventually delete the antigay and antilesbian provisions of the Immigration Act in a comprehensive revision that passed in 1991.

At the state level, the gay and lesbian movement's fight to overturn government-sanctioned discrimination focused on criminal laws. From its inception, the movement has sought to repeal laws that prohibit private, adult, consensual same-sex behavior, and laws that prohibit behavior for homosexuals that is legal for heterosexuals. Despite great progress, nearly half of the states still criminalize gay and lesbian sexual behavior. Many states eliminated their so-called sodomy laws in the sixties and seventies, as part of a modernization of state penal codes, which dropped a host of unnecessary statutes. But only three jurisdictions have decriminalized sodomy in the 1990s: Nevada and the District of Columbia had their sodomy laws repealed by legislation, while Kentucky had its law struck down by a state court.

In 1986, our effort to eliminate criminal laws ran into a roadblock when the U.S. Supreme Court handed down a sweeping and controversial decision, *Bowers* v. *Hardwick,* which upheld the constitutionality of the Georgia law under which a gay man was arrested for engaging in sex in his own bedroom. A closely divided majority declared that the Constitution did not shelter gay and lesbian behavior in the same way that it protected the private sexual behavior of heterosexuals. Citing the "millennia of moral teaching" against sodomy, a majority of the Court affirmed the right of states to legislate against homosexual behavior. The Supreme Court's decision has since been cited repeatedly to justify many different kinds of discrimination against lesbians and gay men.

Even though direct criminal prosecutions under sodomy laws (like that of Michael Hardwick) are rare, collateral uses of the sodomy law are frequent. Unusually, several recent cases have invoked sodomy laws in civil contexts involving lesbians. In the past ten years, such laws have been invoked to deny visitation to a lesbian mother in Missouri; to defend the refusal to hire gay police officers by the Dallas Police Department; to prevent two lesbians from establishing a lesbian-feminist retreat center in Mississippi; to oppose the grant of guardianship to Karen Thompson, the lover of Sharon Kowalski, who fought for seven years before winning, in Minnesota; and to deny gay schoolteachers the right to work in Oklahoma. These cases represent just a fraction of incidents that garner public attention or make it to court. Despite such prosecution, the focus of most of the gay and lesbian movement since 1986 has not been on sodomy law repeal.

Gay and lesbian families undergo enormous stigma and discriminatory treatment. Our relationships are treated as illegal; gay parents must fight to keep custody of their own children merely because they are gay; we are denied the ability to be foster parents and to adopt; and some would even deny to single people (straight or gay) the opportunity to raise children. Marriage remains the aspiration of large numbers of lesbian and gay people; it is a quest that gay people have pursued in courts for several decades.

In 1992, the Hawaii Supreme Court agreed to hear a lawsuit, brought by lesbian and gay couples seeking the right to marry, which argued that the marriage law was invalid under the state's constitution. The case is pending, and its favorable outcome could mark a turning point in this long-desired, but so far unavailable, goal of many gay people. Although same-sex domestic partnership is nationally recognized in Denmark and Norway, few American jurisdictions recognize such relationships; despite scores of lawsuits, no state yet has recognized same-sex marriage by legislation. Same-sex unions are now performed by some religious denominations, and if they were legalized, their frequency would probably surprise many heterosexuals. Still, the idea of gay and lesbian marriage is opposed by fundamentalist, Catholic, and Orthodox Jewish religious leaders. They argue that the sacrament of marriage is specifically defined as a heterosexual rite (and right) and should be so limited.

Without the opportunity to cement our relationships through the institution of marriage, gay and lesbian people have resorted to a creative array of contractual arrangements that attempt to win legal recognition for gay families on nonmarital grounds. The domestic-partnership benefits movement is an example of this approach. The spouses of heterosexual employees can receive health care benefits, bereavement leave, rights of inheritance, and other benefits, discounts, and travel awards, all of which are unavailable to unmarried straight and gay couples. Elimination of such marital status discrimination is controversial to those who believe that heterosexual marriage should be accorded "special treatment" and that it is, as Dan Quayle said during the 1992 campaign, the "preferred option." Domestic partnership remains controversial even within the gay and lesbian community, because some activists argue that it is but a stopgap measure until we win the right to marry.

Another area of antigay and antilesbian discrimination that persists involves restrictions on, and barriers to, parenting by gay people. Literally millions of us are already parents, some through heterosexual marriages before we came out of the closet, others through adoption, or foster-parenting, or through bearing our own children as single mothers. Many more gay people would like to become parents, since our desire to be parents stems from the same desires for family and nurturing that heterosexuals feel. But courts still stigmatize gay and lesbian parents in custody cases. Results of such cases vary from state to state, but the trend is not necessarily toward liberalization. In 1993, two widely covered adoption cases dramatized the different results state courts can reach. In Virginia, a state supreme court denied a lesbian mother the custody of her own child, ruling her unfit; the Bottoms case was upheld on appeal in 1995. But in Massachusetts, the Supreme Judicial Court allowed the adoption of a child by the lesbian lover of the mother. When the facts of these two cases are examined more closely, it is clear that the different outcomes depended in part on the different economic status of the two sets of mothers. The Massachusetts couple was well off, while Sharon Bottoms was a struggling working mother. This suggests the truth that financial status likely affects the experience of discrimination of differently situated gay and lesbian people. Upper-middle class gay people are the first to benefit from the progress the movement makes—but such progress is not automatically available to working-class or poor gay people.

In other parenting situations, barriers to foster care, adoption, and artificial insemination remain in place against gay people in a number of states. Florida and New Hampshire prohibit gay foster care and adoption outright. Under the watchful eye of arch-conservative Gary Bauer, who served as head of President Reagan's White House Domestic Policy Council and is now the director of the Family Research Council, a 1988 White House Task Force on Adoption opposed adoption and foster-parenting by lesbians and gay men. Also that year, the antigay Massachusetts foster-care policy became a national issue for gay and lesbian voters when Michael Dukakis was chosen as the Democratic nominee for President. Dukakis refused to meet with gay and lesbian organizations on this issue, but his antigay policy was ultimately declared unconstitutional by the Massachusetts Supreme Judicial Court, in a lawsuit brought by New England's Gay and Lesbian Advocates and Defenders.

Lesbian and gay youth experience an especially pernicious form of discrimination. A Reagan-Bush administration study on youth suicide issued in January 1989, but suppressed by the White House and the Department of Health and Human Services until August 1989, concluded that a large number of young people attempt suicide because they have nowhere to turn to address questions about their sexual identities. (The number accounts for 30 percent of youth suicides.) Entitled *Report of the Secretary's Task Force on Youth Suicide,* the study became the target of antigay former Congressman Bill Dannemeyer (R-CA), who succeeded in getting Louis Sullivan, Secretary of Health and Human Services, to repudiate the report because it made a series of gay-friendly recommendations. As a result of organizing led by the New York–based Hetrick Martin Institute (HMI) for lesbian and gay youth, a national coalition of youth advocates formed in 1993 to tackle the public policy needs of gay, lesbian, and bisexual youth. Despite enormous progress, and despite the excellent track records of a number of youth service programs, the problems of gay youth remain largely invisible to the mainstream and unaddressed by most school districts. Indeed, curricula and books that teach tolerance toward gay people are the targets of extensive attack by the far right. In 1993, the Rainbow Curriculum was defeated in New York as a result of the systematic organizing efforts of the Christian Coalition and the Catholic Church. The national mobilization to support gay students, teachers, and educational reformers is one of the brightest new directions in the gay and lesbian movement.

Gay and lesbian people are not thought of as a people with faith, but this myth is shattered by the truth that the largest grassroots organizations in our communities are religious. Each week, millions of lesbians and gay men worship at synagogues, churches, and temples. But few mainstream denominations welcome or recognize this devotion.

The abandonment of gay people by mainstream religious denominations actually reverses a trend toward tolerance and inclusion that guided church practices into the 1970s. In the sixties, the Council on Religion and the Homosexual, formed in San Francisco, was influential in calling for fair treatment of gay people by the police and the state. The council actually helped ease the senseless harassment of gay and lesbian organizations and bars that was pervasive in San Francisco in the early sixties. Similar coalitions have since helped enact gay rights legislation elsewhere. For example, in 1982 a broad-based religious coalition helped Wisconsin gay rights activists pass the first gay rights bill in this country. Attacks on the gay community galvanized the formation, in 1992, of People of Faith Against Bigotry, a large religious coalition in Portland, Oregon, which helped defeat the antigay ballot measure.

Two forces came together in the late seventies and early eighties to militate against lesbians and gay men within mainstream religious denominations: first, evangelical Christian denominations began to grow dramatically while old-line churches lost members and faced shrinking financial support; and second, the Christian Right began to organize as an explicitly political bloc, increasing its influence in the Republican Party through its key role in the coalition that elected Ronald Reagan. These shifting economic and political realities gave new life to the hard-liners in each denomination who suddenly began to resurrect medieval arguments against homosexuality (it's an "abomination," a "crime against nature").

As a result, the last fifteen years have seen a series of pitched battles within most mainline churches over the issue of homosexuality, battles often lost by those favoring more progressive policies toward gay and lesbian people. Methodists, Lutherans, Episcopalians, followers of Conservative Judaism, and Baptists have all faced this issue and come

out with varying versions of the Catholic Church's admonition to love
the sinner but hate the sin. Yet organized religion does neither. Instead,
this ambivalent stance leads some mainline churches to actively oppose
gay rights bills. The Catholic Church stepped up its antigay rhetoric in
1986, when the Vatican issued a "Letter on Homosexuality," outlining
its opposition to gay rights laws. This letter was reiterated and expanded
upon by the Pope in 1992 in his Letter to the Bishops.

A handful of progressive churches and denominations have put
forth a different view. The Quakers, the Unitarian Universalist Church,
the United Church of Christ, and the Union of American Hebrew
Congregations are among religious groups that advocate fair and equal
treatment for gay men and lesbians. Gay rights campaigns across the
country have succeeded when broad religious coalitions were organized
to support us, and failed when we could not muster religious support.

VIRTUAL EQUALITY AND PUBLIC OPINION

What the discrimination our community faces—whether at work or on
the street, at school or within families—actually reveals is the persistence of homophobia in the public mind. In this sense, discrimination
represents the public manifestation of private attitudes, attitudes documented in public opinion polls exposing America's deep ambivalence
about homosexuality and civil rights. Poll takers tell us that the public
supports fair and equal treatment for gays in most jobs, but when asked
about certain job categories (like teachers or child care workers), or
when questioned about gay or lesbian marriage and about our moral
equivalence to heterosexuals, the public's support withers.

Polling done by news organization, political campaigns, and gay
and lesbian groups also offers insight into the public's resistance to our
full equality. In the spring of 1994, after examining the latest polling
and focus group data available, the political consultant Susan Hibbard
concluded that "consistently more than half of the US public view
homosexuality negatively. At the same time, closer to 75% are opposed
to discrimination. [T]he country is split on the need for protective
legislation."

As a threshold matter, polls about sexual orientation raise a number
of troubling issues. For one, such polls call into question their accuracy;

many people lie when asked about their sexuality and their sexual behavior. Researchers note this slant and attempt to adjust for it in their
methodology or analysis, but their data always remain somewhat suspect. Also, people are less than forthright in declaring their opinions
about such controversial subjects as sex or race. The tendency to say one
thing and do another has been demonstrated repeatedly in voter preference polls done when black candidates run against whites or when
antigay civil rights measures are on a ballot.

Second, polling has become ubiquitous and easily manipulated. As
the old adage goes, "Statistics don't lie; statisticians do." Unfortunately,
public opinion polls dominate the discourse of politics today. Instead of
being guided by principles or political ideology, most politicians, like
Newt Gingrich, are directed by focus groups and the "popularity" of
their proposals. Polls have become the moral conscience of politics. As a
result, we witness policymaking by popularity contest; decision-making
by small focus groups; leadership by "sound bites"—or the essence of
Ross Perot, who cited polls as the basis for many of his positions. I find
this tendency in American politics depressing, but like all political activists today I use those polls which are advantageous to my position
and discount those which contradict my views.

Finally, public opinion polls create the illusion of representative
democracy—defined as majoritarian rule—but, in fact, they are the
essence of tyranny, because they are so susceptible to manipulation and
unpredictable influence. Results depend on what questions you ask,
who asks them, how they are asked, what form of interview is used
(phone, live, written), who is asked, and when they are asked. The most
insidious and damaging polls in recent years have been those cited by
our enemies to "prove" that a tiny minority of Americans are gay or
lesbian. During the week preceding the Third National March on
Washington for Lesbian, Gay, Bisexual Rights and Liberation, held on
April 25, 1993, front-page stories in major news dailies asserted that 1
percent of the American male population was gay. The statistic itself
was based on an AIDS-related study of sexual behavior among men,
conducted on a small national sample. That 1 percent of respondents in
the study self-identified as exclusively homosexual was seized upon by
the Christian Right as proof that the gay rights movement was nothing
more than a radical fringe that had disproportionate power compared to
its actual size. The statistic was widely repeated by major news outlets,
including the *New York Times,* despite the sheer impossibility of its

veracity. Although subsequent articles were published about the limitations of this study, few achieved the massive visibility of the first wave
of coverage. The statistic stuck, although it is inaccurate.

For the past twenty years, the National Opinion Research Center's
Annual General Social Survey has consistently reported that between
70 and 77 percent of the American public believe that homosexual
relations are "always wrong." This moral condemnation has changed
little despite the greater visibility of gay and lesbian people in recent
years. Thus, in the eighties, 66 percent to 75 percent of Americans
thought homosexuality was immoral; in surveys done in the nineties, 50
percent to 66 percent of those surveyed thought the same.

Polls also reveal that America is confused about its attitude toward
gay sexuality, about the existence of antigay discrimination, and about
the need for protective gay rights legislation. Americans remain split on
whether or not to decriminalize same-sex behavior; a 1993 Gallup Poll
found that 46 percent favored such decriminalization, while 48 percent
opposed it, and the rest had no opinion. This split over gay sexuality has
not changed since *Bowers* v. *Hardwick.*

Paradoxically, at the same time that the majority of Americans
think being gay is morally wrong, a bigger majority condemn antigay
discrimination. The American people do not like unfairness. This sentiment was best summarized by a statement from a man in a focus group
in Oregon. He voted against the antigay ballot measure but said, "I
don't think being gay is right. It's immoral. It's against all religious
beliefs. I don't agree with gays at all, but I don't think they should be
discriminated against." Thus, large majorities of Americans (ranging
from 74 percent to 81 percent) answered yes to the question "Should
homosexuals have equal rights in terms of job opportunities" in polls
done over the past two years. But, not surprisingly, the percentage by
which respondents condemned antigay discrimination decreased significantly when they were asked about specific job categories. Only 41
percent favored nondiscrimination against a gay person employed as an
elementary school teacher; 47 percent to 53 percent favored nondiscrimination in employment of gay people as high school teachers; and
only 43 percent favored employment of gay people as members of the
clergy. Negative public attitudes toward specific job occupations reflect
irrational fears and misconceptions about the prevalence of child molestation, and reflect the ambivalence fostered in the average person's mind
by the condemnation of homosexuality by religious leaders.

In recent years, as antigay groups have brought ballot petitions to challenge or ban passage of gay and lesbian rights laws, the issue of gay rights legislation has been debated in towns and communities from Lewiston, Maine, to Alachua County, Florida; from Idaho to Missouri; and from Washington State to Michigan. As these debates rage, new research on public attitudes toward homosexuality has been carried out. Hibbard notes that focus group data from the 1992 referenda campaigns in Oregon and Colorado, from a set of groups convened in 1993 in New York by the Empire State Pride Agenda, and from groups convened by the Human Rights Campaign Fund's researchers in 1994 in Michigan and Florida produced the following conclusions:

1. that public opinion all over the country is deeply split over the need for protective gay and lesbian rights legislation;

2. that gay and lesbian rights protections are closely connected in people's minds with more general distrust of "minority status, civil rights legislation, affirmative action, preferential treatment, employment quotas and special rights";

3. that large numbers of Americans remain confused about what antigay and antilesbian discrimination means. Some question how a "chosen behavior" can claim discrimination. Others question whether gay people are stigmatized like other so-called legitimate minorities. And many people still do not know what kind of discrimination we experience. Finally,

4. that the messages we develop about gay and lesbian legislation in ballot campaigns are vitally important to educating the public about gay and lesbian lives in general.

More than just documenting opposition, focus groups and polls do help us to understand why people oppose gay and lesbian rights. In July 1993, *U.S. News & World Report* reported data on "the top ranking influences on voters' attitudes on homosexuality." In the poll, 29 percent of those surveyed identified religious organizations as the principal source of their views on homosexuality; of this group, 79 percent opposed gay and lesbian rights. Another 18 percent said that knowing someone gay shaped their views on homosexuality. Not surprisingly, 66 percent of those who knew someone gay or lesbian supported full civil rights. A third group in the poll—17 percent—said that the media were the main influences on their views toward homosexuality. Of this segment, 44 percent said they opposed gay rights. Finally, 15 percent said their families shaped their opinions on homosexuality. Of these individuals, 47 percent opposed full gay and lesbian equality.

A growing body of social science research confirms and clarifies these figures from the popular press. Nationally renowned psychologist Gregory Herek has pioneered much of this research in original studies on the causes of homophobia, AIDS-related stigmas, and antigay and antilesbian prejudice. Presenting social science data from several studies, Herek argues that the research supports the following ten conclusions about those who hold antigay attitudes:

1. that people most hostile to lesbians and gay men are those with limited contact with them;

2. that those expressing antigay attitudes are more likely to come from rural areas, small towns, from the Midwest or South;

3. that those who are older and less formally educated are more likely to hold antigay attitudes;

4. that adolescent and college-age males hold more strongly negative views of homosexuality than middle-aged males and females;

5. that those who are highly religious are more likely to espouse negative views about homosexuality;

6. that those with antigay attitudes "are more likely to view male homosexuals as effeminate and female homosexuals as masculine, and more likely to believe in conforming to traditional, restrictive gender roles";

7. that people with antigay attitudes are more likely to hold a negative or restrictive view of sexuality in general;

8. that those who are antigay display "high levels of authoritarianism and related personality characteristics, such as cognitive rigidity, dogmatism, intolerance of ambiguity, and dependence on authority";

9. that those who believe that homosexuality can be "spread" or that it is a choice are more likely to hold negative views; and

10. that a number of studies have found that males held more negative attitudes toward homosexuality than females.

In addition to drawing these helpful profiles, Herek's research has attempted to understand what causes antigay attitudes. He argues that such prejudice actually stems from, and serves, specific psychological functions for those holding these biases. He postulates that understanding the function which such prejudicial attitudes serve will allow us to develop effective interventions. Herek proposes that the following major functions are served by antigay and antilesbian attitudes: experiential, anticipatory, value-expressive, social-expressive, and ego-defensive. Or what we might call: who you know, what you expect, what you believe, and who knows you.

We all base our attitudes on our past experiences, whether direct or indirect. If people have no direct experience, they still have attitudes based on expectations or anticipation of what gay people are like and how contact with us will affect them. Herek terms these the experiential or anticipatory functions. Soon after I came out to my parents, my father asked me what women in lesbian bars looked like, and he was surprised when I told him we looked like a crowd of women in a mall or on the street—varied and completely familiar. Based on the stereotypes he had heard and read, my father expected gay women to look more masculine than straight women. The best way to change my father's attitude was to change his experience. As I introduced him to different lesbian friends, who look as ordinary, glamorous, sometimes feminine, sometimes butch as any comparable assemblage of heterosexual women, his understanding of gay women has broadened. The experiential and anticipatory functions of prejudice explain why people who know someone gay often have very different attitudes from those who don't.

Similarly, people who are deeply religious or socially conservative hold the attitude that homosexuality is morally wrong, or what Herek terms an "expressive function." What we believe can serve a value-expressive function (meaning that gay and lesbian people raise a value conflict within the person), a social-expressive function (binding together people with antigay attitudes), or an ego-defensive function (because gay and lesbian people symbolize an "unacceptable part of self"). For example, I have had many conversations with religious people genuinely troubled by what their faith teaches about homosexuality. These people struggle to connect what their faith asks them to believe with the reality of gay and lesbian existence. Very often, such conflict is genuine and far from hostile: people of faith often strive to harmonize their doctrine with the practice of tolerance. At other times, religious-based opposition is more overtly hostile. My mother, for example, has moved from hostility toward the idea of my lesbianism to a grudging but growing acceptance. Her objection remains at its core faith-based. In the context of her religious faith (Hinduism), she believes she cannot fully embrace my sexual orientation. Yet, as time passes and she gains more knowledge and experience of the realities of lesbian and gay life, the way she resolves her internal conflict of values has changed.

This social science research, along with the polling data, reveals much about what America thinks about gay people and why. In the process, it defines some realities our movement must recognize and confront. First, the contradictory public sentiment measured by public opinion polls clearly explains the ambivalence politicians display to the gay and lesbian movement. Such polls have a chilling effect on the support politicians and public officials offer. Even from supposedly liberal politicians, gay and lesbian people enjoy an uneasy and fickle support. A quick review of gay and AIDS votes in Congress reveals that most moderate-to-liberal politicians have failed to support gay rights unless the vote was completely "safe" or noncontroversial. Conservatives, on the other hand, fall into two categories: libertarians, who consistently support individual freedom, and moralists, who do not hesitate to condemn homosexuality. Political allegiance is directly proportional to the shifts in public opinion polls. When we begin to change poll numbers, we will count more friends in political office.

In order to change those numbers, the social science research suggests, the gay movement must strategically go after those segments of the population who are most reachable. As the political consultant Celinda Lake has noted, those most likely to be reached by the gay rights message are women. But dominated as it is by men, the gay rights movement is not focused on systematically reaching more women voters. The coalitions the gay movement has forged with traditional feminist groups are mainly legislative coalitions, not electoral ones. Indeed, despite the commonality created between white and middle-class gay men of all colors and poor women of all colors by the government's poor response to AIDS, few in our movement have tried, through projects, to forge a greater alliance between these historically opposed constituencies. Notable exceptions are Gay Men's Health Crisis under the leadership of its former director, Tim Sweeney; and a handful of progressive, minority-led AIDS organizations, like the National Minority AIDS Council and the National Task Force on AIDS Prevention. At present, the movement at the national level has no proactive strategy to solidify support for gay and lesbian equality among potentially supportive voters. The chief national organization with a commitment to changing public attitudes and doing cultural, rather than political education, about gay and lesbian lives is the Gay and Lesbian Alliance Against Defamation. But even GLAAD has so far been a reactive group; it acts as a watchdog on the print media, television, and film rather than as a cultural advocate for homosexual people. Some local GLAAD chapters have begun proactive campaigns to develop and influence school curricula, but these efforts lack a nationally coordinated and fully funded strategy.

GLAAD's success in shaping our media images and thus voters' perception of us, however, is in line with another lesson of the social science research data: that the gay and lesbian movement needs to concentrate far more on culture than on politics as we strive to win deeper acceptance and genuine equality. Religious organizations and leaders, media and pop culture, and our families are pivotal sites for shaping people's views of homosexuality. But to date the gay and lesbian movement remains focused primarily on political and legal reform rather than on these cultural spheres of influence. Our focus has reflected the historical necessity of eliminating draconian laws and harmful social policies. The time has come for us to shift that focus somewhat in order to win the larger battle of full equality.

The importance of educating the public, young heterosexuals, and all segments of the population in the truth about homosexual lives and our aspirations for equality cannot be overstated. Straight people still believe dangerous and mistaken myths about homosexuals. Our exclusive focus on legal, legislative, and administrative policy reform helps end blatantly discriminatory practices, but it leaves these myths intact. By engaging homophobia in the cultural spheres, we challenge such myths where they originate and where they are perpetuated. Such a broad cultural front would tackle another conclusion of social science data; namely, that opposition to gay and lesbian equality is not monolithic: people oppose gay rights for different reasons. A broad-based cultural strategy aimed at straight America's sites of opposition could address these differences.

Opponents of gay and lesbian rights themselves could be grouped into three categories: the concerned, the ignorant, and the hostile. (We may glibly label them the good, the bad, and the ugly.) Like the man from Oregon quoted above, concerned opponents are those who think discrimination is un-American and wrong, but are not quite comfortable with us. This category also includes the genuinely confused and religious among us, who struggle with the question of the morality of homosexuality. It includes moderates, conservatives, and liberals who want to do the right thing, but fear disturbing the status quo. These could be dubbed the "concerned" opponents to gay rights, because if their concerns and fears are addressed, they can still be reached by the gay and lesbian movement. They are open to electoral persuasion and can be engaged on a deeper level as well. Their votes are ours if we wage an informational campaign to secure them; and their lasting support may be won if we try to answer their fears.

The next category of gay rights opponents are those we might term the "ignorant." These are the folk who say they have never met a gay person. They believe many of the most untrue myths about us, and they accept at face value the information they are given about us by the religious right and other "authorities." In this category of opponents are the thousands of average Americans mobilized by Donald Wildmon and the American Family Association to campaign against the National Endowment for the Arts' supposedly pro-gay bias; they include the forty thousand people who sent letters to Secretary Louis Sullivan asking him to keep in place the ban on HIV-positive immigrants (even though every credible medical authority supported an end to the ban); they are the participants in the talk-radio and television shows who react to the gay people on the shows' panels with fascination and revulsion. The ignorant opponents are those who look to their religious and political leaders for guidance on how to think about us. At a time when most of these leaders do not champion us, it's no wonder that most Americans won't go out on a limb either. I label this category the "bad" opposition because they are so difficult to target. Moreover, they are bad news for a movement unable to tailor its message to the questions on the minds of most people. Underneath the ignorance of some individuals lies genuine hostility toward us. Nevertheless, gradual change in polling data over the years suggest that we can reach those who are ignorant through the ongoing process of public education and one on one interaction, and, to the extent that we can continue to enlist the vocal support of major religious and political leaders, we may influence this segment even further.

The third category of opponents we face are those we must sadly characterize as "ugly," for they seek the deformation of American democracy into American theocracy. The fusion of church and state is the logical conclusion of the political views of the Christian Coalition and its allies. Against these opponents, we have little hope of persuasion. But we do have the opportunity to counteract their narrow view of us with the truth, and meeting their exclusionary messages with inclusive responses that embrace them even as we oppose them. We must be very clear that the gay movement does not oppose religion or the rights of people to practice and live by their faith. In a civil society, there is room for both religious worship and secular practice. Gay and lesbian people embrace the most welcoming and pluralistic notions of American democracy. What we oppose is the persecution of any religious majority or minority group in this country. In addition to a commitment to the tradition of democratic pluralism, including a commitment to religious freedom for our enemies, we face the more difficult project of articulating that we are ourselves a moral people, of a wide variety of religious faiths, anchored by values to which we feel deeply bound: values of freedom, equality, inclusion and justice. Indeed, out members of the clergy, lesbian and gay rabbis, and gay members of religious organizations stand in stark contrast to the bigoted religious conservatives who seek our suppression. By being out about both their gayness and spirituality, such individuals challenge the certitude of those who oppose homosexuality on moral grounds.

Openly religious gay people have embraced perhaps the simplest yet most painful lesson the polling research teaches us: that coming out of the closet is a highly significant contribution each out person makes to the realization of full gay, lesbian, and bisexual equality. People who know someone gay in their lives (a family member, a friend, a colleague) are considerably more supportive and understanding of gay rights than those who claim not to know a single gay person. (Sixty-six percent of the former supported gay rights in the *US News* poll.) But another sad truth revealed in that poll was that only 18 percent of those surveyed reported knowing someone gay. This means that 82 percent believed they did not know anyone who was gay or lesbian. The data on how many people report knowing someone gay or lesbian varies from poll to poll—by age and geographic location of respondents.

VIRTUAL EQUALITY AND THE CLOSET

As Lesbian Avenger cofounder and community organizer Maxine Wolfe wryly observed, when I asked why she thought the gay movement was so small, "We're so small because we're still married!" Maxine's answer tells a disconcerting truth about the vast majority of gay and lesbian people: most of our own people remain inside the institution of heterosexuality because of their fear, self-hatred, confusion, or shame at being openly homosexual. Statistically, few people who engage in gay, lesbian, or bisexual behavior self-identify as homosexual or bisexual; and of those who do self-identify, very few are actively involved in the lesbian and gay political movement.

Studies done from the late 1940s to this day reveal that large numbers of people report same-sex attraction and even engage in same-sex behavior. But far fewer respondents call themselves gay or lesbian or bisexual. The Kinsey Report on Human Sexual Behavior, for example, found that 37 percent of adult men and 19 percent of adult women "had homosexual experiences to the point of orgasm at some point in their lives," but a far smaller number of the men—4 percent—identified themselves as exclusively homosexual. The Janus Report, a nationwide sexual behavior survey done by the sexologists Samuel and Cynthia Janus over a five-year period, from 1988 to 1992, reported that 22 percent of the men and 17 percent of the women from their sample (which totaled 2765 individuals) reported having had homosexual experiences. Of those who had homosexual experience, the Januses reported that 39 percent of the men and 27 percent of the women reported having gay sex frequently or in an ongoing way. A 1988 Harris Poll study of 1834 men and women aged sixteen to fifty found that 18.3 percent of men and 17.4 percent of women had homosexual attraction and/or experience since the age of fifteen. While only 4.1 percent of the men and 2.3 percent of the women reported having exclusively homosexual sex, an additional 1.9 percent of men and 1.2 percent of women reported having such contact "fairly often," and yet another 3.6 percent of the men and 2.9 percent of the women reported same-sex contact "rarely." Finally, the national Sex Survey conducted by the respected National Opinion Research Center and published in 1994 concluded that 9 percent of men and 4 percent of women reported having same-sex contact since puberty; this survey found that the proportions shifted depending on whether respondents came from urban, suburban, or rural areas. In urban areas, an even higher number of men and women reported same-sex experience or gay identity.

Gay and lesbian activists have long cited the Kinsey data for the claim that approximately 10 percent of the population is gay or lesbian. Subsequent studies have shown this figure to be statistically inaccurate. In fact, Kinsey found that a far smaller number of men and women reported having exclusively gay or lesbian sex, but that far more than 10 percent reported having had gay or lesbian sex at some time in their lives. Antigay activists now routinely cite low statistics as "proof" that homosexuality is far less widespread than supposed, and they accuse gay activists of lying in order to advance a political agenda. In fact, the data suggest that gay and lesbian activists have actually demonstrated great restraint in claiming only the 10 percent figure. We have not claimed, for example, the many millions of Americans who have nonexclusively engaged in gay or lesbian sexual behavior. In other words, bisexual people may be far more numerous than either gay or straight people acknowledge. Yet neither camp will claim that constituency.

Statistically and methodologically reliable data on sexual behavior remain hard to obtain because they are so politically charged. As *U.S. News* reports, the Sex Survey released in 1994, for example, was "originally proposed in 1987 by the National Institutes of Health to help scientists fight AIDS. But Congress killed funding for it in 1991 [actually congressional opponents stopped funding for the Sex Survey twice, in 1989 and 1991] after conservatives caught wind of its intimate questions. It re-emerged after private foundations agreed to back a less ambitious project." Even the researchers of the 1994 survey, hailed as one of the most exhaustive sex surveys to date, acknowledge that their work has "only scratched the surface of what there is to learn about sexual man and woman."

Accurate data are also hard to obtain because so many people are in the closet—a state of both virtual reality and virtual equality. The closet is such a pervasive fact of life within the gay and lesbian movement that the contortions organizations go through to accommodate it are taken for granted. Even today, nearly all gay and lesbian rights organizations do not mail newsletters or mailings in envelopes that identify them as gay or lesbian. The irony of this is profound: an out-of-the-closet group like the National Gay and Lesbian Task Force never mails anything to its members with its full name spelled out on the cover. Executive directors of nearly every gay or lesbian group that does direct mail solicitation can tell stories of receiving distraught phone calls from people who have gotten these "closeted" mailings, demanding to know how their names were obtained by a gay group. Often, the callers acknowledge they are gay but are angry, because they are not out and are afraid that they will now be exposed as gay to their neighbors, co-workers, or employers. In the 1970s and 1980s we used to joke that none of the gay or lesbian bars in Boston had windows that could be looked into from the street.

While thousands (and even millions) participate in the annual gay and lesbian pride rallies and celebrations held each June across the country, only a small fraction are members of local, state, or national gay and lesbian organizations. So, for example, an estimated 130,000 people attended the 1995 Gay and Lesbian Pride Celebration in Boston; this number surpasses the combined mailing lists of *all* Boston-area gay and lesbian organizations (even without accounting for the inherent duplication of these lists). The pattern is true in every city in which gay or lesbian pride events are held: more people live and participate in gay and lesbian communities than support, volunteer for, or get involved with our movement's cultural and political organizations.

Of the gay and lesbian people who are out enough to be "card-carrying" members of gay political organizations, few are out in every aspect of their lives. I often run into successful, talented people in every profession, seemingly comfortable with their sexuality, out in the media and in their community, who tell me they have not yet come out to their family back home. Or have yet to tell their boss. Or who tell me, "Well, I wouldn't deny it, but I don't see a need to broadcast it." Or who say, "I'm sure they know." In fact, "they" do not know until we make it explicit. Until each gay and lesbian person tells the truth about his or her life—by coming out every day, everywhere, and in every situation— the heterosexual world will be able to deny the existence of homosexuality. Denial about sexual realities seems to be an integral part of heterosexuality as it is defined today. The military fight and the so-called compromise that resulted proved that heterosexuals need the gay and lesbian closet in order to feel comfortable about themselves. But why do we participate in this denial of our own existence?

Homosexuality always involves choice—indeed, it involves a series of four major choices: admitting, acting, telling, and living. Even if scientists prove that sexual orientation is biologically or genetically de-termined, every person who feels homosexual desire encounters these four choices. The first involves whether we will admit the existence of our desire: Will we acknowledge to ourselves that we feel same-sex attraction? The second choice is whether to act on this desire: Will we risk engaging in this love? The third is whether to acknowledge to other people that we are gay, lesbian, or bisexual. Several questions come up here: Do we tell our entire family or just the siblings we are close to? Do we come out to an employer or list our gay work on our résumé? Do we tell our doctor that we are gay, tell the insurance company, tell the parent teacher association at the local school our children attend? Do we keep a picture of our partner on the desk at work, in a wallet? Do we take our lover home for the holidays? These questions never end, be-cause the process of coming out to other people never ends. The final choice each gay person makes is how to live a queer life. Will we integrate our homosexuality into everything we do, treating it as natu-rally as heterosexuals treat their sexuality? Or will we separate our "personal" life from "nongay" aspects of life, allowing ourselves to be gay only in the comfort and "privacy" of gay and lesbian spaces?

Ultimately, gay and lesbian people make very different choices when confronted with these questions, and they always will. Most people who feel same-sex desire suppress it—out of fear of stigma, fear of the condemnation by their religious faith, or shame at being a queer. Such repression leads many men and women to act on their sexual desire furtively. They live straight lives but seek gay sex. Men frequent rest stops, men's bathrooms, male porno theaters, and other public sexual spaces. Women experiment with women they know, more privately, since public sex is not a domain available to most women. Many others hide their sexual orientation even as they live gay lives.

Most of us who are out of the closet live by the rules, try to find work, pay our bills, pay taxes, do our best, raise children, and lead ordinary, productive lives. But we are still treated as outsiders the minute we come out. The very act of coming out forces us outside the system. If one is discovered, one can be witch-hunted out of the military, fired from a job, beaten up—for being openly gay or lesbian, even though we embrace every value, every dictate, every aspect of the status quo. We are told that being out forecloses certain options. One can't be the President, a senator, a CEO, a priest, a good mother or father if one is openly gay. Yet being openly gay allows us to develop strong, unashamed, and whole selves; in essence, what those options require. Moreover, being in the closet forecloses those same options, since closeted people always live in fear of discovery.

Like other ethnic or religious minorities that have been stigmatized for their difference, lesbians and gay men face the paradox that we can "pass" as something that we are not. Our ability to pass as heterosexual makes us able to be both insiders and outsiders. This ability to pass confuses us about our ability to mainstream ourselves. We think we can, and the American tradition of immigrant assimilation says we can, but our own experience exposes this aspiration as foolish. The more open and comfortable we are about our homosexuality, the farther outside the cultural, political, and religious norm we are kept.

Passing as straight allows us to be inside heterosexual society and culture completely; being out about our difference opens up a different experience of both heterosexual society and our homosexual life in it. Some of us become hard-core defenders of things as they are, including the status quo of antigay oppression, in an effort to protect our insider status. After all, we can be "inside" the system, our churches, families, the status quo, and enjoy all the benefits that position affords as long as we don't rock the boat. "Don't ask, don't tell" grants us this qualified immunity.

The gay-activist movement has always argued that passing as heterosexuals deforms us. Ironically, today a newly out-of-the-closet breed of gay conservative makes the bizarre counterargument that being out is somehow pathological, a fetish rather than an aspiration for freedom. This is the nonsensical rationalization of the newly out, made to justify their long stay in the isolation of the closet. The truth is that in order to change homosexual status, we must be forthright and open about what it means to be and to live as homosexuals. Nothing will change as long as we pretend to be people we are not.

I take an increasingly hard line against the closet, but I am torn. On one hand, my militancy still does not lead me to condone the tactic of outing, which many gay activists privately endorse but publicly condemn. In early 1995, the papers were filled with news of a British gay group, OutRage, whose outings of Anglican bishops in England has renewed the simmering debate over outing. Despite the impassioned and extremely persuasive arguments made in books by proponents of outing, like the journalist Michelangelo Signorile, Professor Larry Gross, and the philosopher Richard Mohr, I cannot ethically rationalize the coercive aspect of outing, which forcibly discloses another's sexuality and justifies the use of force as self-defense. The argument is made that we are outing hypocrites or homophobes who are killing us with their duplicity. What I am unable to reconcile in my militant desire to out the world is its conflict with the principle of sexual autonomy, which I also cherish. As a woman, I fight for the principle that control of my sexual and reproductive life should rest with me—not with my parents, my spouse, my church or synagogue, not with my government, and certainly not with the censorious "general public" or the community I come from. How, then, can I seize that autonomy and control from another? For me, there is no easy answer to this basic and difficult ethical dilemma presented by outing.

On the other hand, I share the urgency felt by proponents of outing about the need for a new gay community ethic about the closet. Why does each lesbian, gay, or bisexual person not feel a moral imperative to come out of the closet? In most circumstances, I have not encountered situations in which I believed staying in the closet was the better or more "appropriate" alternative. Of course, there are gay and lesbian people living in extremely dangerous situations, where to come out might be self-destructive: teenagers, for example, who live inside a homophobic family; the international gay activists fighting harsh political repression in Latin America; or gay people who face possible execution in countries like Iran if they are discovered. These are not the people or situations to whom I speak. Rather, I am thinking of the successful professional who refuses to tell her co-workers she is a lesbian. Or the gay man who listens quietly to the jokes and homophobic taunts of clients or co-workers. Or each adult who opts not to speak to his or her family about being gay. I have heard everyone's excuses, from my own to those of terrified activists, about their need to remain inside the closet. After much conflict, I have come to believe that none of the most common and widespread reasons is defensible.

Most days, I feel so discouraged and disgusted by the closet that I think only a dramatic attitudinal shift on the part of gay people will weaken its hold. I remain stymied by what a political movement can do about individual decisions to stay in the closet—pulled on one hand by a sense of ethics regarding individual autonomy, and on the other by the negative consequences of our self-imposed marginalization. The urgency of transforming virtual equality into genuine freedom urges us to develop a new moral ethic about being open. Whatever path we take out of the closet, W. H. Auden's words ring true; there will come a time when each of us "will have to leap."

Finally, it bears stating that coming out does not in itself transform the nongay culture in which we live. This is most evident in the co-existence of gay and lesbian ghettos and massive discrimination. This point is one that colleagues have vehemently debated with me. The journalist Masha Gessen, who emigrated to the United States from Russia, once cautioned me not to dismiss the political and material necessity of the ghetto. She pointed out the crucial importance of shelter and safety for a people as stigmatized as we have been. As we have created ghettos to shelter us from the judgment and disdain of a hostile world, we have in many ways created a communal closet. It is roomier in here, more comfortable than the closets we lived in during the 1950s, but the ghetto ultimately proves to be as restrictive as the individual closet. What does it mean if we are willing to be queer only in the confines of certain businesses, certain bars, and certain resorts? What if our gay life is limited, by fear of disclosure, to the reading of certain newspapers, furtive participation in gay community events and spaces, and passive "checkbook activism"? Is that enough, or is that merely a start toward something more meaningful? The goal of a liberation movement must be to eliminate the need for gay and lesbian ghettos: we fight for the option of gay people to live with, work in, be a part of, and affect the whole society, not just the gay and lesbian world.

If we are to transform our state of virtual equality, evident in pervasive discrimination, ambivalent public opinion, and the persistence of the closet, we must begin with ourselves—both individually and as a movement. Coming out is the one step each gay, lesbian, or bisexual person can take to shatter virtual equality and move closer to the genuine equality with heterosexuals that is our birthright as moral human beings. Our challenge as a movement requires an examination of the strategies that have brought us to this troubling juncture.

CHAPTER TWO

LEGITIMATION, LIBERATION, AND HISTORY

History is made and preserved by and for particular classes of people.

—*David Wojnarowicz*

After the midterm elections of 1994, Rich Tafel, the president of the Log Cabin Republican Club, proclaimed, "This election marks the definitive end to the Stonewall-generation of politics . . . Now that the old generation has been repudiated, the next generation of Gay leaders has the opportunity to refine the movement." His interpretation of the 1994 elections was wishful thinking at best and calculated opportunism at worst. Most of all, it was empirically untrue.

Tafel's thesis—that the shift in the gay vote toward the GOP in 1994 represented the repudiation of gay and lesbian liberation politics—is plausible only if several assumptions are made. First, that "Stonewall-generation politics" have in fact dominated the gay and lesbian political movement. Second, that the politics of liberation have so dominated the Democratic Party that an electoral shift of 5 to 8 percent in the gay vote (between 1992 and 1994) can be read as an emphatic repudiation of such politics. And finally, that gay liberation actually failed the movement. History proves each of these assumptions wrong.

For one, the Stonewall-era ideal of liberation and radical social change ceased to dominate the mainstream of gay and lesbian politics nearly twenty years ago, in the late 1970s. From that period on, the gay and lesbian political movement pursued social, legal, cultural, and political legitimation—what I call mainstreaming—rather than social change. The dramatic but partial end-point of the legitimation strategy has become clear in the 1990s. Neither a significant gay and lesbian electoral turnout in 1992, nor our carefully husbanded political and financial clout, not even a liberal President has been enough to secure us the genuine equality we seek.

Second, the Democratic Party of the 1990s can hardly be characterized as a bastion of left politics or even of liberalism. A pitched battle for control of the party has been under way for years, and so-called New Democrats (who would do better to call themselves New Republicans) have worked effectively to move the party to the right. In this context, the shift in a percentage of the gay vote toward Republicans is more likely to stem from anger at Democratic abandonment of the gay community (during the military fight and in AIDS policy) than from a "repudiation" of liberalism, much less Stonewall-generation politics. The gay shift, in fact, could be read as a repudiation of the posturing of New Democrats; gay people would rather vote for genuine conservatives than fake ones.

Finally, and most paradoxically, despite the dominance of legitimation strategies on the political front, gay and lesbian liberation politics remain relevant culturally. The cultural revolution in gay and lesbian visibility, our progressive empowerment, and sense of pride have been undaunted by the many political setbacks we have suffered in the past few years. Lesbians and gay men appear in television shows as regular characters, from Amanda Bearse to Sandra Bernhard. Drag has become a mainstream phenomenon, with RuPaul and Dame Edna, and movies with drag leads are popular *(Priscilla, Queen of the Desert* and *The Crying Game)*. Meanwhile, gay men are more visible than ever in every corner of the culture, from Broadway to Hollywood to the fashion industry to literature to politics. This cultural explosion is a byproduct of the very liberation politics that Tafel and other neoconservatives deride. Rather than refining our movement to reject what has worked, it would be more logical for us to refine gay and lesbian liberation politics in order to make them relevant to the changed circumstances of a twenty-first-century movement.

Neoconservative sniping at liberation is itself nothing new.

Throughout the history of our resistance to prejudice, gay people have clashed over a fundamental question about the overall goal of our movement. Are we a movement aimed at mainstreaming gay and lesbian people (legitimation), or do we seek radical social change out of the process of our integration (liberation)? Gay and lesbian history could be read as the saga of conflict between these two compatible but divergent goals. Legitimation and liberation are interconnected and often congruent; the former makes it possible to imagine the latter. But our pursuit of them takes different roads and leads to very different outcomes. For some gay and lesbian people, mainstream integration is the paramount goal of our political movement. For others, the transformation of mainstream culture holds the key to genuine gay and lesbian equality. Some of us believe that our political movement exists solely to fight antigay and antilesbian prejudice. Others believe that the elimination of homophobic prejudice is intimately related to the end of gender inequality, the end of racial prejudice, and the institution of a moral economic system.

Gay and lesbian legitimation seeks straight tolerance and acceptance of gay people; gay and lesbian liberation seeks nothing less than affirmation, represented in the acknowledgment that queer sexuality is morally equivalent to straight sexuality. Legitimation seeks to change hearts and minds by educating the general public to understand that gay and lesbian people are human beings. Liberation seeks that same shift in consciousness, but it also looks for a transformation in social institutions—in government, family, religion, and the economy. Legitimation strategies stem from the discrimination that gay and lesbian people face as a minority; the goal of our movement is to end that discrimination and protect our rights. The movement for gay and lesbian liberation, on the other hand, focuses on the suppression of sexuality itself. Viewing categories like gay and straight as constraining, gay liberation seeks to "liberate an aspect of the personal lives of all people—sexual expression." Today, the split between the political center and the political margin has changed from a dialectical tension, whose synthesis keeps us honest, to a deepening breach that divides two hostile camps.

Proponents of legitimation argue to the straight world that gay people are "just like" straights, that we are merely a minority, and that prejudice against us is, therefore, irrational and unconstitutional. Within gay and lesbian communities, legitimationists—like writers Hunter Madsen, Marshall Kirk, Bruce Bawer, Andrew Sullivan—have urged us to narrow the focus of our movement from cultural transformation to public discrimination. Some have called for the movement to minimize the public exposure of drag queens, sadomasochists, effeminate men, butch women, political radicals, multiculturalists, and anyone not aspiring to join the middle-class mainstream. This suppression of internal dissent is called "education" by some neoconservative voices. According to Bawer, "The general guiding philosophy of the gay populace should be one not of confrontation but of connection, not of agitation but of education, not of revolution but of reform."

Proponents of liberation argue that gay, lesbian, bisexual, transgendered, and straight people are all subject to an oppressive sexual and political order, what Adrienne Rich calls "compulsory heterosexuality." Liberationists devised the strategies of visibility and coming-out to challenge the cultural stereotypes that flourished because of gay invisibility. They began the process of cultural reconstruction by building alternative institutions and communities, and they urged the movement to set its sights beyond education and reform, to a radically new relationship with the straight culture, one that saw gayness as an aspect of all straight people, not merely a genetically based queerness in some.

As a formal political movement, gay and lesbian liberation was short-lived. Having emerged in the post-Stonewall period, it had largely disappeared as a national force by the early 1980s. But the ideas, values, and criticisms made by gay and lesbian liberationists survived and flourished in queer culture. This dissonance between a gay culture that embodies values more radical than the political movement that defends it continues to be a source of tension within the contemporary gay and lesbian movement.

Organized political resistance to antigay and antilesbian discrimination is largely a twentieth-century story. The stages of gay and lesbian history can be divided crudely into six periods: 1) the pre–World War II era, at and after the turn of the twentieth century; 2) the post–World War II period, marked by the emergence of the "minority status model"; 3) gay and lesbian liberation, which began in the late sixties and lasted until the early seventies; 4) gay and lesbian lifestyle or identity politics, lasting from the mid-seventies to this day; 5) the eighties, marked by AIDS, an antigay backlash, and internal conflict over racial difference; and 6) the present period of virtual equality, in which we have yet to reap the benefits of a strong nationwide movement. The stages sometimes overlap, and the last three continue to this day. In each of these historical periods, the conflict between margin and center, between the goals of legitimation and liberation, affected the direction of the emerging gay and lesbian movement. Here I consider the dialectic of legitimation and liberation in the first four periods: the pre–World War II era; the postwar period; the Stonewall era of gay and lesbian liberation; and the post-Stonewall era, marked by an emerging queer culture.

PRE–WORLD WAR II ERA

Same-sex behavior is as old as desire itself, but the categories of homosexual and heterosexual are twentieth-century inventions. In a fascinating book on the social anxiety generated by the *fin de siècle*, the literary critic Elaine Showalter explains that "the 1880s and 1890s were decades of 'sexual anarchy,' when all the laws that governed sexual identity and behavior seemed to be breaking down. [I]t is precisely in periods of cultural insecurity, where there are fears of regression and degeneration, [that] the longing for strict border controls around the definition of gender as well as race, class, and nationality, becomes especially intense." Indeed, the first period of backlash against homosexuality in Europe coincided with the start of this fledgling public discussion of sexuality at the end of the nineteenth century. Carried out through public morality campaigns, police crackdowns on homosexual solicitation, and increased enforcement of criminal laws, the backlash was dramatically publicized through the prosecution and conviction, in 1895, of the British writer Oscar Wilde on charges of "gross indecency."

Fortunately, this reaction sparked the formation of early organizations to promote greater tolerance toward homosexual people. The first known gay rights organization was founded in Germany on May 15, 1897, by a doctor named Magnus Hirschfeld. Called the Scientific Humanitarian Committee, it held educational forums, published a journal, and worked to reform criminal laws. Significantly, the SHC had an early relationship with the German feminist movement, and sponsored conferences on new ideas about homosexuality. Hirschfeld also founded two other organizations: in 1919, the Institute for Sex Research in Berlin; and in the 1920s, the World League for Sexual Reform, which boasted 130,000 members worldwide.

Not surprisingly, the Nazi movement destroyed this pioneering German homosexual emancipation movement. On May 6, 1933, Nazi students destroyed the headquarters of the Institute for Sex Research, and burned its library. When the SHC was also suppressed by the Nazis in 1933, Hirschfeld fled Germany for France, where he died in 1935. Exhibits at the Holocaust Museum in Washington document the persecution of gay and lesbian people, who were exterminated by the Nazis, alongside Jews, Gypsies, and others deemed undesirable. The Dutch historian Dr. Klaus Mueller, who was a consultant on gay and lesbian history to the Holocaust Museum, notes that historians have verified that at least ten thousand to fifteen thousand gay men, and an undetermined number of lesbians, were killed by the Nazis in concentration camps.

Before its collapse, the early German gay movement inspired Henry Gerber, an American immigrant from Bavaria, to establish the first U.S. gay rights group, in 1924. The short-lived Society for Human Rights was founded by Gerber and five others, in Chicago, "to combat the public prejudices" against homosexual people. The society folded in 1925, when newspaper coverage of its existence brought the harassment of its founders, Gerber's arrest and trial, biased and negative publicity, and the loss of Gerber's job with the U.S. Post Office, for "conduct unbecoming a postal worker." Years later, Gerber wrote about the experience of founding the society in *One* magazine, the first American gay periodical. In *Gay American History*, Jonathan Katz reprints Gerber's analysis. Prefiguring the sentiments of generations of gay and lesbian activists, Gerber wrote: "One of our greatest handicaps was the knowledge that homosexuals don't organize. Being thoroughly cowed, they seldom get together. Most feel that as long as some homosexual acts are against the law, they should not let their names be on any homosexual organization's mailing list any more than notorious bandits would join a thieves' union. Today [1962] there are at least half a dozen homophile organizations working openly for the group, but still the number of dues-paying members is very small when we know that there are several million homosexuals in the U.S."

In a concise history of the international gay and lesbian movement, Barry Adam distinguishes between the presence of same-sex behavior and the existence of a self-conscious community: "What distinguishes the modern lesbian and gay world from anthropological and historical examples of homosexuality is the development of social networks founded on the homosexual interests of their members." Adam dates the emergence of such organized networks for gay men to the early

1700s in England, France, and the Netherlands, and for both gay men and women in America to the late 1800s.

This distinction between same-sex behavior and community, and the impact of gender identification, sexuality, and social status, is examined in detail in George Chauncey's remarkable history of the gay male community in New York City, *Gay New York*. Chauncey brings to life the vibrant, complex, and relatively open gay male culture that existed in New York City at the turn of the last century. Contrary to modern myth, a visible gay male culture not only flourished, but was integrated into the straight communities around it and was widely tolerated, especially in working-class communities. Chauncey notes that three flourishing gay male neighborhoods existed in New York at the time—the Bowery, Greenwich Village, and Harlem—and he draws the unique class, ethnic, and racial portrait of each.

Chauncey's work is especially breathtaking in its insights into anti-gay prejudice and the evolution of gay and lesbian resistance. Revealing the primacy of gender and of the cultural meaning of femininity and manhood in the formation of modern gay male identity and communities, Chauncey details the impact on gay male identity, and on straight culture, of the male "fairy," a highly visible, effeminate style of being gay that men adopted at the start of the century. "As the dominant pejorative category in opposition to which male sexual 'normality' was defined, the fairy influenced the culture and self-understanding of *all* sexually active men . . . The determinative criterion in the identification of men as fairies was not the extent of their same-sex desire or activity (their 'sexuality'), but rather the gender persona and status they assumed."

Chauncey explains how homosexual desire was then seen as a subset of gender, not as something independent of it. "The fairies' sexual desire for men was not regarded as the singular characteristic that distinguished them from other men, as is generally the case for gay men today. That desire was seen as simply one aspect of a much more comprehensive gender role inversion (or reversal) which they were also expected to manifest through the adoption of effeminate dress and mannerisms; they were thus often called *inverts* (who had 'inverted' their gender) rather than *homosexuals* in technical language." He goes on to detail the complexity and specificity with which nineteenth- and twentieth-century gay men developed their identities in relation to this culturally visible type of homosexual. Some men engaged in same-sex behavior but never identified as fairies. Others took only a traditionally masculine (active) role in sex; yet others took a traditionally feminine role. "By the 1910s and 1920s, men who identified themselves as different from other men primarily on the basis of their homosexual interest rather than their womanlike gender status usually called themselves 'queer.'"

Chauncey's observations about the centrality of gender nonconformity in determining the identities of gay men before World War II is echoed in a book by Elizabeth Kennedy and Madeline Davis that traces the history of a working-class lesbian community in the pre– and post–World War II eras, *Boots of Leather, Slippers of Gold.* This history of the lesbian community of Buffalo, New York, in the 1940s and 1950s reaches similar conclusions about the central role played by gender nonconformity in the formation of modern lesbian community and identities. "At a time when lesbian communities were developing solidarity and consciousness, but had not yet formed political groups, butch-fem roles were the key structure for organizing against heterosexual dominance. They were central prepolitical forms of resistance. From this perspective, butch-fem cannot be viewed simply as an imitation of heterosexual, sexist society. Although they derived in great part from heterosexual models, the roles also transformed those models and created an authentic lesbian lifestyle."

Another significant contribution both of these books make to our understanding of modern gay and lesbian history is the story of middle-class and working-class people, of patrons of gay and lesbian bars, and of many different kinds of gay people previously hidden in more elite-dominated gay and lesbian literary, political, and intellectual histories. By so doing, these books provide fresh insights into class tensions among gay and lesbian people and suggest how our class allegiances affect the movement we have created. For example, Kennedy and Davis demonstrate the inaccuracy of the idea of one community simply by documenting multiple lesbian working-class subcommunities. "Minimally, we could document three public working-class communities in Buffalo in the 1950s—the upwardly mobile, the tough Black crowd, and the tough, primarily white, bar crowd . . . In the particular setting of the late 1960s and early 1970s, a lesbian politic that was based on a unified sense of identity actually severed existing ties between different lesbian subcommunities: 'the lesbian' became white and middle class."

Chauncey argues that it was middle-class gay men who rejected the traditional femininity of the fairy and invented the notion of the "queer," who desired men but was not effeminate. Chauncey quotes from a number of men from the early 1900s who "blamed antigay hostility on the failure of fairies to abide by straight middle-class conventions of decorum in their dress and style." Sounding a lot like gay conservatives today, one man described his frustration that the most extreme and visible type of gay man comes to define the more moderate, but less visible, majority: "As the cultured, distinguished conservative Jew or Negro loathes and deplores his vulgar, socially unacceptable stereotype, plenty of whom unfortunately are all too visible . . . so does their homosexual counterpart resent *his* caricature in the flaming faggot . . . The general public [makes no distinction], and the one is penalized and ostracized for the grossness and excesses of the other."

Another of Chauncey's fascinating observations about class concerns the way men "recast gay cultural styles." He shows that "forms of speech, dress or demeanor that might be ridiculed as womanly, effeminate, or inappropriate to a 'real' man in one cultural group might be valued as manly, worldly, or appropriate to a 'cultured' (or 'sensitive') man in another . . . Thus while many fairies created a place for themselves in working-class culture by constructing a highly effeminate persona, many other gay men created a place in middle-class culture by constructing a persona of highly mannered—and ambiguous—sophistication . . . While the fairy intended his style to mark him as a sexual invert, however, the queer intended his style to deflect such suspicion." The adoption of upper-class values in the belief that they protect us is a strategy that middle-class gay men and women rely on to this day.

Finally, Chauncey echoes Jonathan Ned Katz's contention (developed in Katz's book, *The Invention of Heterosexuality*) that the turn of the century marked not only the invention of the homosexual, but the invention of the heterosexual. He identifies several cultural sources of the binary homosexual and heterosexual identities that we today take for granted: first, the high visibility of fairies; second, rising social anxiety among middle-class heterosexual men as women's roles changed in the late nineteenth century and as a women's movement emerged; third, competition between middle-class and working-class heterosexual men over the meaning of manhood, of who was more of a "real" man; fourth, the development of co-gender social networks in the 1900s to replace the single-sex social networks of the late 1800s; and fifth, the appearance of heterosexuality as a normative category in the medical discourse of the day.

By showing the ways that gender and sexuality were integral to the formation of gay male identity in the early 1900s, and how they diverged into the binary reality of heterosexuality and homosexuality, Chauncey's research exposes three fallacies of our contemporary movement. The first holds that gay and lesbian oppression is singular and disconnected from sexism and women's social status. The second fallacy is that all gay and lesbian people have similar interests, regardless of their economic class. And the third fallacy is that homosexual sexuality is merely the queer version of heterosexual sexuality. Throughout this book, these fallacies will surface to illustrate how our current situation remains blind to the lessons of history and the illusions that undergird and reinforce our virtual equality.

The first fallacy—that oppression based on gender and sexual-orientation discrimination is not connected—is evident throughout our movement. Gay male leaders talk about a coalition with the women's movement as if it were something separate to begin with. Conversely, the mainstream women's movement has retreated from its critique of gender itself to the less threatening critique of gender inequality. Lesbian activists who bridge both movements are handicapped by the sexism of the former and the homophobia of the latter, and have been unable to make either acknowledge the value of accepting both movements as subsets of one common movement. To anyone reading these two new histories, the connection between homophobia and gender-based prejudice is inescapable.

The practical impact of avoiding these connections was most clearly evident in 1993, in the failure of both movements to challenge the sexist roots of the military's antigay and antilesbian policy. The military discourse was primarily about manhood, but our movements waged the fight in the language of fairness. As an institution, the military was fighting for heterosexual survival: to justify itself, heterosexuality must enforce rigid and restrictive ideas of femininity and masculinity on all people. The military man's fear was that he would be regarded as less than straight if he acknowledged that he loved his gay military buddy as strongly as his straight male military buddy. The military woman's fear was of being labeled a dyke because she was doing nontraditional female work. Our movement never directly answered each of these fears, but focused principally on the politicized language of constitutional law, civil rights, and patriotism. Perhaps our defeat is as much a product of our avoidance of the intersection of gender and homophobia as it is a function of Sam Nunn's ego and President Clinton's abdication.

The second fallacy under which we labor is that class differences among gay and lesbian people are somehow irrelevant to the agenda and unity of purpose of the gay and lesbian movement. In fact, the movement lacks a common agenda precisely because the class interests of gay people diverge. Our movement is led by middle- to upper-middle-class people who act on their economic interests as frequently as they act on their sexual politics. Gay Republicans, who are the most honest about the importance to them of economic issues, have begun to acknowledge this divergence in recent months. So, for example, after the 1994 congressional elections, Rich Tafel of the Log Cabin Republican Club argued that large numbers of gay voters had shifted to the GOP because the party leadership had toned down its antigay rhetoric, and they were able to vote their economic interests. Tafel said, "It's something I've been saying for a long time: if Republicans focus on economic and other issues, and there's no Gay-bashing involved, no anti-Gay attacks, they will get a bigger chunk of the Gay vote."

The phenomenon of opting for economic self-interest over gay and lesbian interest is not limited to gay Republicans; prominent gay Democrats have done this for decades. A recent example involved the nationally known gay Democratic leader David Mixner. During the health care debates of 1993 and 1994, queer progressives, gay, and lesbian health clinics and many of the largest AIDS organizations actively pushed for a single-payer plan. In California, the effort involved an attempt to pass a statewide single-payer initiative known as the California Health Security Act, or Proposition 186. According to Paul DiDonato, an attorney with the San Francisco AIDS Foundation, Proposition 186 represented "our absolutely best hope for Californians with HIV and AIDS for achieving equal access to health care." But David Mixner was hired by the political action committee opposing the single-payer measure to lobby against gay and AIDS community support for the bill. According to an investigative report in the *L.A. Village View,* during September 1994 Mixner lobbied the AIDS Project Los Angeles (APLA) board to oppose Proposition 186, without disclosing that he was being paid to lobby against the measure. By October 1994, he had been paid at least $34,000 from the Taxpayers Against the Government Takeover (the No on 186 group) and had received an additional, unspecified amount of money for his representation of another Prop 186 opponent, Aetna Life and Casualty Insurance Company. In the fall of 1994, the No on 186 committee reportedly donated $45,000 to the Access Network for Gay and Lesbian Equality

(ANGLE), a political action network of wealthy LA gay and lesbian people of which Mixner is a founding member. ANGLE used the funds to distribute 400,000 ballot slate mailers, recommending how voters should decide on a number of measures, including a negative vote on Prop 186.

The final fallacy in our movement that we must confront is the idea that homosexuality and heterosexuality are merely two sides of a common coin called sexuality. Many of us genuinely believe that being homosexual differs from being heterosexual only in sexual object choice. We cite new scientific evidence of a biological basis for homosexual orientation as if that fact proves our essential similarity to heterosexuals. This view of sexuality actually holds us back. The histories of gay and lesbian emergence suggest that "sexual identity is much more fluid than the dominant conceptual system allows us to entertain. The boundaries between heterosexual and homosexual have always been difficult to draw . . . We have before us the challenge of thinking of new ways of drawing the boundaries, free from nineteenth-century moral imperatives." In a society whose institutions embody a presumption of heteronormativity and homosexual deviance, arguing that we are just like every one else convinces no one. Further, the argument may not be true: we are just like heterosexuals in the fact of our humanity, but I believe we differ markedly in our view of sexuality, gender, power, and morality. The values around which we have built gay and lesbian relationships, made family, and formed communities are not identical with the values that we were raised to hold by our heterosexual parents—nor are they merely the gay and lesbian mirror images of those straight values. They are values that are uniquely our own, arising out of our experience as outsiders, built out of the experience of resisting sexual repression. I believe that social science research may well prove that homosexual and bisexual people have strikingly different ideas from those of straight people about gender, sexual behavior, relationships, nonbiological family ties (including the importance of friends as family), and power.

These three contemporary fallacies are contradicted by the historical record of pre–World War II gay and lesbian communities. Yet few of us are aware of this early history or take it into account. Reading new histories of our communities should lead us to question the values and assumptions that underlie our movement.

THE POST–WORLD WAR II MOVEMENT

In the United States, World War II marked a turning point in the development of modern gay and lesbian communities. Allan Bérubé's landmark history, *Coming Out Under Fire,* suggests several ways in which the war aided the emergence of a modern gay and lesbian identity and movement. For one, Bérubé states that the war brought previously isolated homosexual men and women into contact with one another. Thousands of people thereby learned that they were not the only ones with homosexual feelings, and many came to accept themselves as homosexual. Second, Bérubé observes that the sex-segregated environment of the service fostered "situational homosexuality": many previously heterosexual people had same-sex experiences because they had the opportunity to, and through these experiences some realized their homosexuality or bisexuality.

Third, and perhaps most significant, Bérubé suggests that World War II changed the expectations of gay and lesbian people themselves. This shift in consciousness was dramatic and irrevocable, and represented the first step toward the shattering of public silence about homosexuality. Bérubé and the historian John D'Emilio both believe that the raised expectations of the postwar generation facilitated the formation of the first American gay and lesbian communities, and aided the organizing of social and support organizations in the 1950s. As Bérubé observes,

> Previous generations had invented the closet—a system of lies, denials, disguises, and double entendres—that had enabled them to express some of their homosexuality by pretending it didn't exist and hiding it from view. A later generation would "come out of the closet," learning to live as proud and openly gay men and women and demanding public recognition. But the World War II generation slowly stretched their closet to its limit, neither proclaiming or parading their homosexuality in public, but not willing to live lonely, isolated lives.

Bérubé reports that the postwar period witnessed an explosion in the spread of gay and lesbian bars and clubs, and marked the beginning of the mass migration of people to major cities like San Francisco and New York, where they could live gay and lesbian lives. This nascent postwar community of gay men and women was, like its nongay counterparts, ripe for political organizing. As the climate grew more overtly hostile toward gay men and lesbians, a new social movement came into being.

The visibility of returning servicemen and women who were gay, and the escalation of the Cold War, also intensified antigay and antilesbian crusades. Witch hunts against gay service members increased as the war wound down and the government no longer needed every available body for the fight. "Undesirable discharges," which prevented veterans from receiving health, pension, and unemployment benefits and also limited their ability to secure work, were issued regularly to gay and lesbian service members. In this climate, the first gay and lesbian membership organization in this country—the Veterans Benevolent Association—was formed in 1945 to provide support, referrals, and a social network for veterans facing such discharges or trying to adjust to life after the war. The VBA continued to support gay and lesbian service members until 1954. Bérubé notes an early alliance between the VBA and the NAACP in the late 1940s as they found a disproportionate number of black service members receiving undesirable discharges. Through a media and political lobbying campaign, the two groups succeeded in ending the use of this category against black soldiers, but it continued to be used against gay and lesbian veterans.

John D'Emilio's compelling history, *Sexual Politics, Sexual Communities,* details the parallel rise of homophobia and anticommunist witch hunts in the postwar era. The Cold War mentality of the early 1950s led to an early—and false—connection between political and sexual subversion: homosexuals were suspect precisely because they were deviant. Campaigns to purge homosexuals from government agencies multiplied as the decade progressed. Given the hysteria surrounding the perceived communist threat, it is remarkable that a gay and lesbian movement was born. What makes it all the more remarkable is that it was a small group of communist and progressive gay men in Los Angeles who founded the first modern gay rights organization, the Mattachine Society, in April 1951.

The Mattachine Society provided support and camaraderie for gay and lesbian people, and held discussions about homosexuality. Jonathan Katz summarized its "mission and principles" statement as follows:

"TO UNIFY" those homosexuals "isolated from their own kind," to provide a principle from which "all of our people can . . . derive a feeling of 'belonging.'" The second principle is "TO EDUCATE" homosexuals and heterosexuals. In reference to education, the society is said to be developing an "ethical homosexual culture . . . paralleling the emerging cultures of our fellow minorities—the Negro, Mexican and Jewish people." The third purpose is "TO LEAD"; the "more . . . socially conscious homosexuals [are to] provide leadership to the whole mass of social deviates. An additional "imperative need is for "political action" against "discriminatory and oppressive legislation." The society is said to assist "our people who are victimized daily as a result of our oppression," and who constitute "one of the largest minorities in America today."

Because of the hostile social climate at the time, Mattachine was organized as a secret society, composed of autonomous guilds. Although historians differ on the source and meaning of the name Mattachine, all agree that the name was apt, for it evoked the notion of a masked people who met secretly. The *Oxford Dictionary of English Etymology* offers a multilingual root for the word *matachin,* citing French and Spanish sources and tracing it to the Arabic *mutawajjihin,* which meant to assume a mask *(wajh* means face). John D'Emilio reported that the name came from a mysterious society of "medieval figures in masks." Randy Shilts believed the origin of the name was the Italian *"matachinos . . .* [or] court jesters who, behind a mask, could speak the truth to otherwise obdurate rulers." Toby Marotta said the name was that of "a secret fraternity of unmarried French townsmen who, in the Middle Ages, conducted dances and rituals at festivals." The Mattachine founder, Harry Hay, told Katz that the name came from the French *"sociétés joyeux"* one of which was called Society Mattachine.

These . . . lifelong secret fraternities of unmarried townsmen who never performed in public unmasked were dedicated to going out into the countryside and conducting dances and rituals . . . Sometimes these dance rituals, or masques, were peasant protests against oppression—with the maskers, in the people's name, receiving the brunt of a given lord's vicious retaliation. So we took the name Mattachine because we felt that we 1950s Gays were also a marked

> people, unknown and anonymous, who might become engaged in
> morale building and helping ourselves.

What is fascinating about this cultural archaeology is how appropriate
the name turns out to have been. Every definition denotes the masking
of identity on one hand and the use of joy, jest, and art as a protest on
the other. Mask and camp became the hallmarks of gay and lesbian
existence and resistance.

By May 1953, membership in Mattachine numbered twenty-five
hundred. The society sponsored nearly a hundred discussion groups
from San Diego to San Francisco, and launched *One* magazine. This
gay publication, in Los Angeles, became a separate organization in
January 1953. By 1955, the first lesbian organization—called the
Daughters of Bilitis (DOB)—was founded by a group of more moderate, and equally courageous, women. DOB was launched in San Francisco through the efforts of eight lesbians, including the long-time
activists Del Martin and Phyllis Lyon, who chronicled their pioneering
work in the book *Lesbian/Woman*. Founded as an alternative to the bar
scene, DOB offered a safe space in which lesbians could meet, support
one another, and begin to educate the broader society. In 1956 the
DOB started a publication, *The Ladder*, which it continued to publish
until 1973.

By the early 1960s, both the Mattachine Society and DOB had
gone national, with active chapters in New York, Washington, and San
Francisco. The number of activists remained small, but the growing
readership of movement publications revealed that a broader group was
being influenced by the militancy of this small cadre. From the late
1950s to 1968, homophile groups launched campaigns to protest police
harassment in New York and San Francisco, defended in court their
right to congregate, and became involved with the New York mayoral
race and with Democratic Party activity in San Francisco. Militants like
Frank Kameny (founder of the Mattachine Society of Washington), the
late Craig Rodwell (founder of the Oscar Wilde Memorial Bookshop,
the first gay bookstore in the country), and Barbara Gittings (founder of
the Daughters of Bilitis chapter in New York) organized the first widely
publicized gay rights pickets in Washington in 1965. The demonstrations targeted the Pentagon, the White House, and a host of federal
agencies to protest employment discrimination against gay men and
women. The movement grew in the Midwest and South, and sponsored
a series of networking conferences and regional associations.

At least three of the five gay men who founded the Mattachine Society were intimately involved in Communist Party activity. The founder, Harry Hay, born in 1912 and still going strong as a founder and spiritual guide of the Radical Faeries, worked in the Communist Party for nearly fifteen years, doing dramatic propagandist theater and union organizing. A co-founder, Chuck Rowland, came home from the army after World War II and helped organize the American Veterans Committee, for which he worked over the next three years. He joined the Communist Party in 1946, but left it within two years after becoming disillusioned and afraid of the growing anticommunist tide in the country. Bob Hull, another Mattachine founder, remained a member of the party into the 1950s, working in one of its cultural units in Southern California. Two other Mattachine pioneers were a gay costume designer indicated by John D'Emilio only as R and later identified as Rudi Gernrich, and the Los Angeles writer Dale Jennings, who had worked on behalf of Japanese-Americans during the Second World War.

The impact of the Mattachine Society's founding by people who were outside the political mainstream was twofold. First, the tensions between the radical founders and conservative members of the society created a political split that still exists. Seen narrowly, the split between radicals and conservatives was about whether the communist background of the founders would harm the newly formed organization. Seen more broadly, the disagreement centered on the vision and goals of the progressive founders. Fights within Mattachine quickly broke out over its agenda and the direction of the movement. Red-baiting, an activity from the McCarthy era, scared moderates and conservatives away from the gay communist founders. Leftists still evoke such a harsh reaction in the movement. Last year, Rich Tafel argued that gay voters were frustrated with the "liberal social agenda of the 1960s . . . [and] the old traditions of Gay activism." More recently, critics attacked the NGLTF for hiring an executive director, Melinda Paras, who had been involved with communist organizations.

A second way the radical background of the Mattachine founders affected the movement was entirely conceptual. Calling their analysis "startlingly radical," the historian Martin Duberman wrote, "This small group of some dozen men pioneered the notion—which from mid-1953 to 1969 fell out of favor in homophile circles, only to be picked up again by gay activists after 1969—that gays were a legitimate minority living within a hostile mainstream culture." Reviewing gay and lesbian history almost fifty years later, it is hard to comprehend why the "mi-

nority" concept was, and remains, so controversial. But the idea that
homosexuals constitute a sexual minority, entitled to the rights and
benefits of any ethnic or cultural minority group, marked a profound
redefinition of homosexuality. D'Emilio suggests that the conception of
homosexuals as a distinct minority aided the gay political movement in
three crucial ways: it helped homosexuals define themselves rather than
being defined by a hostile straight culture; it gave focus to homosexual
political organizing by directing us to pursue civil rights; and it introduced the radical view that homosexual orientation was something distinct from, but morally equivalent to, heterosexual orientation.

From the outset, the minority group model gave early activists a
nonjudgmental definition of homosexuality: as a sexual minority. Every
other characterization of homosexual behavior defined us in a negative
and condemning manner (sinners, criminals, psychotics, and so on).
Defining us as a sexual minority also moved homosexuality from the
domain of illness and sociopathic deviance and into the public domain
of civil rights. As a sexual minority, we challenged claims that our
deviance was bad, pointing out instead that it was unfairly stigmatized.
The idea that homosexuals were a minority gave a material and political
stature to gay existence that in turn helped the movement to grow: if
lesbians and gay men were "one of the largest minorities in America
today," as the Mattachine mission statement asserted, then politicians
had better pay attention. Finally, the minority group framework located
gay and lesbian people within a long liberal democratic tradition of
ethnic, racial, and cultural minorities. Gay and lesbian people were like
immigrants who came to America and made a home, but had to overcome prejudice and irrational fears along the way. We urged society to
see us as it saw the Irish, the Jews, or any other ethnic or racial minority.

Ultimately, conflict over political ideology and the view of gay people as a minority played a central role in causing a split in the Mattachine Society. In 1953, gay conservatives challenged the leadership of
the radical founders and won control. The drive to purge communists
from Mattachine grew, ironically, out of the first mainstream media
coverage the group garnered. That year, an article in the *Los Angeles
Mirror* reported that "a strange new pressure group for perverts," the
Mattachine Society, had sent questionnaires to candidates for public
office. The piece also noted that the group's legal adviser, Fred Snider,
had refused to testify at the anticommunist hearings of the House Un-
American Activities Committees (HUAC). Believing that this publicity

of their political activities was beneficial, the Mattachine founders sent thousands of copies of the news article to their members. Their enthusiasm backfired, as more conservative members became alarmed. Harry Hay remembers that more than five hundred people attended the regularly scheduled annual convention, held in April 1953. Hay's speech—"Are You Now or Have You Ever Been a Homosexual?"—mimicked the leading question asked by the committee. Hay explained that Mattachine was not only free from partisan and party influence, but that it was well aware that the left had gone out of its way to repudiate gay people. He argued forcefully that the organization should take an independent course—free of the influence of the left or the right. But Hay's unrepentant defense of Snider's refusal to cooperate with HUAC alienated conservatives. At the convention, it also became clear that HUAC was expanding its investigation to Hollywood. The pressure to dissociate the fledgling group from the taint of communist influence was intense. Rather than see the society fall apart completely, the founders all resigned and gave the organization's name to the convention to use as it willed.

Discussing the split years later with the historian Jonathan Katz, Harry Hay described it as a conflict in vision. "The original society was based upon this feeling of idealism, a great transcendent dream of what being Gay was all about. I had proposed from the very beginning that it would be Mattachine's job to find out who we Gays were (and had been over the millennia) and what we were for, and on such basis, to find ways to make our contributions to our parent hetero society." The moderates who took over the society in 1953 saw accommodation to straight norms as critical to the movement's success. They argued that homosexuals should "adjust to a pattern of behavior that is acceptable to society in general and compatible with the recognized institutions of home, church, and state." At the April 1953 convention, Marilyn Rieger, a member from Los Angeles, argued, "We know we are the same . . . no different than anyone else. Our only difference is an unimportant one to the heterosexual society, *unless we make it important*" [emphasis in original]. Rieger reasoned that stressing a homosexual culture distinct from the dominant one would only exacerbate the hostility of society, and she pleaded with the delegates to reject such a position. Equality for gay men and women would come, she said, "by integrating . . . not as homosexuals, but as people, as men and women whose homosexuality is irrelevant to our ideals, our principles, our hopes and aspirations." To activists like Rieger, the founders' insistence on defining gay and lesbian identity and claiming a distinct minority status created a chasm between gay and straight people. As John D'Emilio observes, "The emphasis that proponents of the gay minority status placed on being different aroused the antagonism of individuals who yearned above all for simple acceptance of who they were."

Jonathan Katz asked Harry Hay to explain how the mainstream leadership that emerged from the 1953 split differed from the radical founders of the society. Hay answered in language that could describe what gay conservatives and radicals fight over in the 1990s. "The Mattachine after 1953 was primarily concerned with legal change, with being seen as respectable—rather than self-respecting. They wanted to be dignified by professional 'authorities' and prestigious people, rather than by the more compelling dignity of group worth." Gay conservatives today believe the movement should highlight the respectability of the queer mainstream, to "bring the public image of homosexuality into closer alignment with the reality of the majority of gay lives." Their assumption is that gayness can be explained, and will be accepted, as respectable by the heterosexual majority. This notion glosses over the fact that such respectability is limited by race, class, and gender assumptions in the concept. Some gay people will always be considered more respectable than others because of factors having little to do with sexuality. Further, history shows that the quest for middle-class respectability for gay men and lesbians is contingent on a broad redefinition of the place of the sexual, which has not yet been formulated. Our culture continues to be driven by panic and titillation about sex. When a public health expert like former Surgeon General Joycelyn Elders can lose her job for merely acknowledging that people masturbate, sex itself is not respectable, and queer sexuality has a long way to go.

STONEWALL AND THE BIRTH
OF GAY AND LESBIAN LIBERATION

The post-Stonewall generation of gay and lesbian activists picked up on the unanswered questions about what we stood for and what we represented. Initially, these activists rejected the pursuit of respectability, and embarked instead on a process of self-discovery. They affirmed gay sexuality and celebrated it. But by the mid-1970s, like the revolutionary movements on which it modeled itself, the political wing of the gay and lesbian liberation movement was following a far more moderate course, for legal and political legitimacy.

What happened at the Stonewall Inn in Greenwich Village on June 28, 1969, has been described by a number of writers, most vividly by Martin Duberman in his book *Stonewall*. The Stonewall explosion, and its lingering impact, was unusual because the raid that precipitated it was so ordinary. Indeed, Stonewall was neither the worst example of police brutality against gay people in New York, nor was it the first time that gay people had fought back. Across the country, gay and lesbian bars faced routine police raids, battled persecution by liquor-licensing and law enforcement agencies, and experienced election year harassment as mayoral candidates looking for votes got tough on "deviants." In 1965, the Mattachine Society of New York launched a campaign to reduce police incursions in the bars, holding a media-oriented "Sip-In" to challenge antigay serving policies, and forcing the mayoral candidate John Lindsay to address the matter. Early bar raids in San Francisco spawned the funding of a gay business group, the Tavern Guild, and helped activists coalesce into the Society for Individual Rights, an independent local political group. A gay bar in San Francisco named the Black Cat became the first gay establishment there to challenge successfully the revocation of its liquor license in court; the California Supreme Court in 1948 affirmed the constitutional right of homosexuals to assemble. This victory earned the Black Cat the protracted animosity of the local police department, which harried the bar for fifteen years and eventually forced it to close. The repeated raids so frustrated a drag performer named Jose Sarria that he ran as an openly gay candidate for the San Francisco Board of Supervisors in 1961, winning fifty-six hundred votes.

But two things made the 1969 raid against Stonewall different: first, the existence of gay and lesbian political organizations that were able to use the Stonewall riots to build a movement; and second, the volatile climate in which the riots occurred. At the time of the riots, a small band of gay and lesbian activists was in place to galvanize the movement. After the first night of rioting, Mattachine Society organizers prepared a leaflet condemning police harassment. The community meetings that were then held engendered the radical Gay Liberation Front. As the gay journalist Donn Teal remarked, after Stonewall a "New Homosexual was born."

Significant in the emergence of this New Homosexual was the time and the climate: 1969 was a volatile moment in which several national movements for social change involved and radicalized tens of thousands of people. The moderate black civil rights movement of the 1950s had given birth to a more radical student movement represented by SNCC (the Student Nonviolent Coordinating Committee), which was formed in 1961, SDS (Students for a Democratic Society), and the antiwar movement. By the late 1960s, a black power movement emerged, represented best by the Black Panther Party. It incorporated some existing black nationalist and pan-Africanist movements. At the same instant, the second wave of the women's movement took off, with the founding of the National Organization for Women (NOW) in 1965 and the arrival of radical feminism in 1968. Thousands of politically active women abandoned the New Left to build an autonomous women's movement, in part out of frustration with the sexism they encountered.

The antiwar movement and the New Left itself were badly splintered at the end of the decade, with deep splits between white and black radicals, advocates of nonviolent change and violent overthrow, men and women, advocates of a counterculture and those who wanted to reform existing institutions. Yet the antiwar movement remained strong in the early 1970s, hosting the largest demonstrations against the Vietnam War and eventually forcing a change in government policy and a collapse of confidence in the Nixon administration. The unnoticed ingredient in this cauldron of activism was the involvement of lesbian and gay people in each of these movements, sometimes as leaders. For example, one of the national presidents of SDS was a gay man named Carl Wittman. He wrote the still relevant and fresh "A Gay Manifesto" in 1970, and was active in the progressive gay movement until his death from AIDS, in 1985. Scores of leaders involved in the New Left and the women's movement were lesbians, including Robin Morgan, Charlotte Bunch, and Leslie Cagan. Lesbians and gay men worked inside the black civil rights movement and the radical black power movement as well. Most are still in the closet. Among the most prominent of these activists was Bayard Rustin, who served as the chief organizer of the 1963 March on Washington—although behind the scenes, so that his sexuality would not cause a scandal.

What is remarkable about the Stonewall generation is its vision for gay freedom—reflected in the institutions it built, and the values that guided its activities. The Stonewall generation of the 1970s built the frame of the gay and lesbian movement of the 1990s. Out of nothing, and with a fraction of the money at the disposal of the movement today, the members of that generation founded institutions that served the broad spectrum of gay, lesbian, and bisexual people; they started publications; they created literature and culture; they made access to political leaders; and they started the lesbian and gay self-help health and social service organizations that allowed us to respond so quickly to the AIDS crisis in the 1980s. If the Stonewall generation of leaders remains influential, the values that anchored them deserve the credit. They shared an almost spiritual faith in human rights and human dignity, an optimism about democracy and justice, the possibility of sexual freedom and fairness. These values inspired the Stonewall generation of gay and lesbian leaders to target the injustices of the straight world with a righteousness that is not matched in the self-serving politics of today's movement.

Indeed, gay and lesbian liberation lasted far longer and had more influence in stimulating ideas than it did in devising political strategies. The gay and lesbian liberation movement introduced four ideas into the existing homophile movement: (1) the notion that coming out and pursuing gay and lesbian visibility held the key to our freedom; (2) that queer freedom would profoundly change gender roles, sexism, and heterosexual institutions like the family; (3) that gay, lesbian, and bisexual people were an integral part of the broad demand for social change and needed a political philosophy that made connections to race, gender, and economic issues; and (4) that the creation of a gay and lesbian counterculture was an essential part of establishing lesbian and gay identity. These ideas were controversial when introduced, and some remain wildly unpopular. Coming out retains the central relevance and urgency today that it did three decades ago. The idea that gay and lesbian equality unsettles gender roles and undermines heterosexism is also widely understood within our movement. The third idea of gay liberation remains the most controversial: the intersection of race, sexuality, gender, and class is not at all agreed upon by gay activists, nor has a clear practice been developed by us for acting on all these forms of oppression. Finally, the value of a gay and lesbian counterculture is challenged by conservatives, while notions of gay identity are questioned by progressives.

The aftermath of the Stonewall riots also raised three problems for political activists: how to motivate masses of politically inert people into activism; how to define a coherent political theory and practice for a diverse people; and how to coordinate the activities of a decentralized and personally oriented movement. Throughout the 1970s, the gay movement tried to address these challenges with different strategies.

The response varied according to geography and the political orientation of our leaders. To a large extent, every generation of movement
activists since Stonewall has faced these three problems.

The riots proved that the homophile political movement had little
relevance to the lives and passions of ordinary gay people. Movement
activists had, after all, never been able to get such a large mass of people
onto the streets for a Mattachine protest. Even though protests had
been held throughout the 1960s, the political movement had not captured people's hearts. In part, this reflected the failure of homophile
leaders to engage in community organizing in the fifties and sixties, and
explains why the West Coast movement grew differently from the
movement in the East or in the Midwest and South. From the outset,
the Society for Individual Rights (SIR) in San Francisco and early
homophile leaders in Los Angeles focused on both the creation of
community and social networks as well as on the reform of policy. SIR
hosted dances, brunches, bridge games, and socials; it sponsored a community center; it targeted bars for organizing. The gay pioneer Morris
Kight and others helped found the Los Angeles Gay and Lesbian
Community Services Center in 1972. By contrast, the East Coast
groups did not provide social outlets for their members; and the Mattachine Society in the East Coast expended little energy in community
organizing beyond hosting forums. Another difference was that the
movement in the West built relationships with nongay allies, founding
the Council on Religion and the Homosexual, which in the 1960s
helped push for an end to police harassment. These differences enabled
the movement in San Francisco and LA to build a larger base of members and to organize with more credibility in the straight political process. While the gay movement in New York introduced a gay rights bill
in the city council in 1971, and saw it fail for more than fifteen years,
the movement in San Francisco elected an openly gay candidate, Harvey Milk, to the Board of Supervisors in 1977.

The second political problem that the riots revealed—the problem
of political diversity—has still not been addressed honestly by the
movement. Instead, we began in the 1970s to gloss over our divisions by
promoting the idea of single-issue politics, which centers on determining what constitutes a gay and lesbian issue. The answer depends on
who is being asked. For lesbians, the status of women is a lesbian issue;
for black gay men, racism was a gay issue; for poor gay people, working
to raise the minimum wage and expand job training were gay issues; but
for middle-class white men, stigma due to homosexuality itself was the

issue that mattered most. Single-issue politics flattened these deep political disagreements by promoting the tautology that gay and lesbian rights were the proper province of a gay and lesbian movement. In other words, single-issue politics defined issues pertaining to sexual orientation as the only legitimately gay and lesbian issues.

The preoccupation with single-issue politics split one of the first post-Stonewall gay organizations in New York, the Gay Liberation Front. GLF launched in July 1969, in the aftermath of the Stonewall riots, represented the melding of various strains of the counterculture. The radicals of the homophile movement were represented by members of the Mattachine Society of New York's Action Committee, who were frustrated by the caution of Mattachine's leaders. Leftists, who had worked in each of the leading movements of the day, were drawn by the militant rebellion they saw at Stonewall. Lesbians, who were frustrated on one side by the lack of political activism of the Daughters of Bilitis (DOB) and on the other side by the sexism of Mattachine, were empowered into gay liberation activism by the newly emerging women's liberation movement. And, finally, a number of countercultural types, anarchists, artists, the "beatniks," the "hippies" and "yippies," the street people, transvestites, and bar-goers who had led the rebellion into the streets at Stonewall—all of them felt marginalized within the existing homophile movement. The Gay Liberation Front rapidly expanded across the country, but at the very instant that the Los Angeles GLF chapter was founded (December 1969), the original New York chapter was already facing disarray, as more moderate liberationists split off to create the Gay Activists Alliance (GAA). Actually, fault lines had been present at the outset. Participants could not agree if it should be a consciousness-raising group or should be allied with other militant, nongay movements. There were tensions between those long involved with the homophile movement and newcomers, who had been involved in left or antiwar politics; there were tensions between people who wanted more structure and an organized process at meetings, and those who wanted a more egalitarian organizational process that had no leaders or conventional rules of order.

Like Mattachine, the GLF was ultimately doomed by vehement disagreement among gay activists on the question of single-issue or multi-issue politics. Moderates and conservatives argued against gay and lesbian organizations taking on nongay issues or causes. Rejecting any leftist analysis of gay oppression, they bitterly opposed gay groups joining nongay demonstrations to support the Black Panthers or to end the war, and even resisted lesbians who pointed out sexism within gay organizations. In its preamble and first brochure, GAA declared itself a single-issue organization, which would use confrontation, political activity, and education to promote gay and lesbian freedom. The rhetoric was neither purely civil rights nor revolutionary; it was a hybrid. GAA's five early demands, for example, embodied the narrower focus of the group: repeal of sodomy laws; end of police harassment and entrapment; passage of a fair employment law; assurance of bonds to homosexuals; and an end to police and state harassment of gay bars. GAA's tactics were also hybrids; it engaged in protest as well as political lobbying.

Single-issue politics reached a peak in the 1980s and remains the dominant ideology of the gay movement today. The mainstream of the gay movement is organized under the assumption that gay rights are related to but disconnected from other kinds of civil freedom. Yet the tension between single- and multi-issue politics keeps emerging and dividing us politically. Single-issue versus multi-issue politics splintered ACT UP as recently as 1992, when treatment-oriented activists left ACT UP–New York to form TAG (the Treatment Action Group). Such narrowly focused politics made it possible for gay and lesbian political action committees (like HRCF) to support antichoice candidates until 1989, when pressure from lesbians changed this policy. On the other hand, a narrow, gay-rights-only orientation worked to our advantage in 1992, when the movement was able to persuade large numbers of gay voters to set aside other concerns and vote for the candidate who clearly seemed the best on gay and AIDS issues.

Insistence by gay conservatives on so-called gay issues not only limits the movement from forming meaningful partnerships with civil rights allies in the women's and racial justice movements; it keeps us in a gay policy ghetto. The deficit, crime, public schools, housing, the role of government, national defense, welfare reform, and the shrinkage of the workforce—are all national issues that the gay movement has failed to address. We must end this silence and develop a movement courageous enough to articulate gay liberation's approaches to these broad social crises. Gay people do not fight for the freedom to live in a lavender bubble, but in a more just society.

The third political lesson Stonewall taught was that a grassroots movement can survive without a more centrally directed movement, but the latter cannot succeed without the former. The Stonewall riots were the first examples of an uprising among gay and lesbian people. Other instances were the "White Night" riots in the spring of 1979, precipitated in San Francisco by the lenient jury verdict in the murder of Harvey Milk; the mobilization of the First National March on Washington for Lesbian and Gay Rights, in October 1979, opposed by many in the mainstream movement; and the riots that followed Governor Pete Wilson's veto of a gay rights bill in California in 1991. What these events teach is that grassroots actions conducted by more marginalized queers led to a political opening for moderate gay men and women. The drag queens and the street hustlers who rioted at Stonewall opened the space for conservatives to criticize them as counterproductive twenty years later. Similarly, the organizers of the 1979 march were initially opposed by established national gay and lesbian leaders and organizations, but these same leaders benefited from the appearance of 100,000 people in Washington and from the surge in activism after the march, specifically, a new interest in the national movement. And so it was, in 1991, when the pressure put on Pete Wilson to reverse his veto by gay and lesbian street demonstrations actually strengthened the hand of gay Republicans and moderates to whom Wilson turned for advice on how to undo the damage he had done. One year after his veto, he signed a limited gay and lesbian rights bill. In each of these instances, direct action and protest made our presence known and strengthened mainstream strategies for reform.

Stonewall and gay liberation inspired more people to come out and to come in to gay and lesbian communities. Moderate gay and lesbian activists were able to form new political organizations to harness this energy. Thus, an ironic legacy of Stonewall was the formation of two mainstream gay rights organizations in 1973: the National Gay Task Force and the Lambda Legal Defense and Education Fund.

In 1978, the Gay Rights National Lobby was founded in Washington by long-time activist Steve Endean. At the time of its founding, GRNL was supported by all national gay leaders; NGTF board members sat on GRNL's board. NGTF worked to change administrative regulations and to push the executive branch. GRNL's mission was to lobby Congress and to build a national network of constituent lobbyists. Forging some of the first relationships between national and local gay activists with its field organizing, GRNL earned the lasting loyalty of many. In 1980, Endean and others on the GRNL board, like Lambda Rising Bookstore owner Deacon MacCubbin, established the Human Rights Campaign Fund as the first national gay political action committee at the national level. By 1986, HRCF had grown so strong that it

folded GRNL's operations into its larger organizational structure. Endean went on to work for HRCF, devising many new creative organizing strategies until he died in 1993.

The national gay political movement of the 1970s focused entirely
on the straight mainstream, rather than on community organizing or
gay and lesbian movement building. Such efforts earned a remarkable
series of firsts, the most impressive of which was the removal of homosexuality from the list of mental illnesses by the American Psychiatric
Association in 1973. Other firsts included Bella Abzug's introduction of
a gay and lesbian civil rights bill in Congress (March 25, 1975); the
election of openly gay elected officials; the removal of sexual orientation
as a category disqualifying people from Civil Service (secured by Frank
Kameny); Lambda Legal Defense & Education Fund's early lawsuits
and victories; pioneering media work; a meeting at the White House
with President Jimmy Carter's assistant Midge Costanza (on March 26,
1977); a number of attempts to eliminate the antigay immigration policies; and a protracted battle with the U.S. military to end antigay
discrimination.

The more moderate gay movement of the 1970s coincided with,
and often borrowed from, the gay and lesbian liberation framework, but
its goal was legitimation, pursued by two means: establishing the rights-
oriented movement; and fostering the space for gayness to become an
alternative lifestyle. Indeed, one could argue that two distinct gay
movements came into being in the 1970s: the political and the cultural.
The former pursued the goal of representing gay people; the latter was
absorbed with understanding what our homosexuality meant. The political movement established reformist organizations, began electoral
work, lobbied for bills and against discriminatory laws, and laid the
foundation for gay and lesbian political stature. The cultural movement
established support groups and service, founded alternative businesses
to serve the gay community, and forged bonds among gay men and
lesbians. While the political movement argued that gay people were an
oppressed minority seeking civil equality, the cultural movement argued
that gay people were an alternative to heterosexuality. While the political movement invented a gay and lesbian mainstream, the cultural
movement established gay and lesbian communities.

POST-STONEWALL GAY AND LESBIAN
CULTURAL POLITICS

Neither political nor cultural legitimation was the priority of most gay and lesbian people in the 1970s: living gay and lesbian lives was. To America, the personal may have been political in the abstract sense, but to most gay people it was the paramount issue. During that decade lesbian and gay subculture grew exponentially, as, for the first time, gay people created institutions and organizations that were not centered on the bars. Gay and lesbian ghettos sprang up as tens of thousands of gay and lesbian people migrated from the heartland to San Francisco, Greenwich Village, and large Midwestern and Southern cities like Atlanta, New Orleans, Miami, and Dallas. A number of pioneers founded gay organizations across the country—GLF and GAA chapters in Houston, Chicago, and Kansas City. Feminist coffeehouses, bookstores, social clubs, gay male communes, lesbian group houses, and gay and lesbian businesses flourished. Gay and lesbian professionals started to advertise in gay newspapers and serve their communities with their skills. Homosexuality became a lifestyle, and the term meant very different things to gay men, to lesbians, and to the straight world.

For gay men, this was a time to discover and celebrate sexual freedom. From the disco to the bathhouse to the private sex clubs, from early gay porn to the founding of VD clinics in the gay community, gay men established a new, defiant, and public community. Gay male sexuality is not much different from straight male sexuality in its organization of sex at the center of social life: men prioritize sexual freedom and define it as integral to what it means to be a man. But the gay male community's institutionalization of sexual spaces resulted in several consequences, not the least of which was a very different approach to politics on the part of men than women.

Because the fact of government repression arguably makes every act of gay male sex a condemnation of government and religion, most men did (and still do) see their sexual and emotional freedom in stark political terms: moralism versus libertarianism. A commitment to this notion of individual sexual freedom underlies why gay men are so adamantly opposed to closing bathhouses, sex clubs, or other sites organized to deliver sex. This idea of sexual politics differs (although it is not incom-

patible with) the kind of sexual politics that lesbian feminism developed. A politics focused on sexual availability, no holds barred, still
leaves intact the existing norms of gender role, power, and privilege.
Because lesbian sexual politics so earnestly tried to question all the
power dynamics inherent in sexual relationships, it seemed moralistic
and ponderous, and was quickly dubbed antisex. Undoubtedly, some
lesbian feminists were all those things. The entire women's community
was not.

In this sense, sexual freedom both was and was not a dividing line
between men and women. Male sexuality constructed many of the
places gay men frequented to create community and identity. The
baths, the bars, the backrooms, the bushes developed in part because
men could do sexually what women are not allowed to do in this sexist
culture. In the debates on sex that took place during the 1970s, some
lesbians reacted negatively to this expressly sexual orientation among
men, but, in truth, early lesbian communities had their own free-love
norms. Non-monogamy was an article of dogma among many lesbians;
straight women experimented with bisexuality in large numbers; and a
small but influential group of sexual radicals began writing, organizing,
and thinking about sex in ways that would revolutionize feminist ideas
on sex in the "sex wars" around pornography and sadomasochism that
erupted in the 1980s.

The major difference between lesbians and gay men in the 1970s
was the creation by women of an autonomous lesbian-feminist culture
and the institutionalization, primarily by men, of mainstream gay political organizations. Gay men have long enjoyed a different kind of access
to mainstream culture from that of lesbians. Indeed, as Michael Bronski
notes in his book *Culture Clash,* much of what is called "straight" culture
is heavily infused with a gay sensibility: ballet, opera, Broadway, theater,
art, film have all been shaped by the talents of gay men. Bronski details
in a forthcoming book on gay culture that although this gay contribution is unacknowledged (don't tell), it is the chief impetus for the right-
wing backlash against gay people: the right's cultural war is all about gay
people's influence on so-called straight culture. Lesbians have not, until
recently, been widely visible but have similarly shaped culture in unacknowledged ways. The lesbian cultural explosion of the 1970s set the
stage for the emergence of women we witness today.

The impact of lesbian culture on a modern lesbian identity cannot
be overstated. Completely outside the heterosexual or gay male mainstream, lesbians met one another, developed a sense of community, and

created a political identity through lesbian culture, especially women's music. The euphemistically labeled women's music movement was created by singers like Meg Christian, Alix Dobkin, Linda Tillery, Holly Near, Cris Williamson, Maxine Feldman, and others who began to perform in feminist coffeehouses. In 1975, lesbian activists—some of whom had been involved in the early lesbian collective the Furies—founded Olivia Records, the first lesbian record company, which still exists today. Olivia was a conscious political strategy aimed at building a lesbian movement and at promoting a lesbian political analysis: if we could not find images of ourselves in the mainstream, we would make them ourselves.

Olivia's birth, extremely significant to the creation of a consciousness and pride among lesbians across the nation, spawned an entire cultural-political movement. The artists recording on Olivia, and on independent labels, produced explicitly lesbian work. Among the first such records were the song "Angry Athis" by Maxine Feldman, the groundbreaking album by Alix Dobkin, "Lavender Jane Loves Women," and Meg Christian's "I Know You Know," which changed the lives of thousands of women who heard it. The music and lyrics gave voice to a love that had never proselytized in this way, and the concerts created community, where lesbians met. The records spawned concerts, coffeehouses, clubs, and music and comedy festivals. A network of independent lesbian producers of women's culture sprang up across the country. Like many lesbians active in the gay movement today, I learned how to organize events in the women's culture movement of the late 1970s. The Women's Music Distribution Network was established, resulting in the Ladyslipper Distribution, a group in North Carolina that continues to bring women's music to millions. Finally, this cultural movement created the Women's Music Festivals, the largest of which are the Michigan Womyn's Music Festival, held each August since 1975; the West Coast and Southern Women's Music and Comedy Festivals; and the Bloomington Indiana Women's Music Festival. It is *de rigueur* to mock these festivals as vestiges of another era, but they are the bedrock on which a lesbian political consciousness was founded.

Cultural feminism may have sounded the death knell for radical feminism, as the historian Alice Echols argues in *Daring to Be Bad,* but it also marked the beginning of the lesbian-feminist political movement. Lesbian feminism, unlike the gay political movement, was not centered on either coast. Strong lesbian production companies still exist in the Midwest and Southwest, long after collapsing in the Northeast. Because comedians and musicians traveled across the country, bringing lesbians together as they went, supporting small feminist businesses, and spreading a feminist message, lesbians built a nationwide consciousness, far broader than that experienced by gay men. Cultural lesbian feminism was explicitly political. The artists talked about lesbian, gay, and feminist causes; the producers invited political groups to set up tables and distribute information; and the productions themselves were often benefits. One early example of this was an album put out by Olivia Records to counter the Anita Bryant antigay campaign. With a cover that sported a large frozen orange juice container with women's symbols and the title "Lesbian Concentrate," this exciting array of political songs by lesbian-feminist performers educated a generation of young lesbians who had never been touched by the gay political movement.

This awakening was also enlivened and nurtured by the gay and lesbian press of the late 1960s and early 1970s. The reach of newspapers like the *Advocate, Christopher Street,* the *Washington Blade, Gay Community News, Lesbian Connection,* the now-defunct *Body Politic,* the *Philadelphia Gay News,* the *Windy City Times,* and others was significant. Lifelines for isolated gay people, these papers were often the only vehicles for news about the gay and lesbian movement. The gay and lesbian press not only reported on the community; it helped to create it, through calendar listings, resource guides, and space to debate ideas and strategy. Inspired by the late Craig Rodwell, the movement encouraged communities across the country to hold gay and lesbian pride festivals and marches to commemorate the Stonewall riots. This celebration of pride remains one of the only times that gay people are able to gather in large numbers, to feel the breadth of their community, and to celebrate publicly their heritage. The demeanor and language of the Mattachine Society and the DOB seemed old-fashioned, but its hip, revolutionary, and countercultural stance made gay and lesbian liberation appealing to every half-aware, political queer who heard about it.

The fact that this awakening happened without coordination explains why an organizational chart of the gay movement today resembles the Milky Way. Thousands of autonomous gay and lesbian organizations, of every stripe and order, exist in nearly every town and hamlet in America. Nationally oriented activists were often trapped by the parochialism that dominated gay and lesbian politics; despite years of meeting, leaders of Mattachine, DOB, and other groups had failed to secure anything stronger than a small annual national network, the North American Conference of Homophile Organizations. The spontaneous spread of gay organizations suited everyone fine. It pleased those who feared central control and the loss of their local turf, and it allowed those who wanted to create a national movement to do so without accountability to the grassroots.

Our lifestyle was no longer invisible to the straight world either, but the reaction was not exactly one of celebration. The seventies ended on several ominous notes. On November 27, 1978, the openly gay Board of Supervisors member Harvey Milk was assassinated in his office by a former fellow supervisor and former police officer, Dan White. White also killed George Moscone, the popular and liberal mayor of San Francisco. A series of antigay ballot initiatives was launched against the homosexual movement by the newly visible Christian Right. In Florida, Anita Bryant's Save Our Children campaign stirred up hysteria about gay people being child molesters, despite the statistics showing that 95 percent of molestation of little girls is done by heterosexual men. In California, State Senator John Briggs succeeded in placing on the ballot an initiative to prevent gay and lesbian people from teaching in public schools; the state field director for the Briggs Initiative was Lou Sheldon, whose Traditional Values Coalition is today responsible for the dissemination of distorted videotapes like *Gay Rights, Special Rights*. In Wichita, Saint Paul, and Seattle, communities voted on their newly passed gay rights bills, repealing them in the first two cities, while upholding the Seattle law.

Yet the decade closed with perhaps our biggest cultural success to date, the first National March on Washington for Lesbian and Gay Rights, held on October 14, 1979. The march was organized entirely by the grassroots movement; the national groups were fearful that it would attract publicity and right-wing reaction. According to newspaper accounts, more than 100,000 people came; according to organizers, the count was closer to 200,000. The march also featured a historic conference aimed at increasing organizing among gay and lesbian people of color. The first National Third World Gay and Lesbian Conference drew hundreds of participants from around the country, and sparked the founding of the National Coalition of Black Lesbians and Gays.

Politically, the end of the 1970s marked the beginning of the period when we lost some of the ground we had so rapidly gained after Stonewall, a loss caused by the appearance of a formal, antigay opposition. Yet the same decade saw gay and lesbian culture, community, and life breaking new ground. The flourishing of a movement celebrating gay and lesbian lifestyles masked the lingering resistance to our equality, while the gains of the political movement seduced us into believing that reason would prevail over irrational fear.

Nothing could have prepared us for the decade that lay ahead. The debates and dilemmas of the seventies paled in the face of a crisis whose impact gay and lesbian people still experience. As Ginny Apuzzo remarked, "AIDS robbed us of the sexual liberation piece, because everybody in the world said, 'That killed you. You're crazy to want to continue along these lines.' Circumstances dictated that we drop the ideological position and pick up our friends who were dying. In a sense, we were robbed of making the choice of continuing to be a radical liberation movement because we paused to take care of business."

CHAPTER THREE

AIDS AND TRANSFORMATION

AIDS will do more to direct America back to the cost of violating traditional values and to make America aware of the danger of certain behavior than anything we've seen. For us, it's a great rallying cry.

—*Newt Gingrich, 1985*

January 1994

Walta lies on his side, anxiety and fear in his eyes. The air in the room is still. He had a transfusion two days ago. Michael says he was walking around the apartment, but today he has no energy. Last night, he had diarrhea. I don't think he knows we are in the room.

"Walter?" Michael asks, saying his name as if it had an *r*.

Walta, curled in a fetal position on his bed, does not move.

"Walter?"

There is no response.

"Walter, are you all right? Do you need anything? Walter? Urvashi's here. Walter?"

"Yes."

"Are you all right?"

Walta starts suddenly, as if someone has shaken him. He tries to raise himself and can't. He stares at me blankly, then turns to Michael for reassurance. His right eye is glassy and moves in a different direction from his left eye. Has he gone blind in it, I wonder. I don't ask Michael.

There is a shadow, like a dark bruise, on his left cheek. He is very thin.
"Cheekbones for days," he would have said, as he did about my friend
Betsy the first time they met. "Betsy's beautiful. Cheekbones for days."

Michael tells him, "I'm going to hook up some IV, Walter, because
I'm worried about the fluid you lost last night. Let me find your IV
thing." He kneels beside the bed and fumbles under the covers. Walter
does not move or respond. I stand by, doing nothing.

"Where is that thing? Ah. Here it is." Michael clips the IV bag to
the catheter attached to Walta. He times the drip with a wristwatch.
"One, two, three, four, five . . ." he counts out loud, and adjusts the
flow. "There." Walta lies on his side; his eyes are wide and open,
looking past us.

Michael picks up the conversation exactly where he left off, without
missing a thought. We are talking about what we've discussed so often
in the fifteen years we have been friends: the endless drama associated
with keeping afloat the progressive nonprofit newspaper *Gay Community News*. *GCN* is our common political work, our collaborative creation, our means of resistance, the family network through which we
know most of our friends. It is how we will live forever. The operations
of gay and lesbian nonprofit organizations are like soap operas: love,
passion, excitement, vendettas, jealousy, sex, betrayal.

Walta Borawski, Michael Bronski, and I met in Boston through
GCN in that time before AIDS. I was twenty-one. They seemed so
much older, although they were only in their early thirties. They became two of my mentors in gay and lesbian liberation, and, in a way, I
grew up with them. They were together for nearly twenty years, but
theirs was unlike any marriage I had seen: open and totally committed,
independent and yet stable enough to manage dinner together most
nights, full of love and barbed humor at each other's peculiarities. Together, they were encyclopedic in their knowledge of gay and lesbian
history and culture. Michael is frighteningly smart and totally skeptical.
He's the most original gay critic in the country, an old-fashioned intellectual, with a post-Stonewall race, gender, and class consciousness.
Walta was a poet who could knowledgeably dish out the life and career
of nearly every female torch singer who has recorded an album. Michael
has cooked me more meals than I can count—talking the whole time he
cooks—while Walta sat at the table and smoked, or played his latest
favorite record for us, or told us some Streisand trivia.

Walta would have loved to see Barbra on her big tour during 1994.
But he died on February 9 of that year.

We became friends through endless arguments, all trying to define what progressive gay and lesbian politics meant. The *GCN* crowd was an off-beat, nationwide network of writers, artists, cartoonists, activists, and readers. We organized, analyzed, wrote, traded gossip, fell in and out of love with each other, had feuds, made up, and even lived together in collectives and group houses. The Fort Hill Faggots for Freedom was a collection of gay men who lived in a group of houses in Roxbury in the mid-1970s; in the early 1980s, I lived in an updated, lesbian-feminist version. We shared our lives, food, houses, books, music, films, plays, political organizations, and built friendships around never-ending conversations. We attended hundreds of political meetings, wrote leaflets, articles, and books, produced conferences and readings, planned demonstrations, rallies, and pickets, organized fundraisers, benefits, potlucks, neighborhoods, even unions.

For nearly two decades, we have argued with each other about sex and politics. We fought about whether pedophilia and NAMBLA (North American Man Boy Love Association) belonged in the gay and lesbian movement. We fought about pornography and feminism, about sexual differences and similarities between lesbians and gay men, about bisexuality, about gender, about s and m, about power and sex, about the right and left's dislike of sexual pleasure. We alienated the traditional gay political activists at the national level with articles calling them homocrats; we alienated leftists with articles critical of Cuba; we angered lesbians with sexually explicit illustrations to stories; we angered gay men who were offended by seeing women's breasts depicted in a cartoon; we lost advertisers after reporting on violence outside gay and lesbian bars; we infuriated gay conservatives by arguing that our movement was one that fought homophobia, racism, sexism, and economic injustice; and we reached and educated tens of thousands of gay, lesbian, and straight readers.

It was *GCN*-ers—like John Mitzel and Charley Shively—who organized pickets against Anita Bryant in 1977. *GCN*-ers again led the organizing against police entrapment of gay men in the late 1970s. In February 1979, *GCN*-ers Amy Hoffman, Eric Rofes, and Richard Burns went to the first planning meeting in Philadelphia of the First National March on Washington, and Eric served on the march's steering committee. When I got involved with *GCN* in 1979, I worked on pickets against two homophobic films, *Cruising* and *Windows*. In 1980, we organized two gay and lesbian buses from Boston to Washington to have an openly gay presence at the national demonstration against U.S.

intervention in El Salvador. In 1982, we literally raised *GCN* from the ashes when arson completely destroyed its offices. We started the Prisoners' Project to advocate for lesbian and gay people behind bars. We began to cover racism and sexism within the movement; that led us to cover class in a more serious way. By 1983, we had become one of the principal gay sources of information about AIDS.

When did it all change? When did our lives go from the optimism of people developing a whole new politics to the numbness of a people experiencing survival as a disaster?

Was it the year that Walta started to fade? Was it when Richard, Amy, Kevin Cathcart, Catherine Hanssens, and I had dinner together in 1981, the week that the *New York Times* reported the cases of an odd cancer in five gay men? Was it when Michael wrote about the gay clone as a political phenomenon? Maybe it was in 1987, after the Second March on Washington, when Jesse Helms got nearly unanimous support in the Senate for his ban on federal funds for gay-specific AIDS education. It could have been in 1982, when we all argued against the closing of the bathhouses. Was it in 1984, when I first returned to Boston since moving to Washington and Michael and Walta threw a party to welcome me back? Maybe it all changed in 1985, when Jim was diagnosed. Or in 1986, when the Supreme Court ruled that gay and lesbian sexuality could be criminalized by the states. Maybe it was in 1988, when Bob Andrews died. Or in 1987, when Steve Ansolabehere died. Or in 1991, when Mike Riegle died. Or any week in between, when hundreds of people we knew and loved were diagnosed with AIDS, fell ill, got better, went into the hospital, came out of the hospital, came over for dinner, went to the movies with us, went back to the hospital, came out again, went on an international cruise, and then, always too suddenly, died.

AIDS AND THE MOVEMENT

The AIDS epidemic so transformed the gay and lesbian political movement that, as with our personal lives, we can mark two distinct eras: life before AIDS and life after AIDS. At the outset, AIDS presented a pair of political dilemmas to gay and lesbian activists. How were we going to get a response from an administration that did not care about us? And how were we going to motivate and mobilize a community that was largely in the closet and invisible? The gay movement made a series of strategic decisions to deal with the homophobia that lay under both of these problems. At the time, those decisions seemed the best response possible; we can now consider their long-term consequences.

In recent years, AIDS activists have angrily argued that the gay and lesbian movement has forgotten about AIDS, that we are pretending the epidemic is over. In September 1994, Jeffrey Schmalz, who died of AIDS-related illness that fall, wrote an impassioned cover story for the *New York Times Magazine* making this point. Ironically, at the end of the 1980s, gay and lesbian activists had argued with equal vigor that the movement had abdicated the rest of the gay agenda, a position publicly articulated by the late Darrell Yates Rist in *The Nation* in 1989. Incredibly, both statements are true. As we end the second decade of AIDS, our movement is less focused on the epidemic than it was in the first decade, and more affected by it than ever. For many gay people, AIDS has moved from being a political problem to a medical problem. Yet it stains every aspiration gay and lesbian people have, from the mental and psychological state of gay and bisexual men, to the daily loss of talented friends, leaders, and artists, to the reinforced association between queerness and illness, to the fear of death that now accompanies acts of love or sex, to the fear that the right will use the epidemic to impose draconian measures that somehow pathologize us anew.

Neither the gay community nor our movement was prepared, politically or emotionally, to fight against AIDS as a long-term, semipermanent aspect of our lives. We continue to operate as if the "crisis" will soon end. Our desire for a cure is so strong, we act as if one is on the horizon. We recast the state of perpetual mourning in which so many of us live as temporary, transient, individual, and tragically inevitable. Let us not forget the lives we did save, but if we are to move beyond living with AIDS to moving closer to its end in a real, pragmatic sense, we must admit the failure of the strategies we chose during the 1980s, and begin to create new strategies to cope with the changing realities of this epidemic.

Our apparent lack of priority on AIDS must not be seen as a function of burn-out or inertia; nor simplistically as a sign that HIV-negative people are focused on different issues from HIV-positive people. Nor is it a consequence of having rectified all political and social problems associated with the AIDS epidemic. Instead, the way we deal with AIDS today must be understood as a byproduct of the way we constructed our political response to the epidemic years ago. In the 1980s, gay and lesbian advocates made at least four strategic choices whose results affect us to this day: degaying, desexualizing, decoupling AIDS-specific reform from systemic reform and direct action. We used short-term, quick-fix strategies that yielded dramatic but short-lived gains. As a consequence, we failed to tackle the underlying problems that still exacerbate the epidemic: the problems of homophobia, sexual denial and repression, racism, sexism, and the dictates of a profit-driven health care system.

MAINSTREAM ACCESS AND THE DEGAYING OF AIDS

There is no question that AIDS forced the gay and lesbian movement to institutionalize, nationalize, and aggressively pursue the mainstream. Groups were founded or grew larger, jobs in movement organizations replaced volunteerism, and national politics became the principal, and more glamorous, playing field for a previously local movement. In 1986, NGLTF moved its national office from New York to Washington in recognition of this need to have a more determined and credible national lobbying presence. Lambda Legal Defense Fund established a strong AIDS policy and litigation program. The ACLU created the Lesbian and Gay Rights Project and hired an AIDS lobbyist at its Washington office in 1987. Other gay organizations also came into being or grew stronger, among them the Human Rights Campaign Fund; AIDS Action Council established in 1986; the National AIDS Network in 1984; the National Minority AIDS Council in 1987; the National Leadership Coalition on AIDS in 1988; the Interfaith AIDS Network; National Organizations Responding to AIDS (NORA) in 1986; ACT UP (AIDS Coalition to Unleash Power).

In the early years of the epidemic, gay rights advocates faced monumental problems. How were we going to make gay and bisexual lives visible to straight legislative bodies that had never even known we existed? How were we going to motivate political leaders to spend money on the unpopular segments of society affected by AIDS? In the context of a sex-phobic society, filled with secrets and shameful lies about human sexual behavior, how could we explain a sexually transmitted epidemic in terms that everyone could understand? How could we ensure that the maximum number of people—gay-identified and straight-identified—would protect themselves, and not treat this as someone else's problem?

Degaying AIDS promised an answer. Coined by the activists Ben Schatz and Eric Rofes, *degaying* meant removing the stigma of homosexuality from the stigma of AIDS in order to win the access and attention we needed. In short, homophobia required gay people, nationwide, to create an AIDS-specific movement. We chose to focus on AIDS rather than on homophobia and racism, even though these were the causes of the governmental and societal paralysis. Today, there is broad acknowledgment among gay and AIDS leaders that the degaying of AIDS was a conscious political choice made by gay organizers in the mid-1980s. We degayed AIDS when we put forward nongay public health officials as our spokespersons, and when we pressed forward on AIDS-specific issues while avoiding gay and lesbian rights issues. We believed gay people did not carry the same moral authority or influence as public health officials, so we asked the latter to speak for us.

In a panel at the Fifth International AIDS Conference, held in Montreal in June 1989, Ben Schatz challenged the movement for stating that "AIDS is not a gay problem; it's a human problem," which implied that being gay and being human were not the same. With our frequent pleas to the government to spend funds for AIDS because straights can get ill too, we promoted the homophobic subtext that AIDS would not be as important if only gay or bisexual people were susceptible. Further, when we argued that AIDS affected everyone, not just gay people, we focused attention on sexual acts, not on sexual identities. Yet our life-saving focus on such acts (anal sex and fellatio, in particular) reinforced in the public's mind the essence of our stigmatization—sexual behavior. We drew attention to the worldwide statistics on AIDS, which show that heterosexual sex transmits HIV as easily as homosexual sex. By emphasizing the risks to heterosexuals and playing down the staggering destitution of the gay community, AIDS organizations and many AIDS activists established the fledgling AIDS movement as something separate from the gay and lesbian civil rights movement. In a sense it is—more straight people are involved with AIDS organizations than are in gay groups, and the AIDS-specific movement has focused narrowly on services and securing a response to the epidemic. But in our attempt to get a governmental response to AIDS, we employed a strategy that left the gay movement at the mercy of the homophobic, sex-phobic, and racist government.

From the beginning, the efforts to deal with AIDS were stymied by homophobia, but our strategy of degaying the epidemic prevented us from making this explicit or from tackling the underlying problem of antigay prejudice. AIDS-prevention efforts were frustrated by the closet —in order to get gay people to come forward to deal with their HIV infections, we had to overcome their fear of discrimination. We had to convince gay people not to worry about losing their jobs or having their sexual orientation disclosed to co-workers and families. In addition, homophobia prevented health officials from funding gay-specific AIDS-education programs. As recently as 1994 Jesse Helms continued to lead the fight to deny funding for any federal programs that in his mind "promoted" or even dealt with homosexuality. Even today, no national AIDS-prevention campaign or strategy exists; meanwhile, infections among gay men and straight women are on the rise. Further, the politicization of AIDS by the right wing held back any national response to AIDS for many years. The opposition meant that seven years passed before any major AIDS legislation was passed in Congress. The first comprehensive piece of AIDS legislation made it in 1988, the Ryan White Care Bill in 1990, nearly ten years into the epidemic. The right early on equated AIDS with homosexuality, so AIDS policy became a referendum on gay and lesbian rights. If only we had seen these policy fights in the same way, we might have devised one unified movement rather than the bifurcated one we did create.

Let me be clear: the degaying of AIDS was not a lie; the things we said were true. It *is* true that AIDS is sexually transmitted by and to anyone who comes into contact with HIV: certain acts (like receptive intercourse) are more likely to result in transmission than others (most kinds of oral sex). Worldwide, AIDS *does* affect large numbers of heterosexuals. Moreover, an AIDS-specific movement *was* needed to provide services for hundreds of thousands of HIV-infected people. The tragedy of our separating AIDS from its gay roots is not that we misled America—in fact, we saved a lot of lives by urging heterosexuals to practice safer sex, and by explaining to them how they are at risk. Rather, the tragedy of degaying has been internal, both in terms of more gay lives lost and in the size, scope, and politics of the gay and lesbian movement itself.

Questioning the divorce of AIDS-service organizations from the gay and lesbian political movement, Eric Rofes discussed degaying in *Outlook* magazine in 1989. He cited the repeated refusal of AIDS organizations that grew out of the gay community—like AIDS Project Los Angeles, the Names Project AIDS Memorial Quilt, and the San Francisco AIDS Foundation—to use the words *gay* and *lesbian.* He remembered a 1986 AIDS Walkathon in San Francisco, and a 1988 National AIDS Candlelight Vigil in Washington sponsored by the AIDS Memorial Quilt, at which no gay-identified person spoke. He reminded us of a 1989 dinner honoring only straight volunteers in San Francisco, when no similar dinner was held to honor the gay and lesbian volunteers. Rofes pointed out that this repeated dissociation of AIDS from the very community that was struggling to deal with it prompted the late AIDS activist Michael Callen to write angrily, in the March 1989 issue of the *PWA Coalition Newsline:* "AIDS IS A GAY DISEASE! There. I said it. And I believe it. If I hear one more time that AIDS is not a gay disease, I shall vomit. AIDS is a gay disease because a lot of gay men get AIDS . . . More important, most of what has been noble about America's response to AIDS has been the direct result of the lesbian and gay community."

The splintering of the AIDS movement from its gay roots has depoliticized it as a movement; it is like all the other disease-centered national charities (cancer, cerebral palsy, multiple sclerosis). Degaying AIDS allowed closeted gay men and women to begin to donate to gay (but not gay-identified) community institutions. Until AIDS showed closeted queers that it was "safe" to donate or to volunteer and be associated with a gay organization, few people did. As AIDS activism and fundraising developed a social cachet—through the involvement of straight celebrities and wealthy individuals—more gay people felt comfortable getting involved. Throughout the 1980s, people wrote checks to AIDS organizations who had never supported organizations working on the homophobia that inhibited the federal response to AIDS. This lack of support, before 1992, drastically held back the gay political movement. AIDS was a sexier, more chic, and less controversial issue for closeted gay people to work on than the underlying problem of antigay and lesbian prejudice. It felt surreal, in the late eighties, to be so involved in AIDS issues yet be unable to talk about its connection to antigay violence. Or to point out that the lack of attention to AIDS was the same as the lack of attention to all other gay problems.

Another way to understand the depoliticization is to note that, although the AIDS-service movement reaches thousands of people who are touched by AIDS, it has never systematically organized them into a political bloc for AIDS policy fights. For example, the AIDS Action Council does not have access to the mailing lists of every single AIDS organization in the country. So even on the direct mail level, the AAC

is unable to compete on AIDS policy issues with the religious conservatives who amass millions of names, which they marshal to obtain support and to start letter-writing campaigns. If you accept the premise
that building the gay movement advances the AIDS policy agenda, then
we really failed when we did not treat the Names Quilt as a gay cause or
AAC as a gay organization and failed to channel the efforts to advance
gay political ends. That George Bush, who did so little, could be quoted
on the back of the Names Project book reveals the irony of the depoliticization of the AIDS movement.

Although AIDS did accelerate gay and lesbian political participation, the results were mixed for the mainstreaming of the gay and
lesbian movement. On one hand, AIDS integrated us into the broader
political culture by forcing us to focus on national politics, public policy
development, lobbying, and electoral politics. Driven by the urgency of
anger and loss, gay and lesbian organizations asserted themselves in the
legislative or political sphere; we brought gay perspectives and realities
into areas that had not heard from us before. Legislative bodies, government officials, corporate and business leaders, all started to interact with
openly gay advocates. Through this steady process of interaction, AIDS
issues were partly mainstreamed.

On the other hand, because we had defined our political purpose as
AIDS work rather than gay or lesbian work, our newfound access did
not automatically help our movement for gay and lesbian equality. This
paradoxical truth was one that gay and lesbian advocates faced as we
began to come out of the political closet. We rapidly improved our
AIDS-related lobbying, but gained little ground on gay and lesbian
issues. Gay political organizations remained marginalized in Washington throughout the 1980s, even though gay- or lesbian-led AIDS organizations grew in clout and visibility. So, in the time I worked at
NGLTF, AIDS lobbyists were able to get meetings with high-level
Bush officials while lobbyists pursuing gay or lesbian issues were denied.
NGLTF and I failed for two years to secure a meeting with Secretary
Louis Sullivan on gay and lesbian teen suicide, only to witness representatives of the AIDS Action Council (of which NGLTF was a member)
meet with the secretary at least twice and work closely with his staff on
several AIDS policy matters.

VISIBILITY AND DESEXUALIZATION

The second major impact of the AIDS epidemic was to make our lives and our political movement more visible than ever. Since the fifties, media activism has been a force in the gay movement. Some of the earliest projects established by gay and lesbian activists were publications—community newspapers, small publishing houses, and media action groups. During the cultural explosion of the seventies and eighties, literally hundreds of gay and lesbian weeklies, monthlies, newsletters, and bar rags sprang up, and eventually scores of gay radio and cable TV shows began to appear. By the early eighties, a wide array of small presses had begun to publish work that the straight industry would not touch; notable among these are Naiad Press, Alyson Publications, Spinsters Ink, Kitchen Table Press, South End Press, and Firebrand Books.

Younger gay and lesbian activists are sometimes disdainful of the priority that middle-aged and older queer activists place on, and the paranoia we sometimes display about, queer visibility. Our cultural integration seems so pervasive that it feels secure. But gay paranoia about our visibility is healthy and based on history. Invisibility and silence about homosexuality are our two oldest enemies. As recently as ten years ago, major newspapers refused to use the word *gay*, preferring *homosexual.* As recently as 1991, obituaries in major papers did not mention the surviving lover of a gay person who died. Stories about gay and lesbian organizations, discrimination, homophobia, gay culture, gay ideas, artists, and others were simply nonexistent during most of our lives, and even today are just beginning to be covered. Film and television representations of homosexuality were deeply homophobic, as the film historian Vito Russo has detailed in his seminal book, *The Celluloid Closet.*

Before AIDS, the gay and lesbian media were the principal location of any conversation about gay and lesbian issues. Our communities, our disagreements, our sexual mores, and our institutions were thoroughly debated in the pages of lesbian and gay publications. Even after the advent of AIDS, the gay and lesbian media remained the principal source of information. The mainstream press did not cover AIDS seriously until the late 1980s, when two events triggered the coverage: public shock at Rock Hudson's diagnosis with AIDS, in 1985, and the publication of Randy Shilts's *And the Band Played On,* in 1987. In a very real sense the gay and lesbian press saved many lives. They published much of the early political analysis of the AIDS epidemic. It was gay and lesbian media that covered the first conference of People With AIDS, held in Denver in 1982, and published the Denver principles, which became the rallying cry for an entire movement. It was lesbian and gay media that promoted the idea of safer sex, carried ads for benefits, exposed the government's lack of response, and covered the traumatic early political fights within the gay and lesbian communities (over bathhouses, testing, promiscuity, poppers, and much more). It was in the gay and lesbian press that fights about the value of ACT UP's tactics were conducted. It was our press that carried details of medical treatment and scientific information, teaching thousands of people with HIV how to respond to the crisis long before the medical establishment caught on. Finally, it was the gay and lesbian media nationwide that promoted the growth of AIDS education, outreach, and political organizing.

Ironically, as we have won the slow battle to secure coverage of AIDS and gay issues in the straight media, we have suffered from a collapse of critical thinking and a retreat from political analysis. The gay press used to see itself as an advocacy press. Today, gay publishers operate in far more conventional, businesslike ways. As a consequence, I think, large segments of the gay press have abdicated their responsibility as advocate for the community and gay and lesbian public good—on AIDS or on other civil rights matters that affect our lives. Today, these media are becoming more specialized, shrinking into fewer and fewer niches: porn, lifestyle magazines, conservative newsweeklies, and anarchist 'zines. Along with the specialization, there is a shrinking of political thinking about AIDS. The fact that the straight media are now the principal source of information about the disease also explains why so many gay people regard AIDS as "just another health crisis" rather than a political epidemic. Underlying problems of homophobia, discrimination, and stigmatization have not disappeared; they remain as virulent as they were in 1982. But they are not reported in the straight press, and rarely were even in the 1980s. Nor is the politics of AIDS extensively covered by the gay and lesbian press. For example, a bill was introduced late last year in the 104th Congress to make it a crime punishable by death to engage in sex with another person if one was HIV-positive. I learned about the bill from the Internet, not from a newspaper.

This diminution of critical media consciousness and conscience has occurred at the same time as the celebration of gay glamour, epitomized by *New York* magazine's "Lesbian Chic" cover story. I would argue that such a visibility requires desexualizing our community, which ultimately does not dissipate homophobia but only glosses over its presence. Notably, straight culture has elevated lesbians (seen as asexual women and thus safe) over gay men (seen as sexual problems and dangerous) in terms of cultural appeal. Despite our cultural visibility, the equation for the majority of Americans is not Silence = Death, but Gay = AIDS.

In a sense, AIDS outed our entire community. Perversely put, we won visibility for gay and lesbian lives because we died in record numbers: of the nearly 300,000 Americans who have died of AIDS since 1981, more than 70 percent were gay or bisexual men. The sheer number of these deaths, and the far larger and sobering number of gay or bisexual men and women still living with HIV and AIDS-related illnesses, made us a population impossible to ignore. Families had to come to terms with lovers and friends left behind—even if some chose to ignore them. Co-workers had to confront the unacknowledged homosexuality of people they had worked alongside. Problems like the closet, employment discrimination, loss of health care benefits, the denial of care by medical and service providers, were not news to gay and lesbian people, but through the visibility that AIDS gave to our lives, they became more noticeable to others. Discrimination against gay people began to be reported in the news media for the first time, given urgency by the life-and-death situations in which it occurred. This public spotlight exposed gay male life in particular and the existence of lesbian and gay subcultures in general. Lesbian visibility did not come until the 1990s, but the coverage of gay movement battles—of our fights on Capitol Hill, our leaders, our institutions—educated the nation about lesbians as well as gay men. By the late 1980s, gay and lesbian spokespersons were on the news nightly; politicians and legislative bodies began to meet with gay and lesbian rights advocates; court cases challenged the discrimination we encountered; and literally thousands of individual gay people came out to families, friends, and communities.

But our cultural visibility was not easily obtained. For years, the government ran away from AIDS, the media resisted coverage, and conservative religious leaders were silent or hostile. For example, Greg Herek notes that from 1981 to 1982, the *New York Times* ran six stories about AIDS, though it carried fifty-four stories about death from the contamination of Tylenol. Visibility was won through calculated and sustained mass-media campaigns waged by gay activists to seize the attention of the nation. These campaigns were coordinated by public relations and advertising professionals fighting homophobic referenda, by lawyers and lobbyists pressing for reform, by gay and lesbian media advocates, and, eventually, by ACT UP and the direct-action movement.

AIDS media activists began work to influence straight media coverage from the first reports of the disease, in 1981. The mission was twofold: to secure accurate coverage of the burgeoning epidemic, and to counter inflammatory or homophobic coverage. We saw media coverage as a means to advance our public policy agenda, the way to win more AIDS funding and nondiscrimination measures. For example, in 1987, when the Centers for Disease Control (CDC) announced a national policy-setting conference on mandatory HIV testing, AIDS activists girded for battle. Mandatory measures were seen as counterproductive to our effort to bring the epidemic out of the closet and into the public arena.

In the early years of the epidemic, the CDC was the key agency in the federal government's response: HIV surveillance, confidentiality, reporting, contact tracing, HIV testing, and the very definition of AIDS itself originated there. As the epidemic spread and problems multiplied, the emphasis shifted to other agencies. In 1988, the Food and Drug Administration became the focus of our attention as ACT UP pressed for faster access to experimental drugs. In 1989, the Department of Health and Human Services was targeted by women and people of color with AIDS, and the Office of Minority Health was revamped. In the early 1990s, the National Institutes of Health came under sustained scrutiny, and by 1994, AIDS activists from the Treatment Action Group (TAG) lobbied to create a new Office of AIDS Research within the NIH.

When the CDC convened its national conference on mandatory testing, I was the public information director of the NGLTF, and we quickly leaped into action. With NGLTF director Jeffrey Levi, GMHC deputy director Tim Sweeney, and my media-relations counterpart at GMHC, Lori Behrman, I devised the strategy to respond to the CDC announcement. First, we urged AIDS activists, lawyers, and gay-supportive public health experts from around the country to attend the conference. Then, from these individuals, we solicited statements and position papers on the issue of mandatory HIV testing and assembled them into a press packet. Next, we set up a press operations office at the CDC conference hotel, staffed it nearly twenty-four hours a day, and ran several news briefings and press conferences, featuring prominent public health officials (like Mervyn Silverman, then head of the San Francisco Department of Public Health), scientists (like Dr. Mathilde Krim), medical doctors, attorneys, and gay community activists. Nearly every hour, we steered spokespeople toward the hundreds of media reporters covering the meeting. While sessions were under way, our representatives analyzed the CDC proposals and countered ineffective ones with our own recommendations for making voluntary HIV testing readily available.

By the end of the conference, our organizing and press strategy had succeeded. The news coverage of the conference showed that public health officials overwhelmingly opposed mandatory testing and favored voluntary measures. We had defeated a right-wing initiative. And in the process, we had established a new generation of gay and lesbian activists as credible media spokespersons.

Unfortunately, the occasions in which AIDS and gay activists used the media to conduct public education on AIDS tended to be more defensive than offensive. From 1986 until 1989, the antigay right tried to pass several laws in California requiring draconian measures to handle people with AIDS. The gay and lesbian community steered the costly—and successful—campaigns to defeat four statewide referenda. The 1986 measure, Proposition 64, would have allowed the state to restrict the freedom of people with HIV and AIDS. Defeated by a two-to-one margin after a massive gay community effort, it was renewed as Proposition 69 in 1988, only to be defeated again. Proposition 102, the third measure, initiated by Representative Bill Dannemeyer in 1988, would have done away with anonymous antibody testing, required mandatory contact tracing, repealed nondiscrimination laws that protected people with HIV, and allowed insurance companies to carry out testing. The measure was defeated, 66 percent to 34 percent, after another massive organizing effort by the California gay and AIDS communities. The final 1988 ballot initiative, Proposition 96, actually passed: it allowed the nonconsensual HIV testing of any arrested person when requested by an officer, emergency medical worker, or firefighter.

In waging the fight against these measures, the gay and lesbian movement in California raised millions of dollars (most of it from lesbian and gay people) for public education, media advertising, and community organizing. Through it all, the movement became adept at building coalitions with straight medical and public health associations and with a range of nongay allies. While media campaigns worked to win important electoral victories, we lost ground in a sense. For one, the gay movement was forced to spend millions to defend itself rather than to advance queer equality. In the 1990s, the right has used this strategy quite effectively to frustrate gay and lesbian progress at the state and local level. Second, we were forced into a battle that had some ambiguous consequences. From the outset of AIDS, the right has portrayed the gay community as selfishly concerned with its civil rights at the expense of the public good. The debate on confidentiality and nondiscrimination was falsely framed as civil liberties versus public health, a perspective that dominated the first decade of the epidemic. Gay activists like Jeff Levi and Tom Stoddard eloquently argued that the public good required attention to the former, but the question continued to be framed as a debate. With the initiatives, the right was able to repeat this charge, and others, against gay people.

In many ways, the visibility we have won through AIDS has been double-edged, contradicting myths about gay people as much as confirming them. Among the truths are that gay, lesbian, and bisexual people are a part of every extended family; that we have been genuinely heroic in our response to this tragedy; that our response to AIDS developed new models of community engagement, volunteerism, and activism; and that gay and lesbian people come in every shape, size, color, and type. But public information polls reveal that AIDS has not significantly changed heterosexuals' opinions of us. Gregory Herek concluded "that most attitudes appeared to be unaffected by the AIDS epidemic. Public support for First Amendment rights and employment rights for gay people increased steadily, whereas moral condemnation of homosexuality remained consistently high through the 1980s, with a slight increase in 1987."

But the visibility has also reinforced old attitudes about homosexuality and about homosexuals: homosexuality as illness, gay men and lesbians as uncontrollable sex fiends, gay sexual acts as inherently unhealthy and deadly, and being gay as an immoral condition. Recent studies show that AIDS phobia has persisted, ebbing and flowing but always present. A national telephone survey done in 1991 revealed that a quarter of those surveyed felt disgusted by or angry at people with AIDS; more than a third agreed that people with AIDS should be quarantined and their names published; and more than a fifth that people with AIDS deserved their illness.

As AIDS exposed our sexual cultures to an uncomprehending straight majority, the movement made a set of strategic decisions to explain gay male sexuality and the sexual subculture of the post-Stonewall period. The fight to close bathhouses represented our first grappling with public debate on gay sex, debates that recurred in policy fights about abstinence, sex education, condom use, the production of AIDS educational materials that use sexually explicit images and texts, and promiscuity. Congress enacted a sexual standard into law when it passed an amendment, initiated by Jesse Helms in 1987, outlawing federal funds for AIDS education that "promotes or encourages homosexual behavior." This effectively cut off federal monies to the population most affected in the United States. Known as the Helms Amendment, the measure is attached to every bill that may affect gay or lesbian people.

There was no early consensus in the movement on how to handle AIDS and gay male sex, and there still is not. Initially, there was tremendous denial about AIDS among gay men, who trusted the government very little; given the long history of police harassment, they had good reason. With the emergence of AIDS, it seemed too odd, and too predictable, that government officials now told us to close bathhouses, urge gay men to have less sex, fewer partners, more monogamy, and to abstain from or circumscribe the way they had certain types of sex. AIDS struck at the heart of the value of sexual freedom that many gay men believed constituted gay liberation. It became harder to explain to an increasingly conservative country, which believed gay men were dying because they had too much sex, why gay sexual freedom was important.

The mainstream gay and AIDS movements devised a complex response: distancing itself from the sexual liberation ethic of the seventies, while at the same time developing new ways to talk about sexual practices and transmission (media ads, safer sex workshops, videos, posters, and countless other campaigns). In the first instance, we quickly revised our community's sexual history to point out and play up those in committed relationships, and cited the dramatic decline in rates of new infection among gay men as a sign of gay men's sexual responsibility. AIDS education and prevention instituted what Gabriel Rotello has termed "the code of the condom"—reflected in the message that a condom used properly, every time, for anal sex would prevent the transmission of HIV. In either instance, because of our fear of homophobia, we responded to the cultural visibility that AIDS gave to gay male sexual life with a politically motivated effort to de-emphasize the importance of sexuality in the lives of gay men.

The fear of straight reaction to gay male sex still frames our debates and actions in the nineties. For instance, throughout the epidemic, unsafe sex has continued, but we have explained away those results until now. For several years, studies of new infections among gay men reveal that rates of new infections are climbing, more steeply in some populations than others, but climbing across the board. These data have led a small group of activists, notably Walt Odets, Ben Schatz, and Eric Rofes in San Francisco, to spearhead a nationwide re-examination of AIDS prevention. The debate is heated. Several books on the need for new direction in AIDS prevention are forthcoming from Rofes, Odets, Rotello, and others.

Today, a new bathhouse debate rages in New York City, as the existence of unsafe sex is challenged by some. Rotello and Mike Signorile, in New York, are pressing the city to ensure that monitors in all sex clubs prevent unsafe sex. Others argue that private bathhouse owners, not the city, should regulate such monitors. Still others defend such unsafe sex with libertarian arguments. They suggest that if a person knowingly exposes himself to infection by going to a sex club in the middle of this epidemic, knowing that sero-prevalence of HIV among gay men in New York is high, and still engages in unprotected sex, there is nothing others can do; it's a matter of individual responsibility. These debates highlight the centrality of the notions of sexual freedom and sexual liberation to the future of the gay and lesbian movement.

DECOUPLING AIDS FROM SYSTEMIC REFORM

A basic reality of gay lives is that we take care of our own. AIDS service organizations at once grew out of, and depoliticized, the pre-AIDS gay and feminist health movements. AIDS activists did not so much invent a gay health movement as reinvent it. During the 1970s, the early gay and lesbian health movement established community-based health clinics, like the Howard Brown Memorial Clinic in Chicago, the Whitman-Walker Clinic in Washington, the Fenway Community Health Center in Boston, the Lyon-Martin Lesbian Health Center in San Francisco. It organized the National Lesbian and Gay Health Foundation and held an annual conference.

The pre-AIDS health movement adapted the feminist health movement's critiques to challenge mainstream medicine's pathologized and discrimination-ridden view of homosexuals. Mental health activists took on the American Psychiatric Association and counseled gay people to accept themselves and to handle the homophobia of our culture, instead of counseling them on how to become straight! Lesbian self-help health collectives taught women to use speculums, do breast self-exams, demystified women's gynecological needs, and questioned the heterosexist bias of mainstream medicine. Gay and lesbian associations of medical professionals, starting first as support groups, eventually became strong advocacy groups, like the Gay and Lesbian Medical Association (founded as the American Association of Physicians for Human Rights).

As a consequence of the epidemic, the feminist health agenda became the health agenda of the gay and lesbian movement. This meant that organizations like NGLTF and Lambda Legal Defense and Education Fund began to explore issues they had never before concentrated on, like health insurance reform, welfare reform, eligibility for Social Security Disability income, Medicaid eligibility, access to affordable and quality health care, sex education, and nondiscrimination in health care delivery. But the absorption of this health agenda did not answer the more radical feminist criticism. The feminist movement analyzed the health care system as a politicized arena in which homophobia, sexism, racism, and economic disparity were institutionalized. The feminist mission was the construction of a more just, accessible, and fair health care system, guided by and empowering the people it served. *Our Bodies, Our Selves* perfectly illustrates this purpose.

The AIDS-service organizations, in contrast, positioned themselves squarely within the health care system and sought to accommodate us to it. And the gay movement relied on and tried to strengthen the hand of public health officials: we went for the AIDS fix, and left systemic problems largely unaddressed. While the old gay and feminist health movement was grounded in criticism of the economics of health care, the AIDS service movement reproduced the dominant class, race, and gender biases within the organizations, legislation, and delivery system it created; in fundamental ways it shied away from seeing itself as part of a broad antipoverty, health care reform movement. Largely ignoring how a profit-centered health system does disservice to gay men and lesbians, AIDS service organizations have molded themselves into traditional health care bureaucracies—vying for the same funds, creating the same structures, and adopting many of the same attitudes toward patients that radicals in our movement challenge. Ruth Finkel-

stein, the former director of public policy for GMHC, whose outstanding word on AIDS policy in Washington and New York spans more
than a decade, put it this way in 1993: "I really feel there aren't any
more AIDS-specific fixes. The reason that everything is going so badly
is that what remains to be done in AIDS is [to] deal with the [systemic]
issues we haven't dealt with. There's no more confidentiality to fix.
There are no more categorical programs to design and write and pass.
We've done things I'm proud of: the ADA [Americans with Disabilities
Act], the [Ryan White AIDS] Care Act, a model of community planning, participation, and empowerment [and a source of] money and
services. But we've also done things I'm not proud of. In the face of
systemic problems, we've sought exceptions for our people."

Interestingly, the one part of the AIDS movement that did adopt
the radical empowerment stance of the feminist health movement was
the People With AIDS-Coalition. The embrace of feminist principles
by the PWA had a lot to do with the feminism of one of its founders,
the extraordinary songwriter and singer Michael Callen. Callen lived
with AIDS for over fourteen years, before succumbing in 1994, and was
at the forefront of a number of innovations in AIDS activism. He
pioneered safe-sex education, writing the first safe-sex manual, *How to
Have Sex in an Epidemic;* he helped found the People With AIDS
Coalition; and, before he died, he challenged the gay community to
"rethink" AIDS. Callen advocated a greater voice for people with AIDS
in all aspects of the health crisis, from representation on boards of
organizations to involvement in decisions about medical research, drug
testing, and public policy. But Callen's prophetic voice was not heeded
as often as it should have been, and in this decade the crisis is dealt with
on a more traditional model, in which people with AIDS are the "clients" of a paternalistic health care and social service system, which takes
care of them until they die.

While the explicit goal of the early gay and lesbian health clinics
and VD clinics was community organizing and political reform in addition to services, the goal of AIDS service organizations has largely been
medical and social service delivery. Most of them devote only a small
fraction of their resources to public policy advocacy, to political education, or to community organizing. This lack of emphasis on politics has
been severely, and I think rightly, criticized by AIDS activists from
Larry Kramer to many people working within the organizations. Sadly,
the inattention has limited our ability to mobilize constituent pressure
on AIDS policy fights. Thus, in 1991, we could not defend a change in

AIDS policy we had fought years to gain. Secretary Louis Sullivan had agreed to lift the ban on immigration and visitation by HIV-positive people, but the antigay right generated more than forty-thousand letters against the proposal. The AIDS community could marshal only a few hundred in support. The ban against immigration by people with HIV or AIDS stayed in place until 1993, when the Clinton administration removed it. Without a strong political mission, the AIDS movement turned into just another liberal social service movement. In a sense, it was still a step forward for gay people, because we had never had social service organizations to take care of our needs.

AIDS dramatically changed the composition of the gay and lesbian movement. On the one hand, millions of gay and lesbian people became more "politicized" as they saw the government fail to act while scores of friends and loved ones suffered. Men who had never been political, never considered coming out of the closet, never attended a gay or lesbian fundraising event, began to do so in large numbers. Lesbians who had shunned the mixed gay movement, choosing to work on women's rights, grew alarmed at the exploitation of AIDS by the right, and decided to confront the homophobia of the medical, political, and legal systems. Straight friends, family members, and colleagues of people with AIDS were moved through their personal experience to support a movement they had previously ignored. This awakening took place not only in the consciousness of middle- to upper-class men and women of all colors and types, but also among poor and working-class people. Because AIDS affected so many different kinds of people, a broad segment of America began to turn to gay and lesbian organizations for representation and assistance. In the 1960s and 1970s, the gay rights movement was the province of a small group of "politicos." By the late 1980s, gay organizations were being asked to serve white, black, Latino, and Asian, gay, straight, and bisexual, working-class, middle-class, and ruling-class men and women.

The movement was poorly equipped to deal with this influx of new energy and different kinds of people, which helps explain both the movement's growth and the increased tensions that manifest themselves today. For example, as people of color turned to gay and lesbian organizations for culturally specific and culturally sensitive AIDS services, they encountered a lack of comprehension, outright resistance, and sometimes racial prejudice. To reach these underserved populations, gay people of color established AIDS service groups that were racially and minority oriented. By the late 1980s, each ethnic minority group within the queer community had developed an AIDS-specific project. Black and White Men Together established the National Task Force on AIDS Prevention in San Francisco and Atlanta to educate black gay and bisexual men; the Latino/a Lesbian and Gay Organization established an AIDS office in Washington, and locally led Latino projects sprang up in Texas and California; the Native American AIDS Task Force in San Francisco worked with regional groups in Minneapolis and New York; and the Gay Asian Pacific Alliance began its pioneering HIV work in San Francisco. There is little question that AIDS organizations for people of color have expanded the reach of AIDS education and prevention. But they have not transformed the racial or class politics of mainstream AIDS organizations. In this sense, the failure of the mainstream gay and white-dominated AIDS movements to take up systemic reform must be also seen as a failure to address racism and sexism. Cutbacks in social services, Social Security disability, AFDC (Aid to Families with Dependent Children), and other welfare programs will hurt those people with AIDS and HIV who are most dependent on such services. Yet AIDS organizations have not been at the forefront of opposing these cutbacks. We seem to have bought the myth that we will be all right as long as AIDS-specific expenditures (like the Ryan White bill or AIDS research) are not cut. Since the beginning of the epidemic, billions of dollars in Medicaid and Medicare have made more manageable the lives of scores of gay and straight people with HIV. Is it our racial and class bias that prevents us from seeing as "our issue" the massive cutbacks that Republicans propose? And if so, who will lead us to do something about it?

Perhaps the most notable way in which AIDS changed the composition of the movement was the awakened activism of middle- and upper-class gay white men. Until the epidemic struck, many of these men had never experienced prejudice directly or even through their friends. AIDS exposed their sense of security as false, and when it unleashed the government's negligence, religion's avoidance, and the public's homophobia, gay men and women realized that they had to take care of themselves. As Rodger McFarlane, an early executive director of Gay Men's Health Crisis, observed, "For a white man with a graduate degree and a good job who can pass, [discrimination was] not an issue. Never was. Until [AIDS] really got down to it and you realized they want you to die. If you want to be the way you are and not play their way, you're dead meat. You are literally left to die." The men who founded GMHC are examples of these previously uninvolved individuals whose new activism has so transformed the politics and expectations of the gay and lesbian movement; they were Larry Kramer, Nathan Fair, Paul Popham, Paul Rapoport, Dr. Larry Mass, and Edmund White. Of the six founders of GMHC, several had never been active in the gay and lesbian community or been out of the closet before AIDS. These men came together because their lovers and friends were getting sick, and they feared that no one was acting to save them. The men brought donors, contacts, and experience in mainstream business, medicine, and politics into the gay movement. With these skills, contacts, and resources, GMHC, originally an entirely volunteer organization, has become the largest and most politically influential AIDS service organization in the world, with a staff of more than two hundred and an annual budget of over $20 million. The new energy from the gay and lesbian middle class helped build a social service apparatus throughout the country. Community centers, youth projects, antiviolence projects, substance-abuse programs, housing projects, legal services projects, grew larger or were established. In 1992, there were nearly a thousand AIDS service groups nationwide.

We need to value the contribution that upper-middle-class and professional gay men and women made to the gay movement in the 1980s. The engagement of this stratum in gay politics has been a key factor in the cultural revolution we witness to this day. But I think no one can deny that these gay men and women brought their own values and ideals into the existing gay and lesbian movement. The newly activated gay people made the post-AIDS movement more conservative in at least three ways: by the reformulation of the liberation-oriented goals into reform; by the substitution of institution building for movement building; and in their outright rejection of grassroots political organizing as the best means to build gay and lesbian power. In place of liberation, the AIDS movement substituted nondiscrimination; instead of building a movement, it built agencies and bureaucracies; instead of placing its political faith in training and organizing gay and lesbian people, and our allies, into an electoral coalition, it placed its faith in friends in high places.

The organizational history of the Human Rights Campaign Fund illustrates the conservative worldview of this gay upper middle class. In 1980, HRCF was formed by the Gay Rights National Lobby as a strategy to secure political clout by giving PAC money to national politicians. A number of thoughtful and smart gay leaders, some now dead from AIDS-related illnesses, established the fund. HRCF quickly

engaged the energies of an entire generation of middle-class gay men
and women who had been politicized and driven out of the closet by
AIDS. Starting out in 1982 (in Dallas, New York, Philadelphia, and
Boston), the HRCF dinners became the model and the principal means
for reaching this emerging middle-class population; and, in return, the
HRCF dutifully cultivated "friendships" with politicians, gave away
millions of dollars in PAC funds, and lobbied in behalf of scores of
AIDS-funding and civil rights measures. By 1989, this muted role led
the *Los Angeles Times* reporter Victor Zonana to observe that the gay
movement housed direct-action organizations as well as "the quiet lobbying of such pinstriped organizations as the Human Rights Campaign
Fund. Vic Basile, who served as executive director for six years and
helped define the mission and focus of the HRCF, explains the pragmatic philosophy that guided him: "I recognize my limitations. I mean,
you have the power to change certain things, and I think we develop
power by learning how the system works and being able to manipulate
it. And not to think about changing the system. It's too big a task. I
don't think we can make any difference in that equation."

Throughout the eighties, at a time of enormous challenge for gay
and lesbian people, the fund consistently took a safe, middle-of-the-
road approach. HRCF curried favor, accumulated "chits," and concentrated on seeking what it thought it could get, rather than pursuing
what the gay community genuinely needed. This method led to repeated friction between HRCF lobbyists and lobbyists from NGLTF,
AIDS Action Council, and other AIDS service organizations. I recall,
for example, many heated conversations between NGLTF's director and
chief AIDS lobbyist, Jeff Levi, and HRCF staff, in which Levi pressed
for a commitment on a policy issue but the staff equivocated. I also
remember how HRCF staff ignored the Hate Crimes Statistics Act
until the 1990 session, when it was passed, because they deemed it not a
winner; NGLTF lobbyists pursued the fight throughout. This pragmatic—self-preserving—philosophy guided HRCF until the 1990s,
when Basile's successor, Tim McFeeley, led the group to take more
principled political stands.

The tension between HRCF and NGLTF is rooted in class and
political philosophy. It is a tension that remains to this day, despite
protestations of cooperation and noncompetition between the two
groups. HRCF was founded in 1983 by a different class and kind of
person from those who had founded NGLTF in 1973. While the
HRCF base was professional, largely closeted, and able to give between

$150 and $250 for a place at a fundraising dinner, the NGLTF base was smaller, more activist and grassroots, comprising people out enough to donate funds to a gay and lesbian organization that acknowledged its identity in its name. NGLTF survived, marginally, on small donations from many individuals; by 1988, HRCF had nearly twice the budget and staff of NGLTF. The resentment between the two organizations was inevitable.

The second source of tension between the two groups stems from their different approaches. By definition, as a federal political action committee, HRCF takes a top-down approach to civil rights, working carefully with federal politicians to amass political debts through PAC donations and electoral involvement. NGLTF's mission is to work from the ground up against discrimination on the basis of sexual orientation. It does so by training local activists, developing manuals and policy analyses, and forming coalitions with nongay allies on issues like violence, AIDS, family, employment rights, health care reform, and sodomy law reform. Since 1993, the HRCF board has shifted its thinking and now articulates the same commitment to grassroots organizing and movement building that the NGLTF has practiced since its founding. Because of this shift, many activists today call for a merger between the two groups. According to Tim McFeeley, the only time the gay billionaire David Geffen initiated contact with him was to call in 1994 to urge a merger with NGLTF.

I believe fervently in the competition of ideas, but the rivalry between HRCF and NGLTF has never been a healthy contest fueled by different ideas and strategies. At its core, the tension has been an ego-driven war for power and influence. Empire-building and turf battles have become more important than the good of the gay and lesbian community. Those who want one national organization seek control rather than efficiency. It is in this light that I interpret Geffen's and others' calls for merger. While some may conclude that the merger would benefit the community as a whole, a position I have argued at other times, at this moment I feel it would weaken the movement, because it would merge not merely resources, but two necessary and different philosophical approaches. History suggests that the access-driven politics of HRCF would overwhelm the empowerment-driven politics of NGLTF: who has the money controls the agenda. If the selfish interests of a wealthy gay elite dominate the operations and politics of national organizations, then working-class or middle-class queers lose national voice.

THE DIRECT-ACTION STRATEGY AND ITS DECLINE

Direct-action activism emerged in part as a reaction to the conservatism of the gay mainstream, and significantly affected gay movement strategy from 1986 to 1992. ACT UP marked the first (and only) time that this strategy took center stage in national gay politics. A new generation of activists, committed solely and principally to being queer and promoting queer freedom, came into its own. And the deep impact of AIDS on certain industries—notably, entertainment, fashion, theater, and the arts—brought unprecedented mainstream investment in AIDS-related organizations. These developments catapulted forward AIDS treatment and care and gay and lesbian civil rights, but produced mixed long-term consequences. Among these consequences are a greater degree of polarization among gay people; the triumph of the reductive, sound-bite, and media-driven politics of expediency over the thoughtful, morally grounded politics of social justice; and the weakening of the bite of AIDS activism into the bark of AIDS awareness. The direct-action strategy focused on the glamorous and neglected the obvious. We sought (and got) media visibility, but after our fifteen minutes in the sun, we were left with another round of silence and the need to repeat the old actions, with diminished effectiveness each time. Our coercive moralism and guerrilla tactics eventually alienated and angered the people whose decisions we tried to shape. Ultimately, our neglect of dull systematic political organizing left us in 1993 without the political capacity to fight the right locally for our policy agenda nationally.

On March 10, 1987, the playwright and AIDS activist Larry Kramer gave a speech, at the New York City Lesbian and Gay Community Services Center, reviewing the progress of the gay and lesbian movement on AIDS policy. He passionately criticized the lack of political advocacy and media presence on AIDS and asked the crowd of 250 men and women, "Do we want to start a new organization devoted solely to political action?" Days later, at a follow-up at the center meeting inspired by Kramer's address, and attended by more than three hundred, the AIDS Coalition to Unleash Power (ACT UP) was born. ACT UP–New York became the most influential and largest of all the chapters, drawing more than eight hundred people to its weekly meetings at the New York City Community Services Center. But ACT UP chapters quickly appeared throughout the country. By early 1988, strong chapters existed in Chicago, San Francisco, Boston, and Los Angeles. At the end of 1989, ACT UP boasted more than a hundred chapters worldwide, including scores of chapters in small Midwestern, Southwestern, and Southern cities in the United States.

ACT UP gave to gay people affected by AIDS a vehicle through which to organize. Motivated by their own HIV status or by a sense of outrage at the government's inadequate response to AIDS, thousands of people flocked to ACT UP groups. Fueled in part by anger, many were also driven by a fairly pragmatic and calculated critique of why AIDS was not getting the response it deserved. Kramer correctly pointed out that politicians listened to the media, and that, except in isolated incidents, the media had not yet been reached by AIDS activism. The deepening epidemic and Kramer's urgent call for action tapped an energy that the movement had not before reached on a national level: the desire among gay and lesbian people to engage in direct action on behalf of their own lives.

From the beginning, ACT UP attracted a wide mix of people in New York—from closeted gay professional men who were HIV-positive, to veteran lesbian-feminist organizers, to gay activists frustrated by traditional political strategies, to straight celebrities, to young gay and straight activists whose first-ever political involvement was an ACT UP meeting and demonstration. Indeed, ACT UP grew in part because it provided an easy, local, and direct way to participate in gay politics— something that no national gay or lesbian project had given large numbers of people up to that point, or since. Three influential people involved in ACT UP for many years were the New York activists Peter Staley, Maxine Wolfe, and David Barr. From them, I received a surprisingly consistent interpretation of what went on within ACT UP—the forces that brought people together and made it effective and the forces that ultimately drew it apart.

Peter Staley typifies the gay professional man who became an ACT UP activist. Staley was working on Wall Street as a trader when ACT UP held its first demonstration there, and he described to me how it changed his life. "I got handed a flyer on my way to work, as did many on our trading floor. [There] was quite a discussion on the trading floor before work started, about whether these people outside were justified in their anger, and with quite a few traders saying that the government shouldn't do anything and we should just be left to die. That really got me going . . . but I gritted my teeth and remained in the closet. But I started going to the meetings, and I led this double life for a year, closeted and trading by day and at night going to ACT UP committee meetings and getting very involved." When Staley's T-cells dropped sharply, in 1988, he left his job, went on disability, came out publicly, and dedicated himself full time to AIDS and treatment activism. Staley raised tens of thousands of dollars for ACT UP, and planned countless demonstrations. In 1992, frustrated by the direction ACT UP had taken, Staley and others left and formed the Treatment Action Group, a small network of researchers, lobbyists, and activists working solely on AIDS treatment matters.

The lesbian activist Maxine Wolfe came into ACT UP with a completely different political background and expectation. A mother of two, Wolfe had spent years working on issues of abortion and reproductive rights, with CARASA (Committee Against Reproductive and Sterilization Abuse), wrote the grant that funded the Reproductive Rights National Network (R2N2), and founded a grassroots lesbian feminist group, Women for Women, in the early 1980s, when the homophobia of the reproductive rights movement peaked. She went on to work with the Lesbian Herstory Archives on its fundraising drive (which resulted in the purchase of a building). In 1993, Wolfe and several other lesbians (including the writers Sarah Schulman and Anne Christine D'Adesky) founded the Lesbian Avengers. Unlike Staley and the other treatment-focused activists, Wolfe has continued to work with ACT UP, despite major disagreements over the years. She was a key organizer in the 1988 FDA demonstration, the 1989 demonstration at the Department of Health and Human Services, and a series of national actions by ACT UP women to change the CDC's definition of AIDS so that it encompassed illnesses that HIV-positive women encountered.

In October 1992, she helped organize the political funeral at the White House, at which ACT UP members attempted to deposit the dead body of an AIDS activist, and spread the ashes of several others, on the White House grounds. Wolfe explained the departure of treatment activists from ACT UP in this way: "I think it was really great that TAG left. I hate the term 'treatment activist,' because I am one. But that's the way they separated themselves from us. I think that they've basically become part of the system. But mostly I am happy they left because they really didn't want to deal with the political parts of this crisis. And that same set of people took what was a political focus on a crisis and changed it into a medical focus on a crisis. And believed that if they became the experts they could tell the medical people how to do medicine in this crisis."

Another early ACT UP member, David Barr, influenced in his outlook by progressive parents, started his political activism in experimental theater projects. In his late twenties, Barr decided to go to law school and began to volunteer with Lambda Legal Defense and Education Fund in 1984. One of his first projects was to challenge the licensing of the HIV test in 1985, which resulted in stricter confidentiality guidelines being put in place. Barr started the first legal newsletter on AIDS and began full-time work on AIDS policy matters in 1987. "I went to my first ACT UP meeting in June of '87. The March on Washington was that [year and] everything was about to explode. I knew that, and I knew that ACT UP was a place where I wanted to be. I liked it a lot. I liked the feel. It was, for me, the first time that I ever found a gay community that I could feel connected to." Barr went on to play a major role in the reform of the FDA guidelines on the early release of experimental drugs, and has worked to craft a wide range of federal and state AIDS policies and regulations. In 1992, Barr helped co-found TAG and organized an unprecedented coalition in New York called United for AIDS Action, which produced the largest AIDS demonstration, during the 1992 Democratic Convention in New York.

By 1993, Barr was grappling with the race and gender tensions AIDS exposed. "Now, I'm a white gay man and I love white gay men. You know? Those are the people I'm closest to. But I get upset with my community's failure to acknowledge its privilege and its power. And I don't see them willing to give any of it up. I realize other people have to have a voice in AIDS. We've had a voice from the beginning, and that's fine. We took it and we were courageous, but we're not the only ones with something to say. I really am questioning how I can continue to have a voice—because my community needs one, and we have a lot of expertise, we have a lot to say, our bodies are on the line—[but] how do I continue to have the voice and at the same time not drown out everybody else?"

Direct action works because everyone involved shapes the way it takes place. There is no third party mediating the experience; the idea most often originates with the people who carry it out. Pickets, sit-ins, small demonstrations, rallies, speak-outs, leafleting, carrying a sign into a meeting, risking arrest by committing civil disobedience, writing chants and using a bullhorn, spray-painting, wheat-pasting, preparing placards for a march through the city streets—all these forms of protest are very immediate, very personal. The exhilaration of direct action is profound. And the sense of moral purpose—of being united with the other people one acts with—can be passionate and affecting. As David Barr recalls, "It was really exciting to watch people go through this process of finding ACT UP, getting politicized, figuring out what that means, how they can do some work, and how they grew from that. That was really great."

ACT UP worked because it gave people a sense of belonging and a creative outlet for despair. It became community, family, and faith all rolled into one. Gay men found in AIDS activism the courage to confront their mortality, the vehicle to express their anger, and the hope that, through their action, research and treatment would be accelerated. Lesbian activists, long familiar with systemic inequities, found a way to come home into their own movement through AIDS activism. Hundreds of straight, bisexual, and allied folk got involved with AIDS activism and direct action to express their anger at the government, which appeared to condone the death of people with AIDS. But ACT UP was about more than anger—it was, like religion, about faith.

Why did ACT UP grow so dramatically in 1987, and why had the strategy declined just as dramatically by 1993? By October 1987, AIDS was touching the lives of millions of gay men, bisexual people, and lesbians. This fact, coupled with at least four other historical developments, contributed to the national emergence of ACT UP and accelerated the reach of the direct-action strategy: the intransigent policies of the Reagan and Bush administrations; the impact on gay activism of the 1987 March on Washington; the national media coverage captured by ACT UP; and the inability of traditional gay and lesbian groups to involve the large number of people who wanted to take action on AIDS and gay rights at the local level. But, cruelly, ACT UP and the direct-action movement waned for the very reasons it had succeeded. By 1993, the political climate for gay people and people with AIDS had changed; the media scrutiny exposed many contradictions within the direct-action movement; direct action failed to transform mainstream gay institutions and to build the lasting, grassroots political presence we needed; and, most sadly, many people involved in the group grew sicker, walked away in disgust or exhaustion, or died.

Both the Reagan and Bush administrations behaved reprehensibly in response to AIDS. For several years, Reagan ignored the problem completely. His Secretary of Health and Human Services, Margaret

Heckler, met with gay lobbyists in 1983 and promised to make AIDS a priority. But that promise was frustrated by the internal politics of the administration; the Moral Majority and religious right wanted the government to have nothing to do with gay men. By 1986, when Surgeon General C. Everett Koop began to press for a greater response to AIDS, he encountered opposition from Secretary of Education William Bennett. Koop published and distributed the first government mailing on AIDS over Bennett's objection; he sent it to every household by early 1987. For his moral courage, Koop earned the lasting gratitude of gay and lesbian people. By 1987, the year Reagan first uttered the word AIDS, gay and lesbian anger at the administration's abdication was at a boiling point. Randy Shilts's book on AIDS and politics made the government's irresponsibility vivid to his colleagues in the media and to the public at large. All this set a highly politicized stage for ACT UP's emergence.

The impact of the 1987 March on Washington on all gay and lesbian activism cannot be overstated. Planned for over a year and a half, the Second National March on Washington for Lesbian and Gay Rights was an enormous success, exceeding the wildest expectation of any of its organizers. The timing was right, the word was out at the grassroots level, and thousands upon thousands of people came to Washington for a weekend of protests, culminating in the march on October 11. It drew more than 650,000 people and, for the first time, gave massive national visibility to the epidemic's effect on the gay community. As part of the march, the AIDS Memorial Quilt was displayed on the Capitol grounds, providing an emotional and moral anchor for the protests held throughout the weekend. At the march, the colorful and exciting presence of ACT UP attracted the attention of thousands of gay and lesbian people—and drew widespread media notice. On October 12, the next day, a widely covered, national Civil Disobedience Action at the U.S. Supreme Court by five thousand protestors made direct action by gay and lesbian activists a top national news story. The march weekend ignited gay and lesbian activism; people went home and formed scores of local political, direct-action, cultural, social, and professional groups. The NGLTF national office had a fourfold increase in the number of calls it received from gay and lesbian activists seeking technical assistance, organizing materials, and advice. Each year after the march, the movement seemed to grow, a trend that has in fact continued into the mid-1990s. ACT UP both benefited from and contributed directly to this heightened awareness and activism.

From the start, ACT UP also contributed to a greater awareness of AIDS issues within the gay and lesbian community, and in society at large, through the media coverage it secured. Media interest in ACT UP was immediate—from its first demonstration, on March 24, 1987, at Wall Street, targeting the Food and Drug Administration's bureaucratic logjam on experimental drug development. The coverage ACT UP won remains unprecedented. Never before has an organization of gay and lesbian people been as widely covered by the straight press. The media success was both carefully orchestrated and organic. On the one hand, many early ACT UP organizers were savvy media veterans. Some, like Ann Northrop, worked in the news media; others, like Michelangelo Signorile and Bob Rafsky, were skilled at public relations. ACT UP–New York harnessed the talents of some of the finest visual artists in the country and made their political art, their agit-prop, available to others across the country. Keith Haring, the Gran Fury Collective, the videographers from Testing the Limits, and scores of others produced arresting graphic images that were printed on posters, T-shirts, and leaflets, broadcast on cable TV and national news media, and distributed worldwide. These images made an enormous impression on viewers. The lime-green poster of Reagan with the pink word AIDSGATE emblazoned on it, which we carried during the 1988 Republican Convention protests in New Orleans; the American flag labeled "Bush AIDS Flag," with skulls instead of stars; the red-and-black posters citing the AIDS death toll so far and asking "Where Was George?"—all became graphic reminders of AIDS and communicated a strong message. The media committee of almost every ACT UP chapter, peopled by aggressive and forceful activists, also planned actions with an eye toward media coverage: what was the visual, who would do the press conference, where would we stage the backdrop, what media outlet would be the best to cover this event?

Along with these calculated attempts to gain coverage was the inherent drama, tension, and theatricality of ACT UP demonstrations in particular, and of direct-action protests in general, which made them telegenic and newsworthy. I still remember the orchestrated and chaotic beauty of the 1988 FDA action, at which a thousand protestors surrounded the FDA's bleak building in Maryland; the wit of the 1989 demonstration at the U.S. Civil Rights Commission's hearings on AIDS, at which many in the audience donned clown masks and held up watches to protest the ineptitude and wastefulness of this body; the shock of ACT UP's 1989 Stop the Church demonstration against the Catholic Church. The life and death drama of people with AIDS and HIV being angry and screaming at officials and bureaucrats who opposed them riveted the nation's attention for several years.

Ultimately, such actions also angered many people. It's fair to say that ACT UP was controversial from the start. Many people loathed its confrontational tactics. Some in the community feared that ACT UP would alienate the general public. Others feared that it would jeopardize hard-won political access. Still others feared that direct actions against political friends would estrange them. Yet others deplored the use of direct action in most circumstances, arguing that traditional political activism was the best way to win AIDS policies. The self-righteousness that was the hallmark of ACT UP galled many of its erstwhile supporters. ACT UP chapters seemed to thrive on these controversies and exploited them. Among the most polarizing actions in the history of ACT UP were the following: a spring-summer 1988 "freedom ride" by four members of ACT UP–New York through the South, ending at the Democratic Convention in Atlanta, which both alienated and inspired Southern gay and lesbian activists from North Carolina to Louisiana; a pitched, year-long battle in 1988–1989 over the appointment by New York City Mayor David Dinkins of Woodrow Myers as NYC Health Commissioner; the 1989 protest by ACT UP–San Francisco, which disrupted the opera, and another action, which stopped traffic on the Golden Gate Bridge; the 1989 Stop the Church demonstration at Saint Patrick's Cathedral, in which ACT UP members disrupted mass to protest Cardinal John O'Connor's opposition to condom distribution; a demonstration against Louis Sullivan at the International AIDS Conference in San Francisco in June 1991, at which activists prevented him from being heard; and a 1992 demonstration by ACT UP members at a meeting of gay and AIDS lobbyists with the CDC about its policies concerning women with AIDS.

The anger ACT UP evoked among some, and the anger that many ACT UP members felt toward those who opposed them, came, ironically, from the same source: disdain for the politics and ethics of the other. Direct-action and traditional political activists have always clashed in the gay and lesbian movement. Although some veterans of the post-Stonewall generation embraced ACT UP as a return to the radical politics they felt the gay movement had wrongly abandoned, most gay political veterans looked down on direct action in general.

Conversely, many ACT UP members were contemptuous of and hostile
to the mainstream gay and lesbian rights movement. "People are dying,"
they argued. "This is no time for business as usual."

The resistance of traditional lobbyists to the direct-action strategy
was deep. Some seasoned lobbyists felt that direct action was ultimately
beside the point: substantive knowledge of the issues and specific policy
advocacy were far more important. Others, like Representative Barney
Frank, of Massachusetts, argued that, while there was a time and place
for direct action, it tended to alienate more people than it reached. Still
other traditional activists took a pragmatic, even opportunistic, view:
they supported the street activists as long as they helped "legitimize"
more conventional lobbyists. So, for example, immediately after ACT
UP protested at the FDA in October 1988, a high-level meeting took
place among gay and AIDS lobbyists and the FDA bureaucrats. The
lobbyists put forth the same message that the AIDS protestors had
carried, yet they consciously positioned themselves as the "more reasonable" alternative to the mob outside. Such a technique, while effective
for policy writing in the short term, provoked tremendous ill-will and
lasting distrust between traditional political organizers and street
activists.

Similarly, ACT UP grew in stature by self-consciously positioning
itself as the more effective alternative to traditional political work. In
the late 1980s, when gay organizations seemed incapable of defeating
Jesse Helms or summoning the clout to get federal action on AIDS,
ACT UP claimed that it had the most effective strategy for winning
governmental reform. The unglamorous, behind-the-scenes lobbying
process, it argued, was not only too slow to save lives; it was undemocratic, because it did not allow for the participation of "all" who were
interested. As ACT UP gained more media attention, and as it was
credited with many political successes—some of which it was directly
responsible for and others to which it contributed, alongside traditional
lobbyists—its prestige grew, at the expense of traditional activists whose
work took place behind the scenes. In a real sense, each strategy played
the other off its own source of political strength, with gay mainstream
groups enhanced in the eyes of state power structures and direct-action
adherents idealized by grassroots queers.

Direct-action believers had several different kinds of critiques of the
mainstream movement. Some, like Larry Kramer, grew furious at gay
and AIDS organizations, labeling them the enemy because they failed
to take actions he felt they should or to act aggressively enough on

AIDS. Some, like Maxine Wolfe, believed that direct action was more inclusive, democratic, and honest than closed-door lobbying. Others, like the talented and principled organizer Jim Hull from Kansas City, and Mike Shriver and Laura Thomas from San Francisco, took the position that some mainstream gay groups were not to be trusted. Thus, ACT UP and Queer Nation refused to work at the 1992 Republican Convention within a gay and lesbian coalition that included HRCF, NGLTF, and the Log Cabin Republican Clubs; and in 1991 HRCF director Tim McFeeley was not allowed to speak at a California state rally protesting Pete Wilson's veto of the gay rights bill, because AIDS activists objected. Finally, a handful of ACT UP members have functioned as provocateurs, stirring up conflicts within the movement and thriving on division among gay and lesbian activists.

Ironically, I have experienced the hostility of both sides of the direct-action–traditional political divide. Because I came up from a grassroots wing of the feminist and gay movement, I championed direct action alongside traditional political activism. In 1990, as executive director of NGLTF, I protested President George Bush at his first (and only speech) on AIDS, and incurred the wrath of conservatives on the NGLTF board and in the community at large. But in February 1992, I hastily and mistakenly agreed to be involved in a direct-action protest without thinking through the consequences of what the protestors proposed to do (which I learned an hour before the protest took place). The action called for protestors to handcuff themselves to the gay and AIDS lobbyists attending a small meeting with the CDC. The handcuffing was perceived, rightly, by the lobbyists as a hostile and troubling act. When I objected that people were uncomfortable being handcuffed and wanted to be released, the group refused to unlock them. I then withdrew from the action, because it violated my sense of what was right. This withdrawal was wrong on my part, because of my commitment to serve as a legal observer for the protestors, but necessary because I disagreed with the action. A number of ACT UP members branded me a traitor, while the AIDS lobbyists, many of whom I had worked with for several years, eyed me with anger and dismay.

These twin experiences chart the course that the direct-action movement took over the years—from being externally directed, to being directed inwardly, at gay and AIDS activists themselves. For several years, our anger was aimed at the federal government, at federal agencies, at Congress, drug companies, at the media, and at homophobic politicians. But as we became polarized among ourselves, we turned the protests, anger, and direct action toward proponents of traditional political activism. Refocusing the anger we felt at AIDS on one another, or on fellow AIDS organizations with whose policies we disagreed (as ACT UP did in New York when it picketed the Hispanic AIDS Forum), undermined the solidarity we needed to function as a movement.

Meanwhile, the Bush administration stepped up its rhetorical attack on ACT UP, calling the tactics terrorist and militant. This attack by straight homophobes like Bush was picked up and repeated by gay and lesbian conservatives and liberals, many of whom had never accepted the value of direct action in our movement. The pages of the gay and lesbian press in the early 1990s are filled with the criticism of ACT UP as a strategy that had outlived its purpose. As the strategy ran into greater resistance, some who had participated in or endorsed it backed away. Further, the novelty and efficacy of direct action began to wear off. Once again, it became difficult for AIDS activists to obtain media coverage for their protests. Searching for new angles on a familiar story, the media began to report on dissent about direct action within the gay community. In the process of reporting the argument, the media, gay and straight, deepened the old splits between opponents and proponents. By 1992, despite the visibility of ACT UP activists who challenged presidential candidates on the campaign trail, the consensus among gay people was that direct action was no longer an effective strategy.

Interestingly, those who disagreed most with that notion were feminists and lesbians. As ACT UP's popularity declined among men, some new, largely feminist direct-action groups began: the Women's Action Coalition (WAC), the Women's Health Action Mobilization (WHAM), the Lesbian Avengers (LA). Even within ACT UP, women and lesbians asserted themselves on the agenda, pushing for direct action to change the definition of AIDS for women, and pressing for equal access to clinical trials. These new groups reflected the alienation between progressive lesbians and the mainstream gay movement and, to some extent, the new type of lesbian activist. Ruth Schwartz, an activist, wrote, "Many ACT UP women represented a new dyke generation, more queer than feminist. Next to their early-twenties bravado, punk haircuts, and sticker-plastered jackets, lesbian AIDS service providers often looked like the establishment."

Lesbians are, as a whole, more politically progressive than gay men. Our skepticism about government, family, and patriarchy draws many of us to grassroots political action and to the democratic participation and individual control that direct action fosters. Yet I think there are several key exceptions to this general rule, based to some extent on generational, racial, and class differences. For example, with the exception of some of its founders, those active in Lesbian Avengers chapters are mostly young women, often experiencing their first organized lesbian or gay political campaigns. On the other hand, middle- to upper-middle-class gay professional women are more likely to be active in traditional political organizations, like NOW and HRCF. Sadly, the racial separatism of the AIDS activist movement was simply reproduced in the new wave of lesbian direct action. Lesbians of color are largely absent from either of these circles of activism and are more likely to be involved in nongay, antiracist, or economic justice projects. In the end, direct action neither produced new divisions among us nor contributed new understandings to help us resolve the old splits of political ideology, race, gender, and class. Instead, direct action reinforced them.

As the tide of cultural conservatism launched by the New Right in the 1970s hit its stride in the 1990s, it was no surprise that the popularity of direct action diminished. In addition, the mainstream gay rights movement came into its own during the 1990s, seeming to fulfill its promise of political access, cultural visibility, and social legitimation. After a decade of painful transformation induced by AIDS, mainstreaming gayness seemed to many to be the strategy offering the most clear short-term gains and the best hope for long-term equality.

CHAPTER FOUR

THE PREVAILING STRATEGY

MAINSTREAMING DEFINED

The lesbian and gay movement began to claim that it was a civil rights movement as early as the founding of the Mattachine Society. By pursuing the path of civil rights, we consciously chose legal reform, political access, visibility, and legitimation over the long-term goals of cultural acceptance, social transformation, understanding, and liberation. By 1973, the gay liberation movement was becoming a vestigial movement popular among intellectuals and artists. As a political force, its ideas had been absorbed and reinterpreted by a more moderate civil rights–oriented, largely middle-class gay movement. The tension between the two wings of the movement, however, did not disappear. In 1993, for example, it was evident in the very title of the March on Washington, which defined itself as a demonstration for Lesbian, Gay and Bi Rights, *and* Liberation (emphasis added). The 1993 march also represented the full flowering of the mainstream civil rights strategy, as organizers self-consciously styled the march a gay version of the historic 1963 March on Washington, organized by black civil rights leaders. By 1993, we were a "bona fide" civil rights movement, having achieved the ultimate stamp of mainstream approval, the imprimatur of the new publisher of the *New York Times,* Arthur Ochs Sulzberger, Jr., and its editor, Max Frankel, who were reported to have called the gay rights movement the civil rights movement of the 1990s.

Our movement had in fact actively pursued such mainstreaming through three major strategies: involvement in national and local electoral campaigns; working for legal reform and litigation; and lobbying for enactment of nondiscrimination laws. Each of these strategies differs from the other, yet all together move toward the same goal: civil rights for lesbian and gay people and our integration into the mainstream of politics, law, and society. Electoral strategies are aimed toward the leveraging of money and votes to gain political access and clout. Legal strategies have involved us in efforts to repeal antigay laws (such as those criminalizing gay and lesbian behavior, known colloquially as sodomy laws) or turn to courts to vindicate our constitutional and civil rights. Strategies of legislative enactment have led us to try to modify existing laws by adding sexual orientation as a covered category (colloquially, gay rights laws) or to develop new public policies that specifically address gay and lesbian problems (such as laws to stiffen penalties for bias-motivated violence). I concentrate on the movement's engagement at the national level only because an examination of local and state efforts reveals that the politics and character of the gay and lesbian community in virtually each city or town are unique. I use local illustrations wherever possible, but focus principally on the national manifestation of these strategies.

There are other significant differences between local and national electoral activism that bear mention. While many local activists are organized around the election of gay-supportive candidates or openly gay or lesbian candidates at the local level, national activists have concentrated on legislative and regulatory reform. Until 1992, large numbers of gay and lesbian people were not personally involved in presidential campaigns, because, since the seventies, national politics had been the province of a handful of powerful gay and lesbian leaders. I focus in this chapter on presidential politics because it symbolizes the advantages and pitfalls of mainstream electoral organizing and the mechanism by which we have come to national consciousness.

Gay people have not yet mounted viable national campaigns, although several have tried. Openly gay members of Congress like Gerry Studds, Barney Frank, and Steve Gunderson did not originally win election as out gay candidates. Given gay political progress, however, such national candidacies are only a matter of time, as local gay activists and politicians build bases of support that extend beyond our communities. On the other hand, lesbian, gay, and openly gay-supportive candidates ran for, and won, office as mayors, city councilors, school board officials, and other positions. Groups like Chicago's IMPACT (a local gay political action committee), the Maine Gay and Lesbian Political Caucus, the Stonewall Union in Columbus, the Log Cabin Club of California, and the Dallas Gay and Lesbian Alliance support this electoral activism on the local level. Electing one of our own has to be the most gratifying experience in gay and lesbian politics. Although the numbers of gay and lesbian officeholders are small—the Gay and Lesbian Victory Fund, which exists to elect gay candidates, cited fifty-four openly gay officeholders in 1994—the effect of these candidacies is huge and not merely symbolic.

In most instances, gay candidates help to focus and organize segments of our vast communities. This was the case in Harvey Milk's successful run for office in San Francisco in 1977, a run preceded by two drives that were unsuccessful but that established grassroots support for Milk. Milk's campaigns forged long-lasting coalitions between gay people, labor, and other allies. In 1974, Elaine Noble became the first out gay person to win public office when she gained a seat in the Massachusetts state legislature. The impact of her win was felt far beyond that body; she became a role model for thousands of lesbians and gay men. Electoral victories in the 1980s by Midwestern gay and lesbian candidates, like Karen Clark and Alan Spear in Minnesota, came long before similar victories in urban centers like New York, and helped chart a path that led to Minnesota's passage of a statewide gay and lesbian rights bill in 1991.

In the legal arena, a number of major cities host local gay and lesbian bar associations (New York, Los Angeles, Washington, San Francisco, Chicago, Boston), and more informal networks exist in other cities. Functioning more as service organizations than as social change groups, they serve the social, networking, and educational needs of their members and, less frequently, take on advocacy or policy roles in local political fights. The political strategies of our legal movement tend to come from three sources: lawyers involved in litigation to challenge discrimination, queer legal groups, and legal scholars writing in law reviews. I think law reviews contain some of the most fascinating gay and lesbian political theory—because gay rights litigation is the site of so much precedent-setting activity. Sadly, these journals are not read by most activists, gay media columnists, or even policymakers.

While the process of passing legislation is common to both national and local forums, the history of each bill is unique. Behind every gay rights law—be it a city council resolution, a mayoral proclamation of gay pride week, or a state gay rights bill—there is a story. The legislative process is at once absorbing and frustrating. Although it is extremely satisfying to help pass a law that tackles a social problem our people face, such as discrimination in employment, the tradeoffs, compromises, and back-sliding associated with legislative enactment require an iron stomach.

MAINSTREAM POLITICS AND THE EMERGENCE OF A GAY MAINSTREAM

Gay and lesbian involvement in presidential campaigns formally began in the 1972 election, when Senator George McGovern of South Dakota ran against incumbent Richard Nixon on a strongly antiwar and liberal domestic platform. A major reason for McGovern's strong showing in California was the work of San Francisco gay activist Jim Foster. Discharged from the military in the 1950s for being gay, Foster moved to San Francisco and helped found the Society for Individual Rights in 1964. Boasting a membership of a thousand in the late 1960s, SIR quickly became unique among gay and lesbian organizations. It sponsored bowling nights and brunches, bridge clubs and art classes, a thrift shop, and even established the first gay community center, in 1966. In addition, it sponsored candidates nights, issued endorsements, and educated its members. SIR's use of social events and outlets to organize electoral power proved prescient. By 1971, it could take pride in its first electoral victory, that of the gay-supportive candidate Richard Hongisto as sheriff of San Francisco. In 1971, Foster organized SIR members into the Alice B. Toklas Democratic Club, and his organizing skills soon helped the McGovern campaign. As Randy Shilts noted:

> McGovern had issued a seven-point gay rights plank that satisfied virtually every demand the fledgling gay movement was making, from upgrading dishonorable discharges to banning discrimination against gays. The California primary shaped up as a crucial battle for McGovern. To get his name at the top of the ballot—a slot worth several percentage points—the South Dakota senator needed to be

the first candidate to get all of his nominating petitions into Secretary of State Jerry Brown's office.

Jim Foster devised a shrewd strategy to gather the signatures. On the eve of the first day that petitions could be circulated, one group of gay Democrats went into San Francisco's bars and registered new voters. After midnight, another group went in and recruited the newly registered voters to sign McGovern petitions. According to Shilts, by the time the bars closed that night, Foster's volunteers had gathered more than a third of the Northern California signatures needed to place McGovern on the ballot. This work won Foster the respect of the San Francisco Democratic establishment and an appointment as one of two openly gay delegates to the 1972 Democratic Convention.

The convention's platform committee was presented the same seven-point gay rights plank issued earlier by the McGovern campaign, but the candidate suddenly backed away from his campaign-driven endorsement, and lobbied against the plank before the platform committee. Foster insisted that a minority report urging a gay rights plank be presented to the entire convention, a fight he won. Although the party would fail to pass a gay rights plank until 1980, Foster's work had brought gay and lesbian Democrats into the party structure. On July 14, 1972, the same night McGovern accepted the party's nomination, and despite the active opposition of Southern Democrats, Foster spoke to the convention. "We do not come to you pleading your understanding or begging your tolerance. We come to you affirming our pride in our lifestyle, affirming the validity to seek and maintain meaningful emotional relationships and affirming our right to participate in the life of this country on an equal basis with every citizen." Foster ended his speech by urging the convention to support gay and lesbian rights and to pass a gay rights plank: "These are not conservative or radical issues; these are human issues . . . Regardless of whether this convention passes the plank or not, there are millions of gay brothers and sisters who will say to the Democratic Party: we are here. We will not be still. We will not go away until the ultimate goal of gay liberation is realized, the goal that all people live in the peace, freedom, and dignity of who we are."

When Richard Nixon defeated McGovern, his ascendancy was accompanied by the emergence of a modern, ultraconservative movement. This New Right was organized by men like Paul Weyrich, Howard

Phillips, and Richard Viguerie, with the explicit goal of shifting the balance of our cultural institutions to the right. A reactionary movement, formed by people reacting to liberalism and to progressive and leftist ideas popular in the 1960s, the New Right opposed civil rights, did not share the liberal ideal of racial and gender equality, and sought to conserve power and wealth in the hands of those who already possessed it. The New Right, well funded by a handful of wealthy businessmen, strategically allied itself with conservative religious leaders to extend its reach. By the mid-1970s, the movement found an antigay voice in Anita Bryant.

Between the 1972 and 1976 presidential elections, the gay political movement also grew, without coordinated opposition. Gay Activist Alliance chapters spread across the country; new gay Democratic and political clubs were established in LA and Seattle to organize gay voters; and a number of cities like Madison, Washington, and Saint Paul passed gay and lesbian rights laws. Some of the first college gay and lesbian groups were organized, and an early round of lawsuits forced state universities to grant them official recognition. The LA Gay and Lesbian Community Services Center was established in 1972 by longtime activist Morris Kight, among others; twenty-three years later, the center is the largest gay and lesbian service organization in the country. In 1975, the Washington activist Frank Kameny won a ruling from the Civil Service Commission banning discrimination in federal employment based on sexual orientation, while the Supreme Court denied review of a challenge to the Virginia sodomy law.

By 1976, gay and lesbian Democrats like Jim Foster, NGTF co-chair Jean O'Leary, *Advocate* publisher David Goodstein, and others were poised to pick up where they had left off. They had gained further access to the Democratic Party in the intervening years. During the campaign, Carter stated that he opposed "all forms of discrimination against individuals including discrimination on the basis of sexual orientation. As President, I can assure you that all policies of the federal government would reflect the commitment to ending all forms of discrimination." But as a front-runner, Carter, like McGovern, equivocated and told the *Advocate* that he was not sure he would sign a federal gay rights bill. He said, "I do not feel that people should be abused because of their sexual preference, but I don't know how we could deal with the issue of blackmail in federal security jobs. But with that possible exception, I would probably support this legislation." Both as a candidate and as President, Jimmy Carter wrote the script that Bill Clinton would follow in 1992 and beyond: he tried to appease the party's right wing and he neglected its liberal base.

As President, Carter backed away from his campaign endorsements of gay and lesbian rights and refused to take any direct executive action to ban discrimination based on sexual orientation. During the Carter years, Shilts pointed out, antigay military purges increased "dramatically." Still, Carter was better than Nixon in one respect: in 1977, White House staff, led by the public liaison officer, Midge Costanza, met with representatives from gay rights organizations to discuss their agenda. Among those at this first White House meeting were Jean O'Leary, Bruce Voeller, Steve Endean, and Ginny Apuzzo. Another White House meeting with administration officials took place two days before the First March on Washington, in October 1979, and involved march organizers like the late Brandy Moore, Joyce Hunter, Steve Ault, and others. These meetings did in the 1970s exactly what Bill Clinton's third White House meeting with the gay and lesbian community did in 1993: they demonstrated the administration's symbolic willingness to listen backed by an intransigent refusal to act. The major difference in sixteen years seems to be that we have graduated from meeting with senior staffers to meeting directly with the President. But measured in action, the difference is negligible.

During Carter's tenure a virulently homophobic right campaigned against gay and lesbian equality, as it does today. Anita Bryant launched her campaign in 1977 to repeal the gay rights ordinance of Dade County, Florida. Within a year, similar attempts to repeal gay rights laws were under way in Wichita, Saint Paul, and Eugene. Gay and lesbian activists were well aware of the threat posed by the Christian Right as soon as it appeared. Bryant's campaign helped to motivate and educate an entire generation of lesbian and gay leaders like Amber Hollibaugh and Tim Sweeney, who worked against the right in California in 1978. Lesbian and gay periodicals like *GCN* and *Sinister Wisdom* carried articles analyzing local fights against the right, and individual researchers like David Peterson monitored right-wing publications. In 1981, researcher Jean Hardisty founded Political Research Associates, which today is the leading think tank concentrating on the American right. During the early 1980s, groups like Boston Lesbian and Gay Men Against the Right continued to carry out education and actions.

It was grassroots, direct-action, feminist, and progressive queers who took the New Right most seriously. Mainstream gay and lesbian organizations tended to disregard it or treat it as an aberration. The two camps also disagreed on strategy; grassroots activists favored education and direct confrontation, and mainstream activists believed legislation and straight support were paramount. As a result, a chasm formed between the local political movement and its national counterpart. This break in ideology, strategy, communication, and vision polarized the gay and lesbian movement in the late 1970s and early 1980s. The grassroots gay movement fought antigay repeal efforts, protested police harassment, countered homophobic media coverage, and picketed antigay films; the national movement focused on establishing its presence in Washington.

In 1978, California defeated the statewide referendum called the Briggs Initiative, which would have allowed schools to fire any employee for "advocating, soliciting, imposing, encouraging or promoting . . . private or public homosexual activity directed at, or likely to come to the attention of, schoolchildren and/or other employees." Jimmy Carter avoided taking a public stand against the initiative until a few weeks before the 1978 vote, despite repeated telegrams from Harvey Milk asking him to do so. Randy Shilts described how Carter finally endorsed the No on Briggs position.

> President Carter came to California to campaign for Governor [Jerry] Brown's reelection [in October of 1978]. Carter had finished his speech and was walking away from the podium when a television microphone picked up Brown telling Carter, "Proposition 6. You'll get your loudest applause. Ford and Reagan have both come out against it. So I think it's perfectly safe." Carter walked back to the mike and added, "I also ask everybody to vote no on Proposition 6."

Carter's faint opposition differed markedly from the widespread public opposition to Briggs. State teachers associations, unions, religious leaders, and even the former governor of California, Ronald Reagan, opposed Briggs.

Between the 1976 campaign and the 1980 campaigns, a number of developments enabled Ronald Reagan to win over Jimmy Carter and to win again in 1984. First, the economic crisis hurt Carter. Inflation, high interest rates, an energy crisis caused by the oil cartel's decision to decrease production and raise prices, all contributed to voter disenchantment with the Democrats. Second, the Republican Party was successful in implementing its "Southern strategy" to win over white, conservative Democratic voters. It is no coincidence that three Democratic Presidents in the last thirty years (Johnson, Carter, Clinton) have been Southerners; no one has won the presidency without the South since 1960. Over the past two decades, Republican Party strategists like Lee Atwater perfected the use of emotional social issues to drive a wedge between conservative Southern voters and the more liberal national Democratic Party. Reagan's campaigns appealed to these conservative voters with a strong stance against affirmative action, against abortion, and for prayer in schools. As a result of these tactics, conservative voters abandoned the Democratic Party in droves, proving the explosive political potential of divisive social issues like race, abortion, the role of women in society, the role of the military in a peacetime economy, and, especially, homosexuality.

Ultimately, Reagan won because conservatives in his party forged a political alliance with leaders of the fundamentalist Christian Right, who had begun to organize as an electoral base. This powerful coalition was systematically built by Jerry Falwell, Viguerie, Phillips, and the closeted gay conservative activist Terry Dolan. Dolan, who cofounded the National Conservative Political Action Committee, was credited with personally raising more than $10 million dollars for the 1980 Reagan campaign. Dolan died of AIDS in 1985, but his brother, who worked as a Reagan speechwriter, contributed to the silence surrounding the epidemic for several more years.

The 1980 campaign was indeed the first election in which support for gay and lesbian rights emerged as a distinguishing difference between the Democratic and the Republican parties. Try as he might to distance himself from gay and lesbian people, Carter was portrayed by the Republican Party and the right as a champion of gay rights. Although libertarian and moderate Republicans supported gay and lesbian expression (as an example of the individual freedom no state should threaten), few moderate Republicans opposed the Moral Majority publicly. One Republican who did so was the moderate Illinois representative John Anderson, who made a third-party bid for the presidency that year. As the writer E. J. Dionne, Jr., pointed out in *Why Americans Hate Politics,* Anderson drew more votes from Carter's base than from Reagan's and thereby contributed to the Republican victory. According to Shilts, many gay activists abandoned the Democratic Party in 1980 to support Anderson after he issued a strong endorsement of gay and lesbian rights.

Major Republican candidates, from Ronald Reagan to George Bush to John Connolly, made homophobic statements during the 1980 campaign. Reagan: "My criticism is that [the gay movement] isn't just asking for civil rights; it's asking for recognition and acceptance of an alternative lifestyle which I do not believe society can condone, nor can I." Reagan went on to cite the Bible, "which says that in the eyes of the Lord, homosexuality is an abomination." George Bush: "I don't think homosexuality is normal behavior and I oppose codification of gay rights." Connolly stated that gay people should not be allowed to teach in schools or hold sensitive national security positions. Even Bush's 1988 Willie Horton ads had an anti-gay ancestry: during the 1980 campaign, a Republican ad featured a montage from the San Francisco Freedom Day Parade, with an ominous voice-over: "The gays in San Francisco elected a mayor." As the picture faded into a still shot of President Carter, the voice-over prophesied, "Now they're going to elect a President."

The homophobic tenor of the 1980 Republican platform sounds familiar as well. It rejected the Equal Rights Amendment, explicitly supported an anti-abortion Human Life Amendment to the U.S. Constitution, and endorsed the Family Protection Act, a dangerous and broad antigay bill introduced in the Senate by Reagan's friend Paul Laxalt (R-NV). The FPA sought to legislate one definition of family: the heterosexual nuclear family, with women in their traditional roles. Among other clauses, it banned federal support of textbooks that portrayed women in nontraditional ways; and it would have banned the use of federal funds for any gay and lesbian community service organization. As Shilts wrote, "In no document was the history of the gay movement and the women's movement for the next decade more clearly written than in the 1980 [Republican] Party platform." Twelve years later the seeds planted in the 1980 platform bore fruit as the 1992 Republican Convention became the platform for a dangerous new brand of American chauvinism.

By contrast, the 1980 election marked great gains for gay and lesbian activists working within the Democratic Party. Jim Foster served as Ted Kennedy's Northern California campaign manager and gained him enough votes to defeat Carter in the primary. As a result, Foster and other gay activists won Senator Kennedy's backing for a gay rights plank. The 1980 Democratic platform was the first to put the party on record as opposing discrimination. At the convention, held in New York City, seventy-six openly gay delegates and alternates participated. With

Kennedy's support, the gay and lesbian caucus made a deal that allowed it to nominate an openly gay person for the vice presidency. The New York activists Ginny Apuzzo and Peter Vogel nominated the black gay activist Mel Boozer; Boozer was allowed to address the convention for a few minutes on gay rights, and then withdrew his nomination after the symbolic point had been made. Ultimately, gay and lesbian support for the party's eventual candidate, President Jimmy Carter, was as tepid as his support for gay and lesbian rights. With the election of Ronald Reagan in November came the start of twelve years of antigay national policies.

By the 1984 presidential election, the antigay right's influence over the Republican campaign was firmly in place, but right-wing frustration with its inability to enact its social agenda was growing. The Reagan administration retained the support of this conservative right base by playing to its religiosity and homophobia. In a publication called the *Presidential Biblical Scoreboard,* Reagan praised "the Judeo-Christian tradition" of marriage and family and lamented that "the erosion of these values has given way to a celebration of forms of expression most reject. We will resist the efforts of some to obtain government endorsement of homosexuality." During this election cycle the phrase "San Francisco Democrat" was coined, a code phrase for "fag lover." Moral Majority head Jerry Falwell said, "The Democratic Party is largely controlled by the radical ideas of a dangerous minority—homosexuals, militant feminists, socialists, freeze-niks, and the like."

Despite a greater level of participation in the electoral process, gay influence within the Democratic Party lessened in 1984 and 1988, in part because of the way that the party establishment responded to the rightward shift in the electorate. Even with the efforts of progressive activists like Jesse Jackson, the party began to abandon liberalism and re-invent itself as conservative. The Democratic Leadership Council, instrumental in Bill Clinton's conservative legitimation, was founded in the early 1980s. Democratic National Committee chairman Paul Kirk abolished several constituency-oriented caucuses, including the gay and lesbian and Latino caucus, under the rationale that these groups gave the impression that the party pandered to "special interests." The party tried to appeal to women voters by placing Geraldine Ferraro on the ticket with Walter Mondale, a strategy accompanied by a strong profeminist platform. Because of the Republican Party's Southern strategy and the Democratic Party's still liberal appearance, the 1984 election saw a clear split among the voters according to gender and race:

most white men voted for the Republicans; women and racial minority voters voted against them. The shift in the votes of white men widely reported after the 1994 election echoes this earlier shift in 1984.

Between the 1984 and 1988 elections, the gay and lesbian movement was further transformed by its struggle with AIDS. By 1988, the Human Rights Campaign Fund was mobilizing a large financial constituency for the Democratic Party. In 1985 I began to work with the National Gay and Lesbian Task Force as a boardmember. Excited by the challenges of organizing at a national level, I left the board and was hired by Jeff Levi as public information director in 1986. NGLTF had five staff members in 1986 and nine by 1988, yet it was among the largest of gay organizations. Like a frontier, the movement was peopled by iconoclasts and individualists, local activists who often created and sustained groups through sheer will power. In 1986, the combined memberships of the four national political and legal groups (NGLTF, HRCF, Lambda, and NGRA) totaled fewer than forty thousand. Activism at that time required resourcefulness and creativity. E-mail was rare; NGLTF had one computer, no fax machine, and no copier. Nor was there any formal communication among movement activists. There was one major national conference, the National Gay and Lesbian Health Conference, and several regional gay and lesbian gatherings. Information about the movement could be learned only in the gay and lesbian press.

This changed dramatically after the Second National March on Washington for Lesbian and Gay Rights, held on October 11, 1987. Marches are disdained by traditional political workers because they make everybody feel good but win no tangible political gain. Yet national marches contribute great energy, visibility, and motivation to a movement. While the First National March, in 1979, had generated interest in national organizing, the 1987 march boosted gay and lesbian activism at the local level. Groups like ACT UP spread across the nation, and new political organizations came into existence.

By the campaign season in 1988, the movement was growing larger each day and was active both nationally and locally. NGLTF worked on AIDS policy, hate crimes legislation, and lesbian and gay family issues; HRCF saw its funding base increase dramatically. Lambda, the ACLU, NOW, and NGLTF began work on the antigay military ban and lesbian and gay family issues. Lambda, National Gay Rights Advocates (a West Coast legal group that is now defunct), and the ACLU Lesbian and Gay Rights Project all expanded their work to encompass national legislation. Local groups in Maryland and Minnesota tried sodomy repeal bills, although both failed. Several gay rights measures were raised in state legislatures and local communities; most failed. ACT UP demonstrations made the news on a regular basis, and in the summer ACT UP began to plan a national protest at the Federal Drug Administration.

In April 1988, over dinner with Sue Hyde and Robert Bray, then the public information director of HRCF, I discovered that both HRCF and NGLTF were planning to run media operations at both national conventions that summer. I suggested that we coordinate our plans, and on some cocktail napkins, we sketched out the idea for a national coalition, called Gay and Lesbian VOICE—Voters Organized in Coalition for the Election—which would involve as many interested groups as possible. The coalition's goals would be to increase lesbian and gay visibility throughout the election year, to inform our community about candidates' positions, to educate the media and both parties about gay and lesbian rights, and to get out the gay and lesbian vote. Robert and I took the napkins back to our bosses, Vic Basile and Jeff Levi, who approved the plan. The ad hoc start of this important collaboration reflects not only the informal nature of our movement, but also the intense competition between HRCF and NGLTF. Save for Robert and Sue and our friendship, this collaboration would not have happened.

The conventions in 1988 prefigured the homophobic spectacle of 1992. The 1988 Democratic Convention was largely inaccessible to gay activists who were not delegates. Protestors were kept in a "free speech area," which was a parking lot a long distance from the convention site. Gay and lesbian activists were themselves disunited: some supported Michael Dukakis, others supported Jesse Jackson, and still others supported neither. ACT UP made a splash—with its noise and color—by staging one of its first nationally coordinated actions with representatives from Chicago, LA, Boston, and San Francisco joining New York's chapter to organize AIDS-specific protests at both conventions. Rallies, pickets, kiss-ins, human billboards, town meetings, press conferences, were some of the strategies we used. The 1988 Republican Convention was a muted version of the explicitly homophobic convention to come in 1992. Whenever gay or ACT UP members picketed, delegates would jeer, push, shove, and threaten us. At a Speak-Out Against Homophobia, which Sue Hyde and I organized in New Orleans, several members of Young

Americans for Freedom showed up wearing surgical masks and carrying signs that read "AIDS Is the Cure." Despite the fact that we were practically the only protestors at this convention, gay and AIDS activists generated very little media coverage. As the editor in charge of political coverage for a Louisiana paper told me on the phone, "We're not gonna cover every little horse-shit demonstration you people have." His attitude was more politely echoed by much of the national media, who ignored gay and lesbian briefings and press conferences, reflecting that we may have had a VOICE, but no audience.

Most gay Republicans prominent in the movement today—like Bruce Bawer, Marvin Liebman, Rich Tafel, and David Brock—were not out of the closet in 1988. Nonetheless, 1988 was the year in which gay and lesbian Republican organizing began to come out of the closet. The California activist Frank Richiazzi was among the first openly gay people to lobby the Republican Party. A gay Republican reception held at the convention drew limited media coverage but nearly eighty participants. Ironically, the person most willing to serve as a national gay Republican spokesman in 1988 turned out to be using a pseudonym. I'm still not sure of his real name.

Overall, the 1988 presidential campaign frustrated and angered both mainstream and radical gay and lesbian activists. Some gay and lesbian Democratic Party stalwarts were infuriated by the closed door that greeted them at the campaign of Mike Dukakis, who adopted a contradictory position on gay rights. He embraced equal opportunity and said he supported gay rights protections, but, as governor of Massachusetts, he enacted an explicitly antigay policy that prevented gay and lesbian couples from becoming foster parents simply because of their sexual orientation. (The policy was declared unconstitutional by the Supreme Judicial Court of Massachusetts in 1990.) Many close to the Dukakis campaign believed that his refusal to affirm gay rights more emphatically stemmed from personal discomfort. Tim McFeeley, former director of HRCF, recalls meeting with Dukakis in 1985, after he had endorsed the homophobic ban on gay foster parenting and long before he ran for President. After many circular, legal arguments between McFeeley, Dukakis, and the gay Boston attorney Vin McCarthy, who was also in the room, an exasperated McFeeley said he just did not understand why Dukakis refused to budge on publicly supporting gay rights. Dukakis slammed his fist on the table and said, "Because it is wrong!" Among the lasting ironies of Dukakis's stand on gay and les-

bian rights was that his chief fundraiser was a gay man named Robert
Farmer; the press secretary of the Dukakis Department of Social
Services, which defended the antigay foster care policy, was a gay
woman named Mary Breslauer (who now serves on the HRCF
board); and his deceased brother was widely rumored to have been
gay.

In the 1988 campaign, I saw firsthand how eager the gay and
lesbian Democratic establishment was to establish its "credentials" with
an uncaring and largely straight party hierarchy. National gay and lesbian Democrats like Hillary Rosen, Duke Comegys, Jean O'Leary,
and others refused to challenge publicly the Dukakis campaign's
homophobia and often defended the candidate. More independent activists, like Sue Hyde and members of Boston's Foster Equality Campaign, publicly criticized his homophobia at every media occasion. The
clash between the two sides took place both publicly, in the pages of
Boston's gay and lesbian press, and quietly, in numerous little incidents
like this one, which happened after the convention and before the
election. Kate Clinton, a political comedian, was asked by one national
gay activist to stop telling a joke in which she characterized supporters
of Dukakis as righteous GODS—Gay Opportunists for Dukakis. The
joke was not appropriate, according to this activist. Kate politely declined to stop.

The fact that we found ourselves divided over a frankly homophobic
candidate reveals a truth about electoral politics: for gay people the
choice is often of the lesser of two evils. We are constantly asked to
countenance a candidate's antigay rhetoric, policies, or actions because
of other positions—pro-choice, anti–death penalty. In exchange for
private assurances of access, made to those who have contributed the
most money, gay support is cheaply bought. The logic of the electoral
strategy does not allow a moral way through this dilemma, only a
pragmatic one. Thus far we have played the electoral game solely by the
rules we have been given: of a two-party contest in which our movement functions to lessen the antagonism of both parties toward gay
rights.

This is certainly how the gay community played it in 1988. Believing that the choice between Republicans and Democrats was equal,
large numbers of gay voters voted for Bush. I remember people telling
me that, since there was little difference between the two major candidates on gay and lesbian issues, they would "vote their pocketbook" and
stay with the Republicans. The Bush campaign smartly stoked this

allegiance by responding to gay and AIDS questionnaires issued by movement groups, marking the first time a presidential campaign had given such recognition. In 1998, gay advocates were also allowed to testify at the platform hearings; they held a quiet meeting between California gay Republicans and officials in the Lee Atwater–led campaign. Positioning Bush as a President who would continue Reagan's conservative legacy with a "kinder, gentler" face, his campaign treated gay issues in a manner that marked a clever conservative handling of our movement. Rather than rejecting or embracing gays outright, the Bush campaign created a strategy designed to exploit both pro-gay and anti-gay support. Thus, when questioned about his support for gay rights, Bush answered that all Americans enjoy the same constitutional rights and that he affirmed those rights. Because gay people do not enjoy the same constitutional status as nongay people, the answer was quite devious: it challenged the most basic premise of our movement while seeming to affirm our equality. Similarly on AIDS, Bush pledged to increase funds for AIDS programs and to support nondiscrimination while at the same time he appeased antigay hard-liners with tough talk on the need for "protecting the rights of the uninfected" through measures like mandatory HIV testing.

The juxtaposition with Pat Robertson may also have made Bush seem more moderate than he proved to be. Without question, the 1988 election marked a major advance within the Republican Party for religious conservatives. The coalition put together by Reagan had regrouped uneasily behind George Bush: he was seen an Eastern establishment elitist, who was condescending to the growing white, religious, Southern, working-class, and middle-class elements of the party. No one bought his affectation about pork rinds. The Republican Party's right wing demonstrated its frustration with the party's centrism through the Robertson candidacy, a challenge that did surprisingly well in the primaries. Overall, Robertson managed to use his candidacy to collect a large national database of supporters and volunteers, and after the election, he turned it into the Christian Coalition. Under the leadership of the shrewd Ralph Reed, the Christian Coalition has become the most powerful national political organization in the country. Today, it boasts fifty state offices, a network built from the precinct level up, more than 1.5 million members, and a budget of more than $20 million annually. Neither of the parties can match this extraordinary grassroots system nor the discipline and focus of its members.

Robertson's success as a candidate strengthened the hand of Christian leaders with the Republican Party: it was clear that the party needed the voters he organized. Bush's choice of Dan Quayle was a concession to the right, and for the next four years Quayle's main job was to appease the powerful Christian base. Like others in the moderate wing of the party, gay and lesbian Republicans didn't pay much attention to this right flank, choosing to regard it as a "vocal minority" and Quayle as a buffoon. Bush trounced Dukakis in 1988, but his support among conservative and religious right voters decreased throughout his term.

By the 1992 campaign, both political parties and the gay and lesbian movement had undergone dramatic transformations. For Republicans, the change was precipitated by the emergence of the Christian Coalition. For Democrats, it was led by the resurgence of "centrists," who argued that only by moving to the right would the Democrats recapture the middle. For gay and lesbian people, transformation was brought about by the combined impact of the relentless AIDS epidemic and the emergence out of the closet of larger and larger numbers of young gay and lesbian people. Our movement flourished from 1988 to 1992. Six states and several cities passed gay and lesbian rights bills in the early 1990s. Hundreds of new community groups, service organizations, antiviolence projects, and support groups were organized. The movement's national organizations grew bigger and more visible: annual dinners of HRCF were rounding up over a thousand participants in major cities like Detroit, Dallas, Washington, and Columbus. Gay and lesbian student groups were actively fighting the military's antigay policies by getting colleges to ban ROTC programs from campus. Gay and lesbian employee associations in corporate America were growing at a record pace. By 1992, we were poised at last to make the national impact that gay political leaders had hoped to make for decades.

The 1992 elections capped a year in which gay and lesbian issues became a widely debated source of distinction between the two national parties. Like the 1980 campaign, the 1992 one was marked by the homophobia of Republican candidates. Pat Buchanan ran an explicitly antigay campaign, condemning gay rights in his speeches and campaign materials. In March, he released a television advertisement in the South that belittled gay people and homoerotic art, using footage from Marlon Riggs's *Tongues Untied,* a film about black gay men that had received a grant from the NEA and was broadcast on PBS. At the August convention, Buchanan's fiery address about the "culture war" waged by conservatives alienated many people, although the 1994 elections and the continued rightward drift of the country suggest that this rhetoric appealed to many voters.

At the beginning of 1992, the Bush campaign was cautiously silent on most gay and AIDS issues, but as the year progressed, Bush and Quayle stepped up their antigay rhetoric. By the beginning of 1992, I felt the mainstream movement needed to have direct contact with the Bush campaign and the Republican Party. To bring the issue of gay rights squarely before them, I requested a meeting with the RNC and sought a meeting with the Bush campaign. My letter to the RNC was never answered. But I pursued a personal connection to the Bush campaign and eventually won a meeting with the chairman of the Bush-Quayle campaign, Robert Mosbacher. Our controversial meeting came about through the intervention of Mosbacher's daughter Dee, a longtime lesbian activist from San Francisco. I asked her to see whether her father would talk with NGLTF on gay rights and AIDS issues, and mentioned my fear that a direct letter asking for such a meeting would never reach him. Dee spoke with her dad, and told me he was willing to meet.

Robert Mosbacher, a member of his staff, and four representatives from gay and AIDS organizations met at the campaign headquarters on February 13, 1992. With me were NGLTF deputy director Peri Jude Radecic, media director Robert Bray, and AIDS Action Council senior lobbyist and former NGLTF director, Jeff Levi. From the instant we arrived, it was clear to us that the entire office was aware of our meeting. A gay Republican man named Tyler Franz, who worked at the campaign as a reception coordinator and who resigned under antigay pressure a few weeks later, told us that campaign officials were a-twitter about our presence there. This was, to my knowledge, the first on-the-record meeting between a senior official in a Republican presidential campaign and a national gay and lesbian organization. When we began the meeting, Mosbacher disarmingly said, "I want you to know I'm not just doing this to please my daughter." Still, the meeting itself was much less eventful than the reaction to it. Mosbacher was polite and fair, and seemed genuinely alarmed at our representation that gay and lesbian voters felt that President Bush was not doing enough on AIDS. His main message seemed to be simply that George Bush cared about all constituents, and that he was strongly committed to fair AIDS policies. To our requests for stronger statements on antiviolence, gay rights, and AIDS funding, he promised nothing. He accepted the briefing papers and materials we gave him and thanked us for coming.

Interestingly, this innocuous, thirty-minute meeting unleashed a fire-storm of protest from the conservative and religious right, from the gay left, and even from gay Republicans. Robert Mosbacher was the main person wounded in the crossfire, when competing factions inside the campaign criticized the meeting as an illustration of his naïveté rather than a measure of his basic decency.

The meeting drew an immediate outcry from conservative right leaders. Eight congressional Republicans wrote to the President on February 24, 1992, asking him to "counsel his campaign" that "the NGLTF agenda is not the Republican agenda and should not become a part of your re-election bid." Prominent among them was Newt Ging-rich, then the House minority whip, and several of the most antigay members of Congress—Bill Dannemeyer, John Doolittle, Mel Han-cock, Clyde Holloway, Joe Barton, Phil Crane, and William Zeliff. Ignoring the fact that such meetings are the political right of every citizen's group in a democracy, the congressmen denounced Mos-bacher's meeting with NGLTF as "a slap in the face to every voter who affirms the traditional family." The letter continued, "Offending 98 percent of your constituency to attempt to placate 2 percent is unwise. Not only that, it is politically unfounded. Among the few homosexual voters who identified as Republican in 1988, 63 percent voted for Mi-chael Dukakis." If this statistic is correct, then it meant that 37 percent of the self-identified gay vote in 1988 went to Bush.

Another right-wing backlash to the meeting came in the form of letters to Bush from leaders of the Southern Baptist Convention and other religious organizations. To appease the right, the White House quickly characterized the meeting as a personal favor Mr. Mosbacher had done for his daughter. To lessen the furor caused by the meeting, Bush met at the White House with antigay right-wing leaders, like Lou Sheldon, in April 1992. He dispatched Dan Quayle to speak at right-wing conferences and meetings, like the God and Country Rally held at the Republican Convention. For the first time, Bush himself spoke out against gay marriage and expressed his reservations about homosexual-ity in general. More than any other factor, the Bush shift to the right motivated conservative gay Democrats and loyal gay Republicans, who had helped Bush defeat Dukakis in 1988, to throw their support behind Clinton. Pro-gay Republicans like William Weld and Lowell Weicker increased their stature as statesmen by urging the party to adopt a libertarian stance toward gay rights. Meanwhile, the raw, antigay demagoguery of the extremist Republican right, exemplified by Pat Buchanan's speech at the convention, apparently backfired among voters.

Ironically, at the same instant he was making these antigay statements, George and Barbara Bush hosted Dee Mosbacher and her lover of nearly twenty years, Nanette Gartrell, at the White House. Dee and Nanette told me of attending a small White House reception, given by the Bushes for Robert Mosbacher, in the spring of 1992, when he stepped down as commerce secretary and went to work full time for the Bush re-election effort. Dee made it a point to introduce Nanette as her lover to the Cabinet and senior administration officials at the gathering, many of whom had already met the couple over the long friendship of Mosbacher and Bush. At their home, Dee and Nanette display an autographed photo from George Bush marking one such meeting.

The meeting with Mosbacher also brought to the fore some divisions in the gay and lesbian community. Self-styled queer radicals termed me an "assimilationist" and charged me with selling out for meeting with the "enemy." On the other hand, Log Cabin conservatives criticized me for not bringing them to the meeting. These reactions illustrate two different divides that deepened as the year progressed. One was between gay mainstreamers and those identified with direct action, while the other existed between a newly out, gay conservative movement and the existing liberal and progressive political wings. The clashes between these factions produced odd tensions. So, on the one hand, ACT UP and Queer Nation chapters resisted working with NGLTF and HRCF as part of the Gay and Lesbian VOICE '92 coalition, because they refused to cooperate with the Log Cabin Republican group. At the convention, ACT UP and Queer Nation insisted on separate offices, and disparaged NGLTF, HRCF, and Log Cabin as sell-outs. On the other hand, the fledgling gay Republican movement was establishing a national profile for itself for the first time. It was unwilling to be associated with direct-action radicals and was quite proprietary of its access to the Republican Party and media. Log Cabin criticized mainstream groups for not engaging in bipartisan lobbying, yet criticized us when we did so without their presence. Gay Democrats in turn engaged in name calling about gay Republicans, repeating the insult that to be gay and Republican was to be a traitor.

These tensions were actually the byproduct of splits that were deeper than the question of party affiliation, namely divisions over political strategy, race, and feminism. By the end of 1990, many people inside and outside the movement had grown weary of the direct-action movement's tactics. In the early 1990s, Bush leveled explicit attacks on ACT UP that mirrored gay moderate and conservative criticism of ACT UP's militancy. Not surprisingly, these splits came at the very instant there was more "power" to quarrel over than ever before. The new powerbrokers did not want a scruffy movement of radicals in the streets to undermine the mainstream access they were amassing.

The 1992 election saw the fulfillment of the gay mainstream's strategy of leveraging money and votes. Significantly, the election marked the first time that gay and lesbian activists launched a coordinated national effort to raise identifiably gay (and large) sums of money for one presidential candidate. Clinton's promises on gay and lesbian rights were made in the context of the most pro-gay and -lesbian field of Democratic candidates ever to run for national office. Former senator Paul Tsongas (D-MA) had co-sponsored the federal Gay and Lesbian Civil Rights Bill when it was introduced in the Senate, and in 1992 he proudly claimed that record as evidence that he was a social libertarian. Former California governor Jerry Brown had a long record of supporting gay rights. Even independent candidate Ross Perot changed his position on gay rights midway through the campaign, and appointed Los Angeles–based Deborah Olson as his gay-community liaison. In short, Bill Clinton did not lead in his support of gay rights, nor did he overstep the norms of the 1992 presidential field with the positions he took.

The main reason Clinton courted the gay and lesbian vote was necessity. The Democrats needed to forge a new coalition in order to win, and they needed every voting bloc they could marshal. As Reagan had in the 1980 election against Carter, the Clinton campaign exploited bad economic news. Clinton hammered on Bush's lack of domestic vision and focused on bread-and-butter issues like jobs, health care, education, and welfare. The Democratic Party realigned into a centrist New Democratic coalition, stacking the ticket with two Southerners to win back conservative white Democrats who had fled to the Republican ticket in 1980, 1984, and 1988. Clinton catered to the conservative Democratic voters with not-so-subtle appeals to white racism, evident in his calculated delivery of the Sister Souljah speech. The party also benefited when the Ross Perot campaign siphoned off disaffected conservative voters.

Significantly unlike the Carter, Mondale, and Dukakis campaigns, the Clinton campaign actively sought the gay and lesbian vote as part of this new coalition. Its own pollsters gathered data suggesting that at least 5 to 6 percent of the American population was gay—a figure lower than the 10 percent commonly used by gay activists, but considerably higher than the 1 percent promoted by the right. The Democrats went after the gay vote by sending Clinton and surrogates to meet with gay leaders and to attend fundraisers; by funding gay community get-out-the-vote efforts; and by embracing the gay community at the New York convention. Such efforts were a calculated risk, and they paid off handsomely when the Republican Party tilted to an extreme that frightened away voters who were fiscally conservative but socially libertarian. By 1992, the gay community was extremely responsive to this outreach. Gay people wanted an end to the Bush reign; the rising homophobia and paralysis on AIDS of the Bush-Quayle administration energized even gay Republicans into action against the Republican ticket.

A second reason Clinton promised change to gay and lesbian activists was for the financial benefits of such promises. Gay money was actively courted by the Democratic Party and by gay and lesbian supporters of Clinton. The presence of openly gay advisers like David Mixner and former HRCF co-chair Randy Klose connected the campaign to wealthy gay and lesbian Democratic donors around the country. Klose, who died of AIDS-related complications in 1993, was a particularly tireless fundraiser; he donated and raised several hundred thousand dollars for Democratic candidates. Other important gay donors in 1992 were the New York activists Jeff Soref, Fred Hochberg, and Michael Palm; Wisconsin activists Andrew Barrer and the late Duane Rath; Californians Jim Hormel, David Geffen, Barry Diller, Bob Sertner; and Nebraska-based Terry Watanabe. These donors carefully identified all donations they gave and raised as "gay money." According to Mixner, gay and lesbian people actually raised more than $3 million for Clinton.

After the election, most media pundits dismissed the rise of religious conservatives during the Republican Convention as an aberration. Three years later, the folly of this interpretation is clear but yet to be admitted by those same political analysts. As we approach another presidential election cycle, religious conservatives are firmly in control of Congress and many state legislatures and are the definers of the national debate. This influence is measured in behind-the-scenes facts. Robertson and the Christian Coalition have been the largest financial contributors to GOPAC, the political action committee organized by Newt Gingrich, the most influential politician in the country. Ralph

Reed has repeatedly noted the coalition's pivotal role in mobilizing grassroots support for the Republican Contract With America. On a C-Span broadcast on abortion, on April 1, 1995, Reed cleverly characterized the operations of the disciplined, religious minority group he leads as the will of a majority of the people. He carefully recast the conservative turn of the electorate as an expression of mass discontent rather than showing it for what it was: the careful mobilization of a very small electoral majority in a political election in which only 36 percent of eligible voters participated.

Electoral politics is extremely seductive to all movements for social change; it seems the shortest distance to liberation. The theory is invitingly simple: elect people who support you, and they will do the right thing. But the fact is that when broad-based protest movements—like the black civil rights movement and the women's liberation movement —shifted their major focus from community organizing to electing our own, the movements lost momentum even as they gained mainstream acceptability. Electoral work cannot substitute for grassroots political power, but, indeed, must be seen as a means by which a constituent base can be organized. In other words, engagement in elections is not the endpoint or pinnacle of a social change strategy; it is merely a tool.

Keeping the electoral strategy in proper perspective is a lesson the gay movement has yet to learn from the successful examples of several other social change movements: religious conservatives, the pro-choice movement, and the political experience of African Americans. For one, the varying experiences of these three movements, in recent years, teach us that those who do the long-term work of training and educating their members end up with a more effective constituency than those who rely on national appeals or rhetoric. The Christian Coalition and the New Right invested millions of dollars in training and organizing their members into a presence at every precinct. The pro-choice movement has done similar local training and organizing, albeit far less systematically. But in recent years, African-American civil rights organizations have not invested funds to train new and younger leaders, to educate their constituents on the politics of certain issues through local meetings and campaigns, or to organize a multiracial base for civil rights. As a result, the core constituency of the racial civil rights movement is less strong than the core constituency of the religious right or the pro-choice movement. Except in a handful of cities, notably San Francisco and Chicago, the gay movement has not used elections to organize its supporters. Many gay groups still do not conduct voter registration drives, political education seminars, or leadership training, nor are statewide groups organized to identify, train, and mobilize gay rights supporters in every district.

A second lesson we must draw from the gay experience in presidential elections is that in the face of organized opposition, money buys access, but votes buy clout. The change in gay influence in politics from 1972 to 1992 was attributable to a transitory pandering to the rich, not to a fundamental shift in the view of homosexuality held by either of the two major parties. The gay and lesbian experience with Clinton proves this point. All the access in the world has not strengthened our ability to pass pro-gay legislation or to hold the President to his campaign promises. Instead of funding a coherent political infrastructure for our movement, from the local political district up to the statehouse and on to the national level, wealthy donors are pouring time and money into the bottomless well of political access. If expediency is the chief motivator for politicians like Clinton and Gingrich to meet with gay leaders and listen to us, then that same expediency will drive them away as the winds of public opinion shift.

Finally, recognizing that the power that electoral politics brings us is limited—the power to elect people who will try to enact portions of our agenda—the question becomes how we can most effectively use this strategy. Pragmatically, we must engage the system. But thinking long-term, we must do so in such a way that the electoral process becomes a way to strengthen the movement, not merely to elect a particular candidate. In other words, I urge us to keep the focus on our own interests, rather than subsume them in the interests of a particular candidate. This means we must be open to third-party candidacies—by gay people as well as by nongay independents who support our equality. We are more than the pawns of whichever party pursues us hardest. By striking an independent course, we can focus on building our political strength for the future.

LEGAL MAINSTREAMING AND QUEER STATUS

During my first year at Northeastern University Law School, in 1980, my professor of criminal law began class by saying, "Name some famous gay people." This professor was a liberal, and his remarks were meant as a kindly way to introduce the topic of sodomy laws. Following the lead of traditional criminal law textbooks, he had placed a discussion of the legal status of homosexual people in the middle of the course section on victimless crimes. There we were, alongside laws against prostitution, sexual solicitation, and other odd statutes criminalizing acts that arguably had no victims. As one of five openly gay and lesbian students in the first-year class of 133, I sat in stunned silence.

Fortunately, another lesbian student in the class immediately stood up and challenged our professor. Gay rights required a more complex treatment than this, she argued. Sodomy laws had been revoked by half the states and were under legal attack elsewhere; moreover, to lump them in with prostitution and other sex-based regulations was offensive. She ended by noting accurately that such laws represented an illegal incursion by the state into the private life of ordinary citizens. The professor was chagrined and asked several of us to teach a special class on gay and lesbian issues in criminal law. As we prepared to do so, we discovered that law on gay and lesbian rights was uncharted territory. Excited about this new field, we began a year-long independent study course, which we dubbed "The Course That Dare Not Speak Its Name."

At the time, there were no textbooks and only a handful of course outlines available on gay and lesbian rights in the law. Only a handful of schools taught courses in gay and lesbian law; an even smaller number of openly gay lawyers conducted this litigation. In 1982, when I prepared a national attorneys' referral directory for the gay rights group in Boston called Gay and Lesbian Advocates and Defenders (GLAD), our listings were fewer than a hundred attorneys. We are grateful that much has changed since then.

The legal rights of gay and lesbian people are widely litigated today, with thousands of openly gay, lesbian, bisexual, and straight attorneys handling gay rights cases. Scores of excellent books, textbooks, and legal rights manuals exist. Local, regional, and national legal conferences on gay rights law take place each year. There are scholarly journals dedicated to gay and lesbian legal issues and several large national and regional gay and lesbian bar associations, as well as the National Gay and Lesbian Law Association. Even the stodgy American Bar Association has endorsed gay and lesbian civil rights, a testament to years of educational work by gay legal pioneers like the Tennessee-based lawyer Abby Rubenfeld.

Narrowly defined, legal challenges are short-term strategies that provide relief in emergency situations or give redress to people persecuted by unfair policies, because laws are subject to repeal and or nullification; witness the continual assault on *Roe* v. *Wade.* But on a broader level, the courtroom is the stage on which marginal ideas and groups assert themselves in the mainstream. Litigation on behalf of gay rights has radically changed the expectations under which all gay people live today; we no longer put up with discrimination. In February 1995, I spoke with a gay friend visiting from Georgia. After many years with his employer, a company based in Concord, California, but doing business in Atlanta, and after much success as a senior vice president, he found his position suddenly eliminated. He recounted a pattern of increasing harassment, which ended in his termination. He talked of his intention to sue for wrongful termination, knowing that his case would be an uphill fight. But he was determined. "This is wrong," he said. "They shouldn't be able to do this." The man does not consider himself an activist and has had little involvement with the gay political movement in Atlanta, yet he felt entitled to fair treatment. His raised expectations are perhaps the proudest victory of the gay and lesbian legal movement.

In many ways, the gay and lesbian legal movement is light years ahead of the political movement: in the networks and resources it draws on, the talent it fields, and the vision it displays. Since gay and lesbian legal status shifts over time and varies from state to state, I cannot cover a complete history or address pending litigation. Fortunately, we have venues for such deep and timely analysis. Rather, I want to describe two problems I think the legal movement faces. One involves the way the movement itself operates, and the other has to do with the major legal obstacles it confronts.

Gay rights litigation dates back to the fifties, when gay bars fought to get licensed to serve homosexual people, gay patrons of bars challenged police harassment and entrapment, and gay publications challenged obscenity laws. The first legal reform that significantly affected gay and lesbian rights also dates back to the mid-1950s, as legal scholars associated with the American Law Institute developed a modern penal code, which eliminated consensual sodomy as a criminal act. The ALI's Model Penal Code treatment of sodomy laws had been adopted by nearly half the states by the 1980s. Today, twenty-three states still criminalize homosexual conduct through sodomy laws.

Throughout the sixties and seventies, courageous gay individuals raised a wide range of legal challenges, dealing with federal employment policies toward gay people, denial of security clearances, discharge from the military, enforcement of antigay immigration and naturalization laws, and denial of the right to marry. They sought assertion of First Amendment rights to publish gay books and periodicals, to associate and assemble, and the assertion of a broad band of family and custody rights. In the 1980s, this body of law grew more complex, as gay and bisexual men experienced more discrimination because of AIDS. By the 1990s, the legal rights of gay and lesbian people resembled a mottled map, with "free" and "unfree" territories, and wide disparities between states in their treatment of gay people. So, in 1995, the Commonwealth of Massachusetts offered a state-funded program aimed at gay and lesbian youth and at teaching all young people value-neutral information about homosexuality; while Arizona and Alabama had laws prohibiting local schools from "promoting homosexuality" or teaching that it was an "acceptable" lifestyle.

In a sense, splitting the gay and lesbian legal movement from a political or legislative movement represents a false dichotomy: politics, lawmaking, and litigation are intimately connected. But functionally and historically, litigation, lawmaking, and political organizing in the gay movement have taken place in parallel worlds and not in concert or with coordination. The fact is that the gay and lesbian political movement is quite separate from the queer legal movement. The legal movement operates independently, with separate organizations, its own network of donors and activists, and an agenda that does not necessarily coincide with the political or legislative movement's agenda. Often lawsuits push out into ground that the political movement has not yet charted. Consider the Hawaii marriage case, a locally initiated action that has forced the national movement to prepare for the potential legislative and political backlash to a favorable decision. Even today, the national movement is playing catch-up.

There are four major gay and lesbian legal groups at the national level. The oldest, largest, and most prestigious is the Lambda Legal Defense and Education Fund, based in New York. The second-oldest is the National Center for Lesbian Rights, with offices in San Francisco and New York. A third national group is the Lesbian and Gay Rights Project of the ACLU. Interestingly, the ACLU first adopted an ambivalent policy on gay rights in 1957, supporting due process guarantees for gay people, but accepting the constitutionality of sodomy laws. This policy was changed in 1965, after sustained lobbying by people like Frank Kameny and local chapters of the organization. The newest national legal group is the Servicemembers Legal Defense Network, formed in 1993 to assist gay and lesbian military members fighting discharge under the military's discriminatory policy. Regional and local gay legal groups also make important contributions. These include the Gay and Lesbian Advocates and Defenders in Boston, founded in 1978; the Texas Human Rights Foundation, which has waged a battle against the Texas sodomy law for over a decade; a number of state affiliates of the ACLU, which have done large amounts of gay rights litigation (Illinois, Washington, D.C., Southern and Northern California among them); and the Military Law Task Force of the National Lawyers Guild.

In this part of the movement, as in the political sphere, there is intense competition—for donors, prestige, public recognition. But unlike those in the gay political movement, gay rights lawyers have built structures for cooperation. Since the 1980s, national gay rights lawyers have gathered several times a year in formal conferences to discuss pending litigation and legal strategy. Variously called the Sodomy Roundtable—because of the legal effort to repeal sodomy laws—or the Civil Rights Roundtable, these meetings still take place around the country on different legal issues.

On an operational, day-to-day-level, however, cooperation between legal groups and national political organizations remains minimal. Legal groups pursue litigation, speak before legal and legislative bodies, and speak out in the media in a parallel world to the political groups. Political organizations, too, rarely involve the legal groups in drafting legislation or in debating the merits of various approaches they are considering. This separation results in an awkward and counterproductive situation, where each organization pushes an institutional agenda that overlaps with others; rarely do the groups develop and promote a movement-wide agenda that is strategic or carefully coordinated. Staff members of these groups do not talk with one another on a regular, structured basis and, outside of friendships, do not take each other into their confidence. Instead, they compete—for dollars, media attention, and control over the definition and strategies we use to advance different agenda items.

The lack of coordination between the legal movement and the political movement is even reflected in the forums we have created for communication. Lambda's regular Legal Issues Roundtables are open only to lawyers; I used to be invited because I was a lawyer, not because I was the director of NGLTF. Retreats and policy conferences take place regularly on AIDS issues but less frequently on gay and lesbian rights issues. Although we face a set of intractable, interlinked, legal, legislative, political, and cultural barriers, we pursue each as if it were disconnected from the others.

Imagine the difference if such litigation were conceptualized in a broader context, beyond the confines of the court of law alone. Each test case would present an opportunity for public and legislative education and give us a chance to advance a public policy agenda. If coordination among gay legal and political groups were improved and competition lessened, all interested parties could work together to advance the overall principle for which the case is brought. Such a coordinated approach would require the legal organizations to shift the view of their work from that of nonprofit law firms, essentially doing what lawyers in private practice do, to that of politically driven organizations.

Some in the movement today are trying out this new coordinated process. For example, since 1992, Lambda Legal Defense has done excellent work in Hawaii to advance the pending challenge to the state's marriage law. Recently, Lambda assembled a large coalition of media, political, and community groups that will cooperate in the nonlegal work stemming from the case. Lambda's Marriage Project has also worked with political activists to develop organizing and public education strategies to combat the antigay referenda it has challenged in courts.

While litigation has brought relief from discrimination for hundreds of lesbian and gay plaintiffs, it has made us face an old problem that litigation alone will not be able to solve: how to end the stigmatization of gay and lesbian conduct. The most influential case in gay and lesbian rights jurisprudence so far is the U.S. Supreme Court's 1986 decision in *Bowers* v. *Hardwick*. Simply put, the Supreme Court found that "millennia of moral teaching" required it to uphold Georgia's criminalization of gay sexual behavior (sodomy). As the law professors David Cole and William Eskridge summarized, "The Supreme Court upheld a statute criminalizing sodomy against a due process challenge, finding that it was rationally related to the state's interest in upholding morality . . . [*Hardwick*] is to the growing gay rights movement what *Plessy* v. *Ferguson* was to the civil rights movement and what *Dred Scott* v. *Sandford* was to the abolitionists. Each of the these decisions reflects the Court's failure to recognize the equal humanity and personhood of members of a minority group. Because [*Hardwick*] focused on sexual conduct rather than identity, it appeared to invite rationales like those the military now advances, which separate sexual identity from sexual conduct."

Ever since *Hardwick,* courts have had a difficult time demarcating the line between gay or lesbian conduct (behavior) and gay or lesbian status (identity). The legal scholar and gay activist Nan Hunter explained:

> Left without a privacy-based defense against criminalization of that conduct, advocates and some judges argued that sexual orientation was first and foremost a status, not contingent on conduct. This riddle—is homosexuality status or conduct—was purely an artifact of the categories of legal doctrine and the outcome of a single case. Yet it was picked up, replicated, and amplified in the arguments over the military ban. President Clinton framed his position as opposition to discrimination "based solely on status," and, in response, congressional opponents such as Senator Sam Nunn responded in part by arguing that there was no status without conduct.

The Clinton administration's "don't ask, don't tell" policy worsened the status-conduct distinction by treating speech itself as conduct. A soldier's saying "I am a lesbian" has the same weight under the Clinton policy as that soldier's engaging in lesbian sex. This collapse of speech into the category of proscribed behavior was an aspect of the Supreme Court's decision on a lawsuit by a South Boston veterans' group challenging the city's refusal to allow its members to march on Saint Patrick's Day without allowing gay people into the parade. After twice being rejected by Massachusetts courts, the veterans in 1995 reframed their march from a Pro-Irish celebration to an antigay protest. By doing so, they won. In 1995, the Court overturned a lower court decision in favor of the gay marchers, holding that the First Amendment allowed antigay marches! The case did not answer the sticky questions of the links among speech, expression, and status. As Hunter presciently wrote in 1993, "Is the claim one of expression or of equality when an Irish gay and lesbian group is denied participation in a Saint Patrick's Day parade? Is the exclusion of the group wanting to carry a self-identifying banner based on speech or based on status? Are they being shut out because of who they are, or because of what they are saying? In reality, these distinctions are artificial. In the law, they carry enormous weight."

To date, neither the legal nor the political movement has come up with an effective way out of this box. Professors Cole and Eskridge argue that since gay behavior is expressive, it is protected under the First Amendment. They propose a legal challenge to the military policy as an unconstitutional restriction on conduct. Others argue that the only way to overcome the status-conduct bind is to be more specific about gay conduct when litigating cases in which sodomy laws or *Hardwick* are invoked.

Changing scientific evidence on the origins of homosexuality presents an inviting, but treacherous, option to the gay movement: to overcome the status-conduct merger, we are tempted to argue, "We were born this way." If we were born this way, discrimination against us becomes unjustified, they reason; morality and religion are irrelevant; gay and lesbian people are simply one variation in the human gene pool. Such arguments are enormously seductive: a biological basis for homosexuality is the ultimate kind of legitimation. Seeing us as biologically gay or lesbian makes us more human and comprehensible to the average American, while the idea that we choose our sexual orientation leaves the heterosexual mind threatened, insecure, and nervous at any confrontation with us as sexual beings. The dilemma for gay rights activists is that if we abandon the framework of choice for the framework of biology, we compromise the only guarantee of freedom we currently enjoy. Biology is no protection from tyranny; the history of humanity proves it. From the Holocaust to the history of racial prejudice in America, one can see that being born a certain way does not cushion anyone against persecution. All gay rights proponents need to do is listen to the antigay right to have these delusions of safety shattered. The right says that biologically based traits or behaviors are not always socially sanctioned. In the videotape *Gay Rights, Special Rights,* for example, a speaker notes that society condemns alcoholic behavior even though it recognizes that alcoholism may be genetically based.

After the 1993 enactment of "don't ask, don't tell," we cannot finesse the status-conduct distinction either inside or outside the courts. Conservatives routinely characterize homosexuality as nothing more than behavior. We are nothing more than "sodomites" to many religious conservatives. As Senator Strom Thurmond maintained in 1993, "Heterosexuals don't practice sodomy." Gay conduct is seen as identical with gay status by most Americans, and it is this conduct which the gay movement must now demystify and destigmatize. While the courtroom and the legislature may not be the best sites for widespread cultural education about sexual behavior, they remain the places where we must fight aggressively and try to win.

Nan Hunter is right to characterize the status-conduct distinction as an "artifact of the categories of legal doctrine." Homosexuality is far more than a lifestyle, a status, or a sexual act for most of us who are gay. Gayness is our identity, our life, our family, our being. Hunter points out that the gay legal and legislative rights movement's central battle has become one against "state-imposed penalties on identity speech—on speech that promotes or professes homosexuality." From the Briggs Initiative to state laws that disallow the promotion of homosexual "life-style" in AIDS and sex education, to the "don't ask, don't tell" policy—which was recently declared unconstitutional by a federal court in New York—all of these state actions involve the suppression of what Hunter terms "self-identifying expression" or "identity speech." Gaining and preserving legal protection of such pro-gay expression forms a central goal of our legal movement as we head into the next century. In a sense we have come full circle. Many of the earliest and most far-reaching gay rights cases have involved the First Amendment. These lawsuits gave us the right to assemble, publish, create gay-oriented businesses, dance with each other in nightclubs, take same-sex dates to the high school prom. Today, it is the First Amendment that is most implicated in the challenge to stop state suppression of gay and lesbian identities. Indeed, both of the Supreme Court cases on gay rights heard in 1995 focus on First Amendment rights: the Boston Saint Patrick's Day case centered on freedom of political speech, while the Colorado Amendment 2 case focuses on the right of gay people to participate in the legislative process.

THE LEGISLATION OF CIVIL RIGHTS

Our movement's pursuit of legislative mainstreaming has reached its second decade at the national level. At the local level, gay rights ordinances have been sought since the early 1970s, but an organized local and state-based movement for legislative reform remains in its infancy in most parts of the country. Legislative work aims to add sexual orientation as a category to existing laws and to eliminate a long list of discriminatory statutes and regulations that still litter state and federal legislative codes. Relatively few states (9) and municipalities (150) have added sexual orientation to their nondiscrimination policies, while anti-gay and antilesbian laws are on the rise. These laws come in two pack-ages: those which would ban the extension of civil rights to gay people (like the Colorado Amendment 2, which was declared unconstitutional in the case now pending on appeal to the U.S. Supreme Court) and those which target gay people for special discriminatory treatment (like a law, pending in 1995 in the Washington state legislature, that would ban gay adoption or foster care). A number of laws against gay people exist on the books but are not enforced. Virginia once had a law that banned any public establishment from serving alcohol to a known ho-mosexual. After Virginians for Justice, the state gay rights organization, joined with NGLTF to challenge this law in 1991, the state attorney general issued a finding that the law was unconstitutional. But until the gay groups made the public aware of the law and contested its legality, the statute was a tool available to zealous politicians and prosecutors.

Among the truisms of American politics is that you have to give to get, pay to play, lose some to win some. The legislative process is about this kind of interplay between power and compromise. Compromise is venerated as an art among the members of the "permanent government" in Washington—the professional politicians, lobbyists, public relations experts, news media establishment, opinion shakers, and bureaucrats—literally thousands of largely white, largely upper-class, largely male members of what once was aptly labeled "the establishment." They are the curators and archivists of the status quo. And to them compromise is democracy. If one is not willing to compromise, one is considered stupid, naïve, unaware of how the "game" is played. But the side that holds more power induces the compromise, a fact that bases every compromise on coercion. Thus, the trickiest part of any Washington compromise lies not in its negotiation, but in its representation or in the spin one gives it.

Since the emergence of AIDS, the gay and lesbian movement has focused far more on the federal level than on the state or local level. Because we have not built our base from the ground up, we find our-selves in a compromising position nationally. We can get members of Congress or state lawmakers or city council members to introduce gay and lesbian civil rights bills, but we cannot get the legislative bodies to pass those bills. Indeed, we rally so little constituent pressure (letters, phone calls, faxes to our political representatives) in support of gay and AIDS legislation that I am amazed we have passed as many laws as we have. Starting out in a weak position, gay and lesbian lobbyists must often concede to compromises they dislike.

Gay and lesbian history also shows that in legislative progress the principle of "cover" is higher than integrity, ethics, or values as the paramount motivation. The more controversial (read *unpopular*) the political act under consideration, the more cautious politicians and community leaders will be. Until they have the cover to act without fear of retribution, politicians will stall. The need for cover is common in the private sector as well: when a chief executive—in government or the private sector—is supportive of gay and lesbian rights, the agency or corporation moves in that direction. So, the high-tech industry has led all other industries in passing progressive workplace policies dealing with homosexuality, racial difference, and gender. Why? Because it is led by a younger and more open-minded generation of executives, who share a different ethos from that of the post–World War II generation that dominates corporation leadership in other industries. In the Clinton administration, cabinet secretaries of most departments have all issued executive orders banning discrimination in employment by their agencies, in one swoop eliminating the unequal treatment that threatened the jobs of thousands of gay federal employees. These cabinet members did so in part because they knew they would be supported by their chief executive. Supportive governors of every political stripe have issued executive orders banning discrimination, commissioned studies of gay and lesbian youth or antigay violence, and taken other actions that advanced gay equality—allowing similar action by local mayors, health department chiefs, and police chiefs.

As the national lesbian, gay, and AIDS-specific lobbies grew to deal with the AIDS epidemic, they found themselves waging a defensive war against antigay and antilesbian amendments. On October 14, 1987, three days after the Second National March on Washington, Jesse Helms took to the floor of the Senate during the debate over a federal AIDS appropriations bill. In his hand, he had a copy of a sexually explicit safe-sex comic book published by the Gay Men's Health Crisis, the leading AIDS service agency in New York. Helms alleged that the comic book had been produced with federal AIDS education funds. He alleged that this use of federal funds was immoral and outrageous, that such funds were "misappropriated" to produce a handbook that was "pornographic." A subsequent investigation by federal agencies found that no federal funds had been used to produce the GMHC comic book, but on October 14, the Senate, by a vote of 98 to 2, passed an explicitly antigay amendment that Helms attached to the federal AIDS appropriations bill.

The Helms amendment forbade the use of any federal funds for AIDS education materials that "promote or encourage homosexual activity." This amendment's impact was seen by gay and lesbian AIDS advocates as genocidal: it banned the use of federal dollars to conduct life-saving AIDS education for the very population most affected by AIDS, gay and bisexual men. Buoyed by his success, Helms has continued to offer the amendment to each appropriations bill since 1987, and diluted versions of the original one have continued to pass. Despite the moderating language of later amendments, the pipeline to federal funds for gay- and lesbian-oriented safer sex education was cut. Indeed, in 1992 the AIDS Action Council released a report showing that funds for AIDS education aimed at gay and bisexual men and women were not coming from the federal government at all—a government to which all gay and lesbian people pay taxes.

It is interesting to note that the Helms amendment itself was quite similar to the language of the antigay measure championed by the Conservative government of Margaret Thatcher and passed by the House of Commons in Britain in 1989. Known colloquially as "Clause 28," the amendment forbade the use of government funds for any efforts by local government councils and government-funded bodies (such as libraries, public spaces, and so on) that "promoted" homosexuality or the idea that homosexual relationships are "pretended family relationships." Clause 28 worked: it dealt a blow to the British gay and lesbian movement's power by cutting off funds for gay and lesbian projects, homophobia education, and services. The "no promo homo" amendments, as Helms's and Clause 28 quickly came to be known, have reappeared often.

Both principles—of compromise and cover—prevented the gay community from achieving legislative victories on gay rights until the late 1980s. Until then, we lacked the legislative talent to craft compromises clever enough to provide the needed cover for conservative and scared politicians, but tame enough to allow the gay community not to concede its soul. The passage in 1990 of the federal Hate Crime Statistics Act provides a perfect example for examining the impact and implications of compromise in the federal legislative process. Despite the importance of its passage, the Hate Crime bill may well have been a fluke. I cannot imagine another issue on which we could duplicate the unequivocal victory we achieved on this legislation. The clarity of the issue was phenomenal: violence against anyone based on who they are is indefensible. In the legislative battle the ultimate "cover" was provided by the Vatican, which in 1986 condemned hate violence against gays even as it condemned homosexuality as "intrinsically evil." (Even so, there was a vigorous opposition mounted to the Hate Crime effort by Helms and other conservative Republican members of Congress.) On another level, the passage of the bill was unusual because of the active involvement of a number of nongay allies: the Anti-Defamation League, the ACLU, the People for the American Way, and the NAACP all worked closely with the NGLTF to achieve this victory. Without the involvement of these organizations, there is no way the gay and lesbian community could have got the bill passed. Nonetheless, its passage provides insight into the mechanism of the legislative process in Washington.

When the Hate Crime Statistics Act was originally proposed, in 1985, it was limited to data collection on violence based on race, ethnicity, and religion. The addition of sexual orientation to the list of catego- ries required a full-scale campaign, which was waged by Kevin Berrill, the founding director of the Anti-Violence Project of NGLTF, and lobbyists from the American Psychological Association. From 1982 to 1992, Berrill pioneered in national efforts to address antigay violence through the publication of surveys, annual reports, development of policy options, education of law enforcement officers, and the creation of effective coalitions with other groups in society affected by bias-motivated crime. Early opponents to gay inclusion expressed the view that the addition would doom the bill to symbolism, and, indeed, the additional clause went on to become the only aspect of this basic information-gathering bill that was controversial. But Berrill and NGLTF made an effective case for inclusion, and found a sympathetic ear in Representative John Conyers (D-MI), who introduced a new, and inclusive, Hate Crime Statistics Act (HR 3193) in the 99th Congress in August 1987.

Success with the federal bill depended on our completion of four phases of legislative organizing. The first was to make the problem visible and comprehensible. Hate crimes against gay people were regarded in much the same way as violence against women had been before the feminist movement shifted the paradigm of patriarchy. Gay people were told we should not go out at night, not be so blatant, that we invited this violence upon ourselves, that we were murdered because we picked up strangers in bars (the gay-morality version of *Looking for*

Mister Goodbar). By presenting incontrovertible data that shattered these myths, Berrill persuaded the bill's sponsors in the progressive civil rights community and in Congress to add sexual orientation as a category. His campaign to place the issue of antigay violence on the agenda of nongay organizations was a radical departure from the insularity and self-referential stance of the mainstream gay movement of the 1970s. Speaking before any nongay audience, organization, or conference that would listen, Berrill presented the facts on antigay violence. He met with supportive local and national law enforcement officials, developing a good enough working relationship to be invited by the FBI in 1991 to help train police and law enforcement officials; he made alliances with leaders in the racial justice and religious freedom movements, analyzing how hate unites our enemies; and he spent hours of time educating nongay community leaders, board members of nonprofits, and members of the media about the profound implications of violence on the lives of all gay people.

The second phase involved the creation of a broad coalition in favor of the legislation. This effort began in 1987, when many supporters of the original bill championed the addition of sexual orientation. Among these allies were the ACLU, the American Jewish Congress, and the Lutheran Council. The task of mobilizing a coalition became the full-time responsibility of NGLTF's Peri Jude Radecic, who organized a group of more than sixty organizations that met monthly and lobbied effectively. The coalition stayed in existence after the HCSA was passed in order to pursue other bias-crime laws and regulatory reforms.

The third phase involved educating Congress about the massive amounts of violence experienced by gay people. The process of education had begun even before a gay-inclusive bill was introduced. Berrill had worked with Conyers's staff to prepare the first (and only) congressional hearing on antigay violence. Held on September 22, 1986, this hearing collected the testimony of law enforcement officials from cities around the country, gay and lesbian victims themselves, and gay community-based advocacy programs, such as the New York City Gay and Lesbian Anti-Violence Project, which work full time on hate crime prevention and monitoring. The record of the hearing created the legislative foundation for the final bill's passage.

After the bill was introduced by Conyers in 1987, a series of votes in committees provided additional opportunities to educate members of Congress. Another critical element in their education came through the offices of the National Institute of Justice, the research arm of the

Justice Department. In a triumph of perseverance and documentation over ideology, Berrill marshaled such an impressive set of arguments and facts that the Justice Department of Edwin Meese issued a report in 1987 that termed lesbians and gay men "probably the most frequent victims of hate violence in this country."

The final strategy was the generation of constituent support. The Hate Crime Coalition targeted key members who had not co-sponsored the bill and launched letter-writing campaigns from voters in their districts. With this effort, the number of co-sponsors increased. Sadly, what made this constituent effort successful was the lack of an organized opposition on this bill. Although the right tried its best to eliminate sexual orientation, even they were forced to condemn the violence that gay people faced. If they had launched even a small-scale effort to stop the bill, there is no question in my mind that the HCSA would have been stalled. No civil rights group has been able to match the ability of the right wing to elicit constituent letters on any topic. For example, when the Bush administration overturned the HIV-immigration ban in 1992, the right quickly generated more than forty thousand letters to Secretary Louis Sullivan, causing him to rescind his earlier order. The AIDS lobby and civil rights community was able to muster only some five hundred letters seeking the elimination of all travel restrictions. This ability to produce mail has led the right to victories on issues as diverse as NEA appropriations, Washington, D.C., appropriations, and the military. But on the issue of violence, the right did not summon up this volume of mail, and our letter count of several hundred for the bill carried the day with many legislators.

Even with all these building blocks, the Hate Crime bill was extremely controversial because of the sexual-orientation clause. The Hate Crime Coalition and NGLTF fought against the removal of sexual orientation at every single juncture of the bill's passage through the legislative process. The first drama took place in 1987, at the House Criminal Justice Subcommittee and in the House Judiciary Committee. "During debate on the amendments, hostile members called gays 'sexual deviants' and stated that the term 'sexual orientation' was ambiguous and therefore might cover violence against pedophiles and necrophiliacs. They also stated that the bill equated gays with other minority groups and would lead to gay rights." Despite these efforts, the sexual-orientation clause survived the repeated efforts at removal, and the bill passed, 5 to 2, in the subcommittee and 21 to 13 in the full Judiciary Committee in October 1987.

The second benchmark was the full House vote in May 1988. In response to an amendment to delete "sexual orientation" from the bill, a two-part compromise was adopted: "In a compromise arranged by supporters of the legislation, a substitute amendment was introduced defining 'sexual orientation' as 'homosexuality or heterosexuality.' [The compromise] also stated that 'nothing in this bill creates a right for an individual to bring an action complaining of discrimination based on homosexuality.' The HCSA passed the full House by a vote of 393 to 29.

The battle then moved to the Senate, where the companion bill, S702, sponsored by Senator Paul Simon (D-Il), passed the Senate Judiciary Committee by unanimous vote. The bill never made it to the full Senate floor in 1988, though, and the entire process had to begin again in the 101st Congress in 1989. Once again, it moved quickly through the House, but it faced stiffer opposition in the Senate, where the bill's sponsors were unable to outflank Helms, who proposed a daunting four-part antigay amendment. The proposed Helms amendment sought, among other things, to legislate (1) that homosexuality was immoral and unnatural; (2) that sodomy laws should be enforced; (3) that gay and lesbian relationships should never be recognized; and (4) that school curricula should teach that homosexuality is aberrant behavior. The amendment forced the hand of liberal endorsers of equal rights for gay people by requiring them to take a stand on the morality of homosexuality. None of our staunchest allies in the Senate was interested or willing to take such a stand. In the end, it was the Senate leadership's own unwillingness to vote full-force on the Helms amendment that resulted in an eventual compromise.

Intense pressure was put on the gay community to accept an amendment that would modify the original Helms amendment. We faced the bizarre (and, in Washington, the completely ordinary) task of crafting an antigay amendment to a gay rights bill. The procedural ploy known as the "second-degree amendment" is the legislative version of co-optation. At its best, such an amendment is a mechanism to secure consensus; it allows opponents of a bill to have their opposition incorporated in some fashion. At its worst, a second-degree amendment is a tactic used primarily by conservative senators to ensure that no legislation passes without their often undermining influence. When a member of the Senate proposes an amendment to a bill during the floor debate, this is called a first-degree amendment: it proposes to amend the original bill. The second-degree amendment amends the first-degree amendment. Since Senate rules allow only two amendments to be offered on the same topic, once a first-degree amendment is offered, it either passes or is quickly superseded by a moderating second-degree amendment.

Nearly all gay legislative attempts in Congress have resulted in the threat or the actuality of antigay amendments being offered by conservative Republicans and supported by conservative Democrats. No senator is more prolific—or more effective—in the use of this procedural tactic than Jesse Helms. Legislative lawyers in Washington—lawyers who help craft and write laws—have actually developed a specialty in "second-degreeing" such antigay Helms amendments.

During the bill's passage in the Senate, in February 1990, I got a call from Peri Jude Radecic from a pay phone in a Senate office building. She said Senators Edward Kennedy, Orrin Hatch, and Paul Simon had hammered out an agreement on how to thwart the Helms amendment; their suggestion was an amendment that read something to the effect that "traditional family values are the backbone of American society. And that nothing in the bill should be read as a rejection of traditional family values." They wanted our sign-off on the wording. With Peri on the speaker phone, I gathered our Families Project director Ivy Young and Kevin Berrill and called out on two different lines to Nan Hunter, then at the ACLU in New York, and to Tim McFeeley at the HRCF in Washington. Tim thought this was the best deal we could get, and we had to go forward or risk not having a bill until 1992. I argued that the compromise was unacceptable, since it effectively legislated language that everyone from judges to the common person would interpret as excluding gay people and would seriously damage our movement's family agenda. Nan urged us all to think of different language. With Peri pushing us to decide—she in turn was being pressured by Senate staff for a response—we struck on the words *American family values* to replace *traditional family values*. The compromise was acceptable to us, to the Senate staff, and to our coalition partners. We went with it—and the Hate Crime Statistics Act passed, with that bizarre clause.

One of the most effective and shrewd gay rights advocates in Washington is Chai Feldblum, now the director of the Federal Legislation Clinic at Georgetown University School of Law. Unknown to most gay and lesbian people, Feldblum is a legislative lawyer, responsible for the development and passage of key gay rights legislation. She clerked for Supreme Court Justice Harry Blackmun in the mid-1980s, and began to work on AIDS policy issues for the AIDS Action Council and then for the ACLU Legislative Office. At the ACLU, Feldblum helped draft the Americans with Disabilities Act, assisted in drafting the Ryan White AIDS Care Act, and drafted scores of amendments, legislative histories, and legal opinions for a number of lesbian and gay rights organizations. Finally, Feldblum is the author of a new federal gay and lesbian rights bill—the Employment Non-Discrimination Act (ENDA)—which was introduced in 1994 and 1995.

In an interview, Feldblum argued that the gay and lesbian movement in Washington is legislatively weak for one simple reason: it does not construct its legislative campaigns with the systematic and strategic vision used by other civil rights movements. She argues that there is virtually a formula for the passage of federal civil rights legislation, which has five components: an overall political strategist, a legislative lawyer, the lobbyists, a media coordinator, and grassroots support. The first four are the most important; the last can be the most easily manipulated with "smoke and mirrors." In her view, the gay movement's biggest weakness in Washington is its inability to organize such systematic legislative campaigns. The experience of the HCSA bears out Feldblum's theory, as does the experience of bills like the Americans with Disabilities Act and the Ryan White Act. Each passed because these key elements were present.

While this understanding of the federal legislative process has proved accurate, at least three tensions expose the limits of the legislative strategy. For one, the process of passing legislation differs markedly from the process of building a social change movement. Indeed, the two are antithetical. The former requires a fairly obsessive and insular focus on 535 members of Congress, on several hundred staff members, and on the media and opinion-shaping elite that determines the meaning of whatever legislative measure one is pushing. Legislative enactment requires enormous discretion, secretiveness, the shrewdness to play off one political player against another, the ability to compromise and horse-trade on particulars. The building of a movement requires the involvement of large numbers of people in a political process from which they feel estranged. It calls for the motivation of the electorate, openness and candor, and the demystification of insider language into colloquial and commonsense phrases. It works best when ordinary people have an easy way to get involved and when they believe that their leaders stand for principles that will not be compromised away.

A second tension in the legislative strategy is the nature of winning itself. What does it mean to win or to lose? Lobbyists and lawmakers are intently focused on the passage of a piece of legislation, seen as the ultimate win. This limited goal leads them to enter the legislative process ready to bargain and compromise. Thus, rarely does one win what one actually starts out seeking. Many times, in fact, the final bill differs significantly from the measure originally proposed. In Washington, the appearance of victory is more important than the actual language enacted.

Finally, legislative strategies are more vulnerable than any other kind of activism to becoming insular, self-referential, and separated from the interests of the broader community. There is something inherently limiting in the legislative strategy; it requires a kind of conformity to the status quo that neither political organizing, public education, legal argument, nor cultural work demands. To pass a piece of legislation, one has to focus on the needs and self-interest of a handful of lawmakers. They, not the constituents, are the focal point of the effort, and they dictate the terms and outcome. So, in preparing for the passage of the Americans with Disabilities Act, the political strategist for the bill, a brilliant activist named Pat Wright, who heads up the Disability Rights Defense and Education Fund, analyzed each member of Congress to determine what each would need in order to support the bill. Her analysis guided everything—from the drafting of measures, to the bargaining of favors, to the lobbying deals that were negotiated.

Strategies of political mainstreaming have gained gay and lesbian people considerable access. But today we must acknowledge that our progress is stalled by the failure of mainstream strategies to displace the underlying homophobia we face. In 1993, the electoral strategy proved its weakness when President Clinton refused to eliminate the antigay ban on military service. Meanwhile, strategies of legal mainstreaming stalled in the face of the status-conduct distinction. Additionally, strategies of legislative mainstreaming brought us face to face with our movement's inability to defeat antigay amendments or to mount effective grassroots pressure for our agenda. The military defeat reveals, in microcosm, the limitations of each of these strategies.

CHAPTER FIVE

THE MAINSTREAM RESPONSE

DON'T ASK, DON'T TELL

Fraternity comes into being after the sons are expelled from the family; when they form their own club, in the wilderness, away from home, away from women. The brotherhood is a substitute family, a substitute woman —alma mater.

—Norman O. Brown

The story behind the gay and lesbian movement's fight to end the military ban and the resulting "don't ask, don't tell" compromise reveals a great deal about the end-point of mainstreaming. The compromise formalizes a heterosexual denial against which gay men and lesbians have struggled for decades. It mandates the closet for gay, lesbian, and bisexual members of the armed forces, and makes them vulnerable to prosecution simply because of their statements and nonsexual conduct (such as subscribing to a gay magazine). It underscores the idea that no matter how straight-acting, patriotic, normal-looking, accessible, and heroic we are, the straight world resists our open integration into its society. The mainstream is willing to accept homosexuality only to a point and entirely on its terms: if we don't tell, they say they won't pursue. This compromise epitomizes virtual equality; instead of receiving equal treatment, gay and lesbian service troops are subjected to different rules. Yet the Clinton administration government asks us to pretend that the new policy is an improvement over the old, a fact emphatically contradicted in 1995 by a federal court's rejection of the compromise as unconstitutional. Not only does this contest show that straight people see us as unequal; it reveals how easily straight tolerance of homosexuality can coexist with the closet. Indeed, the closet is the *quid pro quo* that the Clinton administration, Congress, and the Joint Chiefs have offered gay people in exchange for their right to serve in the military.

What happened to the gay and lesbian movement in 1993? Why did we lose so dramatically on the military issue? Why did our national movement seem to collapse under pressure just at the zenith of its political access? Everyone has a theory. Some argue that we lost because Bill Clinton caved in to political pressure from the conservatives and the pollsters on his staff. Others argue that we lost because ordinary gay and lesbian people didn't give a damn about the issue; it simply was not as important to them as other problems they face, like violence, health care access, AIDS, and employment discrimination. Still others are certain that we lost because our national organizations were incompetent. Or that they were too involved with infighting and playing inside-the-Beltway power games. Some, like the reporter Jeffrey Schmalz, wrote in the *New York Times* in late January 1993 that the gay leadership was "asleep at the switch." Still others say we lost because we remain weak, disorganized, and politically naïve.

The people most involved in the military fight have not spoken out about what happened in Washington during those years, constrained perhaps by their relationship with key administration officials or worried about the damage the truth would do to their organization. The truth is that the national gay and lesbian movement lost the military battle for two main reasons: Clinton administration abdication and the self-interested and short-sighted way in which the movement acted. Without question, the President caved in under intense pressure to preserve the status quo. On the other hand, instead of designing a coordinated plan to overturn the military ban, gay and lesbian leaders in Washington engaged in a bitter turf war that lost our movement political momentum, prestige, and influence. We failed during the transition period of 1992–1993 to develop a coherent agenda with which to approach the new administration. Instead, many gay and lesbian leaders engaged in the most corrupt kinds of self-promotion, jockeying for the position of powerbroker, engaging in one-upmanship, pursuing job appointments for themselves and their friends, and using the movement as a cover for their selfish pursuits. In the end, Congress codified a bad new policy into law; and the public overwhelmingly backed discrimination against gay and lesbian people. The President subsumed his support for gay rights to political expediency, and the national movement saw its credibility and agenda go offtrack.

Ironically, the people who were blamed the most, the heads of HRCF and NGLTF during 1993 and 1994, took the heat for actions engaged in by a number of others, many of whom have yet to acknowledge their gaffes or their flawed leadership roles. While McFeeley, Radecic, I, and every other head of national gay organizations do bear some responsibility for what we did and did not do in 1992 and beyond, other individuals directly responsible for the gay community's chaotic response include people whose actions have not adequately been assessed. These include David Mixner, who made a series of irresponsible promises to national gay leaders during and after the election season, made a name for himself, and now continues, undaunted, to advocate the same back-room politics of access that led to our defeat; Torie Osborn, NGLTF head from March to September 1993, whose late start and early departure, overreliance on Mixner, and unfamiliarity with Washington politics rendered her less effective than she was capable of being; the talented gay rights lawyer Tom Stoddard, who failed to negotiate an effective relationship between the newly formed Campaign for Military Service, which he was asked to direct, and existing gay and lesbian organizations; donors like David Geffen and Barry Diller, who promised to fund the lobbying effort but then failed to follow through with sufficient money and did not use the administration access they enjoyed privately to help the movement publicly; and an array of lawyers representing military personnel who failed to cooperate and coordinate their efforts.

When we look back on the long history of the fight to end the military ban, it becomes clear that our failure also arose from serious structural weakness in the gay movement; we have no formal grassroots mobilization network in place. Consequently, with every national bill or crisis, we scramble, inefficiently, to create a new structure to carry out the work.

To understand the dynamics of why we lost the fight, we have to answer four questions. First, how did the issue of repeal of the military ban arrive at the top of the gay and lesbian agenda in 1993? Second, why was the movement unprepared? Third, why did the Campaign for Military Service fail? Finally, are we poised to do things differently today?

This critique is informed by my experience as both a participant and an observer. Until December 1, 1992, I was at the helm of NGLTF and knew firsthand the decisions we made and why; but by the time the military story broke in the national media, in January 1993, I was on the sidelines. I have thought hard about how I and others should have handled the Clinton election, the transition, and the military battle itself. I want to make clear that I include myself in my criticism of the movement's actions, because some of what happened in 1993 and 1994 resulted from the failure of leaders like me to do things we should have done in 1992—or even earlier.

Hindsight is a dangerous gift; while it can provide a clarity that was missing when one lived through an event, it can present a view of history that differs markedly from what happened. With hindsight, I think many of us in the movement were shocked that George Bush lost: we honestly did not believe he would. Also, after spending the Reagan and Bush years at work in the gay movement, I know intimately the dramatic shift in visibility and credibility that the movement experienced in 1992. The mainstream movement had been pushing as hard as it could against the doors of federal power since 1972. Suddenly, we broke through. And like characters in a slapstick comedy, we came tumbling through the door, falling on top of each other and stumbling for footing as we adjusted to the sudden lack of resistance. We failed to realize that the resistance had not disappeared; it had changed. The door was still shut, but it was masked by a welcoming façade.

WHY THE MILITARY POLICY?

It is fashionable among gay activists to think that the military issue was placed on the front burner in 1993 not by the gay movement itself, but by crafty, antigay Republicans who pushed it forward because they knew it would discredit the new President. Alternately, some say the prominence of the military issue was Clinton's doing; he wanted to move quickly on his campaign promise. Still others believe the opposition of the Joint Chiefs and their chairman, Colin Powell, was what brought the military issue up front. Elements of all these theories are true. Bob Dole and Republican leaders played their hand brilliantly, holding back until they could sabotage both the policy and the new administration's political credibility; Clinton's promise far exceeded his will to deliver; and opposition by the Joint Chiefs and senior Clinton aides hurt the prospects of an executive order to repeal the ban. But the military policy arose as a top issue primarily because gay lawyers and activists placed it there during the 1992 campaign and early in the new administration's tenure. Military reform was deemed by us to be one of the top three problems facing gay America, the other two being national AIDS policy and a federal gay and lesbian civil rights bill. After a hard-fought campaign, many thought the issue had been sufficiently argued in the media and that it could be easily settled by executive order. In fact, we seriously miscalculated the opposition. The story of why the military ban came to be foremost on the gay movement's agenda long predates the 1992 election.

The historian Allan Bérubé and journalist Randy Shilts exhaustively chronicled the history of the antigay military policy in their books *Coming Out Under Fire* and *Conduct Unbecoming*. Shilts reports that the codification against same-sex conduct in the military occurred during World War I, and that prior to 1919 consensual sodomy was not specifically mentioned as a proscribed act. In the early 1940s, with the United States waging the Second World War, Shilts suggests, the armed services turned to the expanding field of psychiatry to "winnow out those who might not be fit to be good soldiers . . . Since almost all psychiatrists, from the early days of Freud on, had viewed homosexuality as a pathology, the psychiatrists helped formulate regulations that banned all those with 'homosexual tendencies' from the military." Shilts reports that, by 1943, final regulations banning gay people as "unsuitable for military service" had been promulgated. These regulations survived until the late 1970s, when they were modified to read that "homosexuality was incompatible with military service," a formulation that remains intact today, despite the hue and cry of 1993.

These books also reveal that gay opposition to the military ban is long-standing and that the gay Veterans' Benevolent Association was one of the first gay and lesbian support groups to be organized. Changes to the 1943 antigay ban by Carter administration officials came in response to a rising number of lawsuits brought on behalf of gay and lesbian service members in the 1970s by gay legal organizations and the ACLU. It is interesting to compare the two Presidents who have tinkered most with the antigay policy: Jimmy Carter and Bill Clinton. Carter's administration resisted calls to eliminate the policy by executive order, and, instead, played a distancing game with the gay movement. His advisers and aides met with gay leaders, but Carter himself remained aloof and disengaged from the problems of violence, discrimination, and prejudice facing gay and lesbian Americans. In contrast, Bill

Clinton abandoned the gay and lesbian community when the heat rose. He listened to his pollsters and spin doctors, and sacrificed principles of equality, on which he had campaigned, in a doomed effort to appease conservatives. The equivocation of these two Southern Democrats epitomizes the treatment of the gay movement by the Democratic Party: we are embraced to the extent that we are necessary as a useful voting bloc or as fund-raisers, but we are dropped when strong opposition emerges.

One of the most painful aspects of Randy Shilts's vivid history is that so few gay people stood up to fight the military. This may have been a byproduct of the gap between those in the military and those in the movement. For many years, gay members of the armed services had no relationship to the movement outside. And without a political base to which they could turn for support, most people in the military responded to military persecution individually, with shame, self-loathing, and fear. Shilts details the case of American hero Dr. Tom Dooley, an extraordinary pioneer in the provision of medical care in wartime, who founded a major international relief effort but died embittered and ashamed when the military discharged him for being homosexual.

Significantly, Shilts's and Bérubé's histories reveal that, apart from veterans and their lawyers, the political movement did not take up the issue of military reform until the late eighties for several reasons. For one, the gay political movement of the sixties and seventies was tiny. Its organizations had few or no staff and a small membership base. Until 1973, we had no national political organizations and very few national news media. Until AIDS hit our people, most of us never paid attention to national politics, and when the movement finally did develop a legislative presence in Washington, in the 1980s, its agenda was consumed by the problems presented by AIDS.

Another major reason the political movement was slow to tackle the military ban was the ideological bias of many post-Stonewall gay and lesbian activists. Gay and lesbian liberation grew out of the left-leaning antiwar mentality of the 1960s. A significant number of lesbians and gay men are more impassioned about the peace dividend from military industry conversion than they are about opening up access to the military for gays and lesbians. This antimilitary sentiment is closely connected to the middle- and upper-middle-class nature of the organized gay and lesbian movement. To the poor, the working class, and people with moderate means who are disproportionately present in the military, the armed forces represent a chance for a good education, a steady job, a decent income, and health care benefits. Historically, these are not the people who created, staffed, and volunteered for gay and lesbian political organizations, which explains in part why our middle-class, college-educated movement has had such a hard time taking up issues alien to its constituents.

In the context of overwhelming acquiescence by thousands of gay men and lesbians who were discharged, the courage of the early plaintiffs in lawsuits challenging the military policy cannot be overstated. Among these early resisters were Miriam Ben-Shalom, whose lawsuit helped establish that some First Amendment guarantees apply to military reservists; Perry Watkins, a black gay man who was out of the closet for his entire service, and has opposed his termination with enormous dignity and consistency; Leonard Matlovich, a lifelong Republican whose battle to accept his homosexuality was arduous and whose resistance made front-page news; Ellen Nesbitt and Joann Newak, two of the first lesbians in uniform to stand up and challenge their discharges.

Leonard Matlovich's story made the cover of *Time* magazine when I was sixteen years old. I remember seeing the article and wondering why anyone would want to serve in a setting that was so hostile. I remember even more clearly the shocking news of Leonard Matlovich's settlement with the army in 1980, because by then I was a lesbian activist. That year, I was in law school and could not understand why, when he seemed to be winning, Matlovich had abandoned his lawsuit. Shilts's book shed some light for me. Matlovich ended the case, Shilts suggests, because he was exhausted and embittered by being used as a symbol by a movement that abandoned him when the limelight faded. He was also completely broke; he needed the money. Although the movement appropriated him as a symbol of discrimination, it could offer him nothing tangible in return. Matlovich's experience typified that of gay and lesbian veterans, who received very little assistance from the political movement in mounting their challenges to the ban. Until 1988, nongay and gay legal defense organizations (the ACLU, the Military Law Task Force of the National Lawyers Guild, and Lambda Legal Defense and Education Fund, to name the most notable) were the only nonveteran groups to provide tangible assistance to lesbian and gay veterans. But their support was limited to case-by-case advice, not political advocacy. The abandonment Leonard Matlovich felt was repeated on a larger scale in 1993 and 1994. After the Clinton compromise was promulgated, and Congress passed its own version of the antigay policy, the movement to lift the ban evaporated as quickly as it had appeared. Gay political organizations hurried to do damage control on the loss and then moved on, leaving a large number of veterans and service members enmeshed in a legal quagmire as bad as that created by the original policy. Once again, gay and nongay legal organizations, joined now by a brand-new one called the Service Members Legal Defense Network, became the principal advocates to fill this breach.

The recent *political* battle to lift the ban began not in 1993 or 1992, but in 1988, when a handful of national gay and feminist organizations founded the Gay and Lesbian Military Freedom Project. The lesbian organizer Sue Hyde, then serving as the director of the NGLTF Privacy Project, conceived, named, and founded the project. A skillful community organizer, who hailed from the Midwest, Hyde organized the new coalition in direct response to a massive antilesbian witch hunt at the Parris Island Marine Corps Recruit Training Depot. A letter asking for help from one of the women at Parris Island moved Hyde to begin the wave of political activity. During the Parris Island witch hunt, at least two lesbians were tried, convicted, and incarcerated simply for being lesbian, and several others were discharged outright.

From November 1988 until sometime at the end of 1992, the Military Freedom Project was the driving force behind this issue in the media, on Capitol Hill, and in the election campaign. In 1989, Hyde boldly declared that we had a deadline for the elimination of this policy: 1993. The fiftieth anniversary of the inception of the antigay policy would be the anniversary of its fall. We nearly succeeded. Other pivotal members of the Military Freedom Project were Tim Drake, and Tania Domi from NGLTF; Nan Hunter of the ACLU Gay and Lesbian Rights Project; Sandy Lowe and Paula Ettelbrick of the Lambda Legal Defense and Education Fund; Nancy Beurmeyer of the National Organization for Women; a well-connected active-duty gay woman still in the service who gave us invaluable inside information; and Vicki Almquist of the now-defunct Women's Equity Action League. By mid-1989, the Human Rights Campaign Fund, the newly formed Gay, Lesbian and Bisexual Veterans of America, the Military Law Task Force of the National Lawyers Guild, and staffers Kate Dyer from Representative Gerry Studds's (D-MA) office and Irene Rapinsky from Senator Daniel Inouye's (D-HI) office had joined the leadership of the MFP coalition.

Ironically, all the founders of the MFP had politics that today would be characterized as radical feminist or leftist. Each of us, if polled, would have fallen on the antiwar, military-cutback side of the

ideological spectrum. Yet long before flag-waving gay Republicans began to push the issue, this group of radical lesbians had identified
military reform as a high priority for the movement. We knew from
firsthand reports what Randy Shilts's book eventually revealed to the
rest of America: that the government was waging a brutal campaign of
persecution, harassment, and legally sanctioned prejudice against lesbian, gay, and bisexual people. Indeed, during the years Shilts re-
searched his book, members of our MFP coalition connected him to
scores of individual service members who agreed to discuss their experiences with him.

In the gay movement, activists rarely know, much less credit, their
predecessors; our movement's history has barely been written. Every
generation thinks it is facing things for the first time. In a literal sense
that's true, but in a historical sense, most movement battles are repeti-
tious. In addition, to bolster the urgency of their current work, activists
often play down, discredit, or simply ignore efforts that came before.
Perhaps because of my involvement in the founding of the MFP, and
my knowledge of its work, I find particularly curious and offensive the
lack of history that accompanied the fight over gays in the military.
More than any other development, the efforts of the MFP made it
possible for the military issue to loom as large as it did during the 1992
campaign. But few if any reporters for the gay or straight press traced
the political origins of the 1993 fight back to the MFP's work during
the late 1980s and early 1990s.

Even Shilts's otherwise excellent book perpetuates this odd revisionism. Shilts, for example, spoke frequently to Hyde and others involved with the MFP, who referred to him dozens of veterans facing
discharge. We were eager to promote his research because we believed
his book would profoundly deepen the understanding of the abuses
caused by the military ban. In a strictly chronological sense, Shilts
placed the formation of the MFP where it belonged—late in the book.
The fact is that until the eighties the principal fighters against the
military policy were the lawyers and veterans who stood up and challenged their discharges. But Shilts's failure to discuss in depth the
strategies and tactics of the MFP limits our comprehension of the
political defeat we suffered in 1993. Indeed, Shilts's own words about
the MFP belie the lack of attention he gave it in his book: "The
Military Freedom Project represented the first organized effort to protect the rights of gays in the military and to lobby for a change in gay
policies since the Vietnam War. Until the group's formation, gay mili-

tary cases were handled, or not handled, by this or that homosexual advocacy group, with no coordinated strategy for gaining press attention or pursuing legislative channels for a repeal to the antigay policies."

The pervasive sexism of our movement culture contributes to this historical silence. In a largely male-funded and male-dominated national gay and lesbian movement, until men get involved, an issue is deemed not to affect the community as a whole. In the early years of the MFP, by some twist of fate, all the representatives to the coalition's meetings were women. Because we were formed out of the crisis at Parris Island, which involved lesbians, our early political and media actions targeted antilesbian harassment. MFP members exposed statistics revealing that women were discharged for homosexuality at a far higher rate than men, and that sexual harassment of women in the military relied heavily on the threat of "lesbian-baiting." If women refused the sexual advances of men, they were threatened with the label *dyke,* a threat that on its own could trigger a career-ending investigation. It was not until 1992, when rich gay men got behind issue of the military ban repeal (perhaps because they discovered that the issue had political saliency), that the gay press and the straight media began to cover the issue as a movementwide priority. Notably, in 1993, at the height of the public argument, the experience of lesbians in the military became nearly invisible. The main focus of controversy and attention became the morale of straight men following the induction of gay and bisexual men.

Another reason for the lack of interest among many gay men in the early years of the Military Freedom Project was that we started work at a time when AIDS issues dominated the resources of the national movement. Radical activists were drawn to direct action and AIDS work; ACT UP was the hottest organization of the late 1980s. Those who worked on issues like antigay violence, military reform, sodomy law repeal, campus organizing, or gay and lesbian family issues were largely ignored by the media—both gay and straight.

Finally, the MFP's pursuit of inside-the-Beltway strategies to the exclusion of broader political action exacerbated the lack of awareness about its role and contribution. The MFP did its most effective work *within* Washington, to educate members of Congress, raise visibility, and elevate the priority of the military issue. An early MFP action targeted the Defense Advisory Committee on Women in the Service (DACOWITS) in April 1989, to force it to address the problem of sexual harassment faced by lesbians and straight women. For the first time in its nearly forty-year history, DACOWITS heard testimony from out lesbians about the harassment and treatment of gay women in the military. Two of the women who testified at the DACOWITS meetings faced investigations but testified anyway: Navy Lieutenant Mary Beth Harrison and Marine Corps Captain Judy Meade. Two others had been discharged several years earlier for being lesbians: Darlene Chamberlain had been kicked out of the Air Force and Ellen Nesbitt had been discharged from Air Force National Guard. The panel's testimony was riveting. Like the thousands of gay, lesbian, bisexual service members, and scores of nongay personnel swept up in antigay investigations, these women had bizarre tales that few people outside the military could believe. They told of being hounded by Defense Department intelligence agencies, of being pressured to admit to things they had not done, of being threatened with everything from physical harm to discharge and loss of their benefits earned over many years. They testified about excellent service records being disregarded as soon as the rumors about their sexual orientation began. Each of the women told stories about sexual harassment, the lack of recourse to pursue the claims of harassment, and the connection between antilesbian harassment and the sexual harassment of straight women; that is, "lesbian-baiting."

After the panel, the DACOWITS meeting broke into a closed session of the board, invited guests, and armed services staff. The lesbian panel's testimony was reinforced during these closed meetings by Kate Dyer from the office of Gerry Studds, the openly gay member of Congress who was centrally involved in trying to change the military policy. Eventually, DACOWITS issued a recommendation that the Defense Department instruct officers handling sexual harassment investigations to consider lesbian-baiting a form of sexual harassment.

In 1989, Kate Dyer and the Lambda Legal Defense Fund procured copies of a high-level report prepared for the Department of Defense by the Personnel Security Research and Education Center. The PERSEREC report concluded that there was no basis for the military's antigay policy. A Department of Defense effort to suppress the findings backfired when a copy of the report was leaked to the media. The full report was disowned by the Department of Defense even though the consultants who authored it were highly regarded in the military community.

By 1990, the MFP had begun to work with members of Congress, organizing visits by gay veterans and educating congressional staff on the waste and harm of the antigay policy. In 1991, the MFP secured the introduction of a congressional resolution, calling on President Bush to rescind the military ban. Later that year, Representative Pat Schroeder (D-CO) and Senator Brock Adams (D-WA) introduced the Military Freedom Act, which sought to overturn the ban completely. Meanwhile, coalition members like the ACLU Lesbian and Gay Rights Project worked hard on the issue of ROTC discrimination, organizing a national conference in 1991 and securing condemnation of the policy from a number of university and college presidents. The legal groups also stepped up their advocacy, using key cases, like that of the gay naval cadet Joe Steffan, to educate a public that seemed receptive to the idea that the policy was unfair. Staff of each organization in the MFP assisted hundreds of gay, lesbian, and bisexual members facing discharge proceedings by providing advice, referrals, support, and legal help. And MFP organizers like Tim Drake, making a systematic effort to educate editorial boards at major newspapers about the irrationality of the policy, secured a number of editorials against discrimination.

In the early 1990s, the MFP's efforts were highlighted by several events. For one, the Gulf War dramatically focused the attention of the nation on qualified gay and lesbian service members who were willing to serve their nation but were prevented from doing so by the ban. Second, individual cases like those of Tracey Thorne and Greta Cammermeyer drew extensive media coverage. The ongoing lawsuits of a number of gay and lesbian veterans—namely, Perry Watkins, Dusty Pruitt, Keith Meinhold, and Joe Steffan—yielded some excellent legal decisions that further eroded the legitimacy of the military ban. And in 1992 the General Accounting Office finally released a study of the costs of the antigay policy, a study the MFP had asked supportive members of Congress to request in 1990, and pressed for two years to get hold of. The GAO study provided the factual basis for much of the military-ban debate in 1993.

WHAT HAPPENED DURING THE 1992 ELECTION?

The Gulf War brought Pete Williams, the Defense Department's chief spokesman, to national prominence. Williams, a long-time aide to Dick Cheney, had followed Cheney from the Senate to his Defense Department job. Williams was deliberately outed as a gay man in the *Advocate* by the crusading journalist Michelangelo Signorile, with profound repercussions. For one, the event was widely covered in the straight press. For another, it forced Dick Cheney to speak out on the military's ban on gay and lesbian service. He declared that the military did not ban openly gay and lesbian people from civilian jobs, only from uniformed jobs. When asked on television about the policy in early 1992, he called it an "old chestnut," whose time may have passed. Even Representative Newt Gingrich suggested to *The New Republic* that the antigay policy was irrelevant, a position he apparently backed away from in April 1995. In the aftermath of the Williams outing, a chorus of editorial boards and statesmen, ranging from former Reagan Under Secretary of Defense Lawrence Korb to national civil rights leaders, spoke out against the policy.

The issue of gays in the military popped up in two other unexpected ways in 1992: the investigation of the disaster on the U.S.S. *Iowa,* which Naval Investigative Service agents falsely tried to label a crime of scorned gay passion; and the murder of the sailor Allen Schindler. The *Iowa* investigation actually began in 1989, after an explosion aboard the ship took the lives of Clayton Hartwig and three others. The investigators hinted darkly that Hartwig's close friendship with a sailor who survived was the reason for the explosion. One year later, the investigation found that the theory had been completely fabricated by the Navy to deflect attention from its own faulty procedures, and to discredit those seeking to change the antigay military policy. In fact, old gunpowder, aging guns, poor ventilation, and poor operating procedures had led to the explosion. In the case of Allen Schindler, a gay man brutally murdered by another member of his unit, the Navy tried to bury the case, claiming that it was not a case of gay-bashing. The effort of gay activist Michael Petrelis, who kept the case alive in the media and who went to Japan to stimulate publicity during the trial of Schindler's assailant, maintained public pressure and forced the military officially to confront its first prosecution for gay-bashing.

From the earliest responses to gay rights questionnaires, Democratic presidential candidates in 1992 expressed unanimous support for ending the military ban. In the fall of 1991, candidate Bill Clinton pledged to Barney Frank that he would lift the ban, a promise he repeated publicly when asked about his views on the military policy at a forum at Harvard. Clinton again stated unequivocally that he would overturn the policy by executive order if elected President. In January 1992, Clinton responded to an HRCF questionnaire on gay issues by answering: "I believe patriotic Americans should have the right to serve the country as a member of the armed forces without regard to sexual or affectional orientation." The journalist Fred Barnes also reported that the Clinton-Gore campaign book, *Putting People First,* issued in September 1992, promised to "issue executive orders to repeal the ban on gays and lesbians from military or foreign service." This response, coupled with Clinton's appearance at a gay fundraiser in Los Angeles and with the pro-gay stance of the Democratic Party, resulted in the landslide of support for Clinton among previously unmotivated or disinterested gay voters.

Despite the high-level endorsements for change, the antigay ban was not an issue on the minds of most gay and lesbian Americans during the 1992 campaign: AIDS and the antigay right were. AIDS activists dogged presidential candidates on the campaign trail to secure commitments on AIDS issues and to get media coverage. Others worked behind the scenes to craft AIDS position papers and to brief different campaigns on rights issues. In New York, GMHC organized a massive coalition, United for AIDS Action, which gathered more than fifty thousand in Times Square during the Democratic Convention. In Washington, Tim McCarthy produced a video and Greg Scott developed a campaign to get out the vote. HRCF and NGLTF coordinated platform testimony, convention activities, and national press coverage on AIDS and gay rights issues. ACT UP women campaigned successfully to make the Centers for Disease Control expand the definition of AIDS to encompass medical conditions experienced by women. In Houston, ACT UP organized a large health care–focused demonstration that drew some two thousand participants, myself among them. This peaceful demonstration ended at the Houston Astrodome with a vicious police-initiated charge into the crowd, during which I narrowly avoided injury and in which I saw scores of colleagues and friends get beaten by baton-flailing riot police while they lay on the ground, backed away, or tried to avoid being hit.

Meanwhile, the antigay right threatened to increase its ballot crusade, and also embarked on the strategy of running stealth Christian candidates for local school boards and municipal offices. They turned school curricula into battlegrounds as they fought value-neutral sex education and the teaching of diversity.

Throughout 1992, these issues generated more concern and occupied more attention than the military ban. Thus, when the military ban emerged as the first gay issue of the Clinton administration, many gay activists were surprised and upset. As ACT UP member Rebecca Hensler from San Francisco said, "Many of us felt betrayed because we'd been on the front line with our bodies for years, and AIDS was the issue that had mobilized massive numbers of us. Suddenly the first issue championed by the gay leadership with the new administration was one that none of us had worked on." This breach of trust was an obstacle the mainstream movement never overcame. Because the most mobilized lesbian and gay activists were so unprepared to shift their focus, the gay movement was unable to rally strong constituent pressure and grassroots activism against the ban.

Everybody jockeys for access and power during a campaign, and this was especially so in 1992, as the unfamiliar glare of media attention suddenly seemed to follow gay activists everywhere. National reputations were made that year for individuals who had in fact not been significant forces in the national gay and lesbian rights movement. David Mixner gained nationwide prominence because of his personal friendship with Bill Clinton. The outspoken activist Bob Hattoy, a Clinton environmental adviser thrust into a leadership role on AIDS policy as a person with AIDS, gained national prominence from a moving speech at the Democratic Convention. The fundraiser Andrew Barrer appeared at the end of 1992 as a major broker between the movement and the Democratic Party; he went on to serve a term as chief of staff to the former AIDS czar Kristine Gebbie. Seattle ACT UP members Wayne Turner and Steve Michael emerged as new voices on the direct-action movement. But for most of 1992 the jockeying mattered little, because there was so much work to be done, and movement activists took on different pieces of the workload.

One area in which the contest for prestige and clout did matter, however, was the relationship between the gay movement and the campaign of Bill Clinton. Although many gay individuals were involved in the campaign and eventually served on the transition team, leaders of the organized gay and lesbian movement did not enjoy direct access. Communication between gay organizations and campaign officials was mediated through individuals with a role in both, like Mixner and Randy Klose. Even those who were tapped by the campaign to draft briefing papers and policy positions on gay and AIDS issues, like Ben Schatz, now the executive director of the Gay and Lesbian Medical Association, had their approach to the campaign overseen by Mixner and senior policy staff. The wealthy donors in Los Angeles known as ANGLE (Access Network for Gay and Lesbian Equality) enjoyed great access; they held meetings with Bill Clinton and all the Democratic candidates to ask for assurances on gay rights issues. But this elite network claimed no accountability to a broader gay community. While some of ANGLE's members served on the HRCF board, beyond that affiliation the members made no formal attempt to communicate the results of their meetings to organizations like NGLTF, Lambda, ACLU, or AIDS Action Council. The heads of our gay organizations heard information about meetings with presidential candidates informally, at dinners with one another, from gossip on the phone with wealthy donors, or by reading the gay press reports.

Incredibly, while gay leaders met often to coordinate demonstrations and actions, we never met to coordinate the agenda we would present to the Clinton or Bush campaign. Instead, individual organizations lobbied each campaign on their respective issues. For example, AIDS groups pushed hard for Clinton to deliver an AIDS-specific policy address, something he eventually did late in the campaign year. ACT UP pressed Clinton to commit to a Manhattan Project and to appoint an AIDS czar, and was joined in these calls by NGLTF and HRCF, which also pressed for commitments on civil rights measures and the military policy.

In turn, the Clinton campaign handled the gay and lesbian movement organizations skillfully—avoiding and ignoring the full gay rights agenda while throwing bones to each faction. This careful management led Fred Barnes to write approvingly, in the spring of 1992, that "there's a difference between pandering and promising . . . [I]t turns out that although Clinton is eager to curry favor with practically everyone, there's a limit. He's been careful not to compromise himself by endorsing the agenda of every Democratic interest group, most of them liberal . . . Clinton merely panders." But the gay movement did not distinguish between the two: we interpreted pandering as promising.

After Clinton's election, the gay and lesbian movement greatly miscalculated both the commitment of our friends and the craftiness of our enemies. Very few of us in the movement, at any level, had had direct experience in negotiating with or handling a friendly administration. Here, I think, is where we made our first mistake in the military fight. Those of us at the head of the movement failed to gather together more experienced political organizers, veterans of gay rights work in the late 1970s with the Carter administration, as well as grassroots leaders from around the country, in order to develop a strategic approach on handling the new administration. Strangely, we failed to do this even though we had a remarkable degree of unity and consensus on what we wanted. After pressing the Reagan and Bush administrations for twelve years, we were clear about our objectives in national AIDS policy, civil rights, hate and violence, and family issues.

In part, we failed because we were disarmed by the welcoming tone set by a young, hip White House staff that was not at all shocked by or hostile to gay and lesbian people. Overnight, gay donors to the Clinton campaign received invitations to attend inaugural parties, to participate in the invitation-only economic summit held in Arkansas during the transition period, to join transition teams, to write position papers on gay rights issues, to consider being appointees, and even to have dinner with Bill and Hillary. Overnight, people who were gay-friendly were appointed to head federal agencies; some (like Donna Shalala) were rumored to be gay (and denied it, as she did in media interviews before her confirmation). Overnight, a complacent and smug White House press corps, which had never in the first six years of the Reagan administration asked Reagan a direct question about AIDS, which had never brought up a gay rights issue in a press conference or interview with George Bush—this sleepy establishment giant also discovered us.

After the election, a large number of gay and lesbian professionals across the country seemed suddenly to catch Potomac fever; they began to jockey for position and power as soon as the election was over. People who had never been involved in national gay and lesbian politics came out, or moved to Washington in search of work. Adopting a suggestion by Andrew Barrer, the three national political organizations (HRCF, NGLTF, and the GLVF) formed a national project, called Coalition '93, to promote the appointment of openly gay and lesbian candidates to administration positions. In retrospect, we would have been better served had we organized meetings with gay organizations and involved regional activists to figure out what issues to bring before the new administration. Instead, the Coalition '93 strategy involved too many talented people in the role of headhunters rather than policy advocates. It made our relations with the administration at once too cozy and too compromised.

Meanwhile, for the wealthy gay elite, Washington suddenly became the place to live or to be seen. Following their historic role in raising money during the 1992 election, these donors began to flex their newly developed political muscles by taking seats on national boards and calling for drastic mergers and other changes in the structure of the movement. During the inaugural parties, David Geffen and Barry Diller sightings were reported around town. Geffen was rumored to have taken an apartment in Washington. His former political deputy, a man named Bob Burkett, appeared, for the first time ever, at the offices of HRCF and NGLTF to convey Geffen's interest in the military issue, and hint that vast sums of money might be available for the effort. David Mixner shuttled back and forth, enjoying his sudden elevation to a national leadership role through the media opportunities gained by his FOB name-dropping. Donors in New York began to discuss the possibility of founding an ANGLE-style political club in that city. Computer-industry multimillionaire Tim Gill from Colorado emerged as a major national powerbroker, by virtue of his generous pledges of more than $100,000 at one time. It could have been an extraordinary moment; the people with money were finally interested in backing gay rights! The movement would be able to marshal the resources it needed. But like all funds, much of this money came with strings attached. The newly empowered wealthy folk in our movement had their own notions and proposals about how the movement should work and what it should focus on. Merging all Washington organizations, passing a federal gay rights bill, pushing for gay appointees were three examples. History shows that these notions were incredibly naïve and ignored the reality of a far more strategic-minded religious right, which built its base outside Washington.

We were so impressed by the friendly treatment the White House offered that we took to heart campaign promises about which we should have been suspicious. Another consequence of this blind optimism was that we underestimated the strength of the antigay movement. The new administration was, after all, entering a Washington whose permanent government culture is quite conservative. The residue of twelve years would not be wiped away in a few months. Congress had proved itself our enemy, even under a Democratic majority. Yet we foolishly ignored these realities and pushed for an executive order on the military policy.

The weekend after the 1992 election, Tim McFeeley convened a special board meeting of the Human Rights Campaign Fund to discuss that organization's relationship to and expectation of the new administration. McFeeley invited Mixner to speak. At this point, November 1992, Mixner was exuding confidence that the military policy was "a done deal." He made that assurance to me on the phone and repeated it to the HRCF board members at the meeting. He had, by that time, positioned himself as the principal conduit of information and dialogue between the movement and the Clinton transition team. Whether the team saw him as such, I do not know; movement activists did. In the

months after the election, and before the military fight erupted into the
public eye in mid-January, Mixner was so confident of the executive
order that he was barely talking about it to the Washington organizations. Instead, he was proposing the creation of some new civil rights
coalition, a "campaign" that would forcefully push for the languishing
federal Gay and Lesbian Civil Rights Bill, which had been introduced
every year since 1975 but had never advanced. As he said to me in a
phone call, in late November 1992, he believed we had a "window of
opportunity" to pass a federal bill during this administration. He told
me he could raise several million dollars for such an effort; and he had a
vision for organizing a campaign to pass such a bill. I noted to him that,
since I was leaving my job in a few days, it would be better for him to
work with incoming director Torie Osborn and the current deputy
director for policy, Peri Jude Radecic. In fact, Mixner did meet with
Radecic and McFeeley to discuss his ideas for the new Gay Rights Bill
campaign.

Mixner's assurances to us were certainly based on ones he had been
given by senior Clinton staff and perhaps by the President-elect himself. Yet as someone privy to the arguments that went on inside the
Clinton campaign, he above all others knew that opposition to a presidential executive order on gays in the military was stiff and building.
Fred Barnes reported in *The New Republic* that between the November
election and January 17, 1993, when Clinton held a top-level meeting
with his senior staff on the issue, opposition to lifting the ban had
mounted dramatically. According to Barnes, the lawyer appointed to
develop a new policy, John Holum, "proposed to finesse the executive
order. Instead, the President would simply order his defense secretary to
drop the ban and halt efforts to expel homosexuals currently in the
military." Barnes went on to note that the plan drew sharp criticism
from widely different sources. Mixner was reported to have phoned in
his objection and argued that nothing short of an executive order would
work, while Les Aspin, Clinton's secretary of defense, was said to fear a
congressional reversal of such an order. That this internal opposition
was brewing well before the issue erupted in the public eye is now clear.
How widely it was discussed among gay organizations and the military
coalition is unclear.

Complicating the picture was the duplication of effort. Several
squads of people were simultaneously, without effective coordination or
agreement, and sometimes in conflict, working on the same issue.
Among these were: the Military Freedom Project (comprising HRCF,

NGLTF, ACLU, NOW, and other partners); the newly formed Ad Hoc Military Group, led by gay rights lawyers Marc Wolinsky (of New York's Wachtel, Lipton) and Mary Newcombe (an attorney from Lambda's LA office), which drafted a proposed executive order; John Holum, assigned by the Clinton team to draft the new policy on the military; Les Aspin; the Joint Chiefs; the Gay and Lesbian and Bisexual Veterans; Mark Agrast and former Studds aide Kate Dyer for Gerry Studds's office; Barney Frank's staff; Sam Nunn's staff; Bob Dole's staff; and an assortment of people with opinions on the subject, from Clinton's friend Peter Edelman, who solicited individual input from gay rights expert Chai Feldblum, to gay rights lawyers Tom Stoddard, Nan Hunter, and the ACLU's Bill Rubenstein.

Given the intense involvement of Mixner and other gay activists in the postelection transition period, I was startled to read a large *New York Times* story by the gay reporter Jeffrey Schmalz that quoted several leaders, including Mixner, as among those suggesting that the national movement had been "asleep at the switch" and been broadsided by the opposition to the military policy. In fact, our complacency had been fostered by the repeated assurances of Mixner and others in contact with the administration—assurances that we should have questioned. As former director Tim McFeeley wrote in a memorandum dated February 11, 1993, to the HRCF board of directors and governors, "On November 11 (Veterans' Day) after [Keith] Meinhold secured a TRO [Temporary Restraining Order] against the DOD [Department of Defense] and was returned to duty, the mainstream press picked up on this issue and in a series of press conferences and encounters Clinton and Stephanopolous consistently maintained a lift-the-ban position. General Powell and others including Nunn began drawing the line in the sand. This led, I believe, to Holum's attempt to finesse the issue, but we were repeatedly assured that Clinton would fulfill his promise and end the discharges within days of taking office."

The truth is that our leaders in Washington relied on these assurances to a fault. We ignored clear signals that the administration was deeply divided on how to handle the issue, and that congressional opponents were simply biding their time for an all-out attack. In December 1992, at the request of Peter Edelman, Chai Feldblum drafted a memorandum outlining the likely political consequences for the administration of lifting the ban. Relying on her extensive knowledge of how gay issues play on Capitol Hill, Feldblum argued that without a clear head-count indicating support in Congress, an executive order would be dangerous because it could be overturned and a tough antigay policy legislated. She distributed the memorandum to staffers at Gerry Studds's office, to NGLTF and HRCF staff, to Tom Stoddard, and to the ACLU, and further raised the concerns at a January conference call among members of the Ad Hoc Military Group and the Military Freedom Project about the executive order strategy. The consensus of the participants in the call was that the movement should continue to press for an executive order.

Meanwhile, bitter fights were taking place inside the White House and Pentagon. Some have been reported by journalists like Fred Barnes and Elizabeth Drew, but most have not. The true role of those who undermined the Clinton promise has yet to come out, as does the full story of gay and lesbian manipulation. For example, the roles of central Clinton advisers like George Stephanopolous, Anthony Lake, Paul Begala, Morton Halperin, and Bruce Lindsey are far less known. What is clear is that, by mid-January 1993, the issue had become explosive for the administration and for the movement. Senator Sam Nunn, inspired in part by his homophobia and by pettiness at having been denied the office of secretary of defense, announced that he opposed lifting the ban. Colin Powell started to speak up against a new policy.

By the time we became aware that our complacency about the White House commitment to an executive order was mistaken, it was too late to do anything but tread water. On January 24, 1993, Les Aspin was asked on a Sunday morning news program about a memorandum written by him to President Clinton that had been leaked to the press. The Aspin memorandum argued that the move to lift the ban would likely be challenged by Congress, and that the Senate majority leader, George Mitchell, estimated that only thirty of the senators would support the President. According to McFeeley's memorandum, starting on January 25 the phone systems at the White House and Senate were swamped with calls protesting the President's decision to lift the ban. This wave of public reaction was carefully orchestrated by the right and was never matched by gay rights advocates. Although HRCF, NGLTF, and other groups scrambled to react, calling a press conference, organizing phone banks to generate letters and phone calls from members, delivering cables from constituents to members of Congress, the damage had been done, and the President retreated.

On January 29, Clinton announced that he had reached a compromise with Nunn for a six-month delay, during which a Department of Defense Military Task Force would study changes in the antigay policy.

Notably, our movement leaders seemed not to be in the middle of this decision-making process. The compromise was crafted by Morton Halperin, the former head of the ACLU's Washington legislative office, who served as an assistant to Les Aspin for several months. Informal representatives of the gay and lesbian community—Feldblum, Barney Frank and Gerry Studds, David Mixner, and a handful of others—had more contact with the new administration on this issue than the people who purportedly "represented" the gay and lesbian community nationally or represented military veterans themselves. Much as we may disagree with, be frustrated by, or feel let down by the national gay and lesbian political groups, they have an accountability for their actions that is sorely missing among individuals who position themselves to speak for the broader community. There is no way to avoid the reality that skilled advisers will be sought out by politicians and candidates, and that information-gathering and decision-making processes are often more informal than not. But this truth merely places a greater obligation on those who have political access to ensure that their representation of our community is based in reality. Unfortunately, far too many gay and lesbian individuals in positions of leadership operate as lone wolves, and do not consult with, involve, much less inform, their counterparts in other organizations, and their allies. The withholding or selective release of information is part of the game of power in Washington.

The creation of the Campaign for Military Service provides another illustration of the poor communication and the distrust with which our gay leaders operated in this critical moment. CMS was a last-resort strategy, devised in late January and early February 1993, to change the political momentum of this issue. On the intentions of those who pushed for it, I can only speculate, because I watched its formation from afar; without question there is more to the story than meets the eye. At the time it happened, I believed that CMS was a conscious strategy by some Los Angeles–based donors and activists, like Mixner, to create a new national organization they could control.

CMS was formed by people with very different and conflicting political agendas. One set was made of Clinton administration strategists, like Paul Begala and Bob Shrum, whose interest was to protect the President, to provide cover and support for the policy. Another group pushing for the project comprised wealthy gay donors—Barry Diller, David Geffen, among others—a number of whom were new to national gay and lesbian politics. Their interest strikes me as a drive to assert power in the movement, to do damage control of an embarrassing situation, and perhaps to use their considerable influence with the administration to broker a deal. A third group of people pushing for the formation of an autonomous CMS were gay rights activists fed up with the national gay political organizations—frustrated by what they perceived as the ineffectuality of HRCF and NGLTF and stymied by their own lack of influence and control over the national organizations. This group comprised people with a variety of interests.

CMS seems to have been born in the course of one week, late in January, after Clinton announced his six-month waiting period compromise with Sam Nunn. Two of the early meetings at which CMS was conceived were held at the home of Democratic Party consultant Bob Shrum, organized no doubt at the behest of White House political operatives. The first, on the evening of Friday, January 29, 1993, was attended by Bob Burkett (then adviser to David Geffen), Barry Diller, William Waybourn, Mark Mellman, David Craine, Hillary Rosen, Ellen Malcolm, Tim McFeeley, and Bill Rubenstein. Lesbian and gay veterans, congressional representatives interested in the issue, and NGLTF were not involved. Paul Begala arrived late, after a number of participants had left. At this initial meeting, the discussion centered on the need for more grassroots mobilization to encourage constituent support for lifting the ban. Diller and Geffen's representative pledged financial support to do the work, and the national gay groups were assigned the task of eliciting letters and phone calls. A follow-up meeting was held at Shrum's house on February 3, 1993, attended by the original participants, joined by Tom Stoddard, David Mixner, and Peri Jude Radecic.

These meetings established a number of interesting dynamics, which ultimately sabotaged the effectiveness of the Campaign for Military Service. For one, the process took place completely independently of the Military Freedom Project coalition, which included a number of other groups whose involvement was crucial; namely, gay veterans and legal groups like Lambda and the National Lawyers Guild. Second, while all the participants at these elite meetings agreed that a special military-focused campaign was needed to lobby, raise grassroots support, and wage a media and public relations campaign, the participants did not agree on who should control the new campaign. Those most in favor of creating it as an autonomous entity were unhappy with the existing national political organizations: they thought HRCF had mediocre staff and wasted time and money; they thought NGLTF lacked talent, was too poorly funded, and was too radical. These critics did not want to house the CMS within these existing structures. They in effect created a new group, which they controlled. Third, certainly the Clinton administration liaisons and perhaps the newly energized gay activists, like Diller, were more interested in doing the expedient and effective thing, and less interested in its long-term consequence for the gay movement. They did not care who did it, where it resided, or who ran it: they just wanted to defend the President and win the short-term battle. Finally, a range of turf-related tensions simmered under the surface at these meetings. HRCF and NGLTF, with their own history of competition with each other, now feared the consequences of a third permanent national organization in Washington. They saw the LA donors move to create CMS as an effort to destabilize them. Thus, they pushed to make the campaign a coalition among a wide range of groups, with its own special staff, but a staff that would be paid for and funneled through either of their groups. Meanwhile, other tensions simmered. The ACLU Lesbian and Gay Rights Project competed with the others for donors and movement attention; Tom Stoddard had left Lambda angered at how he felt the board and some staff had treated him, which may explain Lambda's absence from these early meetings; Mixner seems to have been interested in using the moment to enhance his stature as a major player.

By the time the second meeting came around, distrust among gay and lesbian participants was rampant. On Sunday, January 31, two days after the first meeting, the *New York Times* had run Jeffrey Schmalz's piece citing widespread anger at the national organizations over their handling of the military campaign. The piece quoted Tom Stoddard as saying that the national gay movement lacked the skills to deal with the crises it faced. The piece provoked a great deal of anger and resentment among the staff of national gay organizations. I called Jeff Schmalz to voice my criticism about the factual inaccuracies of his piece and the obvious bias his story registered against national groups. He heard me out and said he had only repeated what many different critics had expressed to him. Several weeks later, I called Tom Stoddard to say how offended I had been by his comments. I told him I felt he was being manipulated by people who wanted to create a permanent third organization in Washington, and urged him to be sensitive to that perception among the existing gay groups. Tom assured me that a permanent organization was not his intention.

In fact, fears about the hidden agendas of many people in these early meetings were compounded when participants at the second meeting on February 3 discovered that Tom Stoddard had already been asked by Bill Rubenstein of the ACLU to head up the still-in-discussion coalition. This caught Tim McFeeley and HRCF representatives completely by surprise and bred enormous mistrust about who was behind the CMS and why it was being organized. In a later interview, Stoddard told me that he had been informally approached by Rubenstein about his interest in directing the newly formed campaign and was as surprised as everyone else by how quickly the entire process moved. Whatever happened, within a week, Stoddard had become the CMS coordinator, an office had been procured, staff hired, and another national gay rights organization temporarily came into being.

CMS failed for three major reasons: timing, trust, and strategy. While it scrambled to hire staff, raise money, craft a strategy, and begin its work, weeks passed, and the story unfolded without an effective gay and lesbian response. If the idea of CMS had been hatched and implemented two months earlier, the effort might have succeeded. But by the time CMS was formed, the die was cast: powerful political forces had lined up against lifting the ban. Antigay forces had activated networks that CMS was trying to create from scratch, and flooded Congress with negative mail. Senators and members of Congress had taken a position, or been inundated with so much antigay mail that they dared not take a pro-gay rights position. Cowed by his lack of military service and tarred by the label "draft dodger," the President was immediately on the defensive. He kept switching his position to try to appease his critics, a tactic that backfired each time, while a new White House staff showed its inexperience at every step.

Second, because CMS was created in an atmosphere of tension among existing organizations, its staff spent a tremendous amount of time on movement infighting. Serious disagreements erupted over who should be doing what. Work was poorly coordinated among organizations; members of the MFP felt pushed to the sidelines and were frustrated while lobbyists and strategists for CMS itself felt hamstrung by their inability to control and dictate the conduct of the campaign. Had people in the broader movement trusted what CMS was intended to do—and had they trusted the people at CMS more—the result might have been different.

In addition, CMS chose strategies that reflected how out of touch its Washington-oriented staff was with the broader lesbian and gay community. CMS assumed that the masses of gay people understood why the military ban needed to be lifted, and that they supported it. This miscalculation led the campaign to do inadequate public education about the issue. Some of the best education in the military fight came not from CMS, but from the pen of Andrew Sullivan at *The New Republic,* whose editorials and commentary brought great eloquence and urgency to the effort.

Most gay and lesbian people had not really thought about the military policy, and until the publication of Shilts's *Conduct Unbecoming,* in 1993, no one had explained to the nation its destructive impact. What ordinary gay people knew about the policy came from media coverage of individual lawsuits brought by discharged veterans. And although every gay person agreed that the treatment of gay service members was appalling and wrong, not everyone agreed that lifting the ban should be the top priority of the movement. The MFP had never done the widespread and necessary public education. So when massive media coverage began in January 1993, and when virulently antigay arguments began to be raised to keep the ban, most gay people were angry. How could the movement have chosen so weak an issue to bring up as the first thing out of the chute? Why hadn't the movement focused on AIDS and health care, an issue that was a top priority for large numbers of gay, bisexual, and lesbian people?

CMS never addressed this confusion. It simply assumed that everyone who was gay or lesbian would rally behind the lavender flag. At the March on Washington, appeals to support CMS were poorly presented: a symbolic color guard of gay service members carrying the flag may have been an image aimed for the straight television audience, but it did little to inspire the hundreds of thousands of gay, lesbian, and bisexual people on the Mall or watching at home. The mother of the murdered gay sailor Allen Schindler, in fact, made the most moving appeal. CMS appealed to patriotism, duty, and gay and lesbian valor—important to conservatives but not compelling to the ears of most gay people. These issues were not even the ones on which the debate was conducted.

In short, the major reason that CMS failed lay in the very seeds of its creation. The fact that a separate political operation like CMS was needed reflected a profound lack of faith among many gay and lesbian activists in the effectiveness of the existing national political organizations. The formation and ultimate failure of CMS is a powerful morality play whose lesson is that a movement divided among itself cannot win. CMS was an inning of Machiavellian gamesmanship played by a small group of elite-oriented gay men and women. Because of the failure of these individuals to utilize an inclusive, democratic, and honest process, the organization they created was handicapped from the outset by interorganizational warfare, duplication of effort, and waste.

The military campaign pointed out the enormous weakness of the national gay political movement—in structure, manner of organization, skill level and resources. Also, CMS starkly revealed the movement's fallacy *du jour:* that people as despised as we are will win if we merely play the backroom, deal-cutting game that our straight "friends" tell us we must play. In reality, deals work when people have a good hand—and the gay movement has a very weak hand to play. Before we can make clever compromises, we must organize ourselves into a more powerful movement. The consequence of the first lesson from the military defeat is practical; it requires us to discuss and debate the reorganization of our mode of work in Washington, and beyond. And I think our experience requires us to negotiate a new relationship of trust among ourselves. The import of the second lesson is ethical; it calls on us to examine how our infatuation with the mainstream resulted in compromising the value we hold most dearly as gay and lesbian people: the principle that we should be able to be out of the closet without penalty. We must ask, Is virtual equality adequate compensation for mainstream tolerance?

WHERE DOES THIS LEAVE US?

In a sweeping essay titled "The Politics of Homosexuality," written in the midst of this political storm on gays in the military, Andrew Sullivan defined what he saw as the conservative, radical, moderate, and liberal politics of homosexuality. Finding weaknesses in each, Sullivan proposed a modified liberal politics under which the gay movement would focus solely on ending government-supported discrimination. Sullivan argued that narrowing our focus to such "public" discrimination "tackles the heart of homophobia while leaving homophobes their freedom. It allows homosexuals to define their own future and their own identity and does not place it in the hands of the other. It makes a clear, public statement of equality, while leaving all the inequalities of emotion and passion to the private sphere, where they belong. It does not legislate private tolerance, it declares public equality. It banishes the paradigm of victimology and replaces it with one of integrity." From this focus on public discrimination, Sullivan concluded that the two most important issues on the gay and lesbian movement's agenda were the military's ban and government's denial of gay-lesbian marriage.

To Sullivan, the fight to end military discrimination provided the gay movement its best and most clear-cut opportunity to tackle government-sanctioned discrimination. He argued that the "real political power" of the military debate

> comes from its symbolism. The acceptance of gay people at the heart of the state, at the core of the notion of patriotism, is anathema to those who wish to consign homosexuals to the margins of society. It offends conservatives by the simplicity of its demands, and radicals by the traditionalism of the gay people involved; it dismays moderates, who are forced to publicly discuss this issue for the first time; and it disorients liberals, who find it hard to fit the cause simply into the rubric of minority politics. . . .
>
> By conceding, as the military has done, the excellent service that many gay and lesbian soldiers have given to their country, the military has helped shatter a thousand stereotypes about their nature and competence. By focusing on the mere admission of homosexuality, the ban has purified the debate into a matter of the public enforcement of homophobia. Unlike anti-discrimination law, the campaign against the ban does not ask any private citizens to hire or fire anyone of whom they do not approve; it merely asks public servants to behave the same way with avowed homosexuals as with closeted ones.

History shows that Sullivan's analysis was quite idealized, if well stated. Ultimately, the campaign to reform the military led to a more pernicious code than the one we sought to eradicate. In essence, we replaced the "don't do" policy with a "don't tell" policy. Not only was the contradiction between excellent performance by gay service members and their dismissal for homosexual status reinforced (both by the President's new policy and by the congressional re-enactment of the old ban's language that homosexuality was "incompatible" with military service), but the Clinton policy went beyond sexual conduct to stigmatize mere declarations of homosexual desire.

Under the new policy, what Sullivan called the "mere admission of homosexuality" can trigger an investigation that may result in dismissal. In addition, under the new policy, homosexual acts are redefined to include nonsexual acts of affection between same-sex persons; antigay investigations are still allowed, and wide discretion in launching them is given to commanders. The abusive tactics of military investigators— thoroughly documented by Shilts and the MFP—are both legally allowed and explicitly affirmed.

What Sullivan and others saw as the perfect coming-of-age issue for gay politics, an issue that updated Cold War myths about homosexual disloyalty to the state with the image of the all-American gay conservative warrior, played out in a manner that neither he nor others could have predicted. Concessions of gay and lesbian valor and patriotism, made by Generals Norman Schwarzkopf and Colin Powell at the Senate hearings in July 1993, were accompanied by fascinating arguments that open homosexuality undermines heterosexual male bonding, a bonding that was euphemistically called "unit cohesion." The central obstacle to allowing gays to serve openly became not our competency to serve, but the subversiveness of our sexuality itself.

Again and again, the country heard its top generals testify that the problem was not gayness but the open admission of gayness: that open acceptance of gay people would destroy the platonic male-male heroism on which the military depends (some straight guys might not protect a gay guy in a battle), that it would undermine discipline by introducing the uncontrollable factor of love on the battlefield. The entire issue made explicit the extent to which, in the eyes of straight men, the essence of their male-bonding lay in the forcible suppression of undercurrents of homosexual desire. The military debates actually demonstrated the provocative thesis of Eve Kosofsky Sedgwick, that the homosocial basis of society requires the repression of homosexual desire between men. In *Between Men: English Literature and Male Homosocial Desire*, Sedgwick argued that the repression of male homosexuality is the root of compulsory heterosexuality and determines the role women play as buffers between men. In a strange way, Sedgwick and the military agreed: the suppression of the homosexual was essential to the sanctity of male-to-male relationships.

That this debate occurred, and that it focused so directly on issues of male sexuality, with detailed discussions of close quarters in submarines, communal showers, wartime camaraderie and interdependence, and male-male love was astonishing and ultimately helpful in making gay male sexuality (and, to a lesser extent, lesbian sexuality) comprehensible. I agree with Sullivan and others who say that the very occurrence of the debate was a victory for our movement because it focused on so many of the "real issues at stake in dealing with homosexuals." For the first time, a national conversation took place on the subject of how homosexual and heterosexual people get along when the sexuality of the former is openly acknowledged. By the end, the national conversation had exposed the real reason we are denied genuine equality: heterosexual culture's deep-seated sexual anxiety.

While the occurrence of the conversation itself was a good thing, the worst consequence was that it raised fears we did not adequately address. In the scores of television debates, editorials, commentaries, opinion pieces, and polls on the issue of gays in the military, few commentators named and tried to challenge the heterosexual anxiety that ran through the entire proceedings. Of the hundreds of stories about the military policy, the sexual anxiety that lay at the root of the resistance was analyzed in only a handful. Instead of answering the irrational and sexual, gay spokespersons focused on the rational and legal. We waged a classic public policy fight, arguing a reasonable position with great skill. (Tom Stoddard, the director of the CMS, is one of the most effective media spokesmen in the gay movement.) But the issue raised more than a policy question; it touched upon the anxiety in American society about our definition of heterosexual manhood.

Beyond the drama of organizational tension, turf war, and ego-driven power plays is the larger story of how difficult the pursuit of the mainstream is for lesbians and gay men. On an issue that many gay activists regarded as ideal for presenting our case for equal treatment, we were squashed by an opposition whose arguments the movement is still unprepared to answer: about the interaction of lesbian and gay sexuality with heterosexuality, about the meaning of heterosexual masculinity and manhood, about the relationship between gay and lesbian equality and racial prejudice, and about the morality or immorality of homosexual people themselves.

CHAPTER SIX

BEYOND RIGHTS AND MAINSTREAMING

There's an idea that there's this great mainstream,
which may be wide but is shallow and slow-moving.
It's the tributaries that have the energy.

—*Grace Paley*

In many ways, the military fiasco of 1993–1994 revealed the hoax of our mainstreaming. In that political loss, we learned that we had neither overcome the negative cultural images of homosexuality nor created a movement powerful enough to exert its muscle in a major domestic policy battle. Many of us viewed the fight to lift the ban as a logical step in our civil rights strategy, yet despite the years of work by gay veterans who brought lawsuits to challenge the policy, despite the political activity of the Military Freedom Project, despite the visibility of the issue in the 1992 campaign, the large 1993 March on Washington, and even a friendly administration, we ran up against the most abject stereotypes of gay men and lesbians. When soldiers began talking about showers and foxholes, whatever mainstream legitimacy we had assumed, whatever straight acceptance we thought we had earned, vanished without a trace. Arguing this undeniably square issue in the language of fairness and civil rights, we were brought face to face with our essential queerness, that which is most marginalized—our sexualities. The military fight of 1993 and 1994 reaffirmed the ban on gay people in the military (banning status), and added new restrictions to the antigay codes of the military (banning conduct). Today, someone can be kicked out of the armed services for being gay, engaging in gay sex, acting gay, declaring he or she is gay, or for being perceived to have done so.

Given this experience and the virtual equality that the pursuit of mainstreaming has brought us, I believe we must question whether the civil rights paradigm is the best one for us to adopt in our struggle for genuine gay and lesbian freedom. It seems heretical to argue that we must replace a strategy that does work in part, but our experience with political mainstreaming at the national level suggests that the gay movement needs a fundamental shift in order to achieve valid change in our status. We must supplement the limited politics of civil rights with a broader and more inclusive commitment to cultural transformation.

The tension between civil rights and social change has long been argued among us. Both visions have contributed to gay and lesbian progress, but civil rights politics have predominated. I believe this was logical; it was dictated by our characterization as criminal, ill, and somehow less than human. The urgency of fair treatment grew with the spread of AIDS and with its exploitation by the right. But our movement's abandonment of the politics of liberation for the more limited politics of civil rights led us to the insecure status we now enjoy. Virtual equality is the best that the politics of civil rights can deliver on its own. The gay liberation call for cultural honesty about homosexuality has turned into a gay rights movement capable only of "winning" a new code of silence: don't ask, don't tell. The goal to liberate the homosexual in every one of us is now phrased as the modest right to live without discrimination based on homosexual orientation. And the feminist critique of family and gender roles, which was at the heart of gay and lesbian liberation, has turned into our wholesale reproduction of family in gay and lesbian drag.

What gay political history illustrates is that a rights-oriented movement can coexist with prejudice against lesbians and gay men. It can even advance while leaving homophobia intact. This is possible because civil rights can be won without displacing the moral and sexual hierarchy that enforces antigay stigmatization: you do not have to recognize the fundamental humanity of gay people in order to agree that they should be treated equally and fairly under the law. My recognition of the limits of civil rights does not, however, lead me to reject such an approach entirely; a focus on legal and political rights is essential to gay and lesbian civic equality. What I urge instead is expansion: gay civil rights must be seen as part of a broader focus on human rights, sexual and gender equality, social and economic justice, and faith in a multiracial society. As some of us enjoy a seat at the table, our movement must ask itself tough questions about what this access, visibility, and clout mean for the majority of our people. On the crudest level of power politics, it is clear that gay mainstreaming will remain partial and provisional until the underlying religious, moral, and cultural prejudices that stigmatize gay men, lesbians, and bisexuals are transformed. Our movement must strive beyond personal gain to an institutional transformation, beyond mainstreaming ourselves into the center to transforming the mainstream.

Unlike gay rights, gay liberation stands for a broader set of cultural values—like political freedom for all, social justice, and the rebuilding of human community among gay, straight, and bisexual people of all colors, religions, and ethnicities. It also challenges us to articulate new codes of ethics, morality, and individual responsibility. The paradigm shift liberation requires is from the political to the cultural. Rather than rejecting the ghetto, our subculture, or queer forms of expression, thought, and art as byproducts of our victimization, we should see them as keys to our freedom. These queer cultural tributaries embody the threat we pose to the heterosexual order. That gay people are so universally regarded as a threat to be harshly suppressed suggests that gay and lesbian culture contains ideas that are deeply transformational—and, I believe, redemptive—to the political, moral, and social order now in place.

THE CIVIL RIGHTS FRAMEWORK

What are the limits of the civil rights strategies we have pursued and where do we go from here? For one, civil rights are principally mechanisms to gain access, not means to implement fundamental social change. For gay and lesbian people from the outer margins of our culture, simple political access and visibility in the center of society has been an important advance. But we would be short-sighted to consider it the ultimate answer to our stigmatization. The military fight teaches us that access to the electoral, legislative, or legal system is but the threshold from which we must organize to effect genuine change in the status quo. We must forge political coalitions and alliances, because we will never acquire power by operating entirely on our own.

Our political movement for over fifty years has sought integration primarily through a rights-based model. We have asserted our "right" to participate in and benefit from all aspects of civil society. Through demands pursued legally, legislatively, and politically, we have partly legitimated our status. Slogans like "We are everywhere," our attempts to become visible, to come out and speak the truth that we are already a part of society reflect the legitimation model. Conservative gay leaders have long argued that we are "just like straight people." While true to the extent that we are all human, the statement rings hollow to straights and gays alike, but for different reasons. Straight society quickly dismisses our earnest attempts at "straight acting" as just that—acting. This dismissal is reinforced in the propaganda campaigns of the right, whose aim it is to convince America how fundamentally different and depraved gay people are. Likewise, the significant number of gay people who accept the definition of queer as not normal find this argument too assimilationist and unappealing—we do not resemble the status quo and some of us do not accept it.

When we adapted the language and legal framework of the black civil rights movement to the gay and lesbian experience, we did at least three things: we found a language with which to communicate who we were, we moved closer to the center from the marginalized place where we started, and we re-created in the gay context all the problems and limitations inherent in the rights-based framework. First, we defined ourselves as a distinct minority group, not people with a medical condition. We came to understand and to represent ourselves as a people, not a perversion or a behavior. Through its emphasis on the equality of all human beings, the civil rights framework gave us what we most needed, some hope that we would one day be accepted by society as fully as we accepted ourselves. And the adaptation of the minority group model to our experience worked: we achieved some legal and legislative recognition that people ought not be stigmatized because of their sexual orientation. We came to realize that gay and lesbian people shared a common legacy of discrimination, harassment, violence, and rejection, as well as common aspirations of justice, fairness, and human dignity. By explaining our goal as justice, a value treasured by most of our neighbors and families, the civil rights framework helped make gayness itself more comprehensible to mainstream America.

Second, we organized ourselves as a movement for specific legal rights. We wrote legislation and brought lawsuits, ran for elective office, and began to register a gay vote. We argued the truth that equal protection under the law was (and often still is) denied to gay people, and we forged supportive relationships with racial, gender, and religious minorities. But all this resulted in the mainstreaming of only some gay people. Assimilation was an option for those who were willing to mute their queerness: to "not tell" or to pass. For those on the queer margin, like effeminate gay men or butch lesbians, sexual heretics, and gender rebels, the new center still offered an uncomfortable and unsafe refuge.

By adopting the civil rights framework, we have re-created the same obstacles and resistance encountered by our predecessor movements, in particular the black civil rights movement and the women's movement. As a result of the revisionism of the conservative movement and the extremist right, the civil rights paradigm has been stripped of its moral context and placed securely in a materialist context. Today, the granting of civil rights is not seen principally as a moral question of doing what is right or wrong, doing good or evil or justice or injustice. Rather, civil rights are newly defined as a reward given by society for good behavior. Such rights are deemed benefits that society grants to some of its constituents—the deserving minorities—rather than as basic human rights and values. Instead of regarding civil rights as broad and inalienable human rights to which all people are entitled, the right urges us to see them as privileges earned by "responsible" members of society. The conservative linkage of civil freedom to certain kinds of socially sanctioned behavior is especially damaging to gay people still struggling to be seen as human beings rather than as sexual acts.

One consequence of rights redefined as benefits and viewed solely through the lens of interest-group politics is that such rights can be easily eliminated when a different "cost-benefit" analysis is performed or a different political value system is in place. Moreover, the reduction of civil rights to a purely legalistic framework limits what is won.

When framed in the materialist language of law, full civil rights come to mean nothing more than access to the courts by individuals asserting a claim of discrimination. The access to the courts, legally known as a cause of action, reduces the broader idea of human rights; the idea of civil rights becomes more about the realization of access than about the institution of equity. Under a rights-based model, the social contract we seek is fulfilled by access to the system rather than actual equal treatment under it. The grant of a civil right to be free from prejudice, for example, did not eliminate acts of racial discrimination; it merely allowed access to the courts by individuals, of whatever color, who feel they have been wronged by racist actions or policies.

Even though the civil rights strategy has been far from exhausted by us, we have experienced its chief limitation: civil rights do not change the social order in dramatic ways; they change only the privileges of the group asserting those rights. Civil rights strategies do not challenge the moral and antisexual underpinnings of homophobia, because homophobia does not originate in our lack of full civil equality. Rather, homophobia arises from the nature and construction of the political, legal, economic, sexual, racial, and family systems within which we live. As long as the rights-oriented movement refuses to address these social institutions and cultural forces, we cannot eradicate homophobic prejudice.

The mainstream's answer to us has been clear: equal rights and equal protection under the law are not available to queer people. Instead, we are granted the restricted liberty of "don't ask, don't tell." This is the essence of Gingrich's policy of "toleration," a policy consistent with his voting record. In the course of fourteen years in Congress, he encountered forty-six votes on gay, lesbian, and AIDS issues. He voted against the gay community in all but seven of those instances. The idea of toleration is apparently far more limited than equal rights. Nor does toleration mean tolerance: to tolerate people means to put up with them. To be tolerant means to understand them. Neither toleration nor tolerance comes close to the liberation ideals of societal acceptance and affirmation of the human dignity and worth of lesbian and gay people. In the end, Gingrich's ambivalence toward gay and lesbian rights is as unappealing as Bill Clinton's.

The conduct and aftermath of the meeting gay leaders held with President Clinton further illustrates the limitations of civil rights. This was a meeting lesbian and gay political activists had sought for decades —the first meeting in which openly gay and lesbian leaders were welcomed through the front door of the White House. Held just a week before the Third National March on Washington, the meeting on one level marked the pinnacle of our political achievement: we had arrived. During a storm of media coverage about the President's intention to lift the ban, the meeting was seen as an affirmation of the legitimacy of the gay and lesbian movement, a sign that the President was determined to follow through on his campaign promises. In fact, the meeting has come to be a symbol for gay naïveté and powerlessness.

Taking place a month before congressional hearings on the antigay military policy and at the height of the congressional budget process, the meeting offered movement leaders an extraordinary chance to present a national agenda to the new President. By all reports, his welcome and obvious empathy caught all the gay participants off guard. HRCF's Tim McFeeley said, "[I]t was the most wonderful meeting. He could not have been more gracious. I have lobbied hundreds of straight male politicians on gay issues. And they're always twitching. They're always nervous. Bill Clinton was the coolest cucumber for a straight politician. He was fine with it. It was like talking about gay rights with you." McFeeley described the discussion gay leaders had with the President on the military as "almost nonchalant." He said, "[H]e went out of his way to assure us not to worry. And he went into all these anecdotes about how, at every ceremony, one or another uniformed person would come up to him and say, 'Thank you. You are doing the right thing.' Mostly, particularly women. It was clear to us that he felt he was doing the right thing." Others echoed McFeeley's favorable reading. The *New York Times* reported that gay leaders were "starry-eyed" after the meeting, quoting the March on Washington organizer Billy Hileman as saying, "It was the experience of a lifetime." The seasoned and usually cautious Tom Stoddard said, "I had a sense that we were being welcomed into the family that had scorned us for so long."

The meeting held difficult lessons for gay and lesbian leaders. For one, its aftermath underscored the difference between gaining access and wielding power. We got to sit with the President of the United States, but we were not able to prevent his cutting a deal that bargained away our civil rights. Despite his own sense of fairness, within three months of this meeting President Clinton had agreed to the compromise with Senator Sam Nunn that made gay soldiers' lives more uncertain. The compromise not only left the homophobic policy in place, but it allowed the military to discharge nearly the same numbers of gay service members as before it was enacted. White House access did not help our leaders prevent the administration from imposing a policy that was ultimately declared unconstitutional by a federal court on March 31, 1995.

Another difficult truth the meeting revealed is that the political clout of some of our leaders does not affect the substantive challenges we face. The President has backed away from gay and lesbian rights, following the polls, despite the presence of openly gay people throughout his administration and in the White House. Although he has made a handful of statements supportive of equal treatment for gay men and lesbians, such as a letter he sent to the Gay and Lesbian Victory Fund condemning the antigay ballot fights under way across the country, he has not shown the courage of his convictions or loyalty to his friends. Within gay communities, there was disdain for the self-congratulations of the meeting participants. Instead of educating America on the scope and serious nature of gay discrimination, the leaders at the post-meeting press conference sounded like star-struck apologists, patting each other on the back, praising Clinton, and allowing the urgent issues facing gay people to be diverted into the false issue of presidential attendance at the March on Washington.

More disturbing, the meeting proved that the message of gay and lesbian politics itself is far from clear. Americans do not understand the meaning of antigay and antilesbian discrimination. How can we say we are discriminated against as a people when we were invited to meet with the President and were allowed to dominate the airwaves on the military issue?

Finally, I think the meeting showed our lack of sophistication in staging and managing such a spectacle. The symbolism of the meeting was its most significant message. If we had spotlighted the situations of those who have been fighting prejudice based on homophobia and AIDS-phobia, we would have taken better advantage of the platform the meeting afforded. For example, what if Colonel Greta Cammermeyer, Larry Kramer, the lesbian family rights fighter Karen Thompson, and antigay violence survivor Claudia Brenner had participated in the meeting and been present at the press conference afterward? The message of the meeting would have been far less gooey.

Instead, the meeting benefited the White House. It co-opted gay leadership into silence at the instant it needed to be strident. Those who attended were immediately put in the awkward position of defending the President at the very instant he was caving in to right-wing pressure on the military. After all, a meeting at the White House was a big deal, a very public sign of support, wasn't it? This complacency showed a lack of political sophistication. As Ginny Apuzzo remarked, "I think it is very important that we spell out for our community the importance of remembering that it's easy to fight your enemies. It's not easy to fight with your friends. This administration in Washington reminds me of the first Koch administration [in New York City], where the [gay] community mistook access for responsiveness. Access! It's wonderful. I remember the first time I went to the White House. Loved it! I was so excited. You know what? It's another house. It's a nice place to send postcards from. But if you don't go in and come out with more than coffee under your belt, you've got a problem."

The Clinton meeting represented the pinnacle of what the civil rights strategy provides: political respectability. It symbolized a new level of mainstream access for gay activists, but it took place at a time when civil rights are being pummeled and redefined to mean rights for some at the expense of others. We live in a mean, anti–human rights, antigovernment climate. Ironically, this is the moment when gay people, so long estranged from definitions of human rights and civil rights, call on government to protect and defend their rights. No wonder we run into public opposition; we appear to endorse the very ideas of more government, federalism, and civil rights that many people are today rejecting. To be more effective in our quest for equal rights, we must develop the gay movement's positions on these broad policy fights. To my knowledge, no national gay organization mobilized its members against the Contract With America. Yet that ten-point program has threatening implications for gay people. Cuts in Medicare and Medicaid will hurt people with AIDS and HIV; until definitions of family include gay men and women, we can be written out of legislation; calls for an end to affirmative action and the elimination of Title IX do not bode well for a gay movement seeking workplace equity and a movement that values gender non-conformity.

If we are to adopt the civil rights framework, we must defend and define its reach. If gay organizations at the national and state level wrap themselves in the mantle of civil rights language and history, they must take clear stands on the civil rights of blacks, people of color, immigrants, and women. We must have positions on affirmative action, welfare, and economic justice. Our tendency to see ourselves as an exception, as a special category, rather than as one group of many affected by the broad civil and democratic guarantees of the Constitution backfires: we lose the respect of those who could be our allies and we play into the hands of our enemies, who argue that we are a selfish people seeking "special" protection.

While we acknowledge our genuine respect for the enormous contribution the African-American freedom movement has made to broadening the meaning of democracy for all Americans, our use of racial analogies is suspect, coming as it does from a movement deeply splintered over the relevance of racism to the fight against homophobia. Interestingly, even those who believe that the racial justice movement should be completely distinct from the gay rights movement often draw analogies in order to defend gay rights. This dichotomy—between our actions and our rhetoric—leads a largely white gay movement to sound hollow and opportunistic and fuels tremendous resentment. Examining gay and black tensions reveals that we may be too glib, because prejudice against us as gay people differs significantly from prejudice against people because of race. But if we believe our analogies, we must act as if we cared about racial discrimination as much as about homophobia. In other words, if we believe that our situation in the military is similar to that of blacks before the fifties, and if we believe that the treatment of blacks then was as wrong as the treatment of gays today, then what is our position on the continuing legacy of racial discrimination in the armed forces?

The complex experience of black gay and lesbian people is another reason wholesale analogies must be made with care. Gay rights advocates have not been as precise as we should be in our use of comparisons. On the other hand, some of the anger at the analogies itself stems from homophobia—whether it comes from Colin Powell or a local civic leader like the San Francisco School Board member Michael Lumpkin.

To a large extent, black resentment at our use of the racial analogy arises from the persistence of racism, despite the best efforts of a seasoned movement to eradicate it. The evidence of racism in American culture is today evident everywhere, from the racist parody of Judge Lance Ito by Senator Alfonse D'Amato to the serious consideration given to Charles Murray's biased theories about intelligence. Not surprisingly, the atmosphere of great racial polarization breeds anger and distrust. In particular, many African Americans feel discouraged by the strides made by nonracial interest groups while racial inequality remains pervasive and becomes less of a political priority. Black reaction to the gay use of racial analogies exploded in the public eye in 1993 during the congressional hearings on lifting the military ban, and through the divisive efforts of religious conservatives.

In the spring of 1993, at the Senate hearings on lifting the ban, a top-ranking black general who had been second in command in the Gulf War, Lieutenant General Calvin Waller, bristled at the suggestion that antigay discrimination in the military was like discrimination against blacks in the early 1900s. He said, "I had no choice regarding my race when I was delivered from my mother's womb . . . To compare my service in America's armed forces with the integration of avowed homosexuals is personally offensive to me." Colin Powell, former head of the Joint Chiefs of Staff, noted that gay people had served well, but defended their exclusion and dismissed any analogy between sexuality and race as inappropriate.

Throughout 1993, right-wing groups like the Traditional Values Coalition fomented this division, particularly through its release of the inflammatory videotape *Gay Rights, Special Rights*. Discussed at length later in this book, this video made a series of erroneous comparisons between black status and gay status, and argued that the award of gay rights would somehow diminish the realization of civil rights for truly "legitimate" minorities, like African Americans. In addition to releasing this videotape, the TVC directly funds black fundamentalist churches to organize against gay rights within the black community.

Yet despite these efforts on the part of religious conservatives, polls reveal that the black community remains fundamentally more committed to fairness than the white community. A *New York Times*/CBS News Poll "of 1154 adults conducted February 9–11 [1993 revealed that] 53% of blacks thought [gay rights] legislation was necessary, as against only 40% of whites." Polling and focus groups done among African-American voters by HRCF and NGLTF confirm strong support among black voters for nondiscrimination, but also reveal an ambivalence that black voters share with white heterosexuals. As Celinda Lake noted,

> [W]hen the issue is presented as one having to do with rights and discrimination, rather than lifestyle and orientation, African American voters tend to be more sympathetic toward the gay rights movement than is the public at large . . . A whopping 84% of African Americans nationwide believe that gays should have equal rights generally . . . Still, both focus group research and national polling data indicate that African Americans are generally unaware of the status of current civil rights laws as they pertain to gays and lesbians. Sixty-two percent of African Americans don't know that gays and lesbians are not currently covered under civil rights legislation.

Such a level of support is a hopeful sign for the gay movement, but it is not support we can take for granted. Like every other segment of the population, the African-American community is misinformed and believes many myths about the lives of gay and lesbian people. Such focus group research helps identify the kind of education we need to conduct.

Over a front-page article on June 28, 1993, a *New York Times* headline flatly declared BLACKS REJECT GAY RIGHTS FIGHT AS EQUAL TO

THEIRS. The article quoted several people, gay and straight, on their frustration with the use of racial parallels by white gay activists. While noting African-American support for nondiscrimination, the article gave the impression that a deep split existed between blacks and gays, a split into which the reality of black gay and lesbian people simply disappeared. The article quoted a black radio-show host from Chicago named Lou Palmer: "A lot of blacks are upset that the feminist movement has pimped off the black movement. Now here comes the gay movement. Blacks resent it very much, because they do not see a parallel, nor do I." More notably, the article cited Lou Sheldon, head of the Traditional Values Coalition and the right-wing strategist most behind the religious right's effort to organize black fundamentalists, as saying, "The reason gays are making parallels is that it may bring empathy from white men like me, who feel a collective sense of guilt about the way blacks have been treated. The fact remains that this is not a civil-rights issue but a moral issue."

In a *New Yorker* article titled "Blacklash," the Harvard professor Henry Louis Gates, Jr., clarified why black people were so angered at the gay movement's use of the race analogy during the military battle. According to Gates, tensions between blacks and gays are present not only among black fundamentalists, but also among black liberals. He suggested that the racial analogy is problematic in part because it compares gays to the wrong group. Antigay prejudice, he argues, is more akin to anti-Semitism than to racism. In other words, homophobia more closely resembles the cultural myths and stereotypes that confront Jews than it does the myths of racial superiority or inferiority that confront blacks.

While I believe that Gates gives short shrift to the supremacist ideology that underlies heterosexism, our movement would do well to reconsider our easy use of racial comparisons and analogies for the very reasons he outlines. Racial analogies can be crass attempts to claim a history and values of justice to which we must first ask if we are fully committed. In addition, the ranking of oppression remains a peculiar obstacle to a movement of people united by a vision of the world we want to create, not by a particular identity. This tedious tendency toward "victim" politics has been aptly skewered by conservatives and critically described by feminists like Naomi Wolf. Curiously, the newest purveyors of victim politics are the so-called AWM's, the angry white males who have returned after a twenty-year-old backlash to claim their place in the civil rights landscape. Apparently none of us has learned the fundamental lesson of oppression—that the ideal of liberty and justice for all is not demeaned by its enjoyment by one group. Rather, liberty becomes cheapened when a system structurally denies it to some so that others may benefit. Instead of wasting our energies proving to each other how victimized we are, why don't we try to imagine a world in which we can cohabit as free beings?

A second helpful distinction Gates drew revolves around the difficulty African Americans have relating to gayness, which many see as a chosen behavior. He wrote,

> Much of the ongoing debate over gay rights has fixated, and foundered, on the vexed distinction between "status" and "behavior." The paradox here can be formulated as follows: Most people think of racial identity as a matter of (racial) status, but they respond to it as behavior. Most people think of sexual identity as a matter of (sexual) behavior, but they respond to it as status. Accordingly, people who fear and dislike blacks are typically preoccupied with the threat they think blacks' aggressive behavior poses to them . . . By contrast, the repugnance that many people feel toward gays concerns, in the first instance, the status ascribed to them. Disapproval of a sexual practice is transmuted into the demonization of a sexual species.

Gates, like Sheldon, points out that the problem with analogy is not only one of accuracy, but also of morality. Both suggest that our pursuit of equal treatment under the law fails because the civil rights paradigm does not address this source of antigay prejudice: our status is loathed because of our sexual behavior.

CIVIL RIGHTS LANGUAGE AND THE SEXUAL IMPASSE

A critical limitation of the civil rights model for gay people is that it does not give us the language to address the sexual stigmatization that handicaps us; we are ultimately left arguing that sexuality should be protected because it is biologically determined. This is dangerous and unproductive, because it keeps us from tackling the cultural taboos, fears, gender rigidity, and moralism that shape our second-class status. Instead, arguments for gay and lesbian equality based on the biological basis of homosexuality actually undermine the fundamental moral equivalence of gay people: equality, dignity, and justice are human birthrights, not "benefits" society awards to those who are born with a certain gene, a particular skin color, or a particular physical anatomy.

Heterosexual culture has a very schizoid attitude toward sex. On the one hand, sexuality is the engine whose packaging drives everything from consumer culture to attendance in churches. Sex is a commodity designed, produced, and sold throughout the media to entice, motivate, and seduce us into action (mostly consumption). On the other hand, sex is the dirty little secret that can't be revealed. Admitting its true power over our lives threatens the foundations of denial on which we have built what we call social order. Laws enforcing a sexual code have been used against gay men and lesbians for decades. As recently as the 1960s it was illegal for same-sex couples to dance together. During the 1960s and 1970s laws were enforced requiring women and men to wear gender-appropriate clothing. The androgynous cultural space that allows RuPaul to sell records, and *The Crying Game* to win Oscars, is very new, and remains riddled with the titillation and taboo of novelty.

To many heterosexuals, gay people are defined by what they do, rather than as the human beings they are, and this distinction leads straights to challenge how behavior can become a civil rights issue. This question, originated by the right wing, is posed to us across the school boards and city councils of America today. To counter the equation, the gay rights movement has long strived to define gayness as an identity at once rooted in, but more significant than, our sexual behavior alone. Ask any gay, bisexual, lesbian, or transgendered person what defines us as "queer," and he or she will insist it is much more than our sexual lives. But ask any nongay person that question, and the answer rings like a bell: sex is the gay community's calling card. If it were only sex, we would be absorbed into the erotic fringe that lines the edges of the mainstream, the way prostitutes, sex industry workers, and other sexual outlaws are. The deeper threat we present to heterosexual culture lies in the disruption that our sexuality and gender nonconformity make in a society invested in rigid gender roles and the myth that the heterosexual nuclear family should be the sole form of relationship.

In 1991, I appeared on C-Span with Lou Sheldon. Produced with the Close-Up Foundation, the show featured a live town meeting with Sheldon and me in a Washington television studio speaking to high school students at four schools around the country. The kids got to ask Lou and me questions, but before they could get into it, the moderator posed basic questions to us. It was a tense moment for me. Despite many years of television experience, I had never debated Sheldon. An avuncular, balding crusader whose history in the antigay movement is long and determined, Sheldon was the state coordinator for California State Senator John Briggs in 1977–1978, managing the drive to enact the amendment that would have forbidden gay and lesbian people from being employed as schoolteachers. At the time of our debate, his organization claimed to represent twenty-five thousand churches nationwide. The Traditional Values Coalition was behind a smattering of anti-AIDS and antigay referenda in California. It championed a treatment for homosexuality called "reparative therapy," which tries to change homosexuals into heterosexuals, and has been soundly criticized by the American Psychological Association.

Whenever I brought up civil rights, such as the right to equal protection under the law in employment and access to government services, Sheldon brought up sex and AIDS. At first he started talking about anal sex, how loathsome it was, how disgusting and unnatural. He announced that gay people eat feces, put gerbils in their anal cavities, and have thousands of sexual partners in their lifetime. I was stunned, and poorly prepared to see the argument degenerate into a shouting match about gerbils. I kept saying, "You are lying; stop lying. That is not true." And he continued to smile and goad me with his twisted fantasies. The high school kids largely ignored the sexual aspect and asked us questions about equal protection, constitutional law, fairness, and morality. But Sheldon's strategy was clever, because he reinforced the link between sexual behavior and gayness.

Gay and lesbian sexuality remains the biggest obstacle to our full acceptance as human beings by the dominant heterosexual culture. We are hated because of how, with whom, and how much (mythic or real) we do it. To win against the right wing, we have to fight back on the sexual battleground, not run away from it. And to do this, we have to figure out how to talk in mixed company—heterosexual as well as across gender lines—about what sex means to us, about our sexual ethics and sexual morality, about our views on sexual promiscuity, and about our sexual secrets. This is a significant obstacle, one that lies at the heart of the sex phobia of straight culture. Indeed, some activists have observed that no legal and legislative arguments relying on the assertion of the normality of gay sexuality have yet succeeded. On the contrary, as in *Hardwick*, behavior-based arguments fail, while status-based arguments, rooted in the presentation of gay identity as a minority status, have succeeded.

What is it about our sexual selves that is so threatening to the new world order? The heterosexual norm reacts to us as if every act of homosexual sex were an act of terrorism against heterosexuality. In a way, they're right. Gay, lesbian, bisexual, and transgender sex do threaten the mythical norm, but not in ways that negate the moral worth of heterosexuals. For one, we threaten the myth of universal heterosexuality simply by our existence in every culture, color, and time; we repudiate the myth that nature is heterosexual, that there is one dimension to lust. An inverse relationship exists between the acceptance of this sexual truth by avowed heterosexuals: the stronger their avowal of heterosexuality, the less their acceptance of homosexuality. Simply by coming out of the closet to proclaim that we desire each other, we threaten a sexual norm built on the repression and denial of gay sex.

Second, we disrupt the sexist order that decrees women exist for the pleasure and service of men. In this we are a potentially transcendent movement; our full acceptance would necessitate a change in the status of women. Heterosexuality is built on certain roles for women— mother, wife, sexual object. Homosexuals by their very existence pro- pose alternatives to those roles: a man can be a mother; a lesbian can have a wife; a bisexual person illustrates the fluidity of adult sexual desire, a transvestite challenges what it means to be, act, look like a woman or a man; and a transgender person crosses all the boundaries that compulsory heterosexuality works so hard to enforce. As Monique Wittig once wrote, "Lesbians are not women," and, by paraphrase, homosexuals are not men. The gay and lesbian movement makes gender obsolete, redefines motherhood and fatherhood beyond the constriction of biology, redefines family and relationships, and, ironically, has suc- ceeded in making men as objectified as women.

Third, we are threatening because our movement represents the liberation of the most powerful and untamed motivating force in hu- man life: desire. The power of individual sexual desire leaves people uncontrollable, unpredictable, driven by forces that can be threatening and violent, as well as liberating and beautiful. Eros is a force that culture has always tried to control. For the idea of "social order" itself to exist, desire must be controlled. The history of morality-based cam- paigns—legal, cultural, and political—is the history of the futility of this kind of social control.

By extension, gay and lesbian sexuality threatens straight culture because it exposes a limit to the power of the state and the church. We are, with our bodies, engaged in an act of civil disobedience against the moral and legal authority of the church and state. Every time we make love, we challenge the power of government and religious authority to stop us. This power struggle is an old one, going all the way back to the first codification of sodomy laws by Henry VIII. What is new about the antigay crusaders we face now is that they seek to collapse the relatively fragile boundary between church and state. They use the transformative cultural of homosexuality—as they also use morality, race fear, the high divorce rate, teen pregnancy, abortion, and economic crisis—to argue for a fusion of the religious and the secular in order to preserve the status quo. Such a fusion is dangerous to the idea of civil society. In order to resist being defined by our enemies, whose portraits of us lead to rejection by the straight majority, we must wage our struggle on the cultural and sexual fronts, as well as the legal and political.

The theorists Nan Hunter and Lisa Duggan suggest that gay and lesbian people engage in a concept they term "sexual dissent," a useful concept for gay activists to wield against the moralism of antigay rhetoricians like Lou Sheldon. As Lisa Duggan writes, sexual dissent

> forges a connection among sexual expressions, oppositional politics, and claims to public space. Because sexual representations construct identities . . . restriction and regulation of sexual expression is a form of political repression aimed at sexual minorities and gender non-conformists. This is abundantly clear in conservative attacks on the arts that define homoeroticism as 'obscene' and in anti-gay campaigns that attempt to restrict the 'promotion' or 'advocacy' of homosexuality in safe-sex materials or in schools. What the right-wing wishes to eliminate is our power to invent and represent ourselves, and to define and redefine our politics. They know our public sexual expression is political, and that is how we must defend it. Rather than invoke fixed, natural identities and ask only for privacy or an end to discrimination, we must expand our right to public *sexual dissent*.

The formulation of this concept helps us to answer the main objections leveled by our opponents. Framing homosexual behavior in this way exposes that, at its core, we are dissenters from the heterosexual norm. In addition, the idea of dissent invokes the freedom of a people to be allowed to speak publicly about what they seek. Such a defense of public speech helps gay activists respond to the code of silence—the don't-tell ethos—that greets open homosexuality whenever it appears. Finally, I think sexual dissent allows straight people to comprehend why they find us so threatening, while allowing them to see clearly that our difference does not negate their own sexuality.

THE CULTURAL IS POLITICAL

Where this sexual dissent and the threat that it represents have been most visible is in the cultural arena. Although cultural strategies have yielded more progress to gay people than political or legal strategies, we have steadfastly followed the civil rights model. A critical component of building a twenty-first-century movement for gay liberation involves the integration of queer cultural and queer political strategies. Instead of rejecting the gay ghetto, or bemoaning gay and lesbian subcultures as diverting from the fundamental "normality" of all gays and lesbians, we should examine our fear at having these subcultures exposed and debated by the heterosexual order. Rather than rejecting outrageously queer forms of expression and art as evidence of our love of marginalization or proof of internalized gay victimization, we could see them as the keys for unlocking the shame and stigma that gay people must transcend in order to find freedom.

From its birth, the gay and lesbian movement has sought mainstreaming through cultural visibility and media representation. We have increased gay and lesbian visibility in the news media, expanded entertainment industry representation, and effectively characterized ourselves as a lucrative market to be courted. At the same time that we pursue the straight world, we have developed an autonomous culture. An astounding amount of art, film, literature, theater, music, as well as distinct, subcultural rituals, symbols, and queer community norms, bind us together as queer people. Sometimes, this gay cultural production has been absorbed directly into straight culture, as homoerotic images in advertising illustrate. But more commonly, we have tended to see cultural advocacy and political advocacy as distinct. We have bifurcated the pursuit of our open representation in straight culture from the production of our own culture. And we have ignored the many ways in which gay culture is already embedded in straight culture. Neither approach helps us in our goal of gay and lesbian liberation.

Indeed, the dualistic way we have defined culture (ours and theirs) leads us to demand that our own people choose between the categories of assimilationist and queer. The fight between those who supposedly favor assimilation and those who champion liberation is not what we should reproduce. The categories are in fact old and tired, and with different names they have surfaced in every era of the modern gay movement. In the fifties, we called assimilationists "conservative," and those seeking gay rights were termed radicals. In the sixties, we used the terms militant and moderate. After Stonewall, we called people liberationists or legitimationists. In the seventies, the argument raged between grassroots activists and homocrats. In the 1980s, the fight was between those favoring direct action and the gay lobbyists. In the early nineties the term assimilationist was popularized by Queer Nation. By now, these arguments are predictable and too easy. They mask the ambivalence of both sides toward the mainstream culture, as well as the contradictions embodied in each "side." For example, the most "radical" queers love to see us represented in pop culture, and some of the most hardcore of Queer Nationalist sentiment comes from the sheltered regions of the academy. Yet the assimilation of openly homosexual people into institutions like schools, family, and parenting is a profoundly radical step, and the mere fact of open homosexuality or bisexuality is itself still threatening and radical in most contexts.

Culture can be defined as both the means by which human beings organize social life and develop social norms, and the method by which these norms are reproduced and communicated. In the first instance, culture refers to modes of social interaction through which roles and relationships are developed and defined and the means by which an experience of community is created. The family, religious denominations, the workplace, the hometown community, the bar or social gathering place, the kitchen table, the sports arena—are all sites where cultural norms and values are born and reproduced. Our participation in them gives us a sense of belonging, a shared experience, a set of behavioral norms and values that are communicated to each new person entering the circle.

In the second instance, culture refers quite specifically to the media that reflect, represent, and shape our lives. News and entertainment media, visual art of every kind, theater, dance, fashion, literature, music, television, film, radio—are the means of communication, education, and reinforcement of social mores, which reproduce values, which confer and define meaning, and which shape human imagination. Throughout our history, gay and lesbian people have been absent from both of these definitions of culture; absent by the essence of our oppression, invisibility.

Until very recently, there were *no* places for us to develop a gay and lesbian culture. Because of the stigma on the status queer, gay people had to fight one by one, with ourselves, to admit that we were attracted to members of the same sex; to find others like us in order to understand ourselves better; to accept our queerness as normal and natural and healthy; and to communicate this discovery to the world around us —to both the gay world and the straight one. In order to arrive at the invention of gay and lesbian culture, we first had to invent gay and lesbian selves.

Gay liberation as a movement created queer culture by claiming a public space for people to be openly gay. The priority placed by gay liberationists on visibility, on each individual coming to terms with their sexual orientation, moved a private behavior into the public square where it could begin to define itself as a culture. As we made more public space to live gay lives, we created new forms of family, religious worship, and community. Visibility to each other was the precondition for our construction of a gay and lesbian community, movement, and culture.

Today, most gay and lesbian people live their gay lives within the confines of a fluid, semipublic queer subculture that exists separate from —if intimately connected to—the culture that surrounds it. This gay subculture can be found in the smallest rural towns and appears most developed in larger urban centers. It consists of gay and lesbian churches and synagogues, sports leagues, choral societies, musical bands of every genre, writers' groups, recovery groups, support groups, health clinics, community centers, newspapers, nightclubs, computer bulletin boards, employee associations, businesses, resorts, cruise lines, music and comedy festivals, and professional associations. The subculture is indeed a culture that praises desire, that celebrates romance, and has built community out of sexual connection: we are an army of lovers, ex-lovers, friends, and families knitted together by sexual desire. But it remains a culture built amidst, and reproducing, sexual repression.

Our gay communities are still only semipublic at best. Most gay bars still sport shuttered windows against violence and disclosure; most gay publications come in plain brown wrappers; most gay organizations do not have the word *gay* or *lesbian* in their names; and most gay individuals are conveniently not gay all the time. Indeed, most gay people I know would resist the call by liberationists to be completely out of the closet. Some gay people assert, rather illogically, that sexual orientation should be treated by the broader society as a private matter, and should not matter so much, while in the same breath they seek marital rights, family rights, equal employment opportunities, and so on, all of which require a measure of public assertion of homosexual relationships. Today's gay conservatives defend keeping one foot in the closet by arguing that there is something narcissistic or exhibitionist in the call for gay visibility.

The gay and lesbian subculture is most evident to straight people through our public demonstrations—the annual pride parades and rallies across the country each June. America's reaction to these pride marches, in turn, evinces the wide disparity between our culture and theirs in understanding of the meaning of the flamboyance and pageantry of a gay and lesbian pride parade. In most gay communities, gay and lesbian pride has grown into a month-long series of events. They include picnics, softball games, film festivals, poetry readings, performances, town meetings, lobby days at state capitals, and neighborhood potlucks. All culminate at the end of June in some large gathering to commemorate the 1969 Stonewall riots. Sometimes that gathering is enormous, like the 300,000-strong San Francisco Freedom Day Parade. In other communities, like Little Rock, Arkansas, a gathering of two hundred people for a gay and lesbian pride banquet is a significant achievement.

Lesbian and gay pride organizers across the country have had to struggle on two sides to arrange such events. They fight the reluctance and fear of average gay and lesbian people to get them to participate, and they fight the neglect and sensationalism of the local news media's coverage of gay events. The common problem is apathy. Some say gay apathy is a sign of the alienation of the gay mainstream from the more "radical" and "subculture-oriented" movement. I think this is a rationalization. The reason many gay people stay away from pride events and activities is that they do not see their homosexuality in public terms. In part, the view of homosexuality as a private matter is a sophisticated form of staying in the closet; I suspect many people who wear those "nobody knows I am gay" T-shirts are closeted in most aspects of their lives. But in part, the refusal to be public about homosexuality is a refusal to take responsibility for our political movement, something too many gay people still do.

The second apathy, that of the media, is an attitude the gay movement has actively attempted to change. Since the inception of the movement, gay people have worked to transform the news and entertainment industry's coverage of gay and lesbian lives. This advanced the political agenda of the movement by forcing news organizations to report on the injustices facing gay and lesbian people. Greater visibility brought with it greater discussion. Greater discussion about homosexuality lessened the furtiveness surrounding it and educated an uninformed public on how common homosexuality was in every family, culture, society, and time period. The educational process partly quieted the fears many people had about homosexuality, and the lessening of fear allowed a more public place for gay and lesbian people in the culture. But the visibility we gained and the education we achieved through media exposure were secondary to the legitimacy granted to our movement. The fact that gay and lesbian rights routinely were front-page news in 1992 and 1993 contributed directly to the mainstreaming of gay people. In this sense, mainstreaming means the insertion of the gay and lesbian presence into the fabric of normal life.

Such news coverage of gay and lesbian people opened the door for television, music, fashion, and even Hollywood-film attention. Heterosexual mainstream culture started to notice and incorporate gay and lesbian stories and images into its representations in response to several forces. First, cultural representation widened in response to gay people coming out of the closet in each of these media industries. Second, it increased after the agitation of gay and lesbian media activists and artists. Finally, coverage grew with the emergence of news, art, people that the media could report on—and by 1994, there was a lot of gayness "there" for the media to cover.

But as with political access and legislative progress, the cultural visibility gay people have won is contingent, dependent on straight charity, and subject to the barometer of public opinion and public pressure. The skittishness of network television in presenting the image of same-sex affection reveals the vulnerability of this new gay and lesbian cultural access. A kiss is more than a kiss when a gay or lesbian character gives it. The tamest gay kiss is somehow more sexual, more obscene, more erotically charged than the steamiest kiss Sharon Stone or any other heterosexual icon is allowed to indulge in without comment. The Christian Right put so much pressure on the NBC show "L.A. Law" in 1990, after it aired a kiss between a bisexual character and a straight woman lawyer, that several advertisers withdrew and the character's prominence was quickly attenuated. Similar pressure against "thirtysomething" forced advertising cancellations in 1988 after an episode showed two gay characters talking with each other in bed. The most recent example of controversy, in 1994, involved a kiss between television's most popular comedian, Roseanne, and a lesbian character. When ABC asked Roseanne to cut or modify the scene, she refused and threatened to leave the network on principle over the controversy. The episode ran and won a 1994 GLAAD media leadership award.

Our media visibility to date has minimized our difference, especially sexual, and championed our commonality. What this does is leave intact the worst fears and stereotypes of homosexuality—precisely those which involve our sexual difference and are used as weapons in every political fight we wage. Like any political compromise, mainstream cultural activism involves reducing conflict to the least common denominator; a win becomes any representation at all, rather than an image that actually transforms straight fear into acceptance of our lives. Examining how our current visibility was achieved confirms this reluctance to assert our sexual difference and reveals a reliance on straight comfort levels rather than queer self-esteem. How did gay activists convince the straight press and straight Hollywood to cover gay and lesbian news? The answer is twofold: through community organizing and through cause-oriented, celebrity-driven fundraising.

Organizing to increase coverage of gay issues required us to engage in a guerrilla campaign. With little to no money, a handful of computers, in the days before fax machines became common, a small band of gay and AIDS activists blasted through a wall of indifference and ignorance about gay and lesbian rights. We did it by educating news media members, staging media-oriented events, and networking among gay and lesbian professionals who worked in the straight media.

Media education formally began with the Gay Activists Alliance zaps of New York media, like *Harper's* and the *Village Voice,* in the early 1970s. The newly formed NGTF was the first gay organization to have a staff media director, New York activist Ron Gold. He was succeeded by Ginny Vida, who wrote the pioneering book making lesbians visible, called *Our Right to Love.* Vida was succeeded by Ron Najman, a thoughtful and systematic media relations director who brought nearly fourteen years of experience in television news to the NGLTF and the movement. From 1986 to 1989, I served as public information director at the National Gay and Lesbian Task Force and continued the educational efforts my predecessors had begun. At that time, there were only three full-time public relations staffers at any gay or lesbian-identified organization—me, the PR staff at National Gay Rights Advocates, and the director of communications at Gay Men's Health Crisis, Lori Behrman. Not surprisingly, gay and lesbian people remained nearly invisible in the mainstream news media as late as 1986, except for an occasional article about AIDS.

Earlier, I noted how AIDS activists consciously forged relationships with medical and science reporters to broaden the coverage of AIDS, a strategy eventually adopted by gay and lesbian activists. But the process of securing news coverage of gay and lesbian issues was more difficult than getting AIDS reported. The first hurdle we had to clear was the ignorance of the straight media about the gay community. I remember meeting with senior editors of the *Washington Post* in 1990 to discuss their coverage of gay and lesbian issues. In preparation, the NGLTF volunteer Richard Wood had prepared a survey comparing six months of *Post* coverage with comparable coverage in the *New York Times* and the *Los Angeles Times:* the *Post* lagged far behind in quantity and quality of stories. We assembled a cross-section of gay organizational and constituency representatives to talk to editors about the important stories they were missing. We presented lists of story ideas, and a contact sheet so that they could get in touch with gay people who had different kinds of expertise. At the meeting, it was clear the editorial staff was eager to hear our suggestions and had very little idea about what the gay and lesbian community was, who its leaders were, and what political issues it was concerned with. At a follow-up briefing, attended by nearly twenty-five reporters and editors, the need for information exchange became even clearer.

How can the news media cover gay issues if it does not understand them? Until the 1990s, gay and lesbian political groups at the state and local level were largely volunteer or solo-staffed operations, with no media profile or clear agenda. Gay issues were most visible in litigation brought by individuals to redress discrimination or to reprimand zealots who spoke out against us. And because very few paid media and public relations directors worked for gay organizations, media education was not happening. The straight press had no contact names, resource lists, or data on which to base stories. Media relations was seen as a luxury by most gay organizations, even though we spoke often of the need to change how we were represented. The 1987 March on Washington was not able to raise funds to hire a staff person until one month before the march; even the 1993 March on Washington had no media plan or team in place until two months before it took place. One of the most important changes in the priority of media relations came in 1991 with the creation of the Gay and Lesbian Journalists Association. This professional association provided much-needed support to gay people working in straight media contexts, and inspired many of its members to press for more coverage of gay and lesbian issues.

These gains are significant, but by and large we have continued to emphasize our political goals without addressing the cultural basis of straight ignorance—the intractable stereotypes that defeat our agenda. Media coverage in the post–civil rights era of gay politics must substantively challenge persisting antigay stereotypes in addition to seeking visibility. Visibility on its own is no longer enough.

ASSIMILATION OR FREEDOM

The notion of mainstreaming homosexuality has been the dominant objective of legions of gay and lesbian activists since the 1950s. The mainstream has a seductive appeal to those of us who were taught our entire lives that we are sick, immoral, sinful, and depraved. Mainstreaming means integration, social acceptance, political attention, and credibility. To be mainstream is to be a part of a majority, to be safe, respectable, maybe even respected.

But the idea that homosexuals are being mainstreamed is an illusion we hunger deeply to believe because of our years spent in exile. Our hunger stems from the frustration we feel at living on the margin. We deserve to be safe and equal, we deserve to be affirmed, and we have every right in the world to demand our place in the heart of the affairs of our nation and broader communities. But to classify the visibility that a relatively small number of people have won as the start of massive integration or mainstreaming is to be at once profoundly optimistic and drastically limited in our vision. By pretending that we are mainstream, we minimize the deep resistance we continue to face.

We live in a world riddled with the belief that homosexuality is immoral, unnatural, and sinful. When asked whether homosexuality is right or wrong, moral or immoral, an overwhelming number of people answer against us. The forces that originate this view—namely, the Catholic Church, the Christian Right, Orthodox Judaism, Islam, and orthodoxies of every kind—are growing in power and influence. We are exiled when the institutions of our culture—family, church, government

—reject our difference, which we must accept. If we cannot accept being cast out, the closet offers refuge, and we re-enter the mainstream at the expense of our true selves.

The proper questions to ask at this point in our movement are who has been mainstreamed, to what extent, and why? An honest look at the gay and lesbian visibility achieved so far indicates an unsatisfactory and entirely predictable answer. Middle-class gay and lesbian people, those who most resemble the values and appearance of the mainstream culture and political system, are those who have been most integrated into it and who have been promoted by it. In fact, the current mainstreaming of homosexuals reflects an increase in opportunities only for members of gay and lesbian communities that already most resemble the mainstream: in class background, the color of our skin, our political views, our educational background, economic status, and in our access to the skills and people who make and shape public opinion. Discrimination is rarely experienced by those with the tools or skills to mitigate its impact. The sudden popularity of gay conservative voices illustrates this dynamic of the mainstream. Conservatism is enjoying its media moment, and a new conservative establishment seems to be everywhere, promoted in a way that progressive voices have never been championed. Conservatives claim to speak for a silent majority of gay people, but have never worked in the broad-based groups that would bring them into contact with such a gay "majority." They claim to be silenced by gay leftists and liberals, but then they use their media influence to condemn those who disagree with them politically. They claim to be anti-elitist, but care little for democratic dialogue or conversation. In line with the country's current political climate, the voices of gay conservatives are privileged over others: consider the different media reactions to books by Bruce Bawer and Michelangelo Signorile. Bawer was reviewed prominently by the major straight media outlets; his message criticizing the community was widely repeated. Signorile's book gained its success through word of mouth and gay press coverage; his message criticizing the institutionalization of the closet in politics, Hollywood, and in the media was widely ignored. Straight commentators pumped up Bawer's book to be much more than it was—an informed indictment of the excesses of gay political radicals. In fact, Bawer's book tells the coming-out story of a conservative man who really does not understand or credit the gay movement with very much. Signorile's book was written from inside the gay and AIDS movement of the 1980s, but commentators disparaged it as a narrow treatise on outing.

As some of us succeed in pushing our way into the mainstream of American society, the fragile unity we forged in the gay and lesbian communities through the 1980s has frayed. For one thing, homosexuality is not the only way large numbers of us define ourselves. We have other identities that matter deeply: as parents and professionals, in our ethnic identities and political affiliations. Another source of gay and lesbian disunity stems from the new prominence of vastly different kinds of gay people who have conflicting ideas about what gay and lesbian freedom means and how they propose to get it. Gay conservatives have never before been as vocal or visible in gay culture, and the explosive growth of Log Cabin Republican Clubs reflects their growing influence. According to a *GQ* feature on Rich Tafel, the capable and personable president of National Log Cabin Republicans, the group grew in three and a half years from eight to thirty-two chapters and claimed a membership of eight thousand in 1993. For that matter, gay and lesbian anarchists are there as well: a look at the bookshelves full of self-published 'zines of every stripe provides a glimpse of the extensive anti-authoritarian counterculture among lesbians and gay men.

The conservative extreme argues that gay and lesbian people need to stress what is common to us and to heterosexual culture. These writers focus on assimilating us to them. Proclaiming that gay people are indeed just like straights, they argue that loud "subcultural" queers have dominated the media attention and airwaves. They interpret the old gay slogan "we are everywhere" to mean that we are integrated into the fabric of American life, and that we share the values, dreams, and aspirations of our heterosexual counterparts. The opposite extreme revels in the differences gay people represent. Queer Nation is often cited as the originator of this notion, but this is ahistorical: elements of the position can be found in Carl Wittman's 1968 *Gay Manifesto* and in Frank Kameny's famous "Gay Is Good" speech, also from 1968. Queer Nation was a short-lived political organizing strategy whose chief legacy was the popularization of the word *queer* and the related idea that we are, as the word implies, not normal. It appeared in June 1991, but was gone by 1992 from most parts of the country. But the oppositional, confrontational, punk-influenced politics of the Queer Nationalists captured the imagination of thousands of lesbian and gay nonconformists.

Our debates on liberation and legitimation have so far presented the two strategies as mutually exclusive. For most people, the choice of one forecloses the other. Those more comfortable with different styles of gay and lesbian expression are more comfortable accepting the movement's push for both legitimation and liberation. The bromide nearly all people mouth is "Well, we're so diverse, no one strategy, leader, organization will work for us." Or the more conservative expression, "All strategies are valid but there is a time, place, and manner that is appropriate for some and not for others."

It is tedious to continue to wage an argument between so-called assimilationists and so-called militants. Neither is right, and neither is wrong. Acceptance and belonging are human aspirations for all people. In this sense, as the *Village Voice* writer Richard Goldstein wrote to me in a letter, our movement's pursuit of the mainstream is in every way "inevitable," for it comes from within each of us. Goldstein notes that few people can honestly say they want to live outside all social norms, that they do not seek or need validation. "Most of us experience both the yearning for acceptance and the determination to dissent. Virtually every gay person, from disco clone to radical fairy, from lesbian mother to queer national, carries both agendas, and they are frequently in conflict within the same individual. Hence, they are in conflict when we come together in our movement." Rather than seeing this opposition as a war between strategies, we should consider the relationship as a dialectic between two poles that propels our progress. To synthesize these contradictions requires clarifying the contradictions inherent both in ourselves and the mainstream.

Gay and lesbian people in 1995 are in a paradoxical spot: we are mainstreamed at the same instant that we remain marginalized. More precisely, some of us have won mainstream legitimacy and access, but most of us struggle with the same issues that our movement has fought to resolve for decades: whether and where to come out, how to overcome gay self-hatred, how to communicate the real truth of our lives to straight people, how to live free from violence, how to make a living and raise a family as openly gay people. The mainstream attention we now receive is proof that the battle has widened, not that it has ended.

Even those of us who are in the mainstream—as media spokespersons, celebrities, openly lesbian and gay voices in journalism or the arts —are marginalized in profound ways. For example, although gay political organizations are able to communicate their policy objectives through the straight media, these media outlets still insist on "balancing" their coverage of gay rights with the views of opponents to gay rights. Yet every time a Christian Coalition spokesperson or antigay crusader like Pat Buchanan is on the air, the "balance" of secular political voices and leaders who oppose right-wing views is not presented.

The pursuit of equal justice and fairness is essential for a people as stigmatized as gay men, lesbians, bisexuals, and transgendered persons. But the end of stigma will require more than legal declarations, political access for a gay and lesbian elite, or media-oriented tactics that succeed only in increasing the visibility of the media savvy and the telegenic. The development of this new cultural paradigm, or new arm of the movement, requires at the outset an imaginative leap on the part of millions of gay, lesbian, bisexual, and transgendered Americans, a leap that carries us beyond the pursuit of mainstream approval to a commitment to its reconstruction. We must transcend the calcifying dualism of seeing politics as an either-or game—outside or inside, margin or center. We must be willing to risk our security in the ghettos that shelter us, to expose the wildness of our subculture and be prepared to debate it honestly and question it thoroughly, to be politically wise in our constant focus on the principles we as a people stand for, and not on the personalities that interfere with the full realization of those principles. We must face the moral limits of the mainstream we so eagerly pursue and recognize the inequality of the mainstream, which by definition exists in opposition to the margin. In short, the new political paradigm we need requires us to shed the binding hold that the idea of normality has, to leave "normal" behind, as if we did not care.

The practical power of this imaginative leap becomes clear on application. If, for example, we look at the whole issue of assimilation not as a force to be resisted, but as a force to be harnessed, we can see a provocative relationship between the margin and the center. Rather than asking how gay and lesbian people can integrate themselves into the dominant culture, what if, instead, we affirm that our mission is explicitly to assimilate the dominant culture to us? To phrase the question that way suggests at once a pragmatic and transformational mission for our movement, a mission we desperately need. Defining our movement's goal as the assimilation of our heterosexual families, employers, neighbors, and institutions to the normalcy of gay and lesbian people, we clarify the educational work we need to do. Immediately, what we must do extends beyond the law, into the principal sites of daily life: family, work, community, even faith. Instead of arguing about who becomes assimilated and who is left behind, we can discuss how to communicate who we are to the government, family, the communities in which we live. We must attempt to transform rather then reform, apply healing rather than Band-Aids.

This is not to suggest that we as gay people do not need to question the culture we have created so far: I think we do. As Hunter Madsen and Marshall Kirk noted, in their iconoclastic (and ultimately misguided) book *After the Ball,* to say that "gay is good" does not imply that everything gay is good or is equally good. We should continue to develop and debate gay and lesbian values, ethics, and morality in order to understand and define the difference we represent. We will not have unanimity or even unity, but without an open-minded debate of these questions, all we shall have is a cacophony of voices.

This in the end is what I mean by a gay and lesbian liberation-based practice. Such a practice has social transformation as its goal and community organizing as its method. Examining our work on antigay violence, for example, helps us consider how our lives could change if the movement was not focused only on political integration and legitimation, but also on cultural and social transformation. As a concern to both gay and nongay people, avoiding violence is an issue on which broad understanding could be forged. While our civil rights strategies focus on the legal enforcement of certain duties—by the police and state to individuals—a liberation-based strategy targets the sources of prejudice that lead to the violence.

Three kinds of antiviolence movements operate in this country: the citizen-action model of communities mobilizing to mount patrols, run neighborhood watch campaigns, and try to make the streets and neighborhoods safe; the victim-services movement that staffs rape crisis lines, domestic violence centers, gay- and lesbian-specific service organizations, crime victims' support groups; and the racial justice movement that has organized against police brutality, state-sanctioned violence, and violence against people of color in general. Each of these antiviolence movements organizes around the framework of civil rights; each argues that we have the right to be safe in our person and property regardless of who, where, what we are. Each pursues legal reforms through legislative activity—to stiffen penalties, ban handguns, mandate tougher sentences, secure funds for service delivery, increase police patrols, found community-review boards, and much more. Each engages in education aimed at more understanding, awareness, prevention, and support for victims of violence. All of these have been instrumental in securing a modicum of responsiveness from the state to the problem of violence.

Within this framework, the gay and lesbian antiviolence movement has made stunning advances in a very short period. From 1982 to today, the movement has won near-universal condemnation of gay-bashing from governmental, religious, and civic bodies. We got gay-bashing classified as a crime motivated by prejudice and hate, secured passage of bias-penalty bills, produced studies into the causes and solutions to homophobic violence, and secured funding for a range of service programs. But the gay and lesbian antiviolence movement remains isolated, even from the battered women's movement as a whole, with which it shares a constituency. (Both men and women are battered in gay relationships.) The national coalition of antiviolence, civil rights, and police groups that helped to pass the Hate Crime Statistics Act in 1990 never reproduced itself at the state level to protect all the people covered by the federal bill. Anti-Semitic, racist, gender-based, religious, and homophobic violence have all risen in the past several years, but the groups working in each of these areas have not joined forces to work for anything beyond a handful of legislative enactments.

This is the limitation of such a civil rights strategy. It does not extend easily beyond a handful of legalistic or formalistic objectives. In large part the difficulty in bridging constituencies is the minority-group idea itself: identity limits us to the problems faced by "our own" and keeps us from identifying with "others" as "our own." So, as a gay leader, I was criticized for organizing protests against the Rodney King verdict ("What did this have to do with gay people?"), even though the same critics would be the first to point out a lack of response by black civil rights organizations to a brutal gay-bashing by police.

What if our work were defined not as getting for gay people that which other minority groups have won, but as dealing with the violence that threatens all of us? What if we allied in our neighborhoods with all others who fear violence to understand the construction of violent people, and to expose the conditions like alcoholism, drug addiction, insecurity, and economic anxiety that contribute to violence? What if we all worked together to develop neighborhood-based education, organizing, and intervention strategies? It is possible to contemplate such a coalition today, because the basic apparatus for it exists. Ten years ago, there was only a handful of antiviolence projects, and the issue had no national or local visibility. To assimilate the straight world to the gay world would mean bringing straight community leaders into the bars, streets, and homes where we experience violence. It would involve us in educating people who are unfamiliar with us, or threatened by us, on the common problems we face as members of the same community.

To define the principal goal of gay and lesbian liberation as the assimilation of straight culture gives us a clarity of mission that the current goal of civil rights lacks. Civil rights are treated as abstractions by gay and lesbian people; people can feel they have done their bit by merely voting or writing a check. Sadly, liberation has a grandiose ring to it. Gay and lesbian history reveals that abstract notions of liberation do not inspire large numbers of gay people to do anything; terror, fear, danger, and threats do. The periods of growth in gay and lesbian activism have come in moments of grave danger or upheaval. Thus, Mattachine was born in a climate of police repression and antigay witch hunts. Stonewall was the reaction to decades of police harassment and a cultural shift in the credibility of state authority. The gay rights movement grew its first adolescent spurt in the late 1970s as the right-wing crusades of Anita Bryant and the Moral Majority targeted gay people. The movement grew exponentially when the AIDS crisis politicized gay men. Today, as the right-wing assault on our civil freedom intensifies, another wave of gay and lesbian activism is being born. But to wait around for this terror to inspire activism is to accept that we are passive, that our movement's fate is to be reactive. Co-opting that which co-opts us surely presents a more exciting alternative.

Transforming straight culture poses a massive challenge that has room in it for everyone. It actually reflects more clearly than artificial distinctions of culture and politics the way the gay and lesbian movement is organized. Across the country, gay people have created more than ten thousand community organizations—from support groups and choruses to bowling leagues and professional associations—to tackle antigay prejudice where we encounter it. Rather than defining these groups as cultural and proposing that our mission is to make them political, what if we saw them as the political front line, and organized them in a conscious way to do their cultural work more effectively?

To accomplish this shift, we must overcome our resistance to self-scrutiny and engage in the process of self-determination as a community: examining how we define power, our relationship to money, what relationships are possible among gay people and between us and other communities, our response to the right, our need for leadership, and the moral principles by which we want to live.

CHAPTER SEVEN

POLITICS AND POWER

There is difference and there is power.
And who holds the power decides the meaning of the
difference.

—*June Jordan*

On April 26, 1980, the news program "CBS Reports" ran a one-hour special called "Gay Power, Gay Politics." Although gay activists had long pressed to win such straight media legitimation, the CBS show was far from benign. Instead, the program presented the gay community in San Francisco as a threat, its members as sexual hedonists, privileged powerbrokers, and arrogant men scheming to force their "lifestyle" on a recalcitrant public. A biased slant permeated the broadcast. The CBS reporter George Crile peppered the show with negative comments such as this: "There is a consequence to the homosexual life style here. Traditional values are under attack." Later in the program Crile asked the gay community leader Cleve Jones, "Isn't it a sign of decadence when you have so many gays emerging, breaking apart all of the values of a society?" Crile secretly taped men who were allegedly gay walking into bushes in Buena Vista Park and then interviewed children and heterosexual parents about their feelings about gay male cruising.

He tried to goad police officers in the Castro district to make antigay comments, and presented the gay establishment's quest for political power as an ominous and unprecedented effort to seize control and impose a gay agenda on an unwilling straight community. After the show aired, gay leaders protested vehemently, and eventually won acknowledgment of the show's homophobic bias from an independent (and now-defunct) media standards board.

The CBS show featured archetypal footage of waves of smiling, musclebound gay male "clones" in blue jeans and white T-shirts, walking arm in arm down Castro Street. Respectable gay leaders in fancy suits were depicted at political fundraising parties, all touting demographics about the gay vote in San Francisco. Lesbians were invisible in the piece, reflecting the bias prevalent in the media at the time, and partly reflecting the reality that, with few exceptions, lesbians were not leaders in the gay movement. The men depicted in the program were all white, a fact that raised some gay viewers' ire but, again, reflected the outsider status of people of color within the gay political establishment.

The show startled many straight people in America with what was then rare coverage of an out-of-the-closet gay community that had amassed local political clout. Gay power was equated with an invasion of outsiders who move into urban centers and radically change the character of community life. The tone of the CBS show was alarmist and seemed to suggest that gays would soon head out of the Castro, out of the gay bars and bushes that had been their "traditional" domain, and into government offices, board rooms, and, eventually, the playgrounds of America. Despite the gains of the past twenty years, this view of gay power as ominous, male-dominated, and sexually threatening remains pervasive. The makers of the antigay videos in the nineties have patterned their fear-inspiring tapes on this early CBS show.

Another gap between the perception of gay and lesbian power and its reality exists within gay and lesbian communities as well: gay and lesbian visibility in mainstream politics fools us. We think we are stronger and more powerful than we actually are. In the military-ban fight of 1993, for example, many gay and lesbian people were genuinely shocked at the feebleness of our national political organizations. Yet those who had observed gay and lesbian politics in the preceding five years were not at all surprised by the opposition or the outcome. We knew that most members of Congress, including most Democrats, had voted against gay and lesbian interests repeatedly since 1987, their libertarian lip service notwithstanding. More particularly, those who had paid attention to gay politics knew that the movement had never defeated an all-out antigay campaign in Congress.

A discussion of gay power begs an even more basic question: Why do gay people need political power? Some of us believe that homosexuality is a matter of private lives and private acts. Why then do we need a public movement for power? If the challenge we face lies in changing the attitudes of straight people or in winning heterosexual cultural acceptance, then does it matter whether the gay political movement uses a top-down or a ground-up strategy? My answer is simple: we need political power to protect and defend ourselves as we work to eradicate homophobia. This answer may strike some as paranoid or simplistic; but the necessity of a movement that can defend queer people is urgent. Three realities, in particular, frame and frustrate our pursuit of gay political power. The first is how we have defined political power. The second is how this definition informs the structure of our movement. The third is how we are weakened by our continuing resistance to tying our movement's political goals more directly to the specific cultural threat open homosexuality poses.

Whether gay and lesbian political power is defined narrowly as the ability to carry out the policy changes we seek, or whether it is defined broadly, as the writer June Jordan sees it, to "decide the meaning of difference" itself—by either definition, the gay rights movement is far short of the standard. To win genuine equality, a rights-oriented movement and a gay liberation movement are both necessary. Being visible, challenging stereotypes, making queer family and community are all political acts. Conversely, passing laws, electing supportive politicians, and organizing ourselves into a voting bloc are power-oriented strategies, essential to cultural transformation. Because the sexual anxiety of straight culture rises as it encounters open homosexuality or bisexuality, our movement needs the honesty offered by a political theory based on gay liberation. Such a framework freely admits that gay and lesbian equality will change cultural definitions of masculinity and femininity, that it will redefine the family, broaden marriage and its embedded gender roles, and challenge dominant views about sexual and reproductive choice.

OUR DEFINITION OF POWER

In the late 1980s, the Human Rights Campaign Fund launched an aggressive fundraising, marketing, and public relations campaign built around the slogan "Pathways to Power." The subtext was that HRCF, with its access to money and its federal focus, was the best "pathway" to power for our community. HRCF certainly established itself as an effective route to gay and lesbian money for straight politicians: by the end of the 1980s, it ranked among the top ten independent PACs in the country. (An independent PAC is one not tied to any corporation, political party, candidate, or other entity.) In part, the realities of organizing a people in hiding contributed to the popularity of this access-oriented, top-down model of political organizing. The PAC provided a convenient answer to the problem of how to find gay and lesbian people in local political districts. The logic of PACs is easy to understand and compelling to many people; the model worked fabulously in reaching the well-to-do in major cities. Given that the most common gay institution in the 1980s was an antipolitical one—the bar—HRCF's development of the fundraising dinner to reach previously uninvolved people was innovative. Regarded as a sign of the maturity and political savvy of the gay movement, the HRCF strategy for gaining political power through the access of monied gay and lesbian people has become the major one we rely upon today.

According to the top-down approach, power flows from the elite to the masses, from changes at the federal level to the local, from people with money to middle-class citizens, from the laws politicians make to the people whose lives these laws affect. This view of power is alternately described by its proponents as "playing the game," "working the system," "checkbook activism," or, simply, being pragmatic. Concentrating on organizing gay and lesbian professionals and wealthy people, HRCF brought gay elites to Washington to influence their members of Congress with the promise of money in exchange for civil rights support. The gay activist Vic Basile observed, "I think where we develop power is by learning how the system works and being able to manipulate it. And not to think about changing the system. It's too big a task. I don't think we can make any difference in that equation." Basile's pragmatism, I suggest, defines the realm of gay and lesbian politics too narrowly. The system works as much through the construction of voting blocs as through leveraging financial clout.

While Basile is correct that social change is a much bigger task than the more pragmatic process of doing what works within the system, his faith in our ability to manipulate a system that so fundamentally rejects us is misplaced. Despite the delivery of millions of dollars in gay support, the PAC-based strategy for gay power has proved inadequate. As Barney Frank noted at a March 1994 gay retreat, "We have tended to think money buys us more than it can," adding, "Votes will beat money any day." And therein lies the rub. To this date, the gay and lesbian movement has organized in the wrong direction. In the long run, voter registration and the construction of a gay-supportive voting bloc will be far more effective than buying access to friends in high places.

The HRCF approach holds that federal legislative change is the most effective way to reduce antigay discrimination. But to be effective, such a federally oriented legislative strategy must take place in conjunction with a state-oriented and local approach. Without a local base of constituent support, national activism is just so much hot air. Yet at present, none of the national gay political organizations has state affiliates or chapters. The autonomous statewide gay organizations that exist are small and struggling for survival. They are not formally tied, either financially or politically, to the national gay organizations. Meanwhile, state legislatures are becoming the sites of gay rights activity, with both antigay and pro-gay bills being debated every month. Moreover, the Republican Party's dominance at setting the national agenda, and the centrality to that party of antigay Christian votes, suggest that national gay organizations would be wise to direct more of their resources to the growth of a state-by-state gay movement, rather than spending millions in a fruitless effort to pass national civil rights legislation. Focusing on a state and local, ground-up approach to gay and lesbian power could involve national groups in the direct support of state activism, organizations, and leaders. Movement building of this kind would yield long-term benefits at the national level—a fifty-state network of gay rights affiliates would surely marshal more clout in a battle like the effort to end the military ban than does our current strategy for power.

Two recent experiences illustrate other limitations of the road we have pursued. The first is the Clinton administration's rejection of the openly gay San Francisco philanthropist Jim Hormel for a diplomatic post in 1994; the second is the emergence of unaccountable access brokers in our movement. Despite Hormel's many qualifications and his decades of support of Democratic candidates, despite his fealty and financial generosity, he was rejected as an ambassadorial candidate. Many in the gay community believe that the administration turned from him because he is openly gay; it was unwilling to stand up to Senate Foreign Relations Committee chairman Jesse Helms, just as it had been unwilling to handle political pressure in its nominations of Lani Guinier, Mort Halperin, and Joycelyn Elders. Hormel's "place" at the Democratic Party table meant nothing. While Hormel has graciously refused to criticize the Clinton administration for its actions, the snub to him was widely reported by the gay press as another example of the administration's broken commitments. This story exposes the limits of gay access: no matter how qualified, competent, or faithful a party loyalist is, he or she cannot overcome the barrier of homosexuality. Gay people as a political constituency are perceived inside Washington as less dangerous to our liberal friends than are antigay conservatives. Personal gay access does not translate into the power to influence policy decisions.

The second illustration exposes the troubling role that intermediaries play in the elite-based politics of our national movement. Since money is the lubricant of access and conversation in the world of politics, rich gay and lesbian people have become the new powerbrokers in our movement. Indeed, one wonders whether Clinton would have said anything on gay rights issues had he not so urgently needed the money of donors like David Geffen, Barry Diller, Fred Hochberg, Jeffrey Soref, and other gay multimillionaires. The good news is that gay rights and AIDS issues do receive more attention as a result of the influence wielded by these wealthy individuals. The bad news is that the personal clout of rich gay people does not mean greater political power for the gay movement. Mixner had tremendous personal access to the Clinton administration; it meant nothing when the President made the decision to abandon us. Geffen has stayed at the White House and met privately with Bill and Hillary Clinton, yet the AIDS policies of the country remain inadequate and the White House has been frighteningly silent on this massive and deepening crisis. Wealthy gay Republicans abound, yet the Log Cabin Club is unable to stem the homophobia of national party leaders. Elite access must be seen by all of us as merely one step in the road to power, not the end-point that it can too easily become. Not only must the movement continue the less glamorous project of organizing itself from the ground up, but we must see clearly that those in the gay elite who seem to have such great influence are in fact unaccountable to ordinary gay people for the manner in which they represent the gay and lesbian community.

Frankly, the majority of gay people with access—those who attend White House meetings, advise the campaigns of Republican presidential candidates, work on congressional staffs, decide what movies and TV shows will get made, clerk for Supreme Court Justices, or work throughout corporate America—have little sense of responsibility or allegiance to the gay movement. These people generally do not consult with gay leaders or organizations before interacting with the administration, and do not carry any gay movement agenda into the high-level meetings in which they engage. Many gay people with wealth and access are closeted and do not identify as part of the gay movement. They escape personal responsibility through a variety of excuses: they are not out, they do what they can, they do not agree with the more "liberal" or "radical" movement, they can be more effective being silent. All these rationalizations obscure the fact that their inaction contributes to gay powerlessness.

Despite the threat of outing, I think the gay movement has no effective recourse for such an abdication of responsibility. We can talk to people we know and challenge them to do more, but few will. Instead of focusing on the rich, powerful, and the elitist, as we have done for so long, the movement must return its energies to focusing on the ordinary, concerned, and decent gay, lesbian, bi, and straight people who are willing to be better organized, but who have no ready way to access the political movement.

Another problem in the accountability of those who claim to represent the gay community is illustrated by the Los Angeles–based AN-GLE, the Access Network For Gay and Lesbian Equality, in which gay elites purport to represent a community to whom they are not at all accountable. ANGLE's roots lie in the unique way that a handful of wealthy Los Angelenos organized themselves to assert political influence over the past twenty years. In the mid-1970s, the leading gay PAC in the country was a local one, MECLA (Municipal Elections Commission of LA), which issued endorsements of pro-gay candidates for local and county office and pioneered the notion of gay and lesbian political fundraising. The prominent lesbian attorneys Diane Abbitt and Bobbie Bennett were key founders. Other leaders in organizing gay money and clout in LA were the late Sheldon Andelson and David Goodstein, Duke Comegys, David Mixner, and Jean O'Leary. MECLA fell into disarray in the 1980s, as its principals focused on

AIDS and other priorities. In the late 1980s, some of these individuals, including O'Leary, Rob Eichberg, Goodstein, Mixner, Randy Klose, and others, formed a small political network they called the Book Study Group. Members of this informal yet influential group met to discuss national gay political strategy; a number of its members went on to found ANGLE.

ANGLE has carefully defined itself as a private political network, not a public, nonprofit organization. By refusing to become a public organization, ANGLE is accountable to no one but its twenty to thirty members. Yet ANGLE members represented the entire gay community when they formally met with every Democratic presidential candidate in 1992, securing commitments on gay rights from several (including Bill Clinton). Candidates came because they were promised funds. (Several ANGLE donors would write large checks establishing a quid pro quo for the meeting itself.) In turn, ANGLE members' endorsements were seen by candidates as important keys into the broader gay community. The group's privately owned database of over 400,000 gay-supportive California voters is one of its most potent assets; yet I doubt that this database is available on a daily basis to the state's hard-working, Sacramento-based gay and AIDS lobby, the LIFE lobby, for its constituent communications. While ANGLE benefits from and influences the gay and lesbian movement, through its contacts with politicians, it affords the broader movement no opportunity to influence its own positions. Several members of ANGLE (like the Republican activist Rich Colbert, Democratic activist Scott Hitt, and Abbitt) play leadership roles on the boards of the Human Rights Campaign Fund and the Gay and Lesbian Victory Fund. These positions give ANGLE direct influence on the politics of the largest organization in the gay movement—HRCF. But what influence do movement activists not in the ANGLE circle have on the group? Effectively none. The ethics of access-centered politics are troubling: these powerful gay intermediaries gain their political access by claiming that they represent a gay and lesbian community, yet they are not accountable to that broader community. Under the elite-access model of political power, there is no problem with such representation; but under a more inclusive conception of power and leadership, the problem with this model of political organizing is apparent.

The Treatment Action Group (TAG) represents another private, by-invitation network of activists—in this case, not people with money, but all AIDS activists with expertise who split off from ACT UP in

1992 partly because of political differences and their frustration with the group's decision-making process. My name has been on TAG's Advisory Board for over a year, and I confess to being troubled by what my endorsement of this by-invitation-only group means. I endorse it because of my faith in the people who form TAG; but their process is as indefensible as ANGLE's. Because it is small, relatively homogeneous, and well known within the AIDS activist community, TAG produces much good work. But whom does TAG represent? What kind of power is it building? What happens when TAG engages in lobbying with which the broader AIDS community disagrees; how are our debates resolved? These questions have not been answered. By definition, a movement organization ought to be committed to open debate, inclusiveness, representative leadership. Yet these two nationally influential groups are structured in ways that are far less inclusive and democratic than the traditional gay rights organizations.

In addition, what do the existence of ANGLE and TAG reveal about a movement in which talented activists feel they have to form homogeneous, largely white groups in order to "get the job done?" Proponents of such organizations have argued with me that they are pragmatic responses, required by the reality of an unruly movement of such diversity that consensus takes a lifetime to achieve. Isn't it better, they ask, that the political work we all agree needs to be done in fact gets done? This approach flies in the face of feminist ideas of power. Simply put, method or process matters. I think it speaks poorly of our faith in the idea of a movement that the cliquishness that was a historic consequence of gay oppression is now seen as essential to gay progress.

In a sense, ANGLE and TAG's faith in elite access mirrors the definition of power held by the inside-the-Beltway gay organizations. Power is concentrated in the hands of a few and wielded at the discretion of even fewer. All these groups consider the politics of access and top-down change as more effective than the building of a grassroots gay movement. I do not believe that members of ANGLE, TAG, or HRCF would say they oppose such a process; indeed, some may think they engage in movement-building by doing what they do. The reality is that they merely follow the 1980s pathway to power that HRCF pioneered and that the 1993 fight on the military revealed to be entirely inadequate. Whom you know and how much money you have opens doors, but it does not win change. The gun lobby succeeds because it mobilizes money, votes, and the intangible quantity known as influence. The gay movement has established a beachhead in Washington by mobilizing some wealthy people and delivering some votes. But unlike the gun lobby (or the tobacco industry or the health insurance industry or any other major Washington force), we follow a pathway to political power that leads us to the locked, steel gate of antisexual cultural attitudes about homosexuality. The gay movement's use of the politics of access cannot overcome the stigma of homosexual behavior. Money alone will not unlock this gate, and we lack sufficient electoral force to blow it away. What we need instead are tools to dismantle this barrier: these tools are a new movement infrastructure and local organizing.

MOVEMENT STRUCTURE BLUES

The sad reality in any consideration of gay movement structure is that our progress has been achieved more by individual heroism and smoke and mirrors than by the operation of a strong, well-constructed, nation-wide movement. In some ways the decentralized nature of the gay movement is a source of great strength: gay people *are* organizing every-where, against every kind of prejudice. We gain a vitality from being dispersed as homophobia is challenged in every cultural and social insti-tution it manifests itself. But this infrastructure is also disorganized and a source of weakness. We do not act strategically as a national or local movement. We cannot mobilize support for our positions in times of national crises. Our ability to pass gay rights laws remains dependent on a few determined activists and the support of a handful of straight allies, rather than on much larger numbers of gay or straight supporters. In short, decentralization means that we are present everywhere and strong nowhere.

The movement's unquestioned acceptance of the HRCF route to power—top-down, access-driven, steered by the rich and privileged among us—also leaves us with a structure inversely related to what we need to build political power for the twenty-first century. We are top-heavy with strong national groups, while state and local political organi-zations barely exist. The glitter of access obscures the tawdriness of our co-optation. And elite mobilization slowly drives the movement away from the concerns and realities of ordinary gay and straight people, struggling within the broad social reality of pervasive inequality. The following specific problems in gay movement structure must be ad-dressed if we are to move forward: the weakness of all gay political organizations, the separation between social and political activism in gay communities, and the continuing lack of attention (or money) for infrastructure development in the areas of movement communications, training of leaders, and movementwide decision making.

Our biggest structural weakness is the lack of strong political organizations in every state. With the national groups, the gay movement has a roof; with service organizations, we have a foundation; but without state organizations, we have no walls to protect us. There are statewide organizations in approximately half the states, but few are broad based (beyond AIDS), well funded, or even staffed. This weakness is deadly, especially since the battleground for gay and lesbian equality has shifted to the state level. Our enemies at the Christian Coalition, the Focus on the Family, and the American Family Association have state-by-state networks of affiliates, staffed offices, and trained volunteers. In addition, the groups that do exist are generally run entirely by volunteers, usually a handful. If these state groups have staff, like the Empire State Pride Agenda, the Texas Gay and Lesbian Rights Lobby, or the Life Lobby in California, they are tiny or part time. In a vast state like Texas, the Texas Gay and Lesbian Rights Lobby does a heroic job with a staff of three. Money that is raised in states by national groups, like the $3 million that HRCF raises through its dinners, nearly always flows out of state to support federally focused political organizing.

In turn, our national organizations are quite small. A comparison of budgets illustrates the relative size of the national gay movement. The combined annual budgets of four national gay and lesbian political groups in 1992 was $8.4 million ($4.5 for HRCF, $1.29 for NGLTF, $1.6 for LLDEF, and $1.0 for the National Center for Lesbian Rights), far less than the $17 million annual budget of one conservative think tank, the Heritage Foundation. By 1995, the budgets of all the groups had increased dramatically (HRCF had an $8 million budget and NGLTF $3.1 million). But even today, the three biggest national groups have budgets totaling less than $20 million, the budget of the Christian Coalition alone. Again, by comparison, Focus on the Family, the group behind the Colorado initiative, has an annual budget of over $60 million and more than seven hundred staff people! The Eagle Forum, Concerned Women for America, Free Congress Research Foundation, Traditional Values Coalition, American Family Association—each boasts a budget far larger than comparable gay and lesbian organizations. In addition, national organizations of people of color, like LLEGO and the BLGLF, do not even have political organizing budgets totaling even $100,000 apiece.

A comparison of membership rolls of national gay and lesbian organizations reveals the same paucity. It is estimated that 650,000 gays, bisexuals, lesbians, and friends marched on Washington in 1987, and that a million marched on Washington in 1993. In each instance, the U.S. Park Service estimates sharply differed from the larger estimates of the march organizers. The Park Service estimated that 200,000 marched in 1987 and that 300,000 marched in 1993. Whether we choose the larger or the smaller estimate, the truth is that the names on all mailing lists for gay and lesbian organizations totals far less than those who marched in both marches. The membership rolls of the three national groups mentioned above total well under 200,000 people. Even if the mailings lists of other national organizations, like the Gay and Lesbian Victory Fund, the ACLU Gay and Lesbian Rights Project, LLEGO, the Black Leadership Forum, and the National Center for Lesbian Rights were all added together, gay and lesbian names on political mailings lists would number around 300,000. The gay businessman and direct-mail consultant Sean Strub notes that the total of gay and lesbian names on lists is only two million people. This low number presents a significant obstacle to the building of gay and lesbian political power.

Why are the mainstream gay organizations—national or state—so small? Because of the closet, the cliquish nature of gay movement politics, and the fact that we are not organized to work politically where people live culturally. Not only are most gay people unwilling to put their names on gay membership lists, but the closet is the antithesis of a political movement. When vast numbers of us have lived most of our lives in hiding, we are not inclined to drop our defensive behavior in order to work with others for a common purpose. It will take another twenty-five years for the gay and lesbian community to change to the point where most of the people in it have lived most of their lives out of the closet. The effect of these fully out people on the politics, strategies, and ideology of the movement will be fascinating to witness. Until our people allow themselves to be counted—in the census, polls, informal surveys as well as in the neighborhood, local drugstore, and churches of our home towns—political activists will not be able to claim with any integrity how many people we represent, and how many people will be affected by the policies we propose. Until we are not merely out personally, but are organized politically, we cannot expect politicians to take our concerns seriously—and they do not.

Even the act of coming out retains a private and highly individual character that does not lend itself to being organized. Everyone has his or her own story. And each is indeed unique, although there are some typical experiences, such as coming out to parents, siblings, in the media, coming out to co-workers or employers, coming out at the PTA meeting or at a conference with the teachers of one's children. These are stories that gay and lesbian people mostly tell to each other. The straight world tells stories to itself—and mostly pretends that homosexuals are a tiny minority whose emergence from the closet will little affect the conduct of life for heterosexuals.

How can the movement better organize to handle this facet of gay, lesbian, and bisexual oppression? The experience remains individual, even though there are more institutions than ever to support a person who is thinking about coming out. There is virtually no difference in the experience of gay and lesbian teenagers today from what there was twenty or even fifty years ago; in most parts of the country, these young people have nowhere to turn, no one to talk to, and little idea of the kind of community they are entering. Today there is the National Coming Out Day, held each year on October 11, the anniversary of the Second National March on Washington. NCOD itself was invented at a meeting I attended in 1988 called the War Conference. This gathering of some 220 national, state, and local activists was proposed originally by Larry Kramer, who wanted to get gay and lesbian leaders together to talk about how to meet the threat of homophobia, AIDS, and the right. The War Conference was held on February 26–27, 1988, and was an odd, unrepresentative collection of activists who talked nonstop for a weekend about our strategies and made little speeches about what we ought to be doing. Someone proposed that we create our own gay and lesbian holidays and events, and that we encourage celebrities as well as ordinary people to come out of the closet. The National Gay Rights Advocates vowed to initiate this National Coming Out Day, and ran it until 1990, when NCOD became its own organization. Today the HRCF operates the project.

But the closet alone does not account for the lack of appeal that gay and lesbian political organizations have; after all, in the nineties there are more than enough gay people out of the closet to swell the ranks of our civil rights organizations. Gay organizations stay small because they fail to convey a vision of what our movement seeks. Our difficulty in supporting gay leadership disempowers us.

In addition, gay and lesbian organizations are largely undemocratic. To a certain extent, this elitism is a byproduct of our history: gay groups were formed by the very few who were out of the closet. Certain people had more time, opportunity, and willingness to be out and to engage in gay political work. Until the creation of ACT UP, there was no mass component to gay and lesbian political activism. Today the elitism of gay politics is a problem, as large numbers of openly gay and lesbian people come out and want to get more involved in their movement. They quickly find that there are few ways for them to do so. The most attractive aspect of American democracy is its promise of participation: the premise is that genuine power rests in the hands of the many rather than the few. The theory holds that voters, however susceptible to manipulation they may be, have the power to determine their lives. Unfortunately, within the gay movement we have created organizations and structures that afford individual gay people very little opportunity to participate. None of our national political groups has chapters, none holds annual conventions for members, none allows members to elect their boards of directors. Instead, responding to the demands of fund-raising rather than democracy, our groups leave decision-making to the elite who sit on their boards or who give money—largely upper-middle-class professionals, of every color.

Many gay people have no idea how to get involved in gay politics. Whom should they call? What can they do? How can they volunteer their skills? What new volunteers find is that most gay political groups function as cliques; they have not been able to adapt, to absorb new people or share power with newcomers. Sometimes the old guard in gay organizations does not like the ideas and different politics of newer activists. Other times, there is no mechanism for the integrating new volunteers or leaders. With the exception of groups like ACT UP, Lesbian Avengers, and others that are chapter-based, there is little for most card-carrying members to do except write a check. Those who persist and become involved in gay political groups often get discouraged; the infighting and pettiness of our day-to-day politics are intense and unappealing. Often, personality conflicts between local leaders result in the formation of two different organizations; as they did in San Francisco, when Harvey Milk and Jim Foster disagreed. Sometimes when one finds two or more gay political groups in a small town or even in a major city like Boston, their formation can be traced to personality

conflicts between leaders and, less frequently, to actual differences in
political ideology. By splitting off and reproducing, like amebas, the gay
political movement by the 1990s had achieved strength in numbers but
lacked depth. We had scores of organizations for every conceivable
social, cultural, or political aim, but we had no infrastructure for communication, coordination, or support.

Indeed, the movement is organized in a manner antithetical to the
realization of traditional political power, because our structure gives
existing groups no way to coordinate, to effect decision-making in a
time of crisis, to identify an agenda, and to discuss strategy. The lack of
such an infrastructure is evident in the way we organized our national
marches; there was no set process by which such a decision is reached.
In each of the three marches, the desire came from the grassroots, not
the national leadership. The first March on Washington, in 1979, was
opposed by many national leaders until a few months before it took
place. The second march, in 1987, began when a national call for action
was circulated by dozens of grassroots organizers and leaders across the
country. The 1993 march came into being when individuals began to
call for it—most notably people like the late Minneapolis city councilor
Brian Coyle and the late San Francisco activist Drew Siegel. In response to their voices, I convened and facilitated a series of national
meetings in 1991 to hammer out a consensus on when the third march
should take place. Each of these processes was reactive and arbitrary. A
better movement communications system is needed to involve activists
all over the country in making such a strategic decision. Such a system
could take the form of a council of delegates, a federation of organizations, or even a series of electronic town meetings on the Internet. Our
national leadership has not adequately addressed the challenge of turning the decentralized base of gay and lesbian activists and into a coordinated movement.

Our poor communication system contributes to the lack of integration between the decentralized constituency and the centralized power
structure. The Internet may change this, but not all gay political groups
are connected. Political activists communicate poorly with both organized and uninvolved activists. Our principal means of political communication remains the local gay and lesbian press and the straight
media. Unlike any other decade, more gay people learn about the movement through the straight press than from lesbian and gay newspapers,
radio, and TV shows. New lifestyle magazines like *Out* reach tens of
thousands, but their reach pales when compared with the millions who

read a *Vanity Fair* gay story. Gay political organizations have grasped this truth and now aggressively pursue straight media coverage. But this pursuit is troubling. For one, the straight press obviously does not have the same interest as the gay press in reporting gay and lesbian issues. The focus of their stories differ from the emphasis of our movement, as does their basic orientation: the straight press is out for good copy; we are out for justice. Often the straight press anoints as spokespersons those who have limited support or little credibility in the movement but give juicy quotes. To the uninformed observer, these media spokespersons become synonymous with movement leaders. Sometimes they are (as in the case of Larry Kramer); most times they are not. Further, our reliance on the straight media to communicate to our own constituency invariably tempers our ability to talk forthrightly; there is a vast difference between the tone of gay and lesbian voices in our own forums (conferences, workshops, intracommunity conversations, gay media) and the tone of the same voices in the straight media. Finally, straight media coverage is a poor way for gay people to debate and develop strategies across our movement; we need our own media, our own private television networks to train interested activists in how to organize, our own computer hotlines and political action centers. In those gay media which exist, the gay press has moved away from activist journalism to mimicking the straight models of news coverage. Like their straight counterparts, the gay media has an agenda that is masked in the pretense of objective journalism. Sadly, the agenda of most gay newspapers does not include an explicit commitment to building a stronger gay political movement.

In both the short and long run, there is no substitute for gay and lesbian media. We need a muckraking and aggressive gay and lesbian press that is attentive to the movement and unafraid to challenge it to be more honest. Such a press would explain the history, context, and behind-the-scenes deals that accompany gay political activism, and not merely reprint the press releases of those with whom its owners agree. A number of weekly papers—like *Out Front* in Denver, *Bay Times* in San Francisco, *Windy City Times* and *Outlines* in Chicago, *Between the Lines* in Michigan—try to do this kind of reporting. Others, like the *Washington Blade*, offer exceptional analysis and longer behind-the-news stories by reporters like Peter Frieberg and Lisa Keen, but sometimes ape the straight media's view of the gay movement. The gay press is more than a job; it is a part of the movement: it must be the eyes and ears and information processor for the average lesbian, gay, bisexual, and transgender person. Its most important task is to pay attention—to expose the reasons for gay rights victories and defeats, to evaluate the impact of our machinations on our movement, to offer perspective. Only such a press can keep the movement both informed and honest.

The legacy of the closet and problems with intramovement communication are compounded by the inability of political activists to make politics relevant to ordinary gay folk. Countless times, I have been stopped by gay people in my neighborhood (in Boston, Washington, and Provincetown) and asked how they can become more involved. My answer is always halting and unsatisfactory: I tell them to look up groups in the local newspaper and start going to meetings. That answer is not enough if we are to transform an unorganized community into an active movement. The best way to describe the problem of direct contact between the movement and gay people is physically: the site of greatest political activity in our political movement is not where most of us live our daily lives. On a material level, the institutions we have created for political activism, located, as most are, in Washington or in the largest cities of our states, have no relationship to the daily lives of gay and lesbian people. Their counterparts in cities and towns across the country could become the links, but they are, without exception, seriously underfunded and far too weak. In the states and cities where there are staffed gay political groups, we rarely take time to recruit and train volunteers or activists. Instead we engage in crisis management (responding to homophobia) or in behind-the-scenes lobbying. Neither of these is a movement-building strategy.

Some say that gay people are more interested in meeting our social needs than shouldering our political responsibilities. Our failure to turn a personally oriented experience of discovery into a movement for political reform, much less fundamental political change, is a critical barrier to gay political progress. On any given Saturday night, the people in the bars, nightclubs, and discos of one major city would far outnumber the members of gay political organizations. Thus, the primary locus of the gay community in every part of the country remains the gay and lesbian bar, not the gay community center or the gay political organization. In midsize or small cities, the disparity is even more noticeable: a handful of political activists run the all-volunteer political group, yet hundreds of politically uninvolved gay and lesbian people gather weekly at social events, sports leagues, church services, or other community events.

Part of the responsibility for this disparity lies with the political movement itself. Bars and community events give our people something that political groups do not yet give: a place to go, something to do, and a sense of individual belonging. For one, bars are physical places, far more accessible to ordinary gay people than political groups. Most local political groups do not have offices, don't meet on a regular basis, and generally list an answering machine and post office box as their number and address. The promise of community that bars offer, false or real, draws people to them, as much as the alcohol, drugs, sex, and rock-and-roll. The gay movement does not seem as inviting, although I daresay it contains many of the same dramas as our bars provide. Most important, bars capitalize on the lesson gay liberationists learned long ago: sexual politics is not just about legislation, elections, and political power; it is about desire and pleasure. Since culture, not politics, is the domain of such pleasure, we must focus on the sites of family, community, and gay subculture for more of our political organizing.

Most recently, spurred by the availability of local, state, and national funds for AIDS education, prevention, and care, a new kind of gay and lesbian institution has appeared: the gay social service organization. Social service groups were born out of the self-help impulses of gay and lesbian liberation in the early 1970s: gay men's VD clinics, lesbian self-help health centers, hotlines for suicide prevention, counseling centers, antiviolence projects, all sprang up as activists tried to meet community needs that our governments were ignoring. But until AIDS brought home the need for such services to middle-class gay and bisexual men, these organizations did not enjoy the financial support of the gay community nor did they receive any money from government programs created to fund such services for other Americans.

Gay and AIDS service organizations exist because of the abdication of gay people by our society. Yet despite some notable exceptions—like the Hetrick Martin Institute for lesbian and gay youth in New York or the Dallas Gay and Lesbian Alliance—many such organizations fail to see their mission as providing political leadership on gay issues. The rationale used by some organizations to avoid political activity is that they legally cannot do so without jeopardizing their tax-exempt status. For years, the Names Project mobilized thousands of people through the AIDS Memorial Quilt, but failed to connect its constituency with the political movement working for a stronger national AIDS policy. That this argument is used at all shows how narrowly we have defined social services. Indeed, this is an argument that the Christian Coalition apparently disregards! Tax-exempt groups are, in fact, allowed to engage in lobbying activity under IRS rules if they clearly earmark the expenditures incurred in such activity and if they keep the activity to less than 20 percent of their overall operating budget. By failing to act politically, these organizations weaken the movement that enables them to exist in the first place.

If each gay and AIDS organization engaged in even the most basic kinds of political education of its clients, volunteers, and supporters—encouraging them to register and vote, informing them of the voting records on gay and AIDS issues of local politicians, and fostering debate and discussion of the problems gay people face at the national or local level—gay and lesbian communities across the country would be far more politicized and mobilized. The failure to do this kind of political organizing has hurt the AIDS movement immeasurably. Although millions of lives have been touched by loss from AIDS, no AIDS-related political organization has yet organized a massive letter-writing campaign to defeat an antigay AIDS measure. We lost the effort to overturn the ban on visitation and immigration by HIV-positive people in 1991; we were unable to secure drastic increases of AIDS funding until the Democrats came into office; and we have been unable to gain adequate funds for AIDS-prevention programs.

Our failure to see gay social services in a political light is a failure of vision and an institutional limit that may be inherent to service organizations. Eric Rofes suggests that social service agencies will never be forces for progressive social change. To the extent that such groups depend on the government for their financial survival, they will not challenge the government. To the extent that our service organizations depend on private funding from wealthy individuals, their boards are controlled by people with a stake in maintaining the status quo. So, for example, in March 1990, when I asked several of my colleagues to join me in protesting George Bush at a speech we had been invited to attend, the heads of AIDS service organizations all told me they could not do so because several of their funders (corporate and philanthropic) would be in the room.

In addition, Rofes notes, these social service agencies are frequently run by people who do not have activist movement backgrounds, but are instead professional managers, business people, or administrators. Their skills are useful in running complex nonprofit groups, but their lack means the groups are run by managers rather than political leaders. Finally, service agencies deal most often with the symptoms of the problems they address, and rarely establish ways to change the political causes of social problems. It took GMHC at least five years after its founding, and enormous pressure from Larry Kramer and others, to establish a public policy office. Today, GMHC is rare among AIDS organizations in the political advocacy it provides. Similar policy departments in gay community centers in New York City and Los Angeles have propelled these centers into leadership roles for securing attention and funds for the urgent problems facing gay people.

That social service organizations differ so little from their heterosexual counterparts is both deliberate and tragic. The sameness seems deliberate because the more we resemble things as they are, the more respectable and legitimate we appear. The more respectable gay institutions seem, the more often government and foundations will support our projects. And the more funding we secure, the more gay people our institutions can serve. Most gay and lesbian service organizations are trapped in this dance of self-perpetuation, which is the ultimate price of assimilation. The mirroring of straight culture's organizations and operation is tragic because it prevents us from developing fresh solutions to our problems. Are we in favor of the existing social service system, the existing health care system, the existing welfare system? How would we change them, in light of our own experience of health crisis, denial of government services, or welfare? Aping straight social service agencies leaves us in the position of rarely asking such questions.

Despite their limitations, service agencies are our most promising outposts. Such groups can strengthen gay and lesbian political power because they are the bridges between the cultural sphere (where gay and lesbian people live, make family, raise children, and create a life) and the political realm (where the gay movement fights discrimination). They touch people otherwise unreached by the gay and lesbian movement. In one New York City agency alone, the Lesbian and Gay Community Services Center, more than five thousand per week use the building. Even if we assume that only a fraction of those visitors are first-timers, tens of thousands of gay New Yorkers come through the center each year. No gay or lesbian political group in New York counts tens of thousands of members from New York City. The Empire State Pride Agenda, New York's statewide gay rights group, has fewer than five thousand dues-paying members. The same pattern is repeated in social service agencies across the country. Community centers, clinics, hotlines, support groups, and cultural groups draw thousands more participants than do gay political organizations. These thousands of constituents are likely to be unaware of what the major issues are, which political groups exist, and how individuals can get involved.

How we utilize the grassroots communities is a key to the expansion of gay and lesbian political clout. National gay and lesbian groups must develop models for structuring state and local activism, for training and organizing local gay rights supporters into a more coordinated movement. One model could apply techniques that religious conservatives use to build a movement out of their churches. The Christian Coalition takes its religious activists and organizes them by precinct. Each precinct has coordinators who get to know other Christians in their neighborhood. The neighborhood-based activists are given a simple and clear national agenda that they can work on locally (school prayer, opposition to abortion, opposition to sex education and condom distribution, support for the Contract with America). They also receive training in leadership skills, media skills, organizational development, and political organizing. It is possible to organize gay and lesbian communities in a similar manner, but we need national coordination of the effort. The focus of the national movement must shift back to the communities and neighborhood level. That is where the next wave of change for gay and lesbian freedom will start.

The fact that gay and lesbian people have created a growing array of groups and projects suggests that we care passionately about being queer and being able to live our lives. The subculture is our refuge, and we spend a lot of time supporting it. But the movement does not use this cultural infrastructure to reach people not usually motivated by traditional direct mail or media or fundraising events. Even when we do reach out, our communication rarely goes beyond exhortations to join our particular group. We must speak to our people about what it means to be political; tell them why their voice matters inside our movement and outside. And we must do more than speak. I see evidence of such a change among local gay and lesbian organizations like Beyond the Closet in rural Oregon, and the Anti-Homophobia and Anti-Racism Commission in Ithaca, New York. Beyond the Closet counters the disinformation of the antigay right by organizing among gay and straight people. In 1995, it sponsored the speaking tour of Floyd Cochran, a former neo-Nazi, who now speaks out on the dangers of fascist organizing in America. Similarly, the AHRC in Ithaca has formed a straight-gay coalition to oppose the right in school board policy fights, local elections, and local action against racism. These groups, and scores like them, are broadening the purpose of gay organizations by agreeing upon the linkage between homophobia, racism, anti-Semitism, and sexism. They create concrete projects to engage gay and straight participants in joint action.

The biggest obstacle such groups face is the persistence of political apathy and despair among gay, lesbian, and bisexual people. Not that apathy is limited to our movement alone. We live in a cynical time when the political culture of Washington is universally disdained. The left has long criticized traditional politics as ineffective and conservative. The right has defamed most traditional democratic institutions with the epithet of the 1980s, the *l* word, liberal. Caught in the firestorm are most people. What do we think of government, of political institutions, and leadership? Whom can we trust? These questions are asked by us all, and lead many to reject traditional political involvement. Cynicism about politics is a convenient excuse to avoid personal responsibility for action. Only 39 percent of eligible voters participated in the 1994 congressional elections, a sharp contrast to the more than 90 percent who participated in France's 1995 presidential primary. Movements for social change seem anachronistic to many, and, in truth, we may never reach the profoundly cynical. But to those who merely use cynicism as a mask for their fear, movements like gay liberation offer a lifeline. The best way to counter the cynicism and the fear that underlies it is to inspire people with the stories of what we have in fact changed by being organized. It is extraordinary to consider how much social change has taken place because of the activism of relatively few gay, lesbian, and bi people. That any of us can live openly gay lives is a miracle that even the cynical among us must acknowledge.

Apathy is also a consequence of being overwhelmed. The age of information quickly overloads us with details of tragedies and human cruelty that shock and numb us. What can the individual do, in the face of Bosnia, Rwanda, earthquakes, floods, gun-related violence, domestic abuse, corruption, and terrorist bombs? The question of what issue we "pick" to work is like choosing which colored ribbon to wear to publicize our cause. Political action seems symbolic and ineffectual. The problem is one that every political activist encounters personally, and is one that can be overcome only individually. To say that a single-issue movement will help us handle feelings of being overwhelmed is to deny the complexity of the problems we face. We need a holistic approach to our political activism; if we can keep such a frame of mind, what seems overwhelming will shrink because we can appreciate how our small, daily activism helps a far larger political struggle.

A third component of apathy that is particular to gay or lesbian experience is what we might call internal power, or, more commonly, self-esteem. To orient our people toward political consciousness, we must make clear the relationship between our movement for rights and liberation and our quest for gay and lesbian self-esteem. Issues of self-esteem and self-loathing are so central to the conduct of gay and lesbian politics that the veteran activist Tim McFeeley noted that "our movement is more about therapy than it is about politics. It is about people coming to grips with themselves, feeling good about themselves, and not hating themselves. And you've got to get beyond all of that before people actually will pick up the phone, or write a letter." The cultural arm of the movement gains its strength and vitality by serving our need to belong and by providing each of us with a sense of worth. Similarly, fundraising dinners succeed because they give people a sense of empowerment and self-esteem, although they do so in a format that is troubling in its elitism and class bias.

LIBERATION AND ITS DISCONTENTS

The antigay right recognizes the danger of our empowerment; I think this is why we see neoconservatives reviving the idea of shame. In a cover story in January 1995, *Newsweek* held up the beneficial value to America of "shame." The thesis was that perhaps we needed some measure of "propriety" or shame to check our individualism and remind us of individual responsibility for ethical behavior. Nowhere did the article apply that value to the most immodest of cultural forces—the market, which operates shamelessly, without morality or boundary. Shame—the very obstacle so many gay people struggle to overcome—is brandished as a weapon to reimpose our obedience to a moral code that teaches us that we are "intrinsically disordered."

A jarring example of using shame to criticize the gay movement is found in *Democracy on Trial*, the recent book by the straight neoliberal political scientist Jean Bethke Elshtain. The author challenges gay liberation's call for cultural acceptance as part of a "politics of displacement," which, she argues, threatens the fabric of civil society today.

Elshtain defines this politics of displacement as taking two routes. "In the first, everything private—from one's sexual practices to blaming one's parents for ones lack of self-esteem—becomes grist for the public mill. In the second, everything public—from the grounds on which politicians are judged to health policies to gun regulations—is privatized and played out in a psychodrama on a grand scale, that is, we fret as much about a politician's sexual life as about his foreign policy." Elshtain argues that the collapse of public and private undermines "democratic thinking" and opens up the way for antidemocratic social control. She argues that the realm of public life or politics ought to be separated from the realm of private life or the freedom of individuals. While acknowledging its transformative power, she explicitly rejects the feminist postulation that the personal is political, by stating that it diminishes civil rights to individual desires or wants. Her argument for the preservation of distinction between public and private life is illustrated in part through gay and lesbian politics.

According to Elshtain, gay liberation's call for freedom is contradictory: it seeks to get government out of gay and lesbian lives at the same instant that it seeks to have government validate "gay lifestyle." Although Elshtain explicitly endorses the gay and lesbian pursuit of equal treatment and civil rights, she objects to the displacement upon the public sphere of what she considers private choices. In a passage revealing in what it says about this liberal ally's understanding of gay and lesbian politics, she writes,

> The politics of democratic civility and equity holds that *all* citizens, including gays, have a right, as individuals, to be protected from intrusion or harassment and to be free from discrimination in such areas as employment and housing. They also have the right to create their own forms of "public space" within which to express and to reveal their particular concerns and to argue in behalf of policies they support . . . But no one has a *civil* right, as a gay, a disciple of an exotic religion, or a political dissident, to full public sanction of his or her activities, values, beliefs or habits . . . Paradoxically, in his quest to attain sanction for the *full* range of who he is, the cross-dresser or sadomasochist puts his life on full display. He opens himself up to *publicity* in ways that others are bound to find quite uncivil, in part because a certain barrier—the political philosopher Hannah Arendt would have called it the boundary of shame—is harshly breached.

Elshtain misunderstands the devaluation of gayness that is at the core of our stigmatization, a degradation of which unequal treatment is but a symptom. The public-private distinction, like "don't ask, don't tell," reinforces the antigay stigma because it assumes the fundamental illegitimacy of homosexual desire. There is nothing wrong with telling (or asking or pursuing) the truth that we are gay or lesbian or bisexual. The right to privacy, defined as the freedom of the individual to live without the meddling of government, is indeed a vital concept to both the gay liberation and to the gay rights movement. But for Elshtain, as for most liberals, notions of privacy have become confused with the conservative moralism of propriety.

Elshtain correctly notes that new social change movements like feminism and gay liberation challenge old boundaries between the private and the public, but she misrepresents the reasons. The public was defined in such a way as to exclude women and gay people. By asserting that domination based on gender affected who got a job, who wielded power, and how women and men were treated in social institutions, feminism upset the old balance in which private meant home and heterosexual hearth, and public meant the whole wide world in which mainly men were free to roam. Gay liberation similarly challenges the public and private division we have inherited, arguing that since there is nothing inherently shameful about human homosexual response, open homosexuality should not be stigmatized. The apparent contradiction, that government get out of gay lives and that government protect gay lives, is resolved if one accepts the premise that homosexual behavior is not wrong. Elshtain's invocation of shame, as an appropriate boundary between public and private, and the examples of sadomasochists and drag queens that she uses, reveal the persistence of liberal uneasiness with anything but the most "respectable" forms of homosexual being.

SYNTHESIS, POLITICS, AND GENUINE POWER

In journeying from the progressive side of the movement to its civil rights mainstream, and in struggling to make a place there for my multiracial, multi-issue politics, I am struck by the resistance to political debate in our movement. We are a people hungry for simple answers and we often place each other in simplistic categories. Whatever ideology we espouse is what we insist others subscribe to. We say we care about political diversity, but we conduct our political fights like jihads. The slash-and-burn style of political argumentation leaves us little room for growth: one must be for direct action or against it, either a sell-out or a hold-out, either Republican or Democrat, either a conservative or a progressive. The rigidity of political categories has intensified in the past three years. Perhaps because there is more turf (money, access, media visibility) to fight about today, the rhetorical battle over who "legitimately" speaks for the gay and lesbian civil rights movement has heated up dramatically. In the crossfire of invective and sound bite, the truth is the first victim.

So, for example, when gay conservatives state that the Stonewall generation of activists has run the movement and must now move over, of whom are they speaking? I was ten years old when Stonewall occurred; fifteen when NGLTF and Lambda were founded; and twenty-one at the time of the first March on Washington in 1979. Liberals, libertarians, moderates, and conservatives run most of the gay or lesbian organizations I know. Could they be speaking of the army of lawyers and MBAs (educated at Harvard, Yale, Northeastern, Hamilton, Stanford, and Georgetown) who are gay leaders? Does what they say have any relevance to the large numbers of gay and lesbian activists who were children in the sixties, not children *of* the sixties, whose politics were forged out of the horror of AIDS?

Conversely, when queer militants and direct-action advocates write off as too mainstream those who work in certain gay organizations, who lobby, who wear a particular kind of uniform, or espouse liberal democratic views, whom are they identifying with and whom are they against? How do they answer the contradictory experience of their own inclusion? Since 1988, ACT UP has participated fully in federal AIDS policymaking bodies; the most militant Queer Nationalists are thrilled to see gay images reflected in Fox television; the most "radical" actions that Queer Nation undertook were all about visibility, not institutional inequality.

Again and again, we are told we must choose, as if there are always two sides and all of us must be on one or the other. Independent or critical thinking has been replaced by the either-or view of politics in which the two sides never meet, hold dialogue, or transform each other. I find this process stultifying and frustrating. Pressure to make such false choices obscures the political impasse we have reached, and what we must do to build genuine power. Unlike gay conservatives, I believe we distract ourselves from the massive task of building a more powerful movement when we engage in dualistic or reductive fights about strategies for gaining gay power. Our power lies neither in electoral nor in cultural action alone, but in both. Moreover, it begins first inside each of us. Our salvation lies neither with the Republican Party nor the Democratic Party, but with ourselves. Instead, we need a post-partisan ethos and a commitment to cooperation despite political difference. We need a political reality that synthesizes rather than reinforces the dualism of margin and center. Such politics grow out of gay liberation.

Strategies that emphasize grassroots involvement differ markedly from the politics of access. A liberation-oriented approach to gay power would start with two premises: the idea of ground-up power and the related question of its mission. Such ground-up power is about exactly what the words suggest: grinding up the elite-focused politics of access on which we now rely, and replacing them with another conception of power, one that values the participation of each of us. Gay civil participation in the life of our society begins wherever we live—small towns, middle America, the South, or on the coasts. Such civil *citizenship* (a word I use despite its troubling roots in national chauvinism) begins with each of us being registered and politically aware, and it is made real by our action—both in how we live our lives (our praxis) and in how we come together to solve the problems facing both our local gay community and the broader community in which we live. In other words, none of us has the luxury of waiting for the Washington or New York–based movement to solve our local problems; we must dig in ourselves. If no groups exist at the local level, we must start them. Where service groups exist, we must urge them to undertake political training and education. And in the neighborhoods and towns where we live and work, we must do that most important thing—communicate with our families, our neighbors, our co-workers, and our friends about what being gay means to each of us.

Another dimension of such gay citizenship is what I call its mission: What are we seeking power to achieve? A liberation movement's answer differs from the liberal politics of single-issue and gay rights that we currently espouse. A liberation movement seeks fundamental social change: we are for a just world in which racism, homophobia, sexism, economic injustice, and other systems of domination are frankly addressed and replaced with new models. Such a movement begins first of all with an act of faith that the movement and society are possible. Put another way, this faith in social change is what the theorist bell hooks has so elegantly termed "the power of disbelief." We must disbelieve in the permanence of things as they are in order to believe in our ability to launch a new gay and lesbian liberation movement.

CHAPTER EIGHT

MONEY AND THE MOVEMENT,

OR LOOKING FOR MR. GEFFEN

Oh baby, it would mean so much to me . . .
To buy you all the things you need, for free.

—*"Free Money," Patti Smith*

When I was executive director of NGLTF, I launched a campaign to meet David Geffen, the gay billionaire. But like my attempts to meet President George Bush, Secretary Louis Sullivan, and even NAACP head Benjamin Hooks, I did not succeed. In each of these attempts, I sought different things. With Ben Hooks and the NAACP leaders (whom I continued to try to meet even after I left NGLTF in 1992), I wanted to figure out how to improve communication between the gay and black civil rights movements. With Louis Sullivan, I sought to discuss the crisis in suicide among gay and lesbian youth and the urgency of AIDS prevention. With George Bush, AIDS and gay rights were the chief items. With David Geffen, my agenda was money and movement clout.

At the time I began my search for signs of Geffen, the visibility and stature of the gay and lesbian rights movement were far lower than today. The extensive closet in which so many wealthy people lived seemed unattainable by activists like me; we had little access to prominent and powerful people, either straight or gay. In 1989, after all, the media had not yet declared us chic. Fear of the well-organized antigay vote turned the simple task of securing meetings with politicians into a complicated game. It was rare then to find straight, lesbian, or gay celebrities willing to stand up publicly for gay and lesbian equality. The exceptions were those involved in AIDS-related fundraising: advocates like Dr. Mathilde Krim, Dr. Ruth Westheimer, Marlo Thomas and Phil Donahue, Elizabeth Taylor, Judith Light and Robert Desidero, Whoopi Goldberg, Judy Peabody, Barbra Streisand, and a handful of entertainment industry bigwigs. Our problems with access to prominent allies persisted until 1992, when the liberal media discovered the gay and lesbian movement during the presidential campaign. (Ironically, the conservative media discovered us during the 1980s, and homosexuality and AIDS had been a long-standing topic in conservative journals like *The National Review, Commentary*, and the *Washington Times*.) One result of mainstream media attention was that gay and lesbian civil rights became a safe topic of conversation among the rich, the powerful, and the public.

Before this shift in media attention and cultural visibility, movement activists were disdained by wealthy and powerful gay people. Like the fictional Roy Cohn character in Tony Kushner's *Angels in America: Millennium Approaches,* those with power regarded the gay and lesbian movement with scorn. When Cohn is told by his doctor to stop denying that he has engaged in sex with men and face the fact that he has contracted AIDS, he replies,

> AIDS. Homosexual. Gay. Lesbian. You think these are names that tell you who someone sleeps with, but they don't tell you that . . . Like all labels they tell you one thing and one thing only: where does an individual so identified fit in the food chain, in the pecking order? Not ideology, or sexual taste, but something much simpler: clout. Not who I fuck or who fucks me, but who will pick up the phone when I call, who owes me favors. This is what a label refers to. Now, to someone who does not understand this, homosexual is what I am because I have sex with men. But really this is wrong. Homosexuals are not men who sleep with other men. Homosexuals are men who in fifteen years of trying cannot get a pissant antidiscrimination bill through City Council. Homosexuals are men who know nobody and who nobody knows. Who have zero clout. Does that sound like me, Henry?

Even today, few gay people with political or financial clout take responsibility for helping the movement. Like Cohn, perhaps they believe they are special, uniquely powerful, that their contacts and money will insulate them from prejudice. Perhaps they think that if they do not identify themselves as gay or lesbian but do not deny it either, they will be regarded as more than queer by the straight world. That money and social status will insulate them from the prejudice of a Gingrich or a Ralph Reed. It does not. Cohn and Geffen will never be fully equal in the eyes of many, despite their accomplishments and wealth, until we create a society in which homosexuality is regarded as morally and fundamentally equal to heterosexuality. Money changes nothing in this regard.

The activist side of the fence is obsessed with the lives and fortunes of wealthy queer people. Activists trade stories of Geffen sightings and activities the way we trade gossip about the hundreds of other reputedly gay and lesbian celebrities, movie stars, sports figures, journalists, and politicians. Some of the drama of all these Geffen sightings is simply that of chasing a larger-than-life figure. Geffen has at his disposal more money, and therefore more power, than any queer person in the country (maybe in the world!). To us, he lives in this wonderful Gatsby-esque world, jetting among several homes while making fantastic deals in the business world. Some of the drama is about our "Cinderella complex": the prince will come along, embrace the movement, rescue it from poverty and enslavement to an evil stepmother, and make us queen! Geffen, among other rich people, symbolizes everything the movement longs for and does not have: money, access to anyone in the government and private sector, freedom, and power. We dream of harnessing his power, his Rolodex, and his wealth. Again and again, I've heard fellow activists say, "If only someone would leave a multimillion dollar estate to endow NGLTF, imagine how cool that would be," or "If only wealthy people would work together seriously to fund political fights." Clearly, these wishes have yet to come true.

When I began my quest for David Geffen, he was far less publicly connected to national lesbian and gay politics than he is today. He was not fully out of the closet until 1991, when he acknowledged in an interview with *Vanity Fair* that he was bisexual. Even that declaration was arguably made under the duress of exposure. By late 1991, queer mutterings about Geffen's sexual orientation had turned into public calls for his outing after Geffen Records released a homophobic album by the comedian Andrew Dice Clay. Queer Nation–Los Angeles pick-

eted Geffen at various functions, calling him harsh names—from traitor
to hypocrite to simply closet case. Michelangelo Signorile used his
column in *Outweek* to castigate the immorality of wealthy men like
Geffen in not giving more funds, energy, and attention to either the
AIDS organizations or the movement. How he was affected by all this
angry attention, we may never know. But what is clear is that after his
public acknowledgement of bisexuality, Geffen began to be more
closely associated with gay and lesbian projects.

I approached my attempt to get a meeting with Geffen in the same
way I approached the task of securing a meeting with a Reagan-Bush
official: as if it were an all-out guerrilla campaign. First, I did my
research. I gathered information about his donation patterns and philanthropic interests. I read whatever I could find about him. I quietly
asked those who knew him what he was like, what his interests were,
whether he cared about politics, whether he was liberal or conservative,
whether he would meet with someone like me. Someone I called told
me that Geffen had just had dinner with Tom Stoddard. Someone else
had seen him at a party. In 1991, a friend, the producer Cheryl Swan-
nack, told me that her contacts in Hollywood—among them, close
friends of Geffen—were upset about the NGLTF decision to oppose
the Gulf War. Another friend, Tim Sweeney, told me about lunching
with Geffen. "It was the most amazing thing," he said, "I got a phone
call from him to have lunch and he announced that he was giving
GMHC one million dollars!"

Geffen had long given quietly to many charities, nongay and AIDS
charities, in particular. I often wondered whether he knew how closely
his every philanthropic move was watched by a movement with so few
resources. In 1992, 1993, and 1994, his public support for, and level of
giving to, gay and lesbian causes increased. He gave two pledges, of $1
million apiece, to AIDS organizations in New York (GMHC) and Los
Angeles (AIDS Project LA). He donated $20,000 apiece to the fights
against the antigay referenda in Oregon and Colorado in 1992. The
next year, he pledged a five-year grant, totaling $150,000, to Lambda
Legal Defense and Education Fund. Eventually, he increased his grants
to groups like the NGLTF and HRCF from about $10,000 a year to as
much as $50,000. In 1993, Geffen actively attempted to influence the
gay and lesbian movement's agenda and politics when he pledged significant funds for the battle to overturn the military policy. Geffen's and
Diller's promises of financial support were crucial to the launching of
the Campaign for Military Service.

Armed with information, I tried the direct approach. I wrote letters requesting a meeting. In the hope that substance mattered, I sent him copies of NGLTF position papers and reports on antigay and lesbian violence, on domestic partnership and family issues, and on the federal legislative agenda. I called the Geffen Company each time I traveled to Los Angeles to see whether I could arrange a meeting. His staff was unfailingly polite, but our schedules never seemed to match. Eventually, I received a handwritten note from Geffen, apologizing for his busy schedule and his inability to set up the meeting I requested. I appreciated that response. And I was undaunted. So I tried the indirect approach. I asked friends of NGLTF who knew him in Hollywood to arrange an introduction. I asked his acquaintances to talk to him about our work. His friends were used to this kind of attention. Some said, Forget it, he'll never meet with you. Others refused to help in any way. They all said that David is his own man and they had no influence on him.

When I finally met David Geffen, it was anticlimatic and unplanned. We met not at a meeting, briefing, political event, or even a fundraiser, but at a Hollywood birthday party for a mutual acquaintance. I had been brought to the party by two Hollywood friends, former NGLTF board co-chair Curtis Shepard and Hollywood power lawyer Alan Hergott. The house we went to was tucked away in a canyon. A valet parked our car, and we entered a sprawling sea of extremely handsome men. Curt did a quick count and informed me that I was one of three women and one of two nonwhite people in this crowd of several hundred. So what else is new, I said, and we joked that this was perfect, since the whole point of my job was to stand out in a crowd.

We walked right into Geffen. He looked dapper and trim in casual clothes. Alan made the introductions. Geffen was impassive. I offended him almost immediately by thanking him for dumping Andrew Dice Clay, a development the papers had just announced. He informed me he had not dumped Clay for the reasons I suggested and said he'd known Clay for years and that Clay was not at all homophobic. Alan politely tried to turn the conversation to a topic he thought more neutral. He told a story of a young lawyer who had approached him for advice about being openly gay in Hollywood's legal community. Alan remarked how the lunch he'd had with the younger lawyer made him realize again the importance of being a positive gay role model. Geffen poked fun at it all, joking that it was nice that Alan had time to lunch with anyone who called on him, and he thought the importance of role models was overstated. We again argued about the subject of role models and being out until someone distracted Geffen away.

That minor encounter was to be my one and only meeting with this formidable gay man whom I had pursued for several years. I don't single out Geffen because I think he is bad but because he is a symbol of the economic disparity between some gay people of wealth and the larger, far poorer movement. Indeed, I share this story for the things it reveals about me and the movement: our desperation for adequate levels of funding, the disproportionate attention commanded by the wealthy, the debasing nature of the process of fundraising, the pitfalls our political leaders encounter when investing so much energy in fundraising, and the fundamental lack of common purpose among the powerful and wealthy in our communities and those who do the unglamorous work of community organizing and political activism.

My pursuit of Geffen is a tale about the basic corruption of politics —the pursuit of money. This corruption is evident in the 1996 presidential race in which candidates like Phil Gramm boast of how much money they can raise, as if that establishes their merit to govern. It is evident in the demographics of who gets to become an elected official at the national, gubernatorial, or even state level; the wealthy far outnumber working-class or ordinary folk. And it is a corruption our movement does little to question. Chasing money occupies more of our political leaders' time than political strategy does. To raise the money, one must become something that one did not start out being—elite-oriented, compromised politically, and overly solicitous of some people with little to contribute beyond a check.

Fundraising resembles the oldest profession in the world. It may be vigorously denied by some political leaders, but it is the subtext of countless decisions made by lesbian and gay organizations. Fundraising considerations dictate whom we seek out and befriend. Potential donors are the people our political leaders have breakfast, lunch, and dinner with. Fundraising considerations determine where we go for "vacations"; meccas like Fire Island, South Beach, Hawaii, Saint Barts are great places to go to schmooze wealthy queers. Attendance at gay and lesbian fundraisers is an expected part of the "social" life of gay organizational heads.

I have made deep, life-long friendships with people I met during the process of donor cultivation and solicitation. But it is also true that I have spent more hours than I care to remember with people solely to get a $1000 check from them. I have, in the search for money, put up with offensive comments, outright harangues about me and my staff, drunken behavior, idiotic ideas, and enormous egos. During my very first meeting with the late real estate magnate Allan Morrow, who was a major contributor to gay and lesbian causes in New York, he berated me for nearly an hour about all the things NGLTF and every other gay group did wrong. I sat in stunned silence. I felt afraid, then embarrassed, then angry, and above all ashamed—as if I had done something wrong, as if this powerful man who was so sure he was right was, in fact, right. Finally, and somewhat sheepishly, Morrow stopped long enough to ask who I was and what I hoped to accomplish at NGLTF's helm. I left the meeting shaking and furious. But I never said a word to Morrow about it, because NGLTF needed his good will and financial support.

The time and attention we give to wealthy people often takes away from the time and attention we should devote to the politics and programs of our organizations. This conflict in priorities—between the dynamics of raising funds from upper-middle-class and middle-class gay people and the exercise of actual political leadership—is a major reason that we consider so few gay and lesbian organizational heads our genuine political leaders. They spend less time on substance than on managing the process of raising money. Rather than speak at a local high school, arrange for a leadership training of campus activists, hold meetings with potential allies in the straight world, or meet with any number of activists who will generate no money—our executive directors, and even program directors, spend a considerable amount of time worrying about where to find the money to fund their positions. If our leaders have to attend fundraising events nearly every night, when do they read, think, argue with each other, have time to relax and reflect? If our leaders spend all their time in the overprivileged enclaves of wealthy gay and lesbian circles in New York, LA, Chicago, Atlanta, how can they remain connected to the realities faced by the vast majority of our people, who live far more ordinary lives in small towns, the suburbs, or the inner cities? And if our leaders are intent on getting large checks from a small handful of donors, what compromises in politics and program do they make in exchange?

THE ECONOMY OF QUEERNESS

To understand our dependence on donors like Mr. Geffen, we must consider how the creation and the expansion of modern gay and lesbian communities are tied to economic ventures. Unlike ethnic minorities, which transmit their cultural heritage through family, ritual, and tradition, unlike nationalist identity, religious identity, or even gender identity, queer identity is learned principally through the mediation of commercial enterprises. The first time I was in a room full of other lesbian and bisexual women was when I went to a bar near Poughkeepsie, New York. My earliest experiences of lesbian community outside bars came in settings like women's and gay bookstores, women's music festivals, lesbian-feminist concerts and film screenings—all commercial settings (granted, cultural as well). Only after years of being out of the closet, and developing a strong queer familial network, was I able to experience gay community outside a commercial setting. Even today, the public space in which I can be queer is small, contested, and far from "free." This lack of public space is why actions for visibility and public displays of queer identification (buttons, T-shirts, pride rallies, kiss-ins, leafletings, holding hands while shopping) are important: being homosexual is as normal as being heterosexual, and should be judged by the same standards. The public space we occupy today is more often commercial.

In opening remarks to a 1994 conference on Homo/Economics, sponsored by the Center for Lesbian and Gay Studies at the City University of New York, the activist and theorist Jeffrey Escoffier noted that economic or market considerations have played a large role in the development of our communities. He outlined four stages in the postwar economic development of gay and lesbian communities. First was what he called the closet economy, represented by bars, mail order businesses, the sex industry, and other vehicles for queer connection that we invented to circumvent repression. After Stonewall came a liberation economy, anchored still by bars but now expanded into bookstores, coffeehouses, bathhouses, newspapers, businesses, and community organizations. Third was the appearance of what Escoffier termed the territorial economy, or the economy of the gay and lesbian community made tangible or physical. This was signified by gentrification in the 1970s and 1980s, and by the creation of gay and lesbian neighborhoods or by the purchase of land in rural areas, by counterculturalists like the radical fairies and lesbian separatists. The fourth period, Escoffier noted, was the AIDS economy, manifest in the many AIDS service and educational organizations, viatical insurance firms, and a broad range of private and nonprofit health and support services.

Escoffier's conception postulates a set of relationships between each of these queer economies; they did not so much succeed each other as coexist. The economies that underlie gay and lesbian communities are overlapping and interdependent, not exclusive. The closet economy exists alongside the more public liberation economy; the territorial economy shelters gay and lesbian people in and out of the closet, but also shelters us from each other; enclaves of gay and lesbian wealth, like Fire Island, South Beach, the Gold Coast, physically separate and insulate us by class, race, and gender. Many of us, in the closet and out, use the bars as our primary entrance to gay and lesbian territory, to find and interact with our people. The AIDS economy has helped build queer territories, as more organizations, buildings, even housing projects come into existence.

To these four economic stages, I would add a new one, in which we are currently engaged: the queer as consumer and its corollary, the selling of gayness. Positioning gay and lesbian people as good consumers has become a principal aspect of the relationship being negotiated among some queer entrepreneurs, the straight mainstream, and even some of our movement leaders. Brokering this relationship are gay and lesbian people working in mainstream corporations as well as queer activists who believe that the market holds the key to our full integration into society. The consumer economy is evident in the rise of mainstream marketing and advertising aimed at gay and lesbian dollars; ads for Ikea furniture, Calvin Klein, and Banana Republic are just the most overt images in this new mode of marketing. The expansion of gay-oriented services and businesses, by both gay and straight entrepreneurs, reflects another dimension of our consumer economy. Even queer nonprofit organizations regard their members in economic terms. AIDS service organizations and the health care industry in general now describe clients as consumers, while Stonewall 25, the commemoration of a political event triggered in a Mafia-run commercial bar, spent more energy on marketing souvenirs like bottled water, kerchiefs, hats, T-shirts, fanny packs, and buttons than it did on developing a clear political message about where the movement stands. Current national leaders like HRCF's Elizabeth Birch and NGLTF's Melinda Paras pepper their talks with the language of corporate business and commercial enterprise. They speak of "re-engineering" the national organizations to better serve their customers, of using market research and bringing more professional management and marketing skills into the (by implication, previously unprofessional and poorly run) movement.

Similarly, lesbian and gay media, desperate to find ways to survive that do not depend on sex ads and classifieds, have eagerly promoted mainstream advertising's discovery of the queer market. Fueled by the promise of newly available ad dollars, a host of new or revamped gay and lesbian lifestyle–oriented publications have come into print, touting themselves as the conduit to certain "niches" in the broader (and they assert lucrative) queer market: *Out, Genre, Poz, Girlfriends, Advocate, 10 Percent, wilde, Deneuve,* to name just a handful. Advertising dollars also buy corporate sponsorship of gay and lesbian community events. The ironies of these matches are sometimes stark. Liquor and beer companies have been among the most long-standing advertisers and sponsors of gay and lesbian events, pride rallies, fundraising dinners. Yet gay and lesbian alcoholism and drug use rates are very high. In September 1995, groups like New York's Lesbian and Gay Community Services Center and Boston's Fenway Community Health Center—both of which house excellent alcohol and drug abuse programs—hosted a massive bike-a-thon fundraiser for their AIDS programs. It was underwritten by Tanqueray gin.

The model of the market increasingly defines how different segments of the gay and lesbian community are isolated for attention, both by businesses and by nonprofit organizations. Marketing professionals offer us techniques like niche marketing, zip-coded fundraising, targeted direct mail, household profiles, and focus groups. The splintering of queer people into narrow market niches, each pursued and catered to for the special things it cares about, has political consequence: it fragments any sense of community that we harbor. The marketing model splinters community into private individuals with "tastes." We are valued as small queer units of the consumption (couples, households, individuals). We are not approached as a community with shared values and aspirations of freedom.

Not only does niche marketing fray community among us; I think it builds no bridges between us and the straight world. Niches work best when they sell most efficiently. An example of this, taken from the world of mainstream publishing, was raised at the OutWrite 93 conference by the novelist Sarah Schulman. She believes that niche marketing shaped queer communities with the work it promoted (and the work it rejected) and that the concept drastically limits the reach of gay and lesbian writing. In 1993, mainstream publishing discovered a gay and lesbian market—articles appeared in *Publishers Weekly;* mainstream houses scrambled to sign gay writers and put out work to meet the suddenly visible market; bidding wars erupted over the sale of queer books (including mine). By the end of 1994, some industry heavy-weights were declaring that the gay publishing boom was over! The reasons for its launch and termination were equally mysterious. I sus-pect they had more to do with the "popularity" of queer ideas in the mainstream than they did with actual sales figures, no less with the quality of the writing under consideration. The publishing world, like every other entertainment-oriented industry, follows the wind; and the wind has turned against us today. Schulman's second point about niche marketing is equally important. The way gay and lesbian books are sold largely determines who reads them and how seriously they are taken. Why should Schulman's six novels be regarded as "gay" or "lesbian" literature instead of novels about a generation, as the Generation X novels of Douglas Copeland and others are? Why should gay and les-bian books be sold primarily to gay and lesbian people rather than to the general reading public?

My point here is fairly obvious: that markets and success, consump-tion and commodities, all have underlying dynamics that, as Sarah Schulman likes to say, can be "demystified." At the moment we are in a movement that is "selling" gayness uncritically, as if the only problem were with the product we sell (poor role models versus good gay images, gay Republican representatives versus lesbians who might be socialists), not with a heterosexist system that is sustained by maintaining us as a niche market. The reality is that the discovery of the African-American market, of more black images and people on television, film, and in commercials, has done little to stem the persistence and revival of rac-ism. Further, the use of slogans like "You've come a long way, baby," to sell cigarettes to women has not precluded the rise of a right-wing movement intent on "restoring" the authority of the man as the head of the family. Our treatment as a market advances our genuine equality only to the extent that a strong political movement exists.

Ultimately, the market-oriented, queer economy we now witness actually feeds the public perception that gay and lesbian people have above-average disposable income. The truth that some of us do, but many of us don't, gets lost in the marketing. Gay and lesbian elderly, for example, may live on fixed incomes. Queer youth who run away from hostile homes are usually homeless and money-less. Thousands of lesbian and gay students, like straight students, are able to get an education only by going into steep debt. Millions of lesbians and gay men are parents, with the same burdens, responsibilities, and financial pressures that heterosexual families encounter. Many of us support our parents or siblings. The myth that we have huge amounts of disposable income is based on surveys of a small segment of the broader queer community—the readers and subscribers of gay and lesbian magazines. Moreover, this myth is perpetuated because the most visible gay, lesbian, bisexual, transsexual people in a culture obsessed with celebrity are the successful, the wealthy, or the upper middle class among us. The large numbers of gay working-class people, of queers in the hard-working and ever-squeezed middle class, the queers supporting themselves as waiters and retail clerks and hairdressers and computer data entry personnel, as secretaries and factory workers, as low-paid child care workers and teachers, are ignored in the rush to cover the Armani lesbians and the upwardly mobile gay men.

MYTHS AND REALITIES OF GAY AND LESBIAN WEALTH

Three stories help illustrate the myths and realities of gay and lesbian wealth. Each story clarifies the repercussions of not knowing the actual status of gay and lesbian people. On April 23, 1993, the Friday before the National March on Washington, the cover story of the *USA Today* Money section was titled "Courting the Gay Market" and subtitled "Advertisers: It's Business, Not Politics." In the story, the reporter quoted several major companies that planned to promote their products at the march or had already developed advertising campaigns with gay themes. These advertisers included Flowers Direct, Naya Spring Water, Levi's, Calvin Klein, and Banana Republic. Without explanation or attribution for the source of its information, the article recited the following data about gay and lesbian wealth: "To more companies, gay consumers are simply an attractive market. They've got money. The average household income is $51,624 for gay men and $42,755 for lesbians, versus the U.S. average of $37,922. They're educated—58%

are college graduates, versus 21% of all Americans. And they are brand-loyal and appreciative. They even write thank-you notes to companies that advertise in gay publications."

The message of the story was simple: gay people in general, and gay men in particular, have lots of disposable income, advertisers know it and are chasing that money. Jeff Vitale, president of Overlooked Opinions, a Chicago-based gay market research firm, was quoted as saying, "You have the pride parades and gay rodeos and festivals, dozens and dozens of events constantly. [Those attending are] proud, and they're into being gay . . . response rates are tremendous."

The *USA Today* article articulated a message that was incorporated into an effective propaganda tape produced and distributed by the religious right. In 1993, Jeremiah Films, a ten-year-old producer of religious right tapes and materials, produced the video *Gay Rights/Special Rights: Inside the Gay Agenda* for the Anaheim-based Traditional Values Coalition. The well-crafted antigay tape spliced in footage from both the 1993 and 1987 gay and lesbian marches on Washington, footage of Dr. King from the 1963 March on Washington, and footage of African-American people expressing outrage at the claim of civil rights made by gay men and women. Among the civil rights "experts" interviewed were Senator Trent Lott (R-MS), former Justice Department head Edwin Meese, Ralph Reed of the Christian Coalition, TVC director Louis Sheldon, and former Reagan education-and-drug czar, William Bennett. By October 1993, the TVC claimed to have sent out "at least" fifteen thousand tapes, including 535 to Congress. Throughout the spring of 1993, the tape was also distributed widely at the Pentagon by opponents of the effort to lift the military ban against gays and was shown to the Joint Chiefs of Staff while the debate to change the military policy was raging.

Like the TVC's earlier tapes—*The Gay Agenda* and *The Gay Agenda in Education*—the new *Gay Rights/Special Rights* tape is carefully constructed propaganda, filled with partial truths and manipulative argumentation. Chief among its theses is that gay people do not "qualify" for civil rights protection as a "protected minority class" because we fail to meet the "test" for such protection set out by the Supreme Court. Early in the videotape the narrator announces, "According to the U.S. Supreme Court, any person seeking protected minority class status must satisfy three elements: immutable characteristics, financial discrimination, and political weakness." Liz Galst points out in the *Boston Phoenix,* "In fact, for a group to be recognized as a protected-minority class, the statutes require it meet only two criteria, neither of which is mentioned in the video. First, the group must be an 'insular and discrete minority.' Second, group members must show they've been subject to 'arbitrary and capricious' treatment." Further, the tape never points out that the Supreme Court does not decide who enjoys civil rights. That authority comes from the U.S. Constitution and its amendments.

Nonetheless, the videotape goes on to a detailed presentation of purportedly factual economic data, comparing "average homosexual household income" with "average African-American household income." The narrator intones, "Compare the results of a nationwide survey reported in the *Wall Street Journal* between homosexuals and African Americans." Again, without attribution or explanation, the film displays graphics showing that the average "homosexual household income" was $55,430 and the average "African-American" household income was $12,166.

Used by both *USA Today* and the TVC, these income figures come from market research surveys done on readers of gay and lesbian magazines and newspapers. Specifically, the $55,430 figure is from a survey that was commissioned by the gay advertising agency Rivendell Marketing Company. The data were cited in a 1991 *Wall Street Journal* article on the gay market. By contrast, the dramatically low figure of African-American income is from the U.S. Census. If that figure had been taken from market research done on readers of African-American publications, the results would have been different and less dramatic because such readers have higher household incomes.

The *Gay Rights/Special Rights* tape presents three additional "statistics" concerning gay people and African Americans: what percentage went to college (60 percent versus 5 percent); what percentage hold professional positions (49 percent versus 1 percent); and what percentage have taken overseas vacations (66 percent versus 1 percent). Again, the factual bases for these statistics are never reported, and the biases of the data never discussed. The videotape goes on to state that, unlike black people, gay people have never really experienced discrimination or prejudice, because they have never been denied the right to vote, faced legal segregation, been restricted from public restrooms or public businesses and restaurants. Senator Trent Lott, who today serves as majority whip in the Senate and is in line to succeed Bob Dole as majority leader, says, "It makes a mockery of other legitimate civil rights that people have worked for for years . . . To give this kind of recognition is going to undermine all kinds of laws that are already on the books and is going to hurt a lot of people that deserve these kinds of protection."

The small subset of data—culled by market researchers working to increase mainstream advertising in gay and lesbian publications—has been used repeatedly against us by the antigay right. For example, the economic arguments made in this videotape were repeated successfully in Colorado by the homophobic Colorado for Family Values. Indeed, *dollars and sense* magazine reported that the gay firm "Overlooked Opinions got a request for evidence that was used to support the campaign for the antigay ballot initiative in Amendment 2." In the antigay literature it published during the campaign, the Colorado for Family Values asked, "Are homosexuals 'disadvantaged' economically? You decide! Records show that even now, not only are gays not economically disadvantaged, they're actually one of the most affluent groups in America!"

By preying on the economic fears of working-class and even middle-class Americans, such myth-making can produce extreme reactions. In November 1993 in east Texas, three straight men from Tyler brutally murdered a twenty-three-year-old gay man named Nicholas West, one of eight known gay men murdered in Texas since April of that year. Unlike many of the murders, West's resulted in three arrests and, so far, one conviction. In a chilling story about these murders in *Vanity Fair*, the convicted murderer Donald Aldrich described how he and two other young men kidnaped West, robbed him, taunted and humiliated him, viciously beat him, and eventually shot him nine times with three different guns, including a .357 Magnum. The reporter visited Aldrich to learn why he had participated in the murder. Two paragraphs from the story are so revealing that they bear being quoted:

> In Donald Aldrich's view, the queers had everything. He had only his life in a trailer park over in Rockwall, his 10th-grade education, a bad marriage. He had only his go-nowhere restaurant jobs at places like Popeye's to fill the time between the burglary sprees and the prison stints.
>
> "I work all my life tryin' to have something nice and make something of myself," he says. "About the best job I can get is working in a restaurant makin' minimum wage or just barely over it, and it's like, I get no breaks. From the time I was a kid it seemed like there was a lot against me, and yet here they are, they're doing something that God totally condemns in the Bible. But look at

everything they've got, they've got all this nice stuff. They've got all these good jobs, sit back at a desk, or sit back in an air-conditioned building not having to sweat, not having to bust their ass, and they've got money. They've got the cars, they've got the apartments. They've got all the nice stuff in 'em. So, yeah, I resented that.

The article reported that robbery is a frequent ingredient in a number of the incidents of antigay violence in Texas. Aldrich "resented" what he perceived as the greater wealth and better status of men like West. Relative to Aldrich, these gay men looked successful; they had the things he wanted. But since they were sinners, they did not deserve to have such things. Aldrich rationalized the robberies and violence he perpetrated against gay men (West's murder was only one incident) as a way to get even. Smith County Sheriff's Department investigator Jason Waller said, "He [Aldrich] thinks he's a good guy . . . He's not perceiving he's done anything wrong, because this is a fag. This is not a store owner or a preacher. This is a fag."

These stories from the media swirl of the last two years not only reveal the breadth of prevailing misinformation about gay and lesbian economic status, but also illuminate the prejudice that underlies such misinformation. Aldrich's rationalizations for violence echo the anti-Semitic rants of white supremacists. In times of economic turmoil, like these, such excuses for resentment against gay people are likely to thrive.

The truth about gay and lesbian income and wealth is less dramatic than our enemies believe, and not at all what Sheldon's Traditional Values Coalition and other right-wing groups represent it to be. For one, the data that both *USA Today* and TVC's videotape uncritically repeat are themselves fraught with problems. The data were gathered, by Simmons Market Research and by Overlooked Opinions, through surveys of statistically unrepresentative gay and lesbian mailing lists and audiences at gay and lesbian events. The University of Maryland economist Lee Badgett terms these numbers "deceptive because they come from a biased sample of lesbian and gay people." Badgett explains that "to apply information about some subgroup (the 'sample') to the larger group (the 'population'), the sample must be representative of the group. A sample is representative if each member of the larger group has an equal chance of being in the survey." The Simmons Market Research Bureau and Overlooked Opinions surveys were not aimed at representative readers of gay and lesbian magazines, members of gay and lesbian organizations, or participants in gay and lesbian events. Indeed, when Badgett looked into the question of whether "readers of magazines directed toward a particular demographic group" were "economically representative of the group as a whole," she found they were not. She compared average black family income with the income of readers of *Ebony, Essence,* and *Jet,* and found that the magazine readers' income was higher than the average income of families, households, and individual men and women. She found similar disparities when she compared the incomes of families of all races with those of the readers of the *New York Times, USA Today,* and the *Wall Street Journal.* Badgett concludes that it is neither accurate nor reasonable to generalize that the incomes of respondents to readers' surveys conducted by gay and lesbian magazines reflect the income of the general gay population.

Further, data collected by Overlooked Opinions are accurate only for the specific list the company surveys. However, because it is not in the firm's self-interest to acknowledge the gross limitation of the data it sells to advertisers and businesses, Overlooked Opinions and other market researchers hedge and qualify but do not aggressively challenge the right wing's misuse of their data. Additionally, there are inherent biases in the lists and events created by many market researchers; they are not representative of the racial, gender, and true economic realities of gay and lesbian people. For example, Sean Strub's surveys of gay readers of select publications show that the average household income is as high as $63,100, but Strub himself notes the limitations of the list from which he gathered the data. "You have to know what you're looking at: my file is 1 percent black. It obviously doesn't represent the gay population."

Two new studies provide a far more accurate assessment of gay and lesbian wealth. One data set was coordinated by the research firm Yankelovich Partners, based in Westport, Connecticut, and additional data were gathered through analysis of the General Social Survey, conducted annually by the prestigious National Opinion Research Center. In a nationally representative sample of 2503 people, the Yankelovich firm encountered 5.7 percent (143) who described themselves as "gay/homosexual/lesbian." As the *New York Times* reported, "The Yankelovich data indicated little noticeable difference between the homosexual and heterosexual respondents. Among gay men, the mean household income was $37,000, compared with $39,300 among the heterosexual men. Among the lesbians, it was $34,800, compared with $34,000 among the heterosexual women." The survey did in fact identify differences between the gay and lesbian people surveyed and the general public, including higher levels of college attendance, self-employment, and stress—but income disparity was not among the chief differences.

A similar conclusion was reached by Lee Badgett when she analyzed the General Social Survey data set. Unlike the Yankelovich survey, the GSS asks participants if they have engaged in same-sex behavior rather than if they identify as "gay/homosexual/lesbian." Noting that not all GSS respondents were asked all questions in each survey, Badgett identified a sample of 1680 persons (out of 4426 respondents to the GSS surveys done from 1989 to 1991). Flying in the face of myth, Badgett concluded that lesbian and gay people actually make less than their heterosexual counterparts. "The findings of this study provide evidence that economic differences exist between people with differing sexual orientation (as defined by their behavior). Behaviorally gay or bisexual men earn from 9.5 percent to 25.9 percent less than behaviorally heterosexual men. Because this economic disadvantage holds after controlling for education and occupation, the usual economic conclusion is that equally productive gay people are being treated differently . . . Behaviorally lesbian/bisexual women face a smaller sexual orientation penalty, ranging from 13.1 percent to 14.8 percent, which drops to 5 percent when taking occupation into account." Both the Yankelovich and Badgett research suggest that we need much more factual and statistically valid information before we can develop an accurate economic picture of gay people. Meanwhile, the antigay right and its conservative champions within the Republican Party continue to repeat the myths about gay and lesbian privilege every day.

Several factors complicate the ability of gay and lesbian people to counter this campaign of disinformation. For one, most gay and lesbian people still hide or refuse to acknowledge publicly their sexual orientation. Accurate data about the size of our community are difficult to obtain and are plagued with methodological problems. Data about gay and lesbian incomes and lives are also hard to gather. The absence of reliable information makes it easy for myths to be made up and allowed to stand unchallenged. The market research done by Overlooked Opinions, Strub Media Group, Rivendell Marketing, Simmons Market Research Bureau, and others is therefore unique. As Gluckman and Reed write in *dollars and sense,* "Past invisibility has provided a blank slate of sorts, a slate that is rapidly filling up with notions that have more to do with marketing than with reality . . . Marketing teams have devised

elaborate ways to compensate for [the closet], but in the end it's in their
interest to use inflated figures to get corporate attention." Gay and
lesbian market research is itself necessary to queer magazines and newspapers in their search for advertising dollars. While the survival of gay
and lesbian media is vital, media and marketing professionals must use
their data far more responsibly. Each time we overstate the importance
of lesbian and gay magazine readership information or fail to qualify the
data with greater specificity, we create a false impression of gay and
lesbian wealth. That impression, in turn, lends credence to those who
insist that gay and lesbian people are not stigmatized. As an example of
this kind of argument, Gluckman and Reed cite a 1993 article in *The
New Republic* by Jonathan Rausch in which he uses Overlooked Opinion's data and the example of a handful of his economically comfortable
gay friends to argue that gay people are not "oppressed." But money
and income are not the sole measure of freedom or equality; data on
violence, employment discrimination, family discrimination—among
other facts we face—render our equality virtual rather than real.

But Rausch's article underlines an indelible truth: middle-class and
wealthy gay people are far more likely to be visible than are working-
class and poor queers. Working-class and poor gay people are not the
population to whom the gay and lesbian movement's events, newspapers, magazines, enterprises, and efforts at political mobilization are
aimed. Middle-class academicians, middle-class students, business
owners, and professionals of every type constitute the funding base for
the movement. These middle-class queer folk are the ones who attend
gay and lesbian community dinners, cocktail parties, conferences, who
take vacations in queer resorts, who subscribe to papers, who patronize
the arts, buy expensive Broadway tickets, sport trendy clothes, dine out
at restaurants, and drive pricey cars. To the extent that heterosexist bias
pervades nongay agencies serving poor people or the homeless, our
ability to know how many of the clients of these agencies are actually
queer is hampered. I am aware of no poll, data set, or survey of working-class or poor gay or bisexual men, women, young people, or the
elderly. Yet I know from my extensive experience and travels with queer
communities around the country that the vast majority of queer people
are neither upper middle class nor rich. In conversations with working-
class activists in our movement—be they nationally known leaders like
Kevin Cathcart of Lambda Legal Defense and Education Fund, Ann
DeGroot of Minneapolis, Reggie Williams of San Francisco, or the
rank-and-file activists whom I have met and worked with over the years

—I have heard the profound alienation many of them experience with the upper-middle to ruling-class bias of our politics.

Ultimately, we must realize that pretending to be wealthier than we are will, like all pretensions, alienate gay people from one another and separate us from a host of potential allies. Like the world, America is becoming more polarized around wealth. That polarization is present inside our gay and lesbian communities; serious and largely unexplored tensions exist between queers who are rich and those who are not, between middle-class and working-class queers. The tensions range from mild grumbling about the high ticket prices at queer community functions, to serious splits about whether gay groups should fight government cutbacks in aid to the poor (which undoubtedly will hurt large numbers of gay and bisexual people). While liberals, conservatives, and radicals have found ways to enlarge the "accessibility" of our events (sliding-scale fees, low-income prices, sponsorships), we have not tackled the upper-middle-class bias of much of our agenda. The bias is evident every time some gay person argues that "welfare" has nothing to do with the gay agenda. What will the movement do about the single lesbian mother on welfare, or the gay man who receives supplemental Social Security Disability Income, or the queer family that gets Aid to Families with Dependent Children (AFDC)? Why is the voice of the middle-class Republican man eager to reduce his tax bill more credible than the voice of the gay man on welfare?

In truth, the movement rarely debates such questions. When people bring a progressive or even an alternative economic analysis to queer political gatherings, they are soundly trashed. On the other hand, when a conservative economic analysis or agenda is promoted, it is rarely questioned, much less attacked. Two recent examples illustrate this class chasm. At the 1993 NGLTF Creating Change Conference, held in Durham, North Carolina, a handful of participants argued that the pending vote in Congress on the North American Free Trade Agreement (NAFTA) was something the gay and lesbian movement should be concerned about and should oppose. The issue was raised first at a preconference workshop, then at the opening plenary speech given by the Southern activist and author Mab Segrest.

To be honest, I had not thought about NAFTA before I went to the conference. I had read commentaries about it, knew that a vote was imminent, that Clinton wanted it to pass, and that it would most benefit multinationals. But my attitude was one of indifference. At the NGLTF conference, I heard the issue raised by Mab in her plenary speech, and I confess that I was not convinced that gay opposition mattered. Still, I respected her for presenting the issue, and I appreciated the novelty of what she and others were attempting: to urge that the queer movement actually do something to defend and champion the rights of working- and middle-class people in America. Reaction to these fairly mild calls for opposition to NAFTA was fascinating.

Several people denounced the organizers of the conference for allowing such critiques in the first place! The substantive arguments offered by the NAFTA opponents were never really debated; instead, the focus was on the fact that the issue had been raised at all. Conservatives denounced the progressives who had brought it up and accused them of diverting the movement from its real focus on gay rights and AIDS. After the fact, the gay and lesbian media reported the story as if the NAFTA issue had taken over the conference. Conservative columnists used the fact of the NAFTA discussion at the conference to show how "out of touch" NGLTF was, as if the organization was directly responsible for the views of each participant. Liberals either chuckled in amusement at the diversion, or expressed outrage at having been asked to think. The real significance of the conversation that the handful of anti-NAFTA individuals began got lost in the ideological hot air.

The significance of the incident, to my mind, was that a handful of progressive queer activists challenged the NGLTF and the movement to make an economic analysis. This call proved threatening to a movement whose agenda is not only extremely narrow, but is focused principally on securing rights for the upper-middle class folks who control the movement. To these people, the suggestion that we take a stand on a "nongay" issue seemed outlandish. Yet what is a gay or lesbian issue? What makes the pursuit of domestic partnership benefits for middle-class people with good jobs a more important gay issue than the protection of the jobs of gay and lesbian workers threatened by the flight of manufacturers to countries where labor power is purchased more cheaply? Clearly, the reaction at the conference had less to do with NAFTA than with the class and political biases that inform our agenda.

These biases become even more apparent when one contrasts the queer media's reaction to progressive economic views with the views of gay conservatives and Republicans. Since the 1994 elections, gay Republicans have argued that the election proved that our community was more "conservative" than our movement. Expressing no surprise at exit poll data indicating that some 32 percent of gay voters voted Republican in 1994, Log Cabin president Rich Tafel said, "It's something

I've been saying for a long time. If Republicans focus on economic and other issues, and there's no Gay-bashing involved, no anti-Gay attacks, they will get a bigger chunk of the Gay vote." He continued, "A lot of Gay people . . . don't like the welfare state, a lot of them don't like tax-and-spend policies. They voted Republican for the same reason everybody [sic] voted Republican, because they disagree with the Democratic way of solving problems." The Log Cabin Club's interpretation of the election results has been uncritically accepted and even amplified in importance by media analysts. So, for example, an *Out* cover story, "The Newt Era: Is It Good for the Gays?" by *Newsweek* correspondent Mark Miller, flatly stated this gay Republican position as fact: "The truth is that many gay and lesbian voters are more conservative than the leaders of the major gay rights organizations—or most Republicans—like to admit. Until AIDS radicalized the gay community, many of us remained closeted and tended to vote like everyone else: out of economic self-interest." Miller posited that widespread disappointment with Clinton, the diminution of the importance of AIDS to a new generation of gay and lesbian people, and the appeal of Republican fiscal policies all contributed to the pro-Republican gay vote.

Tafel's and Miller's interpretations of the 1994 election clearly make a host of assumptions about gay and lesbian people's economic views—assumptions based primarily on their subjective understanding of certain data. By the same token, Mab Segrest and other critics of NAFTA also made an argument about gay and lesbian people's interests based on data they presented about the economic impact of NAFTA. Yet the economic assumptions of conservatives like Tafel and Miller are treated far more kindly, and as if they had greater validity, than the economic arguments made by progressives like Segrest. I believe the different treatment given to conservative and progressive economic analyses reflects the class biases of our movement, our media, and the agendas that both promote. Rarely does the movement view issues from the perspective of poor gay people (of whatever color). Rarely do the gay and lesbian media report on the lives of working-class or poor queer people. Instead, the assumption is that all of us are middle class or well off, and that all of us share the same economic interests. In truth, the movement is peopled by those from all economic backgrounds. If the gay and lesbian movement is to reach its fullest potential, and secure equality for all its constituents, we must examine how class bias operates within our communities, affecting everything from how we fund our political movement to how we determine and ensure our agenda.

Myths and Realities of Funding the Movement

Throughout our movement's history, two factors have hindered our efforts to raise money for gay and lesbian political, service, and educational projects: the homophobia of nongay institutions and the closet. Institutional funders, like the government, corporations, and the private philanthropic sector, have either ignored us (by failing to recognize us as a subpopulation of other groups, like the elderly or youth) or specifically stigmatized us (with laws banning gay and lesbian people from being foster parents or with discriminatory employment practices). Government support for gay community-based service agencies is itself very new and fraught with danger. With the exception of a handful of cities and states, public funds have not gone to gay and lesbian community-based projects. If one were to eliminate the federal and state funding for AIDS-specific projects, the level of government funding to combat urgent gay community problems, like violence, youth services, elderly services, and so on, would be tiny. Across the country, the fifty gay and lesbian community centers, dozens of hotlines, antiviolence projects, outreach projects, youth support groups, and health clinics we benefit from have been founded and maintained by private donations from gay and lesbian individuals. Even the small level of funding received from government programs is today threatened as the conservative movement attempts to eliminate all government programs except police, military, prisons, and what Secretary of Labor Robert Reich calls "corporate welfare," the huge subsidies given to a handful of powerful corporate interests (like agribusiness). In 1994, for example, the New York City Lesbian and Gay Community Services Center raised 69 percent of its $3 million budget from individuals and rent from its organization tenants; 6% from foundations, and 25% from government contracts. The contracts were for gay-specific work in AIDS education and support, youth outreach and support, alcoholism and drug abuse services, and accessibility of the building to handicapped persons. In 1995, the center faced cutbacks of even this small level of funding as a new governor and Republican legislative majority drastically cut government-funded programs.

The homophobia of government bodies is so pervasive as to be at once self-evident and invisible, so embedded is it within the structure of government services. The conservative myth holds that, to the extent that they should exist at all, government services are currently equally available to all citizens. We don't need nondiscrimination laws or civil rights enforcement mechanisms, because government is color blind, sex blind, and constitutionally required to be even-handed. This myth denies how bias permeates the creation and delivery of government services: higher tax–base neighborhoods get better trash collection than lower tax–base neighborhoods; police response in black neighborhoods differs from police response in white suburbs; government has until very recently refused to recognize, much less address, such gay and lesbian problems as bias-motivated violence, youth suicide, and discrimination in public accommodation and employment. By the end of 1995, Speaker Gingrich has promised antigay leaders, he will host federal hearings on "whether or not taxpayer money is being spent to promote things that are literally grotesque." The hearings will undoubtedly become a national platform for the antigay right to challenge the award of any public funds for gay, lesbian, and bisexual education and service programs.

Following our government's lead, the private philanthropic sector has avoided or ignored gay and lesbian problems. The Working Group on Gay and Lesbian Issues, a national network of several dozen family and private foundations that fund in this area, tries to lobby philanthropies to widen their knowledge of gay and lesbian needs, but the working group numbers fewer than a hundred member foundations (out of the thousands that are members of the National Council of Foundations). Unlike our opponents on the right, who enjoy significant private and corporate foundation support, gay and lesbian projects rarely get funding from the largest foundations (Ford, Rockefeller, MacArthur). Corporate giving to gay and lesbian projects is insignificant or nonexistent. Only a handful of foundations stand out, and they deserve to be recognized: the Joyce Mertz Gilmore Foundation, the Out Fund for Gay and Lesbian Liberation, the Chicago Resource Center, the Public Welfare Foundation, and the American Foundation for AIDS Research.

Although gay and lesbian individuals finance nearly all gay organizations, the closet affects how we raise the money and how much we are able to garner. Individual gay people, joined in recent years by some straight supporters, have been reached by the movement in four principal ways: through grassroots fundraising, through special events (dinners, parties, dances, shows), through direct mail, and through large-dollar contributors known as major donors. The enormous gay and lesbian closet still prevents most of our potential supporters from giving money to gay and lesbian organizations. In short, few people are willing to become "card-carrying members" of queer organizations. Even fewer are willing to donate their time and work publicly on organization boards and committees. The closet also limits the participation of many people in public gay events; to join, attend, march, or speak in support of gay rights is seen by many of our people as tantamount to coming out. Repeatedly, in the past ten years, I've had to address the discomfort of donors reluctant to write "Gay or Lesbian" on their check, or worried about receiving gay-identified mail at their home or office. I've been turned down by potential petition signers unwilling to be identified with a gay or lesbian cause. Pandering to the fear of disclosure is the reason so many gay and lesbian organizations do not use the *g* and *l* words in their names.

From the days of Mattachine and DOB until fairly recently, most queer organizations and projects have been financed out of the pockets of their organizers and volunteers. Even after Stonewall, the GAAs and GLFs that sprang up around the country supported their activism with dances, readings, passing the hat, and individual contributions. Because traditional sources of funding have been unavailable to gay and lesbian projects, fundraising through small-scale, low-dollar events or sales of products (T-shirts, buttons) still provides the fuel for much gay political activism. I have participated in everything from the proverbial bake sale to car washes, from neighborhood dances to house parties at which people paid five dollars ("more if you can, less if you can't"). I've sold lollipops for community programs, raffle tickets, planned concerts, poetry readings, brunches, and even benefit softball games. Quite often, events are based in bars.

It bears repeating that drag performers have played an enormous role in grassroots fundraising for gay and lesbian projects. The Imperial Court of America, a nationwide network of drag activists, raises tens of thousands of dollars for AIDS and gay and lesbian charities each year. In my experience, drag queens and performers are sometimes the most courageous activists in small communities. For example, throughout the late eighties and early nineties, a drag performer named Brandy Alexander owned a gay bar near the Marine Corps's Parris Island facility and daily fought the military's antigay policies. Subjected to regular harassment by the Naval Investigative Service, which would copy license plate numbers of bar patrons or otherwise intimidate Marines who ventured into the bar, Alexander refused to be cowed. He led public protests against the military's discriminatory policy, raised funds for gay organizations, and used his bar as a way to support and organize gay and lesbian service members. His drag act itself was politically charged. I once saw Brandy begin his performance dressed as a woman and end it as a serviceman in uniform. At the end of his metamorphosis, he took off his false eyelashes, earrings, and wig—with great dignity and deliberation—and stood on stage, a proudly gay man in Marine fatigues, and saluted the audience. The act brought the house down and blew apart the macho posturing of the military. Brandy Alexander is but one example of scores of drag queens and transgender activists who help create and strengthen the local movement in many communities. Others include the nationally known Nicole Ramirez-Murray of San Diego and Charles (Coco La Chine) Ching of New York.

Mirroring the decade as a time of economic self-absorption, the eighties marked the coming of age of "professional" gay and lesbian fundraising. Every staffed AIDS or gay organization got a full-time development director; some consultants in fundraising and special events worked solely for gay clients; and the budgets of many local and national groups began to increase. Over the past decade, fundraising has largely shifted from the grassroots or mass-based event to the more formally organized "queer special event." In an atmosphere filled with gay awards dinners, dances, cocktail parties, film benefits, plays, morning parties, evening parties, black parties, white parties, dances on the battleship *Intrepid,* and every conceivable kind of fundraiser, we tend to forget how recent some of these forms of community fundraising are. The fundraising dinner, for example, has been popular only since 1983, when the Human Rights Campaign Fund patented the black-tie dinner as its chief strategy for raising money. Today, it is ubiquitous in the gay nonprofit world. Successful gay groups are today ones with terrific fundraisers—groups like Lambda Legal Defense and Education Fund, the Los Angeles Gay and Lesbian Community Services Center, Fenway Community Health Center in Boston, the New York Lesbian and Gay Community Services Center. The groups that falter are those which moved slowly to professionalize their money-raising—groups like NGLTF, which had no development director or formal fundraising program until 1986, or people of color groups, like the now-defunct National Coalition of Black Lesbians and Gays, which tried unsuccessfully to support a national office in the mid-1980s.

During 1994 HRCF hosted fundraising dinners in twenty-one cities and grossed over $3 million. The dinners were the largest single source of income to the HRCF annual budget of $8 million. The balance was made up by its federal club major donor program, comprising people who give $1500 or more per year ($2 million), direct mail (over $1 million), and a small number of very large contributors and estates (which gave approximately $1.5 million to the HRCF tax-exempt foundation). Grassroots events, low-dollar dances, sales of T-shirts and products made only a small contribution to the group's overall budget.

Fundraising dinners are well regarded as a strategy, as an empowering experience for participants, and as a symbol of our financial clout. The truth is a little less wonderful. At the outset, I want to stress that I think such dinners can serve a politicizing and empowering purpose for many of the people who attend them. The HRCF dinner I attended in November 1994 in Boston, for example, was centered on the theme of coming out. The fifteen hundred people in the room clearly benefited from hearing that message and the inspiring speech of an openly gay schoolteacher from Missouri who was fighting to keep his job. But this dinner, like most others I have produced, run, or attended, was wasteful, elitist, and paradoxically depoliticizing and disempowering.

The waste comes from how much events like these cost to produce, despite partial corporate underwriting. Most dinners and other special events cost at least 50 percent of what they gross; so HRCF in 1994 most likely netted about half of the $3 million it raised. The expenses go to a slew of private vendors, including hotels, caterers, talent, video-segment producers, professional event planners, and printers, among others. An enormous amount of time is spent to produce a smooth event; scores of people volunteer hundreds of hours. But this time is spent on a party. At the end of the night, other than the dollars raised and the blip of media attention garnered, what tangible results do we have to show? None. I think we must examine ways to change some of these party-oriented special events into more effective political opportunities. What kind of education in the movement do the participants get when they leave with a grab bag full of cologne samples and glossy magazines? What if they were to leave with a manual called "How to Organize Your Neighbors for Gay Rights" or a *Coming Out* videotape instead?

The elitism of such dinners is evident in the very construction of the event and from the instant one walks into it. After all, who but the comfortable, the professional, and the wealthy can afford a $250 dinner, or even a $150 event? Because high-dollar fundraising is all about using the appeal of exclusivity to the advantage of the group trying to raise money, the dinners themselves have several tiers of participation. The low end is the basic ticket price—currently $150 per person for the HRCF dinners. The next higher level of giving often adds a predinner VIP reception. The highest level sometimes allows donors to be seated with special political guests, invites them to post-party events at elite clubs, or simply recognizes them prominently during the event. Invariably, the more you give, the more attention you get from the person who heads the organization you support, and the more access you have to express your views. Conversely, the less you give, the less attention, access, and clout you command.

I believe queer fundraising dinners are inherently depoliticizing. For one, checkbook activism is a kind of virtual activism, and it cannot match the power of actual political engagement. A person who comes to a fundraising dinner and writes a check but does nothing else "political" for the rest of the year is doing very little. We have tried so hard to make gay people feel good about donating money to the movement, to create a culture of giving, that we have demeaned the idea of activism. Perhaps we should return to calling ourselves "contributors" if we simply give without getting involved more deeply. After all, contributing itself is an important step. But activism is a far heavier burden, one that more of us need to shoulder. What does it mean that black-tie dinners gather over fifteen-hundred people—largely men—in cities like Dallas and Detroit, while political rallies, conferences, and legislative lobby days may draw five hundred? Even in the midst of the devastation wrought by AIDS, large numbers of professionals and middle-class individuals have remained uninvolved as voters and constituents; they may have written their checks but they have not raised their voices in the discourse over the politics of AIDS.

The truth is that our movement's focus on people's checkbooks has obscured its focus on their hearts, energies, and capacity for political engagement. Big events have become pacifiers rather than motivators. We feel good about getting dressed in finery and dancing with our lover at the annual ball. But it is a lot harder to get dressed up in one's daily work clothes and be openly and fully gay wherever one goes, in whatever workplace or public setting or private family gathering. Money becomes yet another closet in which we can hide, another excuse to stop ourselves from committing more deeply to full freedom and equality. The more money we have, the more elaborate and beautiful our hiding places.

Aimed as they are at one of the most informed and well-connected segments of our communities, these dinners fail to tap or utilize the talents of the people whose lives they touch. I am always struck by the enormously capable people on gay dinner committees whose skills are devoted to working out seating charts and picking floral arrangements. Wouldn't these same organizers be more valuable if they thought about how to turn the two-thousand-person dinner into a genuinely political event, not just one where we dress up and act out a heterosexual political script? Our reliance, during these dinner fundraisers, on straight celebrities or entertainment figures is another part of the formula we have adopted too uncritically. If the purpose of such an event is to deliver a political message to our community and to the media, its content ought to aim higher than the gossip pages. In fact, participants at a gay dinner often leave no more educated or activated than when they entered. We do leave feeling good, but this feeling of empowerment and safety is double-edged, obscuring the reality of how unsafe gay people are. A false complacency is nurtured; "Look how far we have come. I can dance at the Waldorf-Astoria or the Ritz." Yet I suspect few of us would feel safe or comfortable dancing with our lovers at a straight wedding or fundraising dinner. Ultimately, checkbook activism is an unsatisfactory option for people eager to do more. We must supplement it with a political one. At present, only one national, chapter-based organization (GLAAD) exists, and it focuses on media. Few local AIDS or gay rights organizations systematically and strategically motivate, mobilize, and involve gay and lesbian people and our allies where we live.

Two other developments in gay fundraising are worth noting before we examine how gay and lesbian wealths shapes the politics of our movement. These are the limitations of direct mail for gay causes, and our growing reliance on wealthy major donors. Direct mail aimed at gay and lesbian rights supporters is a relatively new phenomenon. Until the late 1980s, when the gay direct mail expert Sean Strub began to work with nonprofit gay and AIDS organizations, none of the national or local groups had professionally run direct mail operations. Lists were barely computerized, membership dues were the only funds groups received by mail, and the idea of purchasing mailing lists to do "prospecting" for new members or using direct mail tricks (like offering special premiums or sending out inflammatory copy) was completely foreign to most gay activists. Strub deserves a great deal of credit for educating a whole generation of gay organizations in the power of direct-mail fundraising. With his help, NGLTF in 1986 used the *Hard-wick* defeat as an opportunity to fund a desperately needed project to repeal sodomy laws.

Direct mail remains a problem because of the difficulty in finding gay-supportive mailing lists. Experts tell us that a very small number of people get involved or give money to gay and lesbian causes. According to Strub, the total number of people who have associated themselves with gay causes in any way (signing petitions, ordering information, giving money) comes to about two million. By comparison, the Christian Coalition alone counts 1.5 million people as members; and right-wing direct mail guru Richard Viguerie marshals mailing lists that total more than thirty million names. Also, mailing is expensive. To identify the millions of gay rights supporters not on current lists would require us to mail widely and indiscriminately, but no gay organization has the deep pockets to finance such prospecting drives. Instead, we have tried back door approaches—targeting gay neighborhoods by zip codes, targeting subscribers to nongay magazines with gay appeal *(Architectural Digest* was one I recall NGLTF testing), mailing to the lists of nongay allies (NOW and the ACLU, for example). Our forays into the world of the straight lists have not been very successful. The best mailing lists that HRCF ever used were those of NGLTF and Lambda; conversely, the best lists for NGLTF were from organizations like HRCF and PFLAG (Parents and Friends of Lesbians and Gays). What happens is that we go back to mailing to the same people, soliciting funds for many different groups. Fortunately, the same people continue to give generously and often.

The basic problem with direct mail for gay and lesbian causes is that no one has invested several million dollars in an aggressive campaign to acquire new names and expand the membership of gay and lesbian organizations. It would take a large commitment of money to raise the numbers of gay rights supporters from the current seventy thousand at HRCF and thirty thousand at NGLTF to match the names that Strub Company has on its database (over 500,000). Once completed, the investment would pay off in fiscal health for these organizations and in political clout. But who will invest the funds for the project?

POLITICAL IMPACT OF ECONOMIC REALITIES

This question brings us to the most complicated aspect of gay funding, the role of the individual person with means. There are many levels of wealth—and the gay community has them all, from students living on $5000 a year, to middle-class families earning $30,000 or less, to couples with household incomes of $100,000, to professionals earning several hundred thousand dollars a year, to millionaires, and ultimately to my long-sought-after Mr. Geffen. In the eighties, gay organizations began systematically to court high-dollar donors through formal programs aimed at getting people to pledge and give $1000 or more per year. Not all of the people who give at this level are "rich." Some have simply made a commitment to the movement. As one man told HRCF's Tim McFeeley, he wrote out three checks each month: his mortgage, his monthly child-support payment, and his monthly pledge to HRCF. Such income has played a major part in stabilizing gay and lesbian organizations.

The emergence of an institutionalized gay and lesbian civil rights movement is in fact linked to the emergence from the closet of professional and middle-class gay, lesbian, and bisexual people. In this respect, we are no different from other reform movements of modern times; reformers seem to be people with the time, luxury, and security to engage in the political process. For example, the founders of the National Gay Task Force, like Barbara Gittings, Nath Rockhill, and Ron Gold, were professionals; Howard Brown was a doctor, while Bruce Voeller and Frank Kameny were scientists. The founders of the Gay Rights National Lobby and the Human Rights Campaign Fund were largely business people, assisted by middle-class campaign consultants, fundraisers, labor movement activists. The founders of GMHC were successful artists, health care professionals, and businessmen. And so on. I suspect that if we were able to survey the backgrounds of the founders of most of our political organizations—at the city, state, and national level—we would find an overwhelming number from upper-middle-class backgrounds. While the leadership of organizations like the now-defunct National Coalition of Black Lesbians and Gays and the Black Lesbian and Gay Leadership Forum and the Latino/a Lesbian and Gay Organization is more mixed in its class background, there is clearly an overrepresentation of well-educated, professional, middle-class people even among the organizations of gay people of color.

The impact of middle-class credentials of large numbers of organizers, volunteers, board members, and leaders has been simple and direct: the goals, methods, and aspirations of these organizations are rooted in our comfortable economic conditions. I think one of the main reasons that gay and lesbian political organizations have been unable to tap into larger numbers of supporters is the middle- to upper-middle-class orientation of their agendas, outreach, and representation. If one walks into a gay and lesbian bar today in any part of the country, one is likely to find a wide range of people: businessmen rub shoulders with college students, who rub shoulders with secretaries, who sit next to artists, who dance with lawyers, who play pool with house painters. In smaller and medium-sized cities with fewer bars and gay gathering spots, men and women mingle much more; drag queens and leather folk, Republicans and radicals, rub shoulders each weekend. In larger cities, each group has its own hang-out, and rarely do circles mingle, except in the dance of dating and mating. But if one walks into gay and lesbian political gatherings, one finds much greater homogeneity in class background, race, and gender. The movement is not as mixed, as integrated, or as economically diverse as the communities we come from. Gay and lesbian service organizations are the most accessible, and therefore the most diverse, of our political organizations; most community centers and community-based organizations, unlike political organizations, don't charge fees for people to participate in their programs.

Major donor fundraising overemphasizes the importance of a handful of people. The math dictates the power: a donor who gives $35 dollars a year as a member has one kind of stature; a donor giving at the level of $50,000 a year has another; a donor planning to leave an estate valued at several million dollars commands an even higher degree of attention. So it is that nonprofit organizations recruit people with wealth and access to positions on their boards. On one level, the principle of necessity requires such action; on another level, our movement suffers significant consequences.

Essentially, the pursuit of wealth by our leadership affects political priorities. For one, fundraising considerations affect an organization's decisions on what programs to create and how to conceptualize those projects. Often a project is begun because it can be funded, not because of a deeper commitment to the issue. An example of this was the decision by HRCF in the late eighties to create the Lesbian Rights staff position. In part, it was the result of the efforts of women on the board to get the group to focus more directly on lesbians. But in larger measure, the decision was about going after a market: HRCF saw the untapped potential of lesbian professional money and determined that a program aimed at lesbians would be the best way to attract funds. The first two Lesbian Program directors, the capable organizers Kathleen Stoll and Tacie Dejanikus, were both frustrated by job descriptions that required them to do fundraising alongside substantive political work.

Organizing ourselves to raise funds from donors capable of giving at this and higher levels occupies at least half the time of most executive directors I know. Major donor fundraising is very gratifying when it succeeds; you can obtain a check for $5000 or $25,000 or $100,000 at one sitting. But it is quite time-consuming in its own way. To gain the trust of the people who give you that kind of money takes time, and it requires that our leaders move in elite circles.

Finally, money affects more prosaic aspects of our organizations, from deciding who gets to sit on the board of directors to who gets noticed and who does not. The political control of a nonprofit organization is supposed to reside in its board, but the boards of most of our successful organizations are made up of the elite, whose interests differ at times from the interests of the queer rank-and-file. Personal agendas are often carried into political policy—as there is more to win (more status, more access, more money to be made on a gay market). Accountability is missing from these elite boards. Creating more representative organizational structures—with chapters, membership-elected board representatives, or national conventions—may be a start, but even these strategies are not sufficient. The main way to incorporate a commitment to represent those not in the room is to incorporate it in the mission of an organization. Ultimately, this is where all our movement debate boils over. Instead of charging gay organizations with missions that reflect a commitment to justice for all, regardless of race, gender, class, and sexuality, we have replicated the inequalities endemic to the broader culture within our groups. If you have money or are willing to raise lots of it, you can join any board in the land. If you don't have access to money, then you are asked to be a volunteer, not a decision-maker.

What impact does the class composition of leaders of the gay and lesbian movement have on its politics today? There is a huge difference between a movement rooted in middle-class values and one focused on the problems caused by poverty. Thus, our movement gets very passionate about issues that deal with workplace discrimination, but that presupposes that people have jobs. We are involved in fighting for domestic partnership benefits, but that presupposes that we work for companies offering those benefits. (Many of us do not.) We are far less passionate about raising the minimum wage, welfare reform, AFDC programs, free school lunches, immigration, poverty, and other issues that affect gay and lesbian families and individuals—but do not affect the middle-class people who are most involved in our movement.

At least one prominent gay fundraiser and donor with whom I spoke, New York's Jeff Soref, denies that the involvement of wealthy people has any particular impact on the agenda or politics of gay organizations. Soref is a major force in New York State and City gay politics. A co-chair of the Empire State Pride Agenda, he is former president of the board of Gay Men's Health Crisis and steered GMHC to greater fiscal strength. He raised hundreds of thousands of dollars for Clinton in 1992, for David Dinkins in 1993, and for Mario Cuomo in 1994. In a frank conversation with me in 1993, Soref expressed great impatience with certain attitudes about wealthy people, which he attributed to movement activists. "You can't take people's money and tell them you don't want them. And the money is in the white gay community right now. The votes and the street power may be elsewhere, and I think we need to use both as, say, GMHC and ACT UP have done. But I think there's still too much contempt for money, too much contempt for professionalism, too much contempt for people who are older or of a different ethnic group."

When I suggested that the tension between moneyed and working- or middle-class activists stemmed from the latter's fear that wealthy people would change the agenda and direction of our movement, Soref sharply disagreed. "It won't change the direction, but it will help accomplish things. That fear is irrational. Our goals are not different from anyone else's goals."

Both of us agreed that the movement suffered from too much internal tension, and that we needed to cultivate more trust and better working relationships between grassroots activists and wealthy professionals, though we expressed very different views of how such a relationship should be constructed. For one, we disagreed on the meaning of the term *grassroots*. I defined it by saying the movement must get "stronger at the local level in a traditional political way." To Jeff, the term "was much more loaded than that. I think *grassroots* implies—I'll be honest with you—poor, disenfranchised, angry." After some back-and-forth about the term, Soref agreed with me about the need to get out the vote, elicit letters, and stimulate constituent pressure for our issues, but insisted that the issue we were talking about was "political control" of the organization by the grassroots.

When I asked Soref how he thought we built power, he answered, without hesitation. "From the top."

"Completely different from my view," I said.

"I think participation and support are implied if you have the correct agenda. I mean, if I went in and said I represent the gay community, rezone my building, it would be suspect! But if you go in and say I'm here to fight for all gays and lesbians, which means equal access, how can somebody quarrel with that?"

"[Building] power from the top; I feel that's what we've been doing," I replied. "And that's what's not working."

"Because we're not building it from the top. I think we've tried to follow a grassroots model. You know, you get volunteers; you get the most active. And you shy away from the professionals, the rich, the people who have made it in the straight world. You stick to the people who work from nine to five and come out for a rally. We all love and respect those people. We couldn't get anywhere without them. You need both. I'm not suggesting to you at all that you ignore the grassroots. GMHC couldn't operate without its volunteers. But I don't think leadership starts from the grassroots up. I think leadership trickles from on high down . . . We need to be a financial force to be a political force. And I think we need to be a professional force to be a political force. But we also need the grassroots."

"But power in the political process comes from mass blocks," I said. "You've got to have the vote to deliver."

"Is the Tobacco Institute a mass block? Is General Motors a mass block?"

"Yeah. A mass of money."

"That's right. That's exactly what it is. It's a mass of money. The system may be changing a little bit, but right now it's still PACs and political contributions and fundraisers. We don't have access to the White House because they like gay people. We have access to the White House because we raised $300,000 [in New York] for Clinton. When we put our foot down and said we're not going to raise any more money for you until this military policy is settled, we didn't hear from them anymore. They moved on. They're trying to find the money elsewhere."

My conversation with Soref embodied all the classic tensions between movement activists and rich people: frustration and defensiveness on the part of the wealthier person; being obsequious, guarded, and supplicant on the part of the less wealthy activist. Soref and I often talked at cross purposes, about different issues, at the same time, instead of sharing information or opinions with each other. Soref seemed defensive, as if he expected me to discredit his formidable achievements as an activist simply on the grounds that he was rich and white. I felt defensive of the hardworking activists I know in the movement, and perversely pleased to have someone so unhesitatingly challenge my most cherished values about organizing.

Soref's questions actually led me to reaffirm those values, which include a faith in ground-up organizing, mass direct mail, low-dollar fundraising, and the building of a movement for power at the state and local level. In fact, the top-down strategy of political organizing fails to motivate the largest segment of our base; ordinary gay people are turned off by the highly visible, high-dollar fundraising that gay organizations utilize. Countless people who told me they don't have money to join the movement were surprised when I noted that membership in most national gay organizations ranges from $10 to $35. Donor-driven politics was practiced by our movement in 1992 and remains the principal strategy employed by groups like HRCF. There is no question it gets results, for those with the privilege to wield such power. What does it get for the rest of our people?

Soref and I disagree about the nature of power and the kind of world we are trying to build. Clearly, we are allies in parts of our struggle, but I am not sure we are fighting for the same cultural vision. Will we ever agree? Probably not. Can we still work together? Of course. How do we come to trust each other? Through concrete actions and practice.

CHAPTER NINE

DIVIDED WE STAND

THE RACIAL AND GENDER STATUS QUO

The old is dying, and the new cannot be born; in this interregnum there arises a great diversity of morbid symptoms.

—*Antonio Gramsci*

It was in July 1989 that I was appointed executive director of the National Gay and Lesbian Task Force, succeeding Jeff Levi. Jeff had worked at NGLTF for six years, more than three as executive director. He had crafted the federal response to AIDS in the hostile environment of the Reagan administration, and had worked hard to establish a credible legislative profile for the lesbian and gay community inside Washington's lobbying world. Jeff got me involved with NGLTF in 1985, encouraged me to run for the board, and eventually hired me as the public information director. We worked well together through many political trials, and I was genuinely sad to see him leave.

The Washington tribute to Jeff was to be the last of seven fundraising parties NGLTF held around the country and was intended in part to introduce me as his successor. My becoming executive director was never a given, and in itself was a minor epic. I organized a political campaign to win the job, securing letters of support from activists across the country and personally meeting with all members of the board to ask for their support. After all, I was not the typical mainstream gay organizational leader. I had worked as NGLTF's Media Director but had never run an organization. I was young (thirty), brown, had progressive politics, came up from the street-action wing of the movement, loved punk rock, and wanted NGLTF to move outside the Beltway and engage more widely in state and local organizing. I had experience, energy, and a vision with which the board agreed; most important, I had the support of many activists around the country. My campaign worked; the board selected me from the nearly eighty candidates who applied.

The week of Jeff's farewell party, a wealthy gay man from Washington called the office to ask how to make a donation in Jeff's honor. This donor had not supported NGLTF before, choosing instead to fund AIDS services and political action committees, but he now wanted to make a contribution. As our associate director of development spoke to him, the donor expressed his strong dismay about my selection as executive director. He was frankly appalled, he said, that the board had chosen me of all people. How could they have selected that radical woman, he asked, "who's practically a nigger." My co-worker, an amiable and infinitely decent man who would never in his life say such a thing, mustered a shocked silence in response. The story entered the office grapevine and reached me almost as soon as the conversation ended. I do not remember what I did when I heard about this comment; I probably fumed and laughed at once. But I can still feel the sting of this man's distrust. He had never spoken to me, had no idea of my values, my background, ideas, or abilities, but because I was "practically a nigger" in his eyes, he would not bother to learn those things. In the course of my stewardship of NGLTF, the man avoided my efforts to meet with him, although I tried many times.

Soon after this incident, I sought advice from Randy Klose on how to revitalize NGLTF's fundraising efforts. Klose was one of the most successful fundraisers in our movement during the late eighties and early nineties. Shrewd and aggressive, he loved the wheeling and dealing of politics, yet he had a generous spirit. Radicalized out of his previously apolitical life by the combined impact of his HIV status and his growing acceptance of himself as gay, Randy dedicated the last years of his life to strengthening the Human Rights Campaign Fund. As co-chair of its board, he traveled the country, tirelessly raising money. Eventually, he moved to Washington in order to push aggressively for more AIDS research, better treatments, and better AIDS care. Before he died, in 1992, Randy was heavily involved in leveraging the power of gay and lesbian money to influence the Democratic Party to support gay and lesbian rights.

I considered Randy a knowledgeable colleague and a friend, so I asked for his ideas on how I should restructure our fundraising effort. We met for breakfast at the Mayflower Hotel in the early fall of 1989. After we had discussed the state of the movement and our respective political organizations, I briefed him on NGLTF's programs and asked his view on how best to raise money for them. Without hesitation, he looked me in the eye and said, "Urvashi, what you need to do is hire a nice white man with a cute ass as your development director." That would help me more than anything else, he added, because it would "balance" me out in the eyes of many donors. In his mind, Randy was only being honest and therefore kind by laying out the truth as he saw it. The blunt assessment should not have surprised me, but it did. Once again, my skin and gender seemed barriers to my surviving in the new job. I politely told Randy that I intended to hire the best person for the job. That turned out, three months later, to be a talented woman named Jamie Grant.

During the next three and a half years, incidents of racial and gender intolerance piled up like grime from exhaust, a byproduct of working in a gay and lesbian movement that labors under the same racial prejudice, gender binarism, and heterosexism that weigh down the broader society. Sometimes the insensitive or frankly racist or sexist behavior came from white gay men and women. Other times, it came from feminists and people of color.

There were countless times when I was the only woman in the room at an important meeting, event, small dinner, or fundraising reception. Or times when I was the only person of some color (a two-for-one, as some call it) on a conference plenary. Scores of people have asked me to speak at their dinner, conference, rally, or fundraiser because they were "interested in diversity." My experience as a political organizer was a secondary bonus. Some people called me to participate in conferences or panels on which I had absolutely no expertise or relevance—because I was the only woman of color in their Rolodex. Others refused to meet with me, for the same reasons that some sought me out—because of my political perspective or reputation, because of my gender, or because of the multiracial movement agenda I advocated.

There were legendary stories—my own and those recounted by colleagues—about the late Allan Morrow, who had had the vision to establish a gay foundation in New York called the Stonewall Community Foundation. Allan often said outrageously insensitive things—sometimes to shock, but more often because he believed them—and was bold enough to express his class, race, and gender views out loud. Once, at a meeting we were both attending, he railed against the grant of funds to an organization serving lesbians, complaining that if he chose to fund an organization that served only gay men he would be charged with being sexist, yet he was expected to fund lesbian-specific projects as a gay man. Another time Allan told a friend of mine that Lambda Legal Defense and Education Fund should not hire a black person as development director because "no one wants to be seen with a black person." On many occasions, he met with activists who ran gay organizations and berated us about what a poor job we were doing, how little we knew, how unprofessional and undeserving of support we were.

There were my own experiences with movement division around gender politics, from arguments over whether gay organizations should change their names to quarrels with friends over their use of the words *cunt* and *bitch* to derogate women with whom they were angry. One example of this tension is the long-term effort of queer feminists to move the gay and lesbian movement toward a pro-choice position. The process is nearly three decades old, having begun in the post-Stonewall era, when lesbian feminists brought their politics into the gay liberation movement. I remember arguing with Vic Basile in 1984 that the Human Rights Campaign Fund should not give PAC money to anti-choice candidates; Vic disagreed. HRCF eventually changed its policy, in 1989, and now funds pro-gay rights and pro-choice candidates. Yet today there are groups like the Pro-Life Alliance of Gays and Lesbians, strangely allying themselves with a right-to-life movement that actively campaigns against gay and lesbian equality. Some gay men and women resist the feminist agenda of reproductive freedom as the intrusion of a "nongay" issue into the gay movement. Indeed, some who support reproductive choice within the movement do so out of a knee-jerk idea that lesbians could need abortions, rather than out of a deeper commitment to the principles at stake. Few gay and lesbian people see the inherent connection between women's reproductive choice and gay and lesbian sexual freedom: the right of individuals to determine their reproductive lives free from the dictates of church or state.

Sometimes gender divisions among us are not as clear-cut as feminists on one side and antifeminists on the other, or women on one side and men on the other. I have experienced many rebuffs from lesbian activists, who told me I was a fool to work with the "boys." The unchallenged antimale assumptions of some lesbians frustrate me tremendously. Such assumptions are reflected in a question I am often asked about AIDS. Invariably a lesbian journalist or conference participant will ask whether I think men would do for lesbians what women have done for men in a crisis comparable to AIDS. This cash-exchange mentality among lesbians makes me angry, because it presumes that the sole reason lesbians get involved in AIDS work is political or genetic. In fact, lesbians work on AIDS issues not because of an altruistic female gene in our bodies, but because we care about the people with AIDS we are losing. Ours is not merely an abstract political or theoretical allegiance to gay men; it is a personal commitment to friends, our brothers and sisters, cousins, sons and daughters.

The lack of trust and solidarity across racial lines is evident in the bitter fights that have erupted over AIDS-related funding, fights that pit largely white gay community–based AIDS groups against racial minority–based AIDS organizations. Such divisions resulted in dissolution of a number of ACT UP chapters in the early 1990s; they fell apart over the question of whether to address issues of race and gender, along with the central issues of AIDS treatment and research. Conservatives derided the 1993 March on Washington as the epitome of "political correctness" for its requirement that all delegations to its national steering committee be gender balanced and racially diverse. When gay conservatives criticized the 1993 march for insisting that 50 percent of all steering committee members be people of color, on the grounds that such representation inaccurately reflected the demographics of the community, what message were they sending to gay communities of color? That they believe people of color will not fairly represent whites? Since many of the same people who objected to the march's targets for racial representation had for years argued that it did not matter that most gay organizations had white-dominated boards and staffs, what were they really saying? That people of color could not represent white gay men and women, but the latter would adequately represent people of color?

The bitterness on all sides is deep and growing. People are in well-dug bunkers, and few people—of any color—attempt to break out of their entrenched positions. The atmosphere of trust and respect that is a prerequisite for work across racial lines is sorely lacking in the gay and lesbian community's struggles with its own diversity. Instead of dialogue, we engage in public attack. Instead of multiracial organizations, we keep inventing more single-race groups. Some gay men in San

Francisco were so incensed at what they perceived to be antimale attitudes that they spray-painted "Stop the Testosterone Bashing" around the Castro in 1993. Some lesbians were so angered at the unwillingness of gay men to address sexism that they split off from ACT UP to form Lesbian Avengers.

In order to move beyond this impasse, I believe progressive activists in particular must subject several of our most cherished sacred beliefs to questioning. In particular, we must ask whether gay and lesbian people "get it" (much less agree) when we argue that our movement must deal with race, gender, and class, along with sexual orientation. Second, we must examine the strategies we have used to foster racial and gender understanding, such as multiculturalism and coalitions, to see whether they actually work. And, finally, we must question our reliance on identity as our principal tool for organizing ourselves.

UNDERSTANDING INTERSECTIONAL POLITICS

Even to bring up racial and gender divisions as a fact of life in the movement is to risk the charge of being divisive. In April 1994, at a conference held at Harvard Law School to commemorate the twenty-fifth anniversary of the Stonewall rebellion, I spoke about what lay ahead for the gay movement. Several challenges face us, I argued: the need to refocus on political power rather than political access; the paradox of our apparent mainstreaming and the persistent underlying sexual and moral resistance; and the obligation to speak out against the racism, sexism, and chauvinism that were resurgent in our movement and in the broader society. After the panel, a friendly but concerned white gay man approached me. He had taken offense when I pointed out that unchallenged racism (as well as sexism and chauvinism) within the gay and lesbian movement was on the rise. I had cited specific examples, noting that such prejudice persisted in large part because we had not articulated clearly how sexual identity, race, gender, and economic realities were interconnected. This failure to communicate the intersection of racism, sexism, and homophobia was augmented by mounting frustration among us all—of every color and gender—at the experience of prejudiced behavior.

The young man had heard my comments differently. He said I was being divisive, that it was wrong of me to characterize the institutions of

the predominantly white mainstream gay and lesbian movement as racist. He was not a racist, he said, and I should be careful before I tagged
groups and people in the movement with that label. When he asked
whether I had any data to prove my claim, I responded that I had
firsthand knowledge, and I reminded him that I had not, in fact, called
any mainstream institution racist. Rather, I had argued (and assumed)
that, because we shared a commitment to work against racism and
sexism, we all needed to do that work more effectively. Surely, I said,
the movement's experience over the past twenty-five years taught us
that there was racial, gender, and even economic bias in our communities and organizations as well as in the broader world. He countered
that specific data were needed to back up such an assertion. Moreover,
he said, people have had many personal experiences that challenge my
assertion. He told me a lengthy story about how he had recently be-
friended a black co-worker, and how that friendship had broadened his
awareness. We argued for nearly forty minutes and parted politely. But
the conversation depressed me for days.

I felt I had failed to communicate my most basic premise in the
speech: that the job of challenging racism, sexism, homophobia, and
other kinds of chauvinism is not someone else's but belongs to each of
us. Later, I realized the problem lay not merely in my presentation, but
in the fundamentally different mindsets and experiences each of us
brought to the topic of race and gender diversity in the gay and lesbian
movement. This man wanted statistics to prove a premise that seems so
obvious it needed no proof in my eyes. My experience of nearly fifteen
years as a brown woman working in a largely white and male-dominated political movement was inconsequential to him, while the mere
mention of what W. E. B. DuBois called "the color line" was seen as
divisive.

Is it possible now, in this climate of sensitivity, to be specific about
racial or gender realities without running into denial, disapproval, or
accusations that one is being "politically correct?" Can we talk frankly
about race and gender realities without being manipulative on one side
or defensive on the other? How am I supposed to describe or define my
own experience? I am, after all, who I am: the first Indian and person of
color to run a mainstream gay and lesbian group. Perhaps in this post–
civil rights era, I must neuter and derace (erase) myself in order to be
heard. The point is that simply pointing out the racial dynamics of a
situation remains controversial.

Around race and gender bias, all of us cushion and hedge our views to conform to the orthodoxies that guide our politics. This caution inhibits the honest and vigorous debate we need. If we are, as we so often claim, a diverse, multicolored, many-gendered, multisexual rainbow of a people, then why should an attempt to bring up racism and sexism in our own movement become a matter of dispute? If most gay people believe—as I think we do—that "none of us can be free until all of us are free," what prevents us from acting on behalf of each other's freedom as if it were our own? Why do we still try to find "one of each" for our conference, meeting, board, newspaper, instead of realizing that we can represent each in one, that we can be the voice speaking out not just on the identity we claim, but for the politics of justice we share. How did a movement about sexual politics—a politics centered on the idea that sexuality is the intersection at which so many of our identities meet—become limited to a movement divided by sexual and racial and gender-based identities? The questions I consider here are not the global ones of why we can't all get along across these vast divisions, but the narrower one of *how* we have tried. But even this pragmatic formulation of how we can work together across race and gender lines begs the question of motivation, which the gay political movement has yet to answer: *whether* we are willing to be a movement aimed at racism, sexism, and homophobia or one about gayness alone.

Historically, the question of how to handle racial and gender diversity in our movement has split gay and lesbian people into several camps: the committed, the resistant, the pragmatic, and the uninterested. Contradicting the harsh rhetoric of conservatives, who argue the movement is obsessively PC and wrong, or the isolation of progressives, who dismiss the mainstream movement as racist and sexist, I maintain that the majority of movement activists are committed to fighting racism and sexism. Evidence of this commitment is found in the greater presence of people of color and women in leadership positions in the movement today. The committed segment of our movement invented theoretical and practical models for undoing the structural manifestations of racial and gender-based prejudice. These strategies included multiculturalism, diversity training, coalitions, racial quotas for boards and representative bodies, affirmative action, and a redefinition of the mission of gay and lesbian organizations. The problems faced by those committed to racial and gender diversity come from the resistance we face and the methodology we have used. As in the straight world, resistance to acknowledging racism and sexism as structural problems and not merely individual failings exists in the gay world, and is shared by conservatives, separatists, and nationalists. But the weakness of these strategies to deal with racial, gender, and sexual diversity is part of the problem, and intensifies the resistance many people have to organizing against racism and sexism.

Although it is convenient to describe as racist or sexist those gay people who are resistant to addressing racial and gender prejudice—and indeed this is too often done—I think to do so is wrong. The resistance comes from both personal and ideological sources. On a personal level, resistance to racial and gender politics springs from some fairly standard emotional reactions. The lesbian theorist Charlotte Bunch identified them in the following way in a concise speech, given more than ten years ago, in which she called on white feminists to get over their "divisive reactions . . . to diversity." She catalogued these reactions as defensiveness, guilt, "overpersonalization," withdrawal, and "acting weary and resentful." The final reaction she described was "limiting outspoken 'minority women' to 'their issues.' "

I'm sure that each of us can recall instances in which the resistance stemmed from one or more of these complex reactions, such as the one I encountered at Harvard. Such defensiveness often stems from overpersonalization; to hear about racism in the movement does not automatically require the listener to defend himself or herself as not a racist. On the other side of the color line, I've encountered a defensiveness among people of color when individuals or organizations are criticized. As the veteran black lesbian organizer Ivy Young wrote to me about an early draft of this chapter, "You're not being at all critical of the POC [people of color] groups, their failure around issues of which they do have some control and their lack of accountability, the 'we-messed-up-because-we're-poc-and-we-don't-have-the-resources-so-what-did-you-expect-anyway' song and dance." Every criticism aimed at a person of color is not based on race; people do have responsibility for their actions and their mistakes. I've seen the paralysis or knee-jerk reactions of guilt-ridden white women and men, and I've been ashamed at the conscious manipulation of that guilt by people of color.

On an ideological level, resistance to tackling racism and sexism comes from gay legitimationists who believe that broadening the movement's scope to encompass race and gender will involve it in issues that are not "our issues." As an activist who favors a broad agenda for gay politics, I've often had to justify political alliances with nongay organizations or work on racial or gender rights. For example, when NGLTF lobbied for the Civil Rights Restoration Act of 1991, a bill that reversed the effect of several Supreme Court decisions stripping the federal government's civil rights enforcement powers, I received phone calls from members questioning the wisdom of our efforts on nongay issues. These (all white) members complained that they supported NGLTF to work on gay rights, not on black civil rights and women's rights. These were not "our" issues, but were more appropriate for the NAACP or NOW. I pointed out that gay and lesbian organizations worked on racism and sexism for several reasons: because it was the right thing to do, because gay people of color and lesbians were directly affected, and because to do otherwise would be hypocritical, since we so often asked nongay organizations to support gay rights.

The most persuasive, and yet expedient, argument I made to these callers was the last one: we were involved in this effort because it would help us get support for gay rights from nongay groups. A quid pro quo from the civil rights community on federal gay and lesbian rights legislation requires our reciprocation. Indeed, only after fifteen years of gay and lesbian presence in the Leadership Conference on Civil Rights did that prestigious national civil rights lobby finally endorse the idea of federal nondiscrimination legislation for gays, in 1992. That such pragmatic and strategic arguments for gay involvement in race and gender matters succeed while moral or diversity-based arguments fail is an indication, I think, of the overemphasis many of us place on gay and lesbian identity. Few of us are solely gay or lesbian or bisexual; we all harbor other identities that matter to us. Yet women and people of color are asked by the movement to suppress those identities in order to participate in the movement. This is nonsensical and unnecessary. Rather than trying to purify gay politics to reflect gay and lesbian issues alone, it would be more honest if opponents of a broader agenda acknowledged that they wanted to preserve the racial or gender status quo, or that they just do not care.

Pragmatism about race is on the rise inside the gay movement because the religious right has upped the ante. In recent years, the right has succeeded in forging strong bonds with black fundamentalists. Right-wing groups like the Traditional Values Coalition have spent hundreds of thousands of dollars to build coalitions with and win the trust of black clergy. In addition, secular black conservatives have also been cultivated and supported; most of these individuals agree with the right's homophobic agenda. Black gay and lesbian activists have argued for years that we need to strengthen our ties with the black civil rights movement, yet no mainstream gay or lesbian group funded such or-

ganizing until 1993, when the religious right released the divisive videotape *Gay Rights, Special Rights*. Because the tape so clearly and effectively divided black support for gay rights by arguing that gay
advancement would undermine black progress, several gay organizations suddenly "saw the light" and began to talk about alliances with
black leaders and community groups. The NGLTF- and HRCF-
funded focus groups and polls conducted in 1993–1994 by the pollster
Celinda Lake marked the first time the gay movement had ever done
research on the opinions of black voters about homosexuality. In 1994,
HRCF lent the time of one staff person to the Black Lesbian and Gay
Leadership Forum, ostensibly to organize nationally in black gay communities. But the staff organizer, the capable Mandy Carter, was given
very few resources to undertake this massive effort. In short, pragmatic
understanding of the importance of a cross-racial alliance between gays
and others sounds great but has translated into little concrete action or
commitment.

   Without ignoring the hundreds of gay and lesbian activists who do
"get" the need to work on racism, sexism, and homophobia all at once, I
believe that most gay and lesbian people neither understand nor value
the importance of multiracial and multi-issue politics. They remain
uninterested and unmotivated. Their failure to grasp it is the responsibility of people like me: we have not communicated the theory nor
developed the practical strategies that would allow concerned people to
become politically involved in multiracial and cogender politics.

   To this date, the gay movement has not carefully distinguished
between these four categories of people—committed, resistant, pragmatic, uninformed. We have tended to see gay people as being in two
camps, our side or the other, which leads us to make generalizations
about the movement that are often untrue. I've heard people of color
complain that no one is doing antiracist work in the gay movement, a
statement that ignores the reality of twenty years of organizing by many
committed white people. I've heard men say that all women are antisexual, a statement that ignores the passionate sex wars waged within the
lesbian-feminist movement since 1982. I've argued with lesbian feminists about whether men can be feminists—and, indeed, have been on
both sides of the argument over a twenty-year period! Perhaps there are
fourteen camps or forty degrees of distinction among us on race and
gender. My point is that the complexities of racial prejudice, sexism,
and homophobia require an equally complex response. To construct a
more effective response to racism and sexism, and to build a stronger

movement against homophobia, we must assess the principal strategies our movement has used to deal with racial and gender diversity among gay people.

At the outset, we should acknowledge that the task of challenging racism and sexism within a movement differs from that of allying our gay movement more closely with other social justice movements. The first task is an internal one, and has been the focus of intense effort by lesbians, people of color, and progressive men. The second task—of building alliances between the gay and lesbian movement and other racial and social justice movements—is one in which very few people are involved. Yet neither task has been fully embraced by the mainstream of the gay and lesbian rights movement or by ordinary gay people. Both propositions remain surprisingly controversial.

We have used three major strategies to address our racial and gender diversity: organizing around individual identity; promoting the notion of diversity politics or multiculturalism; and forging coalitions within the gay movement as well as between gay people and straight allies. Over the course of decades, we have organized ourselves into smaller and smaller identity-based groups, by race and gender and sexual desire. The mostly white-male mainstream is perhaps the largest and, still, least self-conscious of these racial and gender-based projects. The strategies of diversifying organizations, empowering ourselves through single-issue organizations, forming coalitions, working within our racial or gender identities—have all failed to dent racial and gender prejudice. Their inadequacy requires us to examine our inherited orthodoxies. Specifically, I think we must ask: Does identity-based politics work? Does separate but equal work as a way to organize against racism and sexism, much less homophobia? And which coalitions work and which fail?

Gay historians have shown us how gay identity emerged at the turn of the twentieth century, how communities formed after World War II, and how gay identity solidified after Stonewall. But at this moment, our investment in identity-based organizing, and in its corollary, single-issue political organizing, actually holds us back: we are unable to coalesce across identities. I once heard identity politics described as a "necessary mistake," an extremely useful term that summarizes the mixed promise that gay-identity organizing offers to our movement. On one hand, identity has helped us to know ourselves and find each other. On the other hand, identity-based politics is not sufficiently encompassing to serve as a unifying theory or practice.

Discussing the major benefits and limits of identity politics, the organizer and writer Suzanne Pharr defines the problem this way: "Identity politics . . . brings together people who share a single common identity, such as sexual orientation, gender, or race. Generally, it focuses on the elimination of a single oppression, the one that is based on the common identity." She identifies three strengths of the identity-based method of organizing: "clarity of focus in tactics and strategies, self-examination and education apart from the dominant culture" and the "development of solidarity and group bonding." Pharr argues, "Creating organizations based on identity allows us to have visibility and collective power, to advance concerns that otherwise would never be recognized because of our marginalization within the dominant society."

Pharr goes on to point out the weaknesses and limits of this method of organizing, the largest of which is that identity-based organizing cannot countenance the multiplicity of identities of which people are actually composed. She emphasizes that not only does single-identity politics fail to take into account that "[w]hole, not partial people come to identity groups, carrying several identities" but it also fails "to acknowledge that . . . a similar imbalance of power . . . exists within identity groups as within the larger society. People who group together on the basis of their sexual orientation still find within their groups sexism and racism that have to be dealt with—or if gathering on the basis of race, there is still sexism and homophobia to be confronted."

The problem of identity-based organizing is even more fundamental. A false assumption underlies all gay and lesbian organizing: that there is something at once singular and universal that can be called gay or lesbian or bisexual or even transgendered identity. (In fact, homosexual and bisexual people are enormously diverse. The notion that we constitute one community and can coalesce into a unified movement is both a fiction and a prayer.) In addition, we assume that the identity is shared across the lines of gender, class, race, geographic location, and so on; that it is something we can foster, teach, learn, and promote; that while it may change in each historic epoch, it is something that has always existed because gay and lesbian people have always existed.

John D'Emilio terms this the "myth of the eternal homosexual." He clarifies: "The argument runs something like this: gay men and lesbians always were and always will be. We are everywhere; not just now, but throughout history. This myth served a positive political function in the first years of gay liberation. In the early 1970s, when we battled an ideology that either denied our existence or defined us as psychopathic individuals or freaks of nature, it was empowering to assert that 'we are everywhere.'" Arguing that such a conceptualization of gayness limits us, D'Emilio urges instead a historical view of homosexual emergence. In his groundbreaking essay "Capitalism and Gay Identity," he explains how economic changes—specifically, industrialization and its impact on the family, the ability of women to work outside the home, and the existence of wage labor itself—facilitated the emergence of gay and lesbian identity and changed the social meaning of gay behavior.

Belief in this universal gay or lesbian identity informs the work of many activists. They see their work as ensuring the security, safety, and freedom of the status queer, which becomes the unifying project of the gay and lesbian movement. All other issues are nongay. I think this desire for some unification around our sexual identity explains why so many people embrace the word *queer* in this decade. At the very instant that the multiplicity of gay and lesbian identities seemed to require a qualifying adjective for the words *gay* and *lesbian* (black, Latina, Asian, Native American), the term *queer* provides a new anchor to ground us to something shared, stable, and constant. We are not gay men or lesbians; we are queers, defined as much by the contrast and challenge we present to hetero-normativity as by our sexual identity.

In fact, gay and lesbian identity is far from a unitary thing. It is mediated by our race, gender, economic status, history, and other conditions of life. Further, as Pharr notes, each of us is rarely defined by one aspect of our identity: we are all more than gay, more than brown, more than our religion, more than our economic background. I can be at once all or three or four of the identities I embody: a lesbian, an immigrant, a Hindu, an Indian-American, a feminist, an organizer, a lawyer. My identification as a lesbian allies me with other homosexual men and women, but it may or may not ally me with everyone who claims to be gay. For example, while I support the First Amendment rights of homosexual pedophiles (like NAMBLA) to organize, I reject pedophilia as part of homosexual identity and do not support most of the goals of the organization. Nor should I have to. To be gay does not mean one agrees with everyone else who is gay, just as being straight

does not require approval or acceptance of every expression of heterosexuality.

The question of how we understand gay and lesbian identity affects
our political strategy. Sexual identity itself can be seen as a spectrum,
but the way we organize around the categories of *gay* and *lesbian* and
bisexual suggests otherwise—that it is a fixed thing. Some of us are
probably born gay—have known it since we were children and are
finally living the lives we imagined. Others of us may have chosen to be
gay or lesbian or bisexual. Still others may have fallen in love with a
man and later with a woman; what does that make us? The sexual lives
of supposedly straight people are often far more complicated than
the label *heterosexual* suggests; identity does not correspond solely to
behavior.

Yet on the gay left, for example, there is a persistent tendency to
apply universalities to the messy reality of gay and lesbian behavior.
This expresses itself among lesbians as endless navel-gazing about who
is really gay or not, who belongs and who does not; and among progressive gay men in a macho fascination with sexual prowess. Lesbians
vigorously debate the sexuality of lesbians who sleep with women for
years but then have affairs with men. Are they in fact lesbians? What is
a gay man who was married for twenty years before he came out of the
closet? What is a previously straight older woman at sixty-five has
a relationship with another woman? What of a sixteen-year-old who is
confused about how to define herself? Meanwhile, progressive gay men
feel so committed to the ideal of post-Stonewall, pre-AIDS, libertine
sexuality that they rarely listen to the criticism offered by other gay men
that baths and commercial sex clubs feel degrading to them. Such talk is
dismissed as antisexual or is treated as a challenge to their idealized
notions of unfettered gay male sexuality.

Gay conservativism, on the other hand, seems to rest on the belief
that people are born gay or lesbian. Conservatives cite new scientific
data about the possibility of gay genes in the X chromosome, or the
studies of identical twins that show a high correlation between gayness
and genetic similarity, or studies of differences in the hypothalamus.
They argue that because gayness is biological, it is natural, and therefore, that antigay prejudice is wrong. Conservative gay writers often
assert that "most" gays are just like their straight counterparts but for
their sexual desire. By doing so, these conservative writers, the majority
of whom are white and male, universalize their own identities, their
desire for upward mobility, and their pursuit of admission into the

status quo as the aspirations of "all" gay people. When this color-infused formulation of community is questioned, the conservative tendency is to react as if white men are being personally attacked (sometimes they are, but more often they are not). Most of all, our tendency is to deny that which should be admitted as mere fact: our movement is far from color-blind and certainly not free of the stain of racism or sexism.

My problem with conservative views of gay and lesbian identity is twofold: I disagree with the reliance on biology as the reason gayness should be fully tolerated, and I disagree with the idea that single-identity politics is effective. Same-sex behavior may well be related to physical differences between homosexuals and heterosexuals, but if our purpose in this movement is to remove the stigma surrounding same-sex love, then both biologically gay people and those who simply fall in love ought to be embraced by our movement. John D'Emilio put it more eloquently: "Capitalism has created the material conditions for homosexual desire to express itself as a central component of some individual lives; now, our political movements are changing consciousness, creating the ideological conditions that make it easier for people to make that choice."

Organizing around the notion that there is a fixed, definable gay and lesbian identity is far more convenient than organizing around the notion that homosexual desire is a potential in every person. It is also far less threatening to straight America. We are certainly more comprehensible when we speak and act as if there is such a thing as a gay gene than when we attempt to argue that we seek to liberate the homosexual potential in all people! Science may well prove that we are gay or straight because of genetic reasons. But even biology does not limit its expression to one form of being. The fact that homosexual people are as multifaceted as humankind itself means that our effort to organize around one gay or lesbian identity will inevitably fail. We will always be led to the fractured reality of gay and lesbian diversity.

Ironically, the fragmentation of gay and lesbian identity results from our having the space and freedom to learn more about ourselves. Gay people have created interest groups and subcommunities, clubs and networks, organized around the multiple identities we bring to being gay or lesbian. So, today, there is a gay and lesbian Jewish identity, a gay and lesbian Catholic community, an African-American gay and lesbian community, a Latino gay and lesbian community, a Native American gay and lesbian community, and so on. In clinging to the idea of a fixed identity, we have gained and we have sacrificed. The question I pose is whether it has been effective for us to separate into singular racial, sexual, and gender categories. Who has benefited? And where does this identity–based organizing lead and leave our movement?

In response to the persistent racial intolerance in the mainstream gay community, gay and lesbian people of color have found it necessary to form race-specific groups. While their value is uncontested in the empowerment and training of leaders of color and in the priority these groups have given to antiracist work, I remain ambivalent about the long-term impact of race-based organizing. Race-based organizing on the one hand and the racism of largely white gay organizations on the other leave unaddressed the need for a multiracial political movement. The old-guard organizations remain largely white and largely male, while the newer people of color or lesbian organizations are small, with fewer resources and a greater dependency on government grants. During the Clinton years, the gay people of color movement has not gained the level of access or power that white gay and lesbian organizations have achieved.

Since the advent of AIDS in 1981, several hundred racial minority service organizations have also sprung up. The terms "culturally specific" and "culturally competent" and "culturally appropriate" AIDS prevention, education, and services were the terms activists used to criticize the racial bias they felt existed in white-originated AIDS organizations. They claimed that people of color were better able than others to reach their communities with AIDS-prevention messages, and that the racism of largely white organizations kept them from engaging in the work of AIDS organizing in racial minority communities. The critiques were well made, and the challenge well taken. But several problems have arisen from the creation of minority-based AIDS organizations.

They are doing critical, viable, and frontline work with populations that mainstream AIDS organizations do not reach: Haitians, IV drug users, Latinas, African-American women, minority children, straight Asians, and so on. But the existence of these minority organizations prolongs the failure of white organizations to deal with racial and gender prejudice in their own operations. While minority-based AIDS organizations have developed innovative projects with life-saving impact, most of the resources continue to go to the white gay organizations. The laudable increase in government support for projects aimed at people of color accents a deeper problem: the dependence of minority

AIDS organizations on government funds leaves these efforts the most vulnerable to the changing political tides. In particular, it leaves some of our most critically needed organizations prey to the government homophobia that destroyed feminist organizations like the National Coalition Against Domestic Violence in the mid-1980s.

The dilemma of power and resources is even more starkly presented in the case of non-AIDS organizations. The former National Coalition of Black Lesbians and Gays, the seven-year-old Black Lesbian/Gay Leadership Forum, the Latino/a Lesbian and Gay Organization, National Gay Asian and Pacific Islander Network, Asian Lesbians of the East Coast, and the South Asian Lesbian and Gay Association have been among the most active and successful race-based organizations in the country. Yet each of these groups struggles daily to find funds, to generate support, and to be visible in the broader gay and lesbian community. None has the financial or political strength of its white counterparts. Instead, what they have is access to a completely different part of the gay and lesbian community, a very different mission from that of their white counterparts, and a different yardstick by which to measure success. For example, when SALGA mobilized a contingent of forty gay, lesbian, and bisexual people to march in the annual India Day Parade on August 15, 1992, in New York City, their statement for gay rights was as successful as one by the Irish Gay and Lesbian Organization, even though they received far less publicity.

At times I have argued that we should collapse people of color gay and lesbian organizations into larger groups like NGLTF or even HRCF. But I recognize the enormous problems such "integration" could pose: a possible lessening of visibility, priority, and empowerment. I find myself torn about the question of race-specific versus multiracial organizing. My confusion comes from experience with the deep resistance to antiracist work and to multiracial organizing that continues to exist within white gay and lesbian organizations. It is tiresome to have to explain that our repeated assertions about being a multiracial community require our movement to respond to racism and to take a strong stance on what some consider "nongay" issues. It feels much more satisfying and productive to choose to work with like-minded people—people you don't have to convince that working on racism is important.

However, the racial separation we create in our work leads to certain predictable consequences, the most obvious of which is the stunning lack of interaction across racial lines. Unfortunately, the answer to who benefits from this division is difficult to face but ultimately quite clear. At the risk of offending colleagues whom I admire enormously, without whose work in the racial minority AIDS and gay organizations we would not have the visibility and empowerment that allows me to even make this statement, I believe that race-based methods of organizing unacceptably maintain the status quo on racial prejudice. Our work within single-race organizations must be augmented by the presence of a multiracial movement in order to become fully effective.

Historically, in a sense, the parameters for this racial split were set in the mid 1960s, with the emergence of a black power consciousness within the previously integrationist racial justice movement. In 1965, frustrated by the way white activists dominated mixed-race organizations, the Student Nonviolent Coordinating Committee (SNCC) told white activists to go out and organize whites against racism, arguing that the work of organizing people of color was the work of people of color. This has been the dominant view among progressives ever since. After thirty years of this strategy, I suggest that we have failed on two counts: first, whites have not successfully organized whites against racism, and second, the civil rights movement became monoracial and therefore less effective. Instead of advancing the work of eradicating racial prejudice, we have merely deepened it by enforcing segregation anew. The dominant trend is toward more segregation, not less; more nationalist and supremacist thinking, not less; ultimately more polarization than ever.

A similar split within the women's movement during the seventies came to be known as the gay-straight split. Frustrated by the reluctance of women's liberation leaders to challenge heterosexism, radical lesbians split off and formed their own movement. Actually, the women's liberation movement split into three distinct and generally autonomous movements: a cultural feminist component, a liberal feminist mainstream, and a radical lesbian separatist practice. The cultural feminist movement found its most lasting expression in the women's studies movement and in the whole creation of women-oriented social services, such as rape crisis centers and hotlines, domestic violence programs, support networks of women, conferences. The liberal feminist movement focused on the political sphere, dividing into single-issue feminist organizations (working on reproductive rights, domestic violence, sexual assault, comparable work) that chose fights like the ERA, electing women to office, and enacting legal and legislative reform. The lesbian separatist movement focused on the self-conscious task of redefining lesbian identity and establishing lesbian communities. In the mid-1970s, lesbian separatism was the dominant mode of lesbian political activism: the mixed gay and lesbian movement was not where many political lesbians worked.

Within the gay and lesbian movement, the parallel development of lesbian communities and gay male communities resulted in a tense climate of uneasy dislike between lesbians and gay men. I remember being severely criticized by lesbian friends for beginning to work with gay men in 1979. Conversely, gay men who embraced feminism were not seen as part of the gay mainstream, whose attitude was that these dykes hate men and they hate sex, so we have very little in common. A co-sexual movement began in a handful of cities in the late 1970s, principally Boston and San Francisco. Until the mid-1980s, a big topic of mainstream movement controversy was whether gay organizations should change their names to add the L word. With the name change of NGTF to the NGLTF in 1985, this debate finally ended at the national level. Advocacy of feminist objectives (like the ERA and abortion rights) was hotly debated by gay men opposed to "diluting" the movement with nongay issues. At Boston's *Gay Community News* collective, for example, a number of men left the organization rather than work in a co-sexual, pro-feminist environment.

With the advent of AIDS, however, the movement began to be more mixed. Two theories are popularly promoted to explain this development. One could be called the theory of decimation and opportunity; the other, the theory of biology. Neither is accurate, but each appeals to a certain type of misogyny. The first holds that lesbians came into the movement to fill a vacuum created by the loss of large numbers of gay male leaders who got sick, focused on AIDS service groups, or died. This analysis is shallow and wrong. The loss of many gay male leaders was painful and devastating, but more often than not it led to the activism of other men. Leadership in the movement has in fact changed very slowly from male to female, as any quick look at the boards, staffs, and directorships of most gay organizations will reveal. The second theory holds that lesbians simply performed the classic female role of coming in to take care of men as they got sick. This neobiological determinism irritates me, because it reduces the clear political choice many lesbians have made to engage in social service work to our female chromosome. Why not attribute it to a strongly developed sense of justice or morality? Why must we rationalize why women do what they do instead of simply accepting it? Granted, many women are involved in fields like nursing, human resources, social work, health care, education, and so on, but to attribute the association to gender rather than lesbian politics or ethics is to presume too much about women's motivation.

I believe that what most directly brought lesbians into the mixed gay and lesbian movement was political efficacy, not opportunism or gender. By necessity, AIDS broadened the agenda of the gay and lesbian rights movement. A movement whose most visible national effort had been on passing a federal gay civil rights bill, an abstraction that did not touch the lives of many gay and lesbian people, suddenly became engaged in building local gay and lesbian institutions—service organizations that became centers for gay men and lesbians to meet, work, and take care of one another. A male-dominated movement that had rarely ventured beyond "safely" gay issues, like police harassment of gay men in parks and rest stops and bars, was suddenly addressing topics that lesbians and feminists had worked on for more than a decade—the bias of mainstream health care delivery, the expansion of a self-help model of care, Medicaid reform, welfare benefits reform, sex education, the use of reproductive technologies to prevent transmission of disease, racial prejudice, and federal government inaction. When AIDS broadened the gay male movement's agenda, lesbians became valuable in ways we had not been before.

A similar broadening of agenda and involvement—out of a desire for efficacy—has yet to occur in the arena of race. The need for white gay people to take up racism as their struggle could not be more urgent. Today the same white supremacists and militias who terrorize the nation espouse the most vitriolic homophobia present in our culture. The laws closing U.S. borders to immigrants from other countries are directly analogous to laws used to bar openly gay people from visiting or emigrating. The erosion of civil rights and affirmative action laws deals a blow to the gay rights movement's nascent effort at obtaining equal opportunity regardless of sexual orientation. Yet gay opposition to white supremacy still comes more often than not from queers of color and marginalized progressives rather than the mainstream voices in our movement.

Organizing around identity has led us into parallel movements that, in turn, reinforce the particular identity we organize from. Because of identity-based organizing, therefore, we have three separate movements: the civil rights movement, the women's movement, and the gay movement. Identity politics keeps the gay movement separated from straights, whites separated from blacks, lesbians separated from men, people of color separated from each other. We become a devolving series of specific identities instead of a broad community of people bonded by a shared egalitarian politics. Suzanne Pharr clarifies this constriction of our potential when she shows that the white bigotry of the right, forged from an orthodox interpretation of Christian identity, unites the right against all those with whom it disagrees, and the bigotry of the left, forged from its fragmentary identities, divides it from its own potential power. For the right, the exclusionary politics of Christian identity—which pursues the realization of one Christian nation under one Christian God organized around one socially sanctioned definition of family, with clearly defined roles for men, women, and children, all working in a free market economic order—serves as a glue to unify disparate people. Progressives' attempts to forge an inclusionary politics—of diversity or multiculturalism—has failed to unite them in a similar way. The most successful movements on the left have involved single-issue organizing: the antiwar movement, the abortion movement, the divestment movement.

Lesbian and gay people also lack a unifying politics; all we have is our identities. Indeed, identity-based organizing has led us to a kind of nationalism. Both identity-based organizing and nationalism are about belonging, about the need for a community, a tribe, a sense of place. The nation provides a unifying image for a diverse people. When national boundaries fall apart, transformed by the globalization of the world economy as the marketplace becomes the international substitute for national boundaries, profound changes can occur. To many people, such changes are threatening, a force to be opposed at all costs. Thus, the newspapers tell tales of countries like India in which leaders agonize over the "loss of Indian values" as commercial Western culture conquers domestic markets; they talk of blocking access to certain television programs, of preventing certain ideas, people, books from crossing a border. From Bosnia to Rwanda, blood is all that flows from expressions of national purity and ethnic superiority.

Setting up an external enemy builds a national identity more quickly than any other method: leaders from Serbia to Germany to Africa have proved this to be true. In a sense we engage in this process when we set up the Christian Right as our enemy (just as they build up the Christian nation by portraying us as the anti-Christ). This mechanism—externalizing the enemy to unify the nation—propelled the appeal of the short-lived but influential Queer Nation.

The nationalist sentiment is a problem we must confront within our own movement, where it manifests itself in several ways: an overly sentimental view of homosexual difference, a view of homosexual superiority, and in the old formulation of separate but equal. I have often expressed romanticized and idealized notions of how our "difference," our "otherness," or our "outsiderness" makes gay and lesbian people potentially subversive or somehow more compassionate. Because I would like to believe this, it pains me to admit the danger of these views. By definition, homosexuals are different from heterosexuals, but difference connotes no greater insight, moral integrity, or superiority, just as it connotes no lesser value. To paraphrase Montaigne, who said we are all better than we think, the reality is that we are not as good as we think. Being queer does not necessarily make us bad, nor does it make us inherently "good."

In 1990, the manifesto titled "I Hate Straights" was mass-produced and distributed in New York City's Gay and Lesbian Pride Parade, and marked the appearance of the Queer Nation. As Barbara Smith noted in a letter to *Outweek* magazine, one wonders whether, "if queers of color followed [Queer Nation's] political lead, we would soon be issuing a statement titled, 'I Hate Whiteys,' including white queers of European origin." The spirit of QN captured the anger of a community frustrated with the resilience of homophobia and the intransigence of heterosexist institutions. Overnight, QN chapters sprang up, and an anarchist spirit of creative disobedience became its signature: leafleting and kiss-ins at malls, integration of straight bars, promotion of slogans like "Queers Bash Back," and a colorful array of provocative stickers and shirts symbolized the new generation of gay, lesbian, bisexual, and transgender activists who had no trouble questioning orthodoxy of all kinds.

One problem with the manifesto and the group itself was that Queer Nation should more aptly have been called Queer Anti-Nation. The group consisted of people united more by what they stood against than what they stood for. Defined by style, individualism, and an opposition to the idea of normality, the group resisted any definition by substantive politics, political practice, or old notions of community. Queer activists may have been ideologically diverse, but they quickly established a new and fairly orthodox tribal language. QN had a dress code (leather, shaved heads, Doc Martens, and T-shirts with big lettering), an anti-establishment stand (the target mattered little: it simply needed to be more "fixed," and therefore was regarded as more "mainstream" than the Queer Nationalist), and an attitude that spoke to the nineties (postmodern, in their faces, militant). The flourishing underground 'zines published by defiant queers ranted against the assimilation stance of those who used the words *gay* and *lesbian* to identity themselves. Queer became the vanguard; everything else was retro.

Ultimately, Queer Nation collapsed for many of the same reasons that other direct-action groups lost their edge in the nineties: confrontation and polarization became less effective. Direct action was attacked by George Bush, Dan Quayle, and other national politicians as too "militant," too violent a strategy. The implication that direct action was radical, polarizing, and therefore ineffective was picked up by gay critics. Meanwhile, internal fights took place in Queer Nation chapters over racial and gender politics. By 1993, Queer Nation was nearly finished in most parts of the country. Its most lasting contribution was the slogan "We're here, we're queer, get used to it."

One of our earliest major responses to movement racism and sexism was to diversify and integrate our monoracial organizations. We sought such diversity in boards, staffs, and memberships; we invested in outside trainers and facilitators to conduct sensitivity-training sessions; and we paid consultants to advise us on multiculturalism. While laudable, these efforts have been relatively infrequent, modest, and ineffectual. Most gay organizations have not engaged in a conscious consideration of the way they represent or serve gay people of color or lesbians. Among the handful of groups that have made serious commitments to multicultural transformation are Shanti Project, Los Angeles Gay and Lesbian Community Services Center, and the New York City Lesbian and Gay Community Services Center, but the changes have come with a fair measure of internal resistance and dissension.

Multiculturalism was itself a compromise, arrived at by white institutions in response to pressure by gay and lesbian people of color. Throughout the 1980s, gay and lesbian people of color pushed gay groups to diversify in order to better serve the interests of nonwhite communities. Some mainstream gay groups stipulated that at least 20 percent of their board would be people of color. Others hired token staff or found token board members to appease the critics, and thereby brought on upheaval. For example, in the 1990s the Los Angeles Gay and Lesbian Community Services Center and the Shanti Project of San Francisco, under the leadership of the progressive white gay organizer Eric Rofes, embarked on major programs to transform their mission and composition in ways that would make the groups more racially and gender diverse. Working with lesbians of color like Deborah Johnson-Rolon and Melinda Paras, Rofes succeeded in dramatically changing both organizations, and in the process alienated many people who had philosophical or particular objections to the changes. The Shanti Project, for example, made a videotape documenting for staff, volunteers, and clients the difficulties of turning a largely white gay male organization into one that serves different constituencies and itself has women and men of all colors and classes trying to work together. The Shanti Project's materials documenting its three-year campaign are among the only such materials available in the country, an indication of how much lip service is paid to diversity but how little action gets taken.

Similarly, in the late 1980s and early 1990s, AIDS organizations in major cities on the East Coast had to confront a change in their caseload, as more HIV-positive people of color, women, drug users, and immigrants began to be diagnosed and to seek services. Groups like Gay Men's Health Crisis have engaged in extensive self-definition. Whom do they have a responsibility to serve? Only gay and bisexual men, or all people with AIDS? To their credit, most AIDS organizations like GMHC have acted honorably, affirming their primary mission but broadening their services to reflect reality.

Conscious efforts like those at Shanti and GMHC have been the exception, not the rule. Most gay and lesbian organizations have continued to operate as always; they have not made a clear attempt to involve more women, people of color, or poor gay people in their work. By embracing the myth of a united gay and lesbian community, monocultural organizations have been able to label themselves inclusive and representative simply by declaring it so.

Diversity programs have been strongly criticized, by conservatives and progressives alike, as being misguided and divisive on one hand, and tokenist and too modest on the other. These strategies attempt to neutralize racism and sexism with messages of tolerance and to teach respect for different cultural styles. Falsely, they assume that all participants want to learn about and change racial prejudice and that we all want to foster gender equality. A far harsher reality limits the effectiveness of multicultural or diversity politics: many whites don't care at all about black people or other people of color. Some gay people think immigration by Third World people is undermining the U.S. economy and raising their taxes. Others are unwilling to share power with people of color. In addition, lesbians and gay men continue to harbor the most sexist of opinions and attitudes toward each other. Misogynist views are rampant in gay male culture, and antimale sentiment is endemic at many lesbian gatherings. Underlying these gender divisions is the pervasive fear of women's power and the lingering fear and anger at male domination. Given the prevalence of these sentiments, even the simple threshold of embracing diversity cannot be crossed.

An additional problem with these strategies of multiculturalism and diversity training is that they concentrate on reform of the *process* of decision-making within gay and lesbian organizations, not on their *programs, policies, politics,* or *actions.* The theory is that if we change the representation of people of color on the board and staff, we will change the kinds of decisions that are made. That is the same error we make when we mistake access for power. In reality, whether change takes place depends on what people are put into place, what networks they bring to the table, and what kind of power they are able to wield. I've been on a number of largely white gay boards at which the token people of color have done little to push the organization to change its mission, to serve a broader gay community than the white male one that started the organization. Indeed, the person of color brought in to "represent a constituency not previously represented" is disempowered from the beginning, being the only one in the room, or being viewed as a token by other board members. In essence, we reproduce virtual equality within our own community, giving more visibility to people of color but undermining their power to make decisions. Many talented people of color refuse to accept such tokenism and will not serve on mixed-race organization boards or concentrate their work in explicitly race-based organizations.

The problem again is a philosophical one: quotas increase representation but do nothing to expand understanding or effect the change needed to end racial intolerance and gender prejudice. There is no agreement among gay men and women about the importance of working with each other across racial lines, nor is there agreement that such a partnership necessarily involves seeing the gay and lesbian agenda as a part of the broader one for social justice—racial justice, gender equality, and economic justice.

Despite all the rhetoric about coalition politics, the fact is that our movement has failed to use the strategy appropriately. We lack effective alliances between the gay movement and our allies, and we expend little effort on the task of building and maintaining such partnerships. Our inability to form meaningful coalitions with feminist, liberal, civil libertarian, religious, and racial allies can be demonstrated by our relationship with the movement we most often compare ourselves to: the black civil rights movement. Until the seventies, the mainstream gay and lesbian movement had no formal relationship with leaders of the national black civil rights movement. A number of black politicians running for office in the late seventies and early eighties deliberately forged alliances with gay and lesbian leaders and began to speak out on gay rights issues. These pioneers included Marion Barry in Washington, Harold Washington in Chicago, Tom Bradley in LA, Andrew Young, Maynard Jackson, and John Lewis in Atlanta, and David Dinkins in New York. Early work to shape cooperation between the gay movement and the civil rights movement was also carried out by gay and lesbian African-American activists, like the late Mel Boozer, who worked as the NGTF Washington representative, and by the leaders of the National Coalition of Black Lesbians and Gays (people like Gil Gerald, A. Billy Jones, Angela Bowen, and Barbara Smith).

In 1983, this burgeoning relationship suffered a setback when the Washington congressional delegate, Walter Fauntroy, announced that plans for the commemoration of the twentieth anniversary of Dr. Martin Luther King's civil rights March on Washington would not embrace gay rights because, to paraphrase him, gay rights had about as much to do with civil rights as penguin rights did. The "penguin rights" remark provoked an uproar and evoked strong statements of support for gay rights from Coretta Scott King, Jesse Jackson, and other national leaders. Despite the tension, committed gay activists did participate in that event.

Our early AIDS efforts did not receive widespread support from communities of color; the largely white composition of the gay leadership and the heterosexist bias of the civil rights leadership inhibited the development of a close partnership. By 1987, when the National Minority AIDS Council was founded, even the AIDS movement had split along racial lines. In the mid-1980s, the candidacy of Jesse Jackson and his formation of the Rainbow Coalition drew the support of large numbers of gay and lesbian people. The Reverend Jackson sought the support of gay organizations of all colors, and became the only presidential candidate to be invited to address the 1987 March on Washington for Lesbian and Gay Rights. Jackson spoke out forcefully for gay and lesbian rights in his 1988 campaign but received little financial support from the mainstream gay movement.

The most successful coalition between gay and lesbian groups and civil rights groups was formed during the four-year effort to pass the federal Hate Crime Statistics Act. The bill, requiring data collection of hate crimes, was initially championed by the Jewish community (in particular, the Anti-Defamation League) and the civil rights movement (in particular the ACLU and NAACP legislative offices). In 1986, the main sponsors agreed to add sexual orientation to the categories of hate crimes for which data would be collected. By 1987, the ACLU, ADL, NAACP, and NGLTF were close allies in a national coalition of more than sixty organizations working for the bill. When the bill passed, the effort was credited by all as an example of successful teamwork.

But the relationships built between the gay movement, the NAACP, and others did not continue except at symbolic levels. I think there were two major reasons. First, there was no joint legislative cause after the Hate Crime bill to which both movements committed themselves; and second, the gay and lesbian movement became deeply divided by race at the same instant that the broader society experienced a dramatic heightening of racial tension. The *Miss Saigon* controversy, the splits of ACT UP chapters over race and gender issues, the fights between AIDS organizations of color and largely white gay organizations, and a systematic campaign by the right to foster discord among black and gay communities led to widening distrust by 1993. In the larger culture, the deepening racial divide caused by Reagan-Bush economic policies blew up in racially motivated riots in Miami, Los Angeles, and other cities.

Analysts have argued—and our experience with coalitions shows—that necessity is the engine that drives people of different backgrounds to work together. For some of us the necessity is present in our beings; if we are women, people of color, and gay, if we are a mix of identities that are stigmatized or disempowered by the status quo, we have an easier time comprehending the intersection of a number of issues. For others, necessity comes in the form of an external threat that motivates us to take actions we normally would not consider. But necessity alone does not drive progress. The deepening crisis in the cities shows that even where it is clearly necessary for us to work together to fight poverty, crime, and despair, we lack the will. Even as large numbers of gay and bisexual men of color die of AIDS, some white gay AIDS organizations and some minority AIDS organizations act as if all the gay men with AIDS are white, and all the people of color are not gay. We engage in self-serving denial, fight bitterly with each other for crumbs from the government's shrinking pity pot, and persist in the myopic divisions of services around sexual orientation and color and gender, divisions that lead to the existence of more than a hundred AIDS organizations in the San Francisco Bay Area alone.

In these mid-1990s, the logic of necessity dictates that gay and lesbian people solidify their relationship with other social change movements, with people of color, with the Jewish community, with the mainstream women's movement at every level, and with a broad range of civil libertarians. Instead, we are in a period of great insularity. The pessimistic view that it is us against the world coexists with the naïve belief that the changes we witness in social attitudes toward the status queer are irreversible. Doom and gloom about the growing power of the right coexist with the attitude that the right is not much of a threat and will be easily defeated in a national election. The view that AIDS is killing us all, in life and in spirit, overwhelms many political men I know; while a view of AIDS as a disease of an earlier generation of gay and bisexual men colors the wishful thinking of a young generation of gay men. The sense that lesbians need to organize on our own, that people of color need to organize on our own, that white gay men need to organize on our own deepens at the very instant that we need each other's love and support and trust more than ever.

The problem is systemic to the gay and lesbian movement. It pays so little attention to the priority of coalition-building that no gay organization has staff dedicated to such an effort. Instead, the coalitions that get built are paper structures, involving the exchange of signatures rather than the exchange of ideas, bodies, energies, and commitment. This is a fatal weakness for the gay movement as it enters the next century.

THE DREAM OF A COMMON MOVEMENT

At a gay and lesbian retreat we both attended, Andrew Sullivan and I discussed the involvement of the gay movement in racial justice. I argued that tackling racism was inherently important for the gay movement for two reasons: because it was the right thing to do, and because a large number of gay and lesbian people are people of color. I maintained that antiracist work was integral to our work against homophobia because the same forces in society justified both forms of prejudice, and because gay people as a minority need allies in order to win politically. Andrew disagreed. He said that what I described made the gay and lesbian movement sound like a subset of a broader racial justice movement. While he had no quarrel with such an antiracist movement, he thought our gay movement needed to stay focused on gay and lesbian issues alone. He was uncomfortable with broadening the movement on pragmatic grounds, because not everyone in the gay community was committed to racial justice. Instead, he asserted that if we stayed focused on gay rights issues only, concentrating on how to win marriage and end public discrimination, we could unite the gay community.

The resolution of this argument is necessary if our movement is to move forward. There are those who believe we must maintain a single, narrow, gay-rights-only focus. There are those who believe that the gay movement must incorporate in its mission a commitment to end discrimination and prejudice of all kinds. The third position, which I hold, is that those of us who are equally committed to racial and economic justice, feminist values, and gay and lesbian liberation must come together in a common, progressive movement. For those not interested in tackling gender, race, economic justice, or other issues of difference, the gay and lesbian movement as it is currently constructed offers plenty of opportunities for single-issue political activism. Those who are more interested in moving beyond identity politics have two options for building a broader and more harmonious movement: the first involves working more widely with a range of people on issues on which we share common purpose—the coalition-around-an-issue strategy. The second is more ambitious, finding the new path, creating what I call a "common movement."

Those who continue to work inside the gay and lesbian political framework still have the choice of working narrowly or broadly. There is no easy way to transcend differences that are centuries old or to overcome prejudices that are deeply held. But I do think organizers who are interested in building a multiracial and co-sexual movement can have a beneficial impact by being more conscious of race and gender in organizing their work. Practically speaking, I think we organizers should ask ourselves three questions at the start of any political project or campaign: How does this issue affect different populations within the gay and lesbian community? Can we build coalitions with the non-gay community around this issue? How can we educate the different segments of our community on the direct way this project or campaign affects them?

If we gay and lesbian leaders asked ourselves the first question, many of the problems of insensitivity or ignorance could be identified early and avoided neatly. Asking how a particular issue (campaign, slogan, activity, project, program, benefit) affects different segments of the gay and lesbian community requires organizers and leaders to think of people they may not automatically consider. If we do not know the answer to the question, it is important to do some research and educate ourselves!

So, for example, if a gay organization is planning a media campaign to promote a "positive gay and lesbian image," the immediate question of who is the audience may trigger a further caution: will different messages be needed to appeal to white voters and to African-American voters? The answer will require convening an additional set of focus groups. In another example, if Lambda Legal Defense and Education Fund had asked themselves that question when they first thought about hosting a *Miss Saigon* benefit, perhaps their concern would have led them early to conversations with the Asian gay and lesbian community. Such conversations, held while the event was still in the planning stages, could have saved the organization a great deal of pain. Instead, Lambda committed itself to holding a theater benefit slated to bring in a large amount (10 percent) of its annual budget. When Asian activists protested the show's sexist stereotypes and racist casting, Lambda's director reacted defensively. Tensions heightened, despite mediation, until staff and board members were traumatized and a wonderful organization's reputation severely damaged in communities of color; ultimately, Lambda's director Tom Stoddard and a number of staff people were burned out or turned off. One beneficial outcome from this painful controversy was the empowerment it gave to the gay and lesbian Asian and Pacific Islands community in New York and nationwide.

The second threshold question I suggest we ask is one that is rarely raised in our movement: How can we organize to build coalitions between us and nongay allies around any issue? Of our allies, we assume too much, and of our enemies, we assume too little. Instead of conceptualizing a campaign aimed at straight people, we tend to ignore them, demonize them, or assume that they get it. I do not mean that we should shape our goals to the status quo, but we should focus on the segments of the mainstream where education and transformation are possible. Polls show that two-thirds of the electorate are somewhat too strongly supportive of gay and lesbian rights. The people making up that two-thirds should be the targets of our educational and coalition-building efforts. Ironically, the movement more often aims at the reactionaries, who will never be convinced, rather than our families and friends, who can be motivated to become more vocal on behalf of gay equality. Even when a group like PFLAG exists in so many communities, it is too rarely treated as a political resource by gay activists in that same community.

With each new project, a gay organization must consider how to build coalitions on the project between us and nongay allies. This practical matter instantly requires an analysis of who our friends are on any given issue. For example, if the issue is an AIDS-related one, a certain set of community leaders, organizations, ministers, and media outlets can quickly be identified as a possible base for a coalition. Approaching these people, planning forums, press conferences, and doing events becomes the method of organizing. If we engage in this kind of local action—moving beyond our community and beyond the insular world of the gay and lesbian ghetto—we can actually be engaged in the revolutionary work of changing consciousness. I've always found such community organizing among the most exciting work anyone can do, because it puts you precisely where change matters most—between people.

History shows that single-issue coalitions have been the most effective strategies the gay movement has adopted. Replicating the nationally effective Hate Crime bill coalition at the statewide level may well be a useful tool for local activists. In nearly every major city violence against lesbians and gay men is a huge problem. In each of these cities, violence against people of color, against Jews, and against women has reached epidemic levels. Yet few antiviolence or anticrime coalitions exist around the country between us and other community-based or faith-based groups. What if local antiviolence projects were to organize gay victims of violence to speak to every single straight club, church group, or youth group that would listen? Person-to-person education would do more to break down misunderstandings than the media-oriented advertising approaches toward public education we have pursued thus far. Such political education is especially needed today, when the very idea of civil rights is under attack. Whatever one's politics on race or gender may be, every gay person needs to understand that as the legal rights of black people, people of color, or women are eroded, so too are our rights. The same legal and political framework we seek to protect serves to shield other minorities as well. Without political education on the history of gay and civil rights, we remain baffled or forever surprised by the "one-step forward, two-step backward" aspect of gay and lesbian progress.

Asking the third question, how to communicate the importance of a particular issue to the gay and lesbian community, may seem an obvious one, but it is most often neglected by gay organizations. A major criticism of the Campaign for Military Service was that it failed to communicate effectively with, and therefore to mobilize, gay and lesbian people. Many declared themselves opposed to the policy; few activists actually organized forums, went before local community organizations (gay and straight) to talk about the issue and its importance, engaged in leafleting or tabling at the malls, or pursued any coalition-building efforts at the local and state level. As a result, CMS assumed it had a level of support that in fact did not exist. Gay organizations constantly make this mistake. Relying on gay media outlets to print press releases they send out, gay groups fail to realize that their job involves doing basic political education among gays and our allies as much as it involves winning a policy fight. Without an educated constituency motivated to engage in the fight, little can happen. One wonders what effect such community-based organizing might have had on the fight to overturn the antigay military policy.

My own view is that it will take nothing less than a new movement for us to move beyond identity and toward a shared progressive politics. Paraphrasing Adrienne Rich, I pursue this "dream of a common movement," one built from a shared set of values, ethics, and political aspirations. The urgency of this movement's formation has never been greater. Gay people, feminists, women and men who are progressive, non-Christians and tolerant Christians, people of color—people of all backgrounds have a common enemy today. A totalitarian right, invested in notions of religious, racial, and gender-based supremacy, moves closer to political and cultural dominance daily. In the face of this crisis, will we stand divided, or unite to transform our future?

CHAPTER TEN

THE SUPREMACIST RIGHT

We want to see a working majority of the Republican Party in the hands of pro-family Christians by 1996 or sooner. Of course, we want to see the White House in pro-family Christian hands, at least by the year 2000 or sooner, if the Lord permits.

—Pat Robertson, Christian Coalition 1991
Road to Victory Conference

Our culture is superior. Our culture is superior because our religion in Christianity and that is the truth that makes men free.

—Pat Buchanan, Christian Coalition 1993
Road to Victory Conference

Gay and lesbian people tend to see the antigay focus of religious and secular conservatives as something discrete and unconnected to other right-wing objectives. In truth, the homophobic campaigns launched by right-wing organizations have as their goal a far larger target than gay and lesbian people alone. Any review of the history of the religious and secular right in our country reveals that this wing is after cultural and political supremacy. Though profoundly antidemocratic, the right uses the tools of democracy to win power. Their self-described war (more like a jihad) covers many terrains: politics, morality, racial relations, art, education, economics, the role of government, even the methodology by which we analyze the world. At its core, this right-wing movement rejects the two-hundred-year-old experiment of American pluralism and, in its place, proposes a Christian state, a theocracy. Right-wing leaders and organizations explicitly reject democratic values like tolerance, dissent, individual freedom, and compromise. Indeed, the right elevates intolerance to a virtue if it is based on Christian values. This message was articulated quite clearly by Operation Rescue founder Randall Terry: "I want you to let a wave of intolerance wash over you. Our goal is a Christian nation. We have a biblical duty, we are called by God, to conquer this country. We don't want equal time. We don't want pluralism."

Recently, the ever-careful and shrewd tactician Ralph Reed betrayed the true agenda of the religious conservatives in the *Wall Street Journal*. After duly noting that "Moses delivered the 10 Commandments, not a 10-point legislative program," Reed went on to emphasize how "religious conservatives are providing much-needed ground support for the Contract With America" and also outlined the next objectives in their pursuit of cultural supremacy: pro-family federal policies, downsizing government in general and the public school system in particular, replacing welfare with church-based ministry to the needy, and a "religious liberty statute . . . to guarantee that the right of all citizens to freely express their faith in public places is not infringed." In the spring of 1995, the Christian Coalition began a new national campaign to assert its political influence, pushing a Contract with the American Family. This agenda reveals that the right's ambitions go far beyond participating in a broader conservative coalition: their program aims to expand the influence of evangelical Christians into all aspects of American life. Reed's *Wall Street Journal* essay proudly cited evangelicals as an emerging political constituency whose agenda enjoys the support of moderates, deficit hawks, tax cutters, and business groups. He observed, "The differences between these constituencies are becoming increasingly blurred. A recent survey conducted for the National Federation of Independent Business found that 43 percent of all small-business owners are evangelical Christians. Their concern is both the regulatory chokehold of the federal government and the coarsening of the culture." This blurring of the distinctions that once divided the right from the mainstream is a direct consequence of the amazing organizing work done by Reed and other religious right leaders during the past two decades.

Following the direction of the Human Rights Campaign Fund, most gay leaders today use the term "radical right" to denote the homophobic religious and secular conservative movements. The use of this terminology is focus-group driven, recommended by the pollsters Mellman, Lazarus and Lake, who conducted a series of focus groups in early 1994 and found that calling the right "radical" discredited them more with listeners than calling them "religious." Although I understand the decision, I disagree with its accuracy. The right is not seen as "radical" by the vast majority of people who come into contact with it. Emerging as it does from the mainstream of religion, wrapping itself in tradition and the traditional family, the right appeals to many people who are troubled by their powerlessness in a world spinning faster and faster out of their control. Indeed, polls suggest that large numbers of Americans see gay and lesbian people as too militant and radical. So if I call Ralph Reed a radical right-winger, I do little to win the support of voters who find him a reasonable and appealing spokesperson for a movement with which they may not entirely agree, but whose "moral values" they share. On the other hand, if I call Randall Terry a bigot, am I not just stating the obvious? His response would be that if doing Christ's work makes him a bigot, he accepts the label. The use of words like *radical* and *bigot* and *zealot* undermines our credibility more than it does that of the other side.

The other problem with such terms is that they are too unspecific about what makes the right radical, bigoted, and overzealous. Secular conservatives are just as radical in their views of shrinking government as are religious conservatives; they essentially believe in abolishing the federal system (except for the military and prisons). Bigotry based on race, ethnicity, gender, sexual orientation, and even religion appears along the entire spectrum from conservatism to liberalism. Leftist sectarian parties are often grossly homophobic and sexist, and liberals at times join neoconservatives in expressing racial prejudice. Zealotry is not seen in Puritan America as a bad thing; we admire it.

At the risk of contradicting my own position that too shrill a tone alienates the very people we hope to reach (the undecided or shifting middle in all the polls on gay and lesbian issues), I assert that it is supremacist ideology that separates the far right from the conservative middle. Ralph Reed, Pat Robertson, Pat Buchanan, Randall Terry, Phyllis Schlafly, Gary Bauer, Don Wildmon, David Duke, Oliver North, and others are, at their core, supremacists: they believe in the primacy of the Christian religion and would, if they could, impose it on all others. Some of them are white supremacists; all champion male supremacy in the traditional family. Without exception, they are heterosexual supremacists. By comparison, mere conservatives, like Arlen Specter, Orrin Hatch, even Bob Dole, may be right-leaning, but they do not operate from a supremacist ideology. A third category, opportunists, defines people like Newt Gingrich, Phil Gramm, Ben Nighthorse Campbell, Richard Shelby, and Bill Clinton. To keep their moral stand in the foreground, I alternately use the terms Christian Right or religious conservatives. I focus little on the secular right, and refer readers to the excellent work of the journalist Sara Diamond and organizations like Political Research Associates, the Center for Democratic Renewal, and others for more information on the variety of right-wing movements in this country.

I doubt that followers or sympathizers with the right would see their movement as supremacist or totalitarian or even antidemocratic. After years of observing and experiencing the right's organizing efforts aimed at gay and lesbian people, I can come to no other conclusion. The label *supremacy* is not intended to serve as a campaign message or a marketing device; it is an analytic reference to help us better understand the scope of response and urgent action that this Christian Right movement requires. I offer a tough-love understanding of the religious right —despite the objections I expect to hear—for one reason: we are far too complacent and naïve about the violent force this enemy is amassing. That ordinary, peace-loving, deeply faithful people follow the religious right does not disguise the truth that its leaders have organized a militantly antidemocratic movement that is turning American constitutional democracy inside out. The enemy is not religion, God, the Spirit, or people of faith. The enemy is evil. Prejudice, injustice, inequality, intolerance, hatred, violence are all evils being strengthened by the religious and supremacist right.

BACKGROUND OF THE SUPREMACIST RIGHT

The birth of a politicized Christian Right was no fluke, nor was it historically inevitable. The long-time New Right operative Morton Blackwell, who served under Reagan, remarked to *The New Yorker* that Oliver North's 1994 Senate candidacy fulfilled a long-term strategy: "There's more than ten years of work here . . . It began in the nineteen-seventies, when conservative-movement activists made a conscious effort to involve theological leaders in politics." In 1973 and 1974, Paul Weyrich, funded by John Birch Society member and multimillionaire Joseph Coors, founded two leading New Right institutions, the Heritage Foundation and the Committee for the Survival of a Free Congress.

In the early years of the New Right, conservatives actually had to convince religious leaders to get involved politically. Sara Diamond observes:

> Contrary to common perception, Jerry Falwell did not originate the idea of the Moral Majority . . . [I]n May 1979, Robert Billings of the National Christian Action Coalition invited Falwell to a meeting with [Howard] Phillips, [Richard] Viguerie, [Paul] Weyrich, and Ed McAteer who . . . told Falwell of their shared opposition to legalized abortion and pornography, and their intention to influence the 1980 GOP platform. Weyrich proposed that if the Republican Party could be persuaded to take a firm stance against abortion, that would split the strong Catholic voting block within the Democratic Party. The New Right leaders wanted Falwell to spearhead a visibly Christian organization that would apply pressure to the GOP. Weyrich proposed that the name have something to do with a "moral majority."

For more than twenty years, Paul Weyrich has been a central figure in the Right, yet he remains one of its least noticed leaders. Now in his early fifties, Weyrich is the theoretician and mastermind behind a vast number of right-wing organizations. In addition to founding the Heritage Foundation and the Moral Majority, he helped found the National Christian Action Coalition and the American Life League; he serves as president of a series of interlocking organizations funded by the Free Congress Research Foundation, a think tank, and established National Empowerment Television (C-NET), a cable communications network for Christian conservative political activists. "I always look at what the enemy is doing and, if they're winning, copy it," he once said to explain why he started the Heritage Foundation as a "conservative alternative to the Brookings Institution."

In 1987, Weyrich issued a manifesto, "Cultural Conservatism: Toward a New National Agenda," circulated by the Free Congress Foundation, which set the ideological tone for much of the right-wing activity we see today. According to the Anti-Defamation League, Weyrich's monograph defined cultural conservatism as the belief that "there is an unbreakable link between traditional Western, Judeo-Christian values and the secular success of Western societies." Weyrich argued that cultural conservatism would be achieved by "strengthening divorce laws, abolishing abortion, providing private school voucher programs, helping the poor through a new 'conservative doctrine of service,' and reversing court decisions that fail to recognize that a general encouragement of religious does not violate the principle of separation of church and state."

Weyrich's strategy in establishing National Empowerment Television (NET) was brilliant. The network takes advantage of the Christian movement's edge in broadcast communications to create a secular façade for Christian conservatism. NET has several functions: (1) a vehicle by which the right trains activists, through regular seminars, educational programming, and interactive briefings on a wide range of topics; (2) an instant communications mechanism enabling a national office to quickly reach local activists with information and instructions for political action; and (3) a medium for delivering what Weyrich calls "an unfiltered message," about Christian values and policy objectives. On December 6, 1993, the NET expanded its broadcasts from training and internal communications to a twenty-four-hour conservative news network. Among the shows NET carries is a regular cable show featuring Speaker Newt Gingrich.

The mainstreaming of the Christian Right was achieved through its participation in electoral politics and its symbiotic relationship with the Republican Party. The collaboration between the Christian Right and Republican Party operatives was inaugurated in the mid-1970s: the party wanted the right's access to voters and volunteers; the right sought political clout. In particular, the Republican Party needed a device to win over traditionally Democratic Southern voters; the Bible provided the belt. The New Right, in turn, sought political legitimacy and leverage to enact its cultural agenda—an agenda that included tax credits for religious schools, broader access to government funds for conservative programs against abortion, pornography, homosexuality, and nontraditional families.

But what began as a mutually beneficial relationship deteriorated rapidly into distrust during the 1980s. In *The Christian Right and Congress,* political scientist Matthew Moen details the right's frustration with national politics. He describes how the Reagan administration appeased the Christian Right with symbolic speeches, appearances at Christian events, and small policy gestures, but backed off repeatedly from pushing the right's moral agenda in Congress. George Bush continued this policy of co-optation, but without Reagan's personal charm to pull it off, the policy backfired. During Reagan's term, Paul Weyrich warned that the Republican Party risked losing evangelical support because it had "wrongly subordinated moral to economic concerns." Yet in 1993 and 1994, the religious right used exactly this strategy—subordinating moral concerns to economic agendas—to help the Republican Party win control of Congress.

The tension between the Christian Right and the Republican Party during the 1980s was exacerbated by ruptures within the right. By 1987, reports the Anti-Defamation League, "the headline organizations of the religious right [like the Moral Majority], particularly those which had most closely allied themselves to Republican power brokers in Washington, were defunct. Regional, nonpolitical, and low-profile grassroots groups like Concerned Women for America, Focus on the Family . . . and the Traditional Values Coalition continued, with a few exceptions, to labor in virtual anonymity." By the time the sex scandals involving Jim Bakker and Jimmy Swaggart erupted in 1988 (a scandal whose exposure Robertson campaign associates apparently blamed on Lee Atwater), the Christian Right seemed to be finished. Falwell's 1989 shut-down of the Moral Majority signaled to some the end of the Christian era in politics. Instead, his collapse marked the end of one generation of leaders and the rise of another, whose ambitions and achievements have far surpassed those of the first wave of Christian activists.

While Christian Right leaders toed the line and worked for Reagan's re-election in 1984, they simultaneously launched an alternative strategy to win power: promotion of Pat Robertson for President. Sara Diamond dates the Robertson for President campaign to early 1985, when pro-Robertson articles by prominent New Right conservatives began to appear in the media. Paul Weyrich announced, "Robertson, more than anyone else on the scene, is likely to be the national conservative figure who could not only equal what Reagan has accomplished, but can exceed it." Robertson carefully fueled the speculation, stating that he would make a formal announcement on September 17, 1986, and announcing on that day that he would run only if three million registered voters signed petitions pledging support and money. The Robertson forces made the petitions available at churches and conferences throughout the year. Diamond notes the genius of this strategy; "[m]ore than just a vote of confidence, over three million signed petitions became the initial mail and phone lists for the Robertson campaign."

The 1988 Robertson campaign shocked Republican Party strategists into paying attention to their evangelical base. Even though Robertson won only 120 out of 2227 delegates to the 1988 GOP convention, evangelicals accounted for more than a quarter of all delegates present. The volunteers and funds Robertson controlled represented critical resources to George Bush, whose campaign conceded the importance of this organized constituency when it allowed Robertson a prime-time speaking slot at the convention. Other concessions made by the Bush camp included the selection of Dan Quayle as Bush's running mate, and the campaign's focus on symbolic issues like Willie Horton, flag burning, the ACLU, and the Pledge of Allegiance.

The 1988 campaign was fascinating and perhaps unique in American political history because two religious leaders, representing completely divergent political orientations, ran for President. Jesse Jackson's second run for the presidency coincided with Pat Robertson's launch of a political career that is still unfolding. Garry Wills observed that while Jackson's "way up [was] from the margins, with the help of marginal people," Robertson, by contrast, came from a wealthy family and had built a lucrative financial empire in the mainstream of American evangelism before launching his presidential bid. Unlike Jackson, Robertson was, as one of his biographers observed, "a true American blueblood."

Whether Robertson intended to use his 1988 presidential run as a building block for a totalitarian organization, or whether his launch of the Christian Coalition in 1989 was merely the next step in the effort to Christianize America, it is impossible to distinguish. Robertson admits that the Christian Coalition was born when "I acceded to the urging of several key advisers to start something that would give focus and direction to the tens of thousands of Christians who had entered politics for the first time during my campaign with the hope of ensuring a better future for themselves and their families."

At a meeting convened in November 1990 by the Ethics and Public Policy Center, scholars and movement leaders assessed the religious right's past and future. Despite the apparent demise of New Right political institutions, Weyrich and others pointed out that Christian activists had succeeded in shifting the national debate on many social issues; a right-wing position now competed with conservative and liberal positions, and the left was nowhere to be seen. Ralph Reed argued that the religious right was in its "infancy" and "compared the status of the [Christian] movement to the National Association for the Advancement of Colored People of 1939." Reed noted that the NAACP had not won any significant electoral, civil rights, or political victories some thirty years after its founding in 1909, and, presciently, he argued that the proving ground for the right's success lay in the future, in its ability to win at the "state, county, and precinct levels."

From its birth, the Christian Coalition distinguished itself as a force interested in long-term and total cultural power. Today, it is without match in its level of organization, national reach, and leadership skill. The Christian Coalition boasts over a million members, more than 870 chapters, "an additional 350,000 grassroots activists on its mailing rolls, volunteers in 50,000 precincts, full-time staff in 19 states, and a 'pro-family' database of 1 million." As Reed explained in 1994, "The priority has always been to organize, to build a permanent infrastructure. We're looking twenty years ahead, not two years. If we build our movement only against Bill Clinton, once Clinton is gone, in either two or six years, then what will we say?"

In his book *The Turning Tide*, Robertson defined the coalition's goal as a "clear mandate . . . to affirm and support America's historic and traditional political institutions, which happen to be founded upon ethical systems derived from (and strengthened by) Judeo-Christian values." Robertson also outlined the particular strategy for taking power employed by the Coalition, a strategy he called the 15 percent solution. The *Village Voice* journalist Craig Goldin explains the strategy concisely: "Even in a well-attended presidential election, only 15 percent of eligible voters determine the outcome. Here's the simple math: about 60 percent of the qualified electorate is registered, and only half of them vote. Half again of that 30 percent determines the outcome, hence the all-powerful 15 percent. 'We don't have to worry about convincing a majority of Americans to agree with us,' Guy Rodgers, the Christian Coalition's national field director declared at the 1991 Road to Victory conference. 'Most of them are staying home and watching *Falcon Crest.*'"

By the middle of 1994, the Christian Right was positioned to exert enormous influence in key elections in every single election cycle, not just national ones. It controlled the Republican Party in at least eight states, including several states pivotal in national elections: South Carolina, Oregon, Minnesota, Virginia, Texas, California, Idaho, Iowa. In addition, it wielded great influence in the Republican Party in Alaska, Oklahoma, Ohio, Missouri, Louisiana, Nevada, New Mexico, Arizona, and Florida. This clout paid off for Republicans in the 1994 congressional elections, and proved Reed's 1990 predictions. About 39 percent of those eligible to vote in that election actually did, and of those nearly half voted for Democrats. Yet because the Christian Right was able to turn out high numbers of conservative voters through its precinct-level "get out the vote operation," the Republican Party won, though narrowly. Indeed, in the *New York Times Magazine,* Todd Purdum noted that according to one election analysis he had seen, eighteen thousand votes made the difference in the shift we saw in Congress during the 1994 elections.

The early wave of Christian Right activity failed because it was widely regarded as too extreme, a lesson that second-wave leaders have taken to heart. At first, in the early nineties, the religious right developed "stealth" tactics for its candidates, playing down their Christian faith in order for them to pass as moderate. But today the Christian Coalition has disavowed the stealth strategy. Perhaps because it is now too big and noticeable to sneak into an election, it eschews secretiveness for a strategy Reed described in 1993 as "Casting a Wider Net." This strategy is exemplified by three very effective grassroots initiatives intended to broaden the right's cultural and political influence. First, the Christian Coalition and Right-wing organizations actively fund, help organize, and seek support from African-American conservatives and black fundamentalist church leaders. Through this work, they aim to foment black opposition to civil rights and splinter the strong black support that gay rights activists have enjoyed. Second, recognizing that the harsh image presented at the 1992 convention scared voters away, the right has done an effective makeover to convince the public of its moderate and reasonable nature. Reed's essay argues that the way to win electorally is to speak to the bread-and-butter issues of middle-class and working-class people. Minimizing traditional issues or its moral agenda is one way the right casts a wider net for voters. Finally, right-wing leaders have steadily intensified their attacks on the idea of separation of church and state in order to advance their theocratic agenda. To hear Robertson and others talk, one might believe that the very notion of separation of church and state is a liberal plot. While some may regard the First Amendment's intent as clear and dispositive, I am not so sanguine.

Potentially the most significant change in Christian politics is the new alliance with black conservatives and black fundamentalists. This partnership is attributable in part to the visibility the 1991 Clarence Thomas nomination gave to black conservatives, to the efforts of the Republican political leader Jack Kemp, and to the right's desire to appear supportive of civil rights in general. The Clarence Thomas nomination exposed the deep splits between progressives and conservatives within the black intellectual community; while Kemp's long-standing advocacy of economic empowerment as a way to reach African-American voters gave the Republican Party the substance it needed to court the black vote without challenging the anti-civil rights politics it used to hold on to the white vote.

Adam Meyerson, a Heritage Foundation pundit, predicts that an "earthquake" will "rock American politics" by the end of this century, when a majority of blacks identify as conservative rather than liberal. He cites a 1992 poll that found a third of voting-age blacks identified as conservative, and black voters supporting Christian Right positions on school choice, welfare, public housing, and family policy. Meyerson also observes, "Many important white conservative organizations . . . are stepping up efforts to attract black membership. Focus on the Family is organizing an urban ministry program dedicated to restoring the black family. The Christian Coalition is aggressively signing up black and Hispanic members. The Traditional Values Coalition . . . unites black and white pastors in opposition to government efforts to legitimate homosexuality."

Meyerson outlines four reasons that black America is ripe for the conservative message. The first concerns black frustration at the liberal inability to solve persistent problems of crime, economic inequality, and the decline of the family. The second has to do with the shrinkage of public funding. Meyerson cites data claiming that "nearly 30 percent of the black labor force, and roughly half of college-educated blacks, work in the public sector." Since public funding is shrinking, liberal policy will be unable to provide opportunity to blacks, but black entrepreneurship, championed by conservatives, will. Concern among African Americans about the perceived decline of the black family makes them receptive to the right's strong pro-family rhetoric. And finally, he postulates that conservatism will succeed because it "looks to two institutions, above all, to provide greater opportunity to Black Americans. One is black-owned business . . . The second institution is religion."

A progressive perspective on black conservatives comes from the researcher Deborah Toler, who argues that the movement consists of "black bourgeoisie [who hold] long-standing . . . negative attitudes toward poor members of the [black] community." She identifies the major intellectual forces in this movement, analyzes the derivation of black conservative ideas from white neoconservative ideology, and explains that the alliance between black and white conservatives rests on their shared derogation of poor black people. Toler disputes Meyerson's presumption that conservativism has a wide appeal within the black community; she says that black conservatives are "out of step."

Reed articulated the theory underlying the right's efforts in the black community when he wrote that "the pro-family movement has limited its effectiveness by concentrating disproportionately on issues such as abortion and homosexuality." To widen its support among voters, religious conservatives spent 1993 and 1994 focusing on economic issues and social issues affecting the American family, such as crime, tax cuts, and health care. This strategy shift reflects the media and marketing savvy of the Christian Right, whose research and polls showed that for conservative Christians, the "top five issues were the same as everybody else's—the economy and jobs, welfare, the budget deficit, and crime. Abortion ranked eighth as an issue; gay rights twelfth or thirteenth."

As the Anti-Defamation League noted, "The Coalition's 'wider net' strategy included an image makeover." Reed apparently decided to use sports imagery instead of war imagery because the former was more accessible. Christian Coalition trainers advised trainees against using "redemptive language . . . We don't want to use Christianese when talking to an audience that doesn't understand Christianese." The Christian Right may indeed succeed in pulling off this "mainstreaming," because the right always begins with an advantage that neither the left nor gay activists can claim: it represents the interests of two of the most cherished institutions in America—the family and religion. We should have no illusions as to why the Christian Coalition has engaged in this makeover: it wants political power and is willing to be pragmatic and disciplined to win it.

The final strategy launched by the Christian Right during 1993 and 1994 was the rising attack on our common understanding of the separation of church and state. Some New Right leaders have long championed the theory that America was established as a Christian nation. They argue that the First Amendment, which bans the state establishment of religion, does not apply to Christianity. In *The Separation Illusion*, published in 1982, John Whitehead, founder and president of the influential right-wing think tank the Rutherford Institute, asserted, "The [Supreme] Court by seeking to equate Christianity with other religions merely assaults the one faith. The Court is in essence assailing the true God by democratizing the Christian Religion." This view is now more widely articulated by Pat Robertson and other Christian Right leaders. In a November 1993 speech, Robertson said, "They have kept us in submission because they have talked about separation of church and state. There is no such thing in the Constitution. It's a lie of the left, and we're not going to take it anymore."

How democratic can a movement be when it portrays a matter of American constitutional history as a lie of the left? In the fascinating *Under God: Religion and American Politics,* Garry Wills clarifies the apparent paradox of the role of Christianity, in particular, and religion, in general, in secular American politics. Wills examines American history, specifically the 1988 campaign, to argue that religion is central to an understanding of American politics. The separation of church and state, he says, has less to do with the Founding Fathers' idealization of the secular than with their fear of the power of the religious. "Neither Jefferson nor Madison thought that separation [of church and state] would lessen the impact of religion on our nation. Quite the contrary. Churches freed from the compromise of [state] establishment would have greater moral force, they argued—and in this they proved prophets. The first nation to disestablish religion has been a marvel of religiosity, for good or ill. Religion has been at the center of our major political crises, which are always moral crises—the supporting and opposing of wars, of slavery, of corporate power, of civil rights, of sexual codes, of 'the West,' of American separatism and claims for empire."

The Christian Coalition's re-interpretation of the separation of church and state, therefore, is indeed threatening. The right is correct in stating that Christians established America and that the Constitution does not "ban God" or religion. But it is completely wrong when it proclaims that the Constitution authorizes the establishment of a religious state. The First Amendment provides, in part, that "Congress shall make no law respecting an establishment of religion or prohibiting the free exercise thereof." As Americans United for Separation of Church and State notes, "Thomas Jefferson succinctly interpreted this provision to mean that government has no power to prescribe any religious exercise or to assume any authority over religious discipline. The religion clauses [of the First Amendment] . . . were intended to build 'a wall of separation between church and State.' " The issue is far from decided, because during the eighties, in opinions authored by Justices Rehnquist and Scalia, the Supreme Court began to back away from the principle of separation. These new directions, coupled with the Christian Right's communications empire and skill, make the legal question of "separation of church and state" a critical one to those who cherish a secular ideal of democracy.

ANTIGAY CAMPAIGNS OF THE RIGHT

In a provocative book, *Sexuality and Its Discontents*, the British writer Jeffrey Weeks argues persuasively that the decline of the left and the rise of the right are due in large measure to the unwillingness of the former to deal with issues of sexual politics. Weeks says that "[s]exuality is a fertile source of moral panic, arousing intimate questions about personal identity and touching on crucial social boundaries. The erotic acts as a crossover point for a number of tensions whose origins are elsewhere: of class, gender, and racial location, of intergenerational conflict, moral acceptability, and medical definition." Throughout the history of morality-based, antisex campaigns, the right has successfully exploited the potential of the sexual to expand racial, gender-based, and moral fear. As Weeks observes, "The political paradox of the late 1970s and early 1980s is that it has been the traditional moralists—or at least their latter-day progeny—who have recognized the opportunity provided by the new political complexity and the growth of sexual politics; and the old left which has signally failed to respond to the new politics. Increasingly, therefore, the contemporary political agenda on sexual issues is being written not by the libertarian left but by the moral right."

A brief look at the different ways the right and the progressive feminist and gay movements deal with sex today bears out the truth of Weeks's observation. The right focuses directly on the sexual anxiety felt by many parents, young people, and single adults. With their campaigns against pornography, explicit depictions of sexual behavior in popular culture, and sex education, members of the right challenges what it terms an ethic of sexual promiscuity and permissiveness in our culture, blaming it for the rise of sexual activity and pregnancy among young people. Ignoring the reality that young people have always had sex, they blame sex education in schools and the immorality of films and TV for this increase. Therefore, they insist, schools and sex educators must teach abstinence rather than contraception or safe-sex techniques, and they oppose condom distribution as a way to deter AIDS because, they claim, it promotes sexual activity. In place of sexual permissiveness, they propose a "new chastity." In July 1994, the Colorado-based Focus on the Family even took out a full-page ad in the *Boston Globe* (and other dailies) titled "In Defense of a Little Virginity." The right's assault on government funding for the arts rests on the manipulative use of a handful of sexually explicit works of art that were created partly with public support. This war on art and cultural expression has already resulted in legislation banning federal funds for art that is sexually explicit or homoerotic. In short, the right is active on every conceivable front (media, art, government, law, education) with a message that all sex outside heterosexual marriage is bad, and that all sexually explicit images should be drastically regulated, if not suppressed outright.

In response to this coordinated, antisex agenda, there exists a strange alliance of mutually uncomfortable factions. Pornography is defended by the industry and by those feminists who defend expression even while they challenge the exploitation of "sex workers." Arts funding is defended by the gay movement allied with a traditional arts community that was surprisingly reluctant to attack homophobia when the art wars began, in 1989. Sexually explicit speech is defended by civil libertarians from the ACLU and political libertarians who disagree with the ACLU on other aspects of its civil rights agenda. Sex education and condom distribution in schools are defended by educators, abortion rights activists, and AIDS activists, who rarely meet with one another to talk beyond this narrow issue.

Further, while much ink has been spilled analyzing the sexual revolution of the 1960s (or debating whether there even was one), few of the progressive analysts have connected themselves to political organizing. Unlike the right, the left has not created a political movement centered on sexuality. Discussions of sexual politics remain lively within the feminist movement, but the mainstream political organizations of feminism, like those in the gay rights movement, do not like to organize on a pro-sex platform. In the climate of moral panic around sexual activity that is whipped up by the right, such a focus might appear suicidal. Yet that approach remains essential if we are to challenge the interpretation of gay and lesbian sexuality that is projected by the right.

The right has launched three waves of antigay activity—or what Weeks terms "moral panic"—over the last two decades. The waves continue into this day. The first wave took shape in the 1970s, as the gay movement itself was forming. Its chief theme was that gays posed a danger to children. The second wave formed in the 1980s, heightened by AIDS. Concentrating on the alleged inherent danger of gay sexual behavior, it perpetuated the equation of disease with homosexuality. The third wave began in the late 1980s and has yet to crest. Manifest in antigay ballot initiatives, state laws, and school board fights, this wave seeks to delegitimize not only gay people, but civil rights themselves.

Antigay activity came into the national consciousness in January 1977, when Miami's city council, known as the Dade County Commission, joined the gay rights bandwagon by passing the first Southern gay and lesbian civil rights law. Immediately, a coalition of Southern Baptists announced their intention to convince voters to repeal the law. Their spokesperson, Anita Bryant, created the Save Our Children, and within a few months had collected six times the number of signatures needed for a ballot vote. Bryant and Save Our Children won their fight when the Dade County human rights ordinance was repealed by a two-to-one margin on June 7, 1977. Seventeen years later, only seven localities in Florida had gay rights ordinances. An attempt in 1990 to pass a gay rights bill in neighboring Broward County was defeated by ballot measure; the vote was closer, 59 percent against, 41 percent for, but still overwhelming.

After the Dade County win, Bryant made her crusade national and founded two organizations, Protect America's Children and Anita Bryant Ministries, to convert homosexuals into heterosexuals. According to Political Research Associates, Bryant's organizations "were hampered by a lack of political sophistication" in the use of modern techniques of fundraising, voter identification, and political mobilization, as well as by her personal problems (which resulted in divorce and the disclosure that she had been battered). By 1979, Bryant's organizations had collapsed, but other New Right leaders took up her antigay campaigns.

The Dade County experience was the prototypical antigay ballot fight, and one whose successful formula has been replicated and refined in succeeding right-wing campaigns. In the wake of the Dade County vote, several gay rights laws were challenged by ballot measure in 1978 and pro-gay laws were repealed in Wichita, Kansas, and St. Paul, Minnesota. That same year, the Oklahoma state legislature banned both gay teachers and any discussion of homosexuality in the public schools. Ultimately, this law was challenged by the National Gay Task Force and held unconstitutional in a 1984 case argued before the Supreme Court.

Inspired by Bryant and fueled by an ambition for national office, California State Senator John Briggs announced an initiative aimed at preventing gay and lesbian people from teaching in California schools. Although defeated by a two-to-one vote in 1978, the Briggs Initiative in California became the biggest media story after the Dade County defeat. The measure was the focal point of massive, if fractious, organizing efforts by California's gay and lesbian community. In the early months of this campaign, most gay people did not take the Briggs measure seriously. A poll released two months before the election showed that Briggs would pass and shocked many people into action. Randy Shilts wrote that the anti-Briggs campaign was aided significantly by Harvey Milk's motivational leadership, but the campaign also gave a host of newcomers to gay politics a chance to earn their political stripes, among them: Cleve Jones, Tim Sweeney, Amber Hollibaugh, Harry Britt, Sally Gearheart, the pollster Dick Pabich, the political campaign veterans Dan Bradley, Pacy Markman, Jerry Berg, Jim Foster, the late *Advocate* founder David Goodstein, and scores of others.

According to data compiled by the *Washington Blade*, the gay and lesbian movement has lost far more antigay ballot initiatives than it has won. Since 1974, at least sixty-four antigay measures have been brought to voters, and fifty of them have been decided against us. In its fall 1995 term, the United States Supreme Court will decide on the constitutionality of such antigay ballot measures, when it reviews the lawsuit challenging Colorado's antigay amendment, which passed in 1992. The Sixth Circuit's decision in 1995, overturning a lower court's rejection of an antigay ballot measure in Cincinnati, provided an ominous sign of how the Supreme Court could vote, and how the trend in the country runs against civil rights. Recently, the American Family Association proposed a constitutional amendment to forbid the passage of state laws protecting gay people in employment and housing. In 1994, during his unsuccessful campaign for governor of Florida, Jeb Bush (son of George) declared that he favored the repeal of gay rights laws, supported the rights of landlords and employers to reject gay applicants, would not hire gay people himself, and is "totally opposed to the expansion of additional legal rights for people based on their sexual orientation."

The untruth that gay and lesbian sexual behavior is a threat to children has been repeated quite effectively by the right. We can counter that message only by answering it directly, not avoiding it. Yet we are afraid to tackle the subject of children forcefully because we are so afraid of being labeled child molesters. The fear of drawing this charge keeps gay parents and people who work with children in the closet, and that, in turn, as young gay people have pointed out, separates us from the very people who most need our mentoring and support.

Our avoidance merely lends credence to the lie perpetrated by the right. Since we have nothing to hide or be ashamed of in our relations with children, let us stop acting guilty. The vast majority of child molestation and sexual abuse is done by self-identified heterosexual men, but this fact does not result in calls to bar all heterosexual men from becoming parents, teachers, Boy Scout troop leaders, or day care workers. Just as the existence of straight and gay pedophiles (defined as "adults who have a sexual attraction only for children and are unable to relate sexually to adults") does not keep straight or gay people from contact, interaction, or healthy relationships with children, neither should the existence of homosexual pedophiles in groups like NAMBLA be used to label our entire community as such.

Suzanne Pharr suggests that the movement handle charges of pedophilia by taking several steps: articulating a strong position against the sexual exploitation and abuse of children, holding honest discussions with each other of gay sexuality, supporting sex education in schools, and showing greater honesty by coming out of the closet. The most provocative and, in my view, important of Pharr's suggestions is the call that the gay and lesbian movement vigorously debate sexual ethics. We must talk about our values, what we do, what we won't do, what we think is right, and what we believe wrong. Because we have been so stigmatized simply for engaging in gay sex, we tend to avoid such conversations. Yet unless we hold frank discussions about our sexual ethics, the right will easily divide us and put us on the defensive merely by discussing the details of our sexual behavior. Pharr writes, "The Right's narrow view of sexual morality has diverted us from the questions that might help us sort through the differences of sexual orientation, sexual behavior, and sexual ethics . . . Perhaps we could get closer to developing positive community standards if we held all sexual practices up to this ethical question [in a particular situation]: Is there use of power and violence and control to violate the integrity, autonomy, and wholeness of another person? If so, then we know we oppose that behavior." Although such honest discussion will be bitter (as arguments among feminists about pornography have been), we must have such conversations in order to face and overcome the lie that gay and lesbian people pose some extraordinary danger to children.

The second wave of antigay activity portrayed homosexuality as a danger to the public health of the nation. Even before AIDS, the medical model to explain homosexuality had fixed in the public mind an association between homosexuality and disease. With the advent of

AIDS, this equation was solidified, and the right graphically depicted gay male sexuality as unhealthy, deviant, and pathological. For years, right-wing politicians refused to acknowledge AIDS as a disease that anyone having unprotected sex could transmit or receive. Instead, the early language of the crisis emphasized "high risk groups," as if the status itself inevitably resulted in AIDS. The stigmatization of Haitians, another population in whom AIDS emerged, illustrates the focus on groups rather than on behavior.

Jean Hardisty, of Political Research Associates, identifies three major benchmarks in this second antigay wave: the publication in 1982 of an antigay book by Enrique Rueda called *The Homosexual Network*, the influence of the widely discredited antigay psychologist Paul Cameron, and the right's misuse of the AIDS epidemic.

During its second wave of antigay activity, the Christian Right developed the propaganda it routinely cites to this day. Rueda's seven hundred–page tract was commissioned and distributed by Paul Weyrich's Free Congress Research Foundation and in 1987 was shortened, re-issued, and mass marketed under the title *Gays, AIDS and You*. Other texts that were published during this period were *The AIDS Cover-Up*, by Gene Antonio; Bill Dannemeyer's *Shadow on the Land: Homosexuality in America*; and Michael Fumento's *The Myth of Heterosexual AIDS*. These books represent just a fraction of the weaponry in the arsenal of the right's antigay propaganda. In publications like the *Moral Majority Report*, in newsletters of Christian Right organizations, and in the special pamphlets promoted by newly formed "grassroots" groups like Dallas Doctors Against AIDS, the right popularized the term "the Gay Plague" to define the epidemic.

This period also saw the development of the right's condemnation of homosexuality in sexual terms. Descriptions of exotic sexual practices and flagrant and outlandish myths about what gay people do sexually are often based on the "research" of Paul Cameron. Since 1980, Cameron has promoted himself as an expert on gay and lesbian sexuality, on the basis of surveys and studies that have been severely criticized by his peers. In response to complaints from other psychologists, the American Psychological Association found that Cameron had misrepresented the work of others and had used shoddy research methods in his own studies. As a result, the APA expelled Cameron in December of 1983.

Despite his lack of credibility, Cameron remains a major resource for the religious right. His research appears prominently in the antigay videotape *The Gay Agenda*. He has advised congressmen (Dannemeyer and Robert Dornan, chief among them), been called as an expert witness in antigay cases (although the Colorado District Court explicitly cited his testimony as lacking credibility), and recently published a new antigay book. In an article on Cameron, *The New Republic* detailed several examples of the misrepresentations he popularizes with apparent impunity. The article reveals that Cameron's "data" about gay male sexual practices come from two studies: one based on responses from forty-one gay men and twenty-four lesbians (out of 4230 surveyed), and another based on subjects recruited from gay male venereal disease clinics. His widely cited data on the high rate of death among gay men and lesbians come from a "study" he did comparing obituaries in gay publications with obituaries in straight newspapers—hardly a scientific method.

The impact of AIDS on the right and on gay and lesbian communities cannot be overstated. AIDS gave the right the ammunition it needed to expand its war against homosexuality, and AIDS more than any other factor helped build a national gay and lesbian movement. More sadly, AIDS aggravated in profound ways the self-hatred and guilt that gay men, in particular, had long struggled with. The clinical psychologist Walt Odets describes this process culturally as society's "homosexualization of AIDS" and, internally, as our tacit "internalization of AIDS as homosexuality." At a recent conference, Odets argued that this internalization results in several unconscious processes among the gay men he treats, including "transferring feelings about sickness from homosexuality to the literal sickness of AIDS, of transferring feelings about an underacknowledged and hated form of life as a homosexual to a similar vile form of life as a participant in a semiprivate plague; of transferring feelings of inferiority about one's homosexuality to feelings about having AIDS or being part of the humanity that is characterized by AIDS; and, finally, of transferring feelings of guilt about being homosexual to feelings of guilt about having AIDS, not having AIDS, or not doing enough for those who have it."

Politically, this AIDS-related activism can be charted in several ways: in the media coverage of AIDS, in the slowness of the federal response, and in several ballot initiatives related to AIDS and gay rights. Writers have documented the denial, fear, and hysteria that surrounded the media's coverage of AIDS in the early years. The mainstream media, slow as they were to cover AIDS, gave great currency to Christian voices when they finally did, to the great frustration of gay and lesbian activists. A number of Christian Right leaders actually established themselves as national figures through the media visibility they gained from AIDS, among them Dannemeyer, Dornan, Gene Antonio, Michael Schwartz of the Free Congress Research Foundation, Gary Bauer from Reagan's staff, and of course Cameron. Whenever AIDS was discussed, our views had to be "balanced" with theirs, a process that delegitimized our objections as partisan while legitimating theirs as objective.

From the outset, the right characterized AIDS as God's punishment for the sin of homosexuality. In a television debate on ABC on July 17, 1983, Jerry Falwell said, "When you violate moral, health, and hygiene laws, you reap the whirlwind . . . You cannot shake your fist in God's face and get by with it." In July 1983, the Pro-Family Christian Coalition of Reno protested the arrival of the National Gay Rodeo in Reno, taking out full-page ads urging the city to cancel the event. One local minister said, "I think we should do what the Bible says and cut their throats." The early antigay media campaign of the right also relied heavily on Cameron's pseudoscientific articles claiming that the gay community was a "living, breathing cesspool of pathogens."

Congress and the executive branch were the sites of the biggest guerrilla war on AIDS, a war that pitted a new coalition of gay, AIDS, and traditional liberal civil rights groups against mainstream conservatives, a growing collection of religious right groups, and evangelical activists within the Reagan-Bush administration. From 1982 until the 1990s, every appropriation bill became a battlefield between gay lobbyists like Jeff Levi and Republican opponents like Bill Armstrong from Colorado, Bob Dornan, and Jesse Helms, with calls for coercive measures ranging from mass testing to mass isolation. Every dollar authorized by the federal government for AIDS was contested. Surgeon General Koop faced the wrath of the Christian Right when he overruled Education Secretary Bill Bennett and his policy aide Gary Bauer to mail out the AIDS brochure to every household in 1986. There is no question that the presence of the Christian Right as a valued and essential member of the Republican electoral coalition directly contributed to this tardy and tentative response. The constituencies most affected by AIDS—gay men, bisexuals, drug users, immigrants, hemophiliacs, poor women—were far less organized than the antigay religious right.

The religious right further polarized political support for AIDS through the effective use of several antigay California initiatives on AIDS. Both the LaRouche Initiative (Proposition 69), defeated in the fall of 1986, and the Dannemeyer Initiative (Proposition 101), defeated in 1988, sought to force the state to initiate coercive measures, like quarantine, against gay men and people with AIDS. Even though both measures were strongly opposed by every credible public health official in the state and nation, the battle to defeat them cost gay and lesbian organizers millions of dollars. In effect, the right thwarted the potential of the gay and lesbian movement in California to organize affirmatively, by placing it on the defensive. Across the country, religious right groups also initiated more than fifteen petition drives to repeal local gay rights ordinances. Such laws were repealed by vote in Duluth; Houston; Fort Collins and Athens, Ohio; Irvine, California; and Tacoma. According to the NGLTF's records, more than thirty-five localities have been the targets of some kind of antigay ballot vote since 1990.

The third wave of antigay activity developed a brilliant synthesis of the earlier themes by arguing that civil rights laws were not intended for, nor should they be extended to, sexual minorities. According to the religious right, civil rights are special rights, accorded above and beyond what the U.S. Constitution and Bill of Rights grant to each citizen. Defined as privileges, civil rights are reserved for "legitimate" and "deserving" minorities. Religious conservatives argue that gay people do not qualify as a legitimate minority because we do not face the same discrimination or have the same experience as racial minorities; that because homosexuality is a sexual behavior, it is a moral issue, not an issue of justice or rights; and that gay rights constitute the legitimation of homosexuality and therefore bestow a "special" status on gay people.

Ironically, this antigay wave is marked by the recasting of traditional foes of civil rights as their champions. In the *Gay Rights/Special Rights* videotape, Attorney General Edwin Meese, who once called the NAACP "a pernicious lobby" and whose tenure as Reagan's head of the Justice Department marked a sharp decrease in civil rights prosecutions, is portrayed as a civil rights defender. Other experts on civil rights featured in the videotape are Mississippi Senator Trent Lott, who has, according to the Leadership Conference on Civil Rights, opposed every major piece of civil rights legislation for the last twelve years, including the Voting Rights Extension Act and the Martin Luther King Holiday bill; William Bennett, who opposes multicultural and bilingual education, has supported Jesse Helms, and has long opposed affirmative action; and Lou Sheldon, who lobbied against the 1990 federal Civil Rights Restoration Act.

As with its sexual myths, the right has promulgated a fictitious definition of gay civil rights. It has made headway into minority communities by suggesting that gay men and lesbians are not discriminated against and by pandering to widespread racial resentment at the way our movement has benefited from the gains earned by the black civil rights movement. Nowhere in the right-wing videotapes or in the mainstream media coverage of the right are there discussions of black gays and lesbians or gay people of any color. Instead, the myth that all gay people are white is deliberately fostered, allowing the Christian Right to play to the racial anger at whites that is present in communities of color.

The Christian Right's current antigay wave succeeds precisely because it deals with ordinary people's fears and lack of experience with gay men and lesbians. For one, it moves well beyond the discourse of deviance and criminality that has been invoked against gay men and lesbians since the 1950s. Given the wider cultural visibility of gay men and lesbians, the old canards that we are all perverted, abnormal people simply do not work. The right can no longer shock people merely by mentioning the word *homosexual* in a crowded theater. They now try to shock the public by reproducing images of homosexuals celebrating sexual freedom or engaging in camp behavior (footage of bare-breasted women, or drag queens in nun habits, or leather folk is a staple in the right's videos). In every public utterance, they attempt to reinforce the association of homosexuality with sexuality, by talking graphically about anal sex, sexually transmitted diseases, and particular practices like oral sex, rimming, and water sports. But even these images fail to shock at a time when commercials, music videos, and films feature sexy, sometimes bizarre, sometimes outrageous imagery. Postmodern culture admits what was once unsaid—that people are sexual creatures. The idea that gay people have sex is therefore not as shocking as it once was. Indeed, juxtaposed with the violence reported daily in the local news, the banality of the middle-class gay or lesbian or bisexual couple next door hardly seems a threat.

To heighten the threat, the right has augmented its message of deviance with the rhetoric of what University of Wisconsin law professor Jane Schacter terms the "discourse of equivalence": the idea that because gay people are not like or similarly situated to racial minorities, we have no legitimate claim to civil rights protection. Schacter locates the right's success in the ability of this "discourse of equivalence" to differentiate between gay people and other groups that have won civil rights. Schacter notes that "[t]he structure of the new discourse is comparative, focusing on whether gay men and lesbians are sufficiently 'like' other protected groups, and whether sexual orientation is sufficiently 'like' race, gender, disability, religion, or national origin, to merit the legal protection of civil rights laws." In other words, the right invents an additional hurdle for gay and lesbian people to cross in order to qualify for civil rights. For our pursuit of civil rights to be legitimate, we have to be enough like people of color or women or the disabled or others who "merit" legal protection. Since we are a people whose behavior is stigmatized, they say that we are unlike other "choice-less" minorities, and that our claims for civil rights must be rejected. The more we try to argue that we are "just like" African Americans, the more credibility we give to the right's strategy, because black history differs from gay history and from women's history. Suzanne Pharr points out that this strategy threatens the application of civil rights laws to all people, for if we can be deemed "undeserving" of civil rights laws by virtue of our behavior, so can black people who behave in ways deemed "deviant." Pharr predicts:

> When people have come to believe that civil rights are special rights that are bestowed by the majority only upon those who demonstrate "good" behavior, and, when through anti-gay initiatives, civil rights (which they call "special rights" or "privileges") are submitted to the popular vote, a pattern is carefully established to place the civil rights of all people in jeopardy, both in the voting booth and the courtroom. The questions become these: Do people of color deserve civil rights if they are thought of as criminals? Do immigrants deserve civil rights if they are seen as a drain on the economic system? How would the popular vote go? Who ends up in control?

Specifically, the right undermines the gay and lesbian civil rights quest in two conflicting ways: by denying discrimination against gay people and by defending it. First, it asserts that the "*experience* of gay men and lesbians does not reflect the same kinds of disadvantage as that suffered by groups protected by existing civil rights laws. The second argument concedes that gay men and lesbians are objects of discrimination, but *defends* such discrimination as fully appropriate, based on the claim that homosexuality is an objectionable 'chosen behavior.' " An example of the first strategy, Schacter notes, is the right's erroneous use of market surveys claiming that lesbians and gay men are more affluent and politically powerful and therefore do not experience the "same" kind of discrimination as other minorities. The strategy of trying to prove that gay people do not experience discrimination was also effectively used in 1992 by Colorado for Family Values. As CFV director Kevin Tebedo observed, the group's goal was to encourage voters who care about civil rights to vote against their extension to gay men and lesbians, to give them "an intellectual reason for voting yes on Amendment 2. They [gay people] are not oppressed. They make a lot of money. They do just fine. They don't meet any of the criteria. I can vote yes on Amendment 2 and not have to tell anyone the way I really feel."

At the same time, religious conservatives attempt to justify and defend antigay discrimination. Schacter identifies three concepts in the right's efforts to rationalize antigay discrimination: "sameness," "special rights," and "chosen behavior." She defines sameness, or "this new, repressive culture of analogy," as the idea that gay people can qualify for civil rights protection only if the form and experience of the discrimination they face is the same as that of already protected minorities. Such an interpretation drastically misrepresents and constricts the reach of civil rights laws. In reality, as Schacter points out, civil rights laws have long been flexible just so that new judgments are reached by society to determine "what forms of discrimination are deemed unacceptable and about which groups need legal protection against discrimination . . . Characterizing antidiscrimination law as fixed and static . . . enables the [antigay] discourse on equivalents to transform civil rights laws from instruments of social change into instruments for *resisting* social change" [emphasis in original].

The most damaging weapon in the right's arsenal is its use of "special rights" rhetoric. Polling and focus group data gathered by Celinda Lake for the Human Rights Campaign Fund shows that nearly half the voters in key states facing ballot measures in 1994 believed gay men and lesbians were seeking "special rights." Lake also found that only three out of ten people knew that gay men and lesbians are *not* protected by existing civil rights laws: another four out of ten believed they are fully covered, and the remaining three out of ten had no idea.

Suzanne Pharr writes that "it is the racism encoded in the 'special rights' language that makes this argument work so powerfully." An example of the racial coding can be found in the most commonly used argument against gay rights: all people have the same rights granted them under the Constitution and the Bill of Rights. This statement is incompletely true. In fact, the Bill of Rights exists precisely because succeeding generations needed to address gaps and weaknesses in the Constitution (such as the denial of the right to vote to women and the denial of full citizenship to black people). Clearly, civil rights are not constant or forever fixed in the political realities of 1776, and the Constitution's mechanism for amendment indicates that the Founding Fathers had the future in mind.

Historically, the "no special rights" theme was first used against the gay and lesbian community in the Anita Bryant campaign of 1977, the same year that the Supreme Court decided *Baake,* which threw out the admissions policy of a California medical school because it was held to constitute reverse discrimination against white males. As Randy Shilts reported, the Bryant forces argued that "homosexuals were not born that way. They chose to be gay . . . and they could influence young people to choose to be homosexual as well. That was why they wanted gay rights protections, so they could work at playgrounds and public schools and recruit young people to their way of life. They were flagrant lawbreakers and now they wanted 'special privileges' of civil rights guarantees. One antigay pamphlet asked: 'If homosexuals, who break Florida's law against unnatural sex acts every time they perform homosexual sex, can be granted special privileges, then what about other law-breaking sexual libertines—prostitutes, pimps and their ilk?' "

Jane Schacter's article traces the "special rights" language even farther back, to arguments made by opponents of the Civil Rights Act of 1964 and repeated by opponents of the Civil Rights Act of 1991. "Opponents of the [first] law equated civil rights protections with job preferences and aggressively argued that 'it is not civil rights to give one group advantages at the expense of another group' . . . Opponents of the [second] bill argued that it would 'institutionalize color, ethnic and gender preference under the false flag of civil rights.' " Opponents of civil rights laws have successfully convinced large portions of the electorate that such laws are a form of reverse discrimination, that they grant special-interest groups job preferences, quotas, and special treatment, at the expense of the "majority." The power of these views on "reverse discrimination" was evident in the effectiveness of political ads attacking affirmative action devised by Jesse Helms in his 1990 reelection campaign against the progressive black candidate Harvey Gantt. In one advertisement, the viewer sees a close-up of a pair of white hands crumbling a job-rejection notice while the voice-over explains that the worker needed the job, was qualified for it, but lost it because of a "racial quota."

Today, the Christian Right is engaged in defending discrimination by redefining it as discernment. As Mark Olsen, the media director of Colorado for Family Values, explains in the CFV training tapes on how to pass a Colorado-style amendment, "One of our biggest issues is to tackle the D word . . . In the past, people used to refer to discriminating shoppers . . . Does that mean that those shoppers did not frequent African-American stores? No. It meant those people were astute shoppers. They were good at making choices . . . Amendment 2 does not prevent [a homosexual from] holding a job; it prevents [him from] demanding one. Demanding a job is demanding a special right." According to this logic, something that is universally believed to be wrong is now something that is universally believed to be good: to be discriminating is to be astute, judicious, wise, smart, tasteful. CFV executive director Kevin Tebedo states, "When somebody stands up and points at you and says, 'Should an employer be able to hire or not hire somebody just because they are gay?' the answer to that question and the reason we are all fighting for what we are doing, is yes. Is yes! . . . That is not illegal discrimination, that is called making a choice. Yes, an employer should be able to do that."

A final contortion that the right inflicts on the meaning of discrimination is to read into it a specifically behavioral subtext. The right argues that homosexual people are the same as homosexual behavior, and since that behavior is not protected constitutionally, we are not entitled to coverage under civil rights laws. In this argument, the right echoes and popularizes the flawed reasoning of the Supreme Court in *Bowers* v. *Hardwick,* which denied that the constitutional right to privacy applied to private, adult consensual sexual behavior. As Jane Schacter points out, the idea that we seek civil rights protection for our "chosen behavior" involves a complete sexualization of gay people, and also inaccurately limits the application of civil rights laws—which indeed have been applied to behavior. She cites statutes protecting religious practice.

> Because sexual behavior is seen as the defining aspect of gay and lesbian life, homosexuality is all "doing" and no "being." Because civil rights laws protect people only for who they "are" and not for what they "do," homosexuality is not entitled to civil rights protection . . . A Florida anti-gay organizer reduced the idea to the pithy slogan, "Sodomy is not a civil right."

Not surprisingly, this "chosen behavior" argument surfaced in the military-reform fight of 1993. It is, in fact, the core of the Clinton administration's "don't ask, don't tell" policy. For years, a legal distinction was drawn in military cases between "status" and "conduct." Several federal court decisions held that the military could not discharge someone based solely on status; there had to be some conduct that violated the military code of behavior. During the hearings to change the policy, this distinction was erased. Being gay or lesbian was itself enough to warrant exclusion; the presence of openly gay people was deemed disruptive because it equaled the presence of homosexual behavior. The compromise was at its best a misguided attempt to reinstate the status-conduct distinction: if we did not tell, no one would know, and we could still be who we were.

Another aspect of the right's focus on behavior is its emphasis on choice. Because we choose to engage in gay behavior, says the right, we are not entitled to legal protection. Gay activists most frequently respond to this argument with an assertion that homosexuality is innate. We cite scientific studies (of twins, siblings, brains) to argue that homosexuality will eventually prove to have a biological basis. But in doing so, we radically limit the original reach of our political movement. Where once we sought to free the homosexual potential in everyone, by making it safer to be gay, lesbian, or bisexual, we now assert the conservative view that all we want is the freedom to be our biologically determined selves. History shows that the shelter of biology has never protected a people from persecution. The right does not care that we were born gay; they object to us because we are not straight.

OUR RESPONSE, OUR FUTURE

Despite two decades of confrontation, the national gay and lesbian movement did not formalize its response to the Christian Right until 1993. That year, all national gay organizations began to devote a significant portion of their resources to stop the Christian Right. The NGLTF formed the four-person Fight the Right team, anchored by the veteran organizers Sue Hyde, Scot Nakagawa and Robert Bray. In one year, this NGLTF team organized nearly thirty training sessions for more than three thousand activists, and prepared a wealth of written background, polling, and organizing materials. The HRCF funded focus groups in target states, commissioned polls, and hired topnotch campaign strategists, like Anne Lewis, to advise local and state activists. Lambda Legal Defense Fund's Suzanne Goldberg worked brilliantly to file lawsuits challenging both the substantive merits and the procedural technicalities of antigay ballot measures in Colorado, Ohio, and Florida. She worked with activists in nearly a dozen other states to lay the groundwork for additional legal challenges if they became necessary. The Gay and Lesbian Victory Fund hired the campaign organizer Dave Fleischer, who convened several training sessions on campaign management. The Lesbian Avengers created the Civil Rights Organizing Project to support the work of local groups organizing against the right in target states. The Black Lesbian and Gay Leadership Forum launched an initiative to combat the right's inroads into the African-American community. And across the country, hundreds of state and local gay activists came together in organizations like Show Me Equality (Missouri), Arizonians for Fairness, Floridians United Against Discrimination, Don't Sign On Campaign (Idaho), Michigan Campaign for Human Dignity, Campaign for Liberty (Nevada), and Washington Citizens for Fairness–Hands Off Washington.

All these projects are worthwhile and encouraging, but their formation begs two questions: Why did it take us so long to organize against an old enemy? Are we now organized effectively? The answer to the first lies in part with a long-standing misunderstanding of the religious right. For two decades, we regarded it as an extremist movement instead of seeing it for what it truly is, a respectable and very disciplined movement of Christian soldiers. In our disregard of religious conservatives, gay people were not alone. Liberals, moderate conservatives, and people all along the spectrum dismissed the movement until they could no longer ignore its power. The antigay campaigns of the past twenty years provide ample evidence of the true objectives and views of the right. Many religious conservatives agree with Lou Sheldon that gay and lesbian people should undergo "reparative therapy"—to turn us into straights or at least into nonpracticing homosexuals. Others follow R. J. Rushdoony, who demands a strict and literal code of laws based on biblical precepts, including the death penalty for gay people. Still others follow the more modest if equally damaging teachings of the Catholic Church to love the sinner while hating the sinful behavior. Given this spectrum of faith-based hostility toward homosexual and bisexual people, none of us can be complacent about our future as a people.

For more than two decades, we have engaged in dangerous denial of the Christian Right's potential by dismissing it as too extreme. It will never win real power, we said. We comforted ourselves with every wild-eyed statement made by the right's leaders; applauded the media's sensationalized and ahistorical coverage of the right; and breathed sighs of relief when antigay initiatives led by Briggs, LaRouche, Falwell, and Dannemeyer failed. We must, however, take a historical and unsentimental view of the roots, ideology, and intent of the religious right. It is best understood not as religious or moral, but as fundamentally antidemocratic and totalitarian. Researchers have pointed out its authoritarian traditions, but few have identified its current structure and ideology as that of an explicitly totalitarian movement, intent on overthrowing democracy.

The right stands against the most cherished concepts of democratic pluralism. It would rewrite the Bill of Rights to allow for the establishment of a Christian state; it would re-interpret civil rights laws in sharply restrictive terms; it would deny recognition and political equality to persons with whom it disagrees; and it would support the government's enforcement of a narrowly defined "traditional" family structure. In order to defend ourselves against the right, we need a deeper analysis of the totalitarian agenda and vision that its leaders and organizations promote. To read Hannah Arendt's classic study, *The Origins of Totalitarianism,* is to recognize both the success and danger of the religious right.

After studying totalitarian movements in Europe and in the Soviet bloc, Arendt produced a lucid analysis of the structure and dynamics of such movements as communism, national socialism (or Nazism), and fascism. She showed that "totalitarian movements are mass organizations of atomized, isolated individuals. Compared with all other parties and movements, their most conspicuous external characteristic is their demand for total, unrestricted, unconditional, and unalterable loyalty of the individual member. This demand usually precedes the total organization of the country under their actual rule and it follows from the claim of their ideologies that their organization will encompass, in due course, the entire human race."

The right demands this kind of loyalty of all its followers. Granted, the leaders of the right portray such loyalty as faith in God, yet the politics of the right derive from less than divine sources. The tension between this absolute adherence to tenets and the give and take of the democratic process is seen in the tension between the Religious Right and moderate Republicans. In early 1995, Ralph Reed drew widespread criticism from Republicans for declaring that unless there was a prolife plank in the Republican platform, Christian voters would not support the party. Reed's message unmasked the pretense of cooperation under which the coalition and other factions of the religious right had operated inside the party since 1992. Reed's public statements were widely reported in the news media and were quickly rejected by party leaders, but his views were shared by other leaders in the Christian movement. In *Christianity Today,* Gary Norquist predicted that if the Republican Party did not endorse a prolife plank, a third-party candidacy was inevitable. Meanwhile, Gary Bauer, a former Reagan White House official, warned that Christians risked alienating their base if they strayed too far from the moral issues that united them. Interestingly, Reed disavowed his own statements in a conveniently timed op-ed piece in the *Wall Street Journal,* in which he proclaimed that the 1994 elections had proved that Christians and secular moderates could work together in harmony.

The question of ideological adherence to a specific agenda, however, is hardly answered by this calculated exchange of views. Is Reed's earlier statement the real truth, or is his editorial view the true stance of the coalition? Is Bauer saying what Reed would like to say? My point is that a bitter conflict seems to erupt within the Christian Right every time a leader wanders from a fairly narrow ideological line. To a people that are supposedly "politically incorrect," as Reed's book proclaims, purity in politics matters a great deal.

Arendt's analysis of the use of "propaganda" by totalitarian organizations illustrates the role of the right's antigay propaganda. Totalitarian movements make their appeal to the masses through "absolutist, scientific" propaganda; they claim to have divined the laws of nature and history and discovered "the hidden forces that will bring them good fortune in the chain of fatality." Arendt identified "the true goal of totalitarian propaganda [as being] not persuasion but organization." Analyzing the origins of the most effective piece of Nazi propaganda— that a Jewish world conspiracy existed—Arendt showed how the message helped the Nazis to gain power.

In a similar fashion, the Christian Right claims to be guided by divine, natural, and scientific truths about what gay and lesbian people represent. Propaganda videos like *The Gay Agenda* and *Gay Rights/ Special Rights* rest on biblical literalism, misstatements of scientific research or the quack science of people like Paul Cameron. Framing their arguments in the language of reason and logic, the right-wing propagandists portray gay people as unnatural, immoral, freaks who are out to destroy the traditional family and social order. In response, the gay movement has inadequately challenged the factual and pseudoscientific lies promoted in the right's videotapes; the handful of videos and research articles we put together have not been distributed as widely as the right's untruths. Arendt understood that since the goal of right-wing propaganda is not to persuade but to organize, neither truth nor fiction mattered very much.

Arendt's view of the various levels of membership in the totalitarian hierarchy, before it seizes political power, also sheds light on a group like the Christian Coalition. She defines this structure as a "front organization," in which large numbers of sympathetic people engage in the activity of the totalitarian enterprise and serve as a "protective wall" for a small group of leaders.

> The sympathizers, who are to all appearances still innocuous fellow citizens in a nontotalitarian society, can hardly be called single-minded fanatics; through them, the movements make their fantastic lies more generally acceptable, can spread their propaganda in milder, more respectable forms, until the whole atmosphere is poisoned with totalitarian elements which are hardly recognizable as such but appear to be normal political reactions of opinions.

Similarly, today the voices of a Christian minority of well-organized sympathizers are wrongly perceived as the voice of the "silent majority" of the people. While leaders like Pat Robertson and Ralph Reed determine the direction and agenda of the Christian Right, their sympathizers give the illusion that democracy is being served.

Arendt's comprehensive look at the relationship between anti-Semitism, racism, economic imperialism, and the totalitarian state is essential reading for the serious student of gay and lesbian politics today. My point is that if we view the Christian Right as totalitarian, not merely as "religious" or "fundamentalist," we gain a more accurate picture of the objective of the coalition. The burden is on the religious right's leaders to demonstrate how their views are compatible with a democratic political system. It is a burden the right consistently fails to accept.

Our failure to organize until so recently was caused by elements more difficult to face. Chief among them is the handicap of the closet. Until more gay people are willing to be out in their church, workplace, community—indeed, everywhere—our ability to respond to the lies of the right will remain weak. Lies thrive on secrets and silence. Truth requires courageous action. Additionally, we have been slow to respond because we are stretched thin by AIDS. Since the eighties, dealing with

AIDS has been our top priority, and to many of us it remains so. Now we are in a position to do both: to lead more forcefully on AIDS because it devastates our communities, and to organize more emphatically against the right. Finally, our response has been slowed by the lack of funds. Foundations, individual donors, and gay and lesbian organizations themselves have yet to be committed to this effort. A handful of right-wing foundations gives millions to support the small network of religious conservative think tanks, leadership schools, publications, and policy journals. Progressive foundations have not demonstrated the same commitment to promoting liberal, much less progressive institutions. While the leading progressive research center, Political Research Associates, scrapes along on a budget of under $300,000, the right's organizations, like the Free Congress Research Foundation and the Family Research Council, boast multimillion dollar budgets. The journalist John Weir concluded that "[m]ore than just an abomination, homosexuality is damn good business." The financial incentive of producing antigay materials is staggering. Weir reports, for example, that the Springs of Life ministry, a previously obscure and struggling California organization, released the video *Gay Agenda* in 1992. Produced for an estimated $75,000, the tape grossed $1.5 million in one year.

This infusion of cash means that right-wing organizations dwarf their gay rights counterparts. The American Family Association has a $6 million budget. The Traditional Values Coalition claims it represents more than 25,000 churches. The Free Congress Research Foundation spends more than $5 million each year. The Concerned Women for America, at $10 million dollars, is larger than NGLTF and Lambda combined. With more ease than any other political movement in this country, the Christian Right can mobilize large numbers of individuals and funds for its campaigns.

The answer to whether we are now organized effectively pains me, because I know how hard some activists have worked to organize campaigns and the overall movement against the right. But when our efforts are evaluated against the sophistication and skill of our enemies, the gay movement must admit to a continuing failure. Our Fight the Right efforts are as weak as theirs are strong, as scattershot as theirs are coordinated, as insignificant as theirs are effective. We must evaluate and change the ways we have done this work.

As a number of researchers on the right have noted, the current right-wing attack on gay and lesbian equality was prefigured in its campaigns against civil rights for racial minorities and women. Suzanne

Pharr traces the ideological roots of the Christian Right to the segrega-
tionist politics of the 1950s and 1960s. "The Christian Right organized
in response to the Civil Rights Movement. They viewed the Civil
Rights Movement and eventually the legacy of this movement—the
Women's Movement, the Lesbian and Gay Movement—as the cause of
the breakdown of authority, stability, and law and order." In Pharr's
analysis, the antigay, antiblack, antiwoman agendas of the religious and
the secular right are integrally linked. Indeed, the homophobic campaigns have everything to do with dismantling the progress won by
those earlier, and far more successful, movements for social change.
Thus, our response to the right must rest on a strong defense of traditional civil rights strategies—like affirmative action, voting rights laws,
and progressive redistricting which creates minority districts. By staying
silent, we damage ourselves and weaken our alliances.

   With overreliance on the political access of a handful of leaders, the
lack of strong movement infrastructure and organization, and the public's perception that it is extremist or militant, our movement is in a
situation similar to that faced by the Christian Right during the first
Reagan term. And we must do what the religious right did then if we
are to advance. The right shifted its strategy from seeking short-term
political objectives to bringing about a long-term cultural transformation. It placed high priority on infrastructure and leadership development, policy analysis and youth training, strategic planning and development of media, and a change in focus from national to local
organizing.

   Like the gay and lesbian movement of the 1990s, the early waves of
the religious right floundered because they were effectively co-opted by
the Reagan and Bush administrations. The right, even though it helped
elect both Presidents and won unprecedented political access, was seen
by the political operatives in the White House as bringing baggage in
much the same way that the gay movement is seen today. Reagan and
Bush gave symbolic endorsements to Christian Right groups: they sent
supportive letters and telegrams to conferences, held meetings with
leaders, and offered rhetorical endorsements of certain agenda items.
Key Christian Right activists held positions in the Reagan White
House, but were unable to wield much control over policy battles: Gary
Bauer, head of the Reagan Domestic Policy Council, lost to Surgeon
General Koop in his effort to prevent federal involvement in AIDS
education. The Bush campaign in 1988 made overtures to gay and
lesbian Republicans (Atwater met with gay Republicans), just as it

made overtures to the religious right. But when it came to action or laying out some political capital, Reagan and Bush backed off. School prayer amendments, tuition tax credits, and even abortion votes lost momentum in Congress.

A chilling parallel to this exists in the relationship between the gay and lesbian movement and the Clinton administration. Symbolic and rhetorical support, telegrams to conferences, and statements at marches and rallies have been accompanied by abdication on policy matters whenever antigay opposition appears. Some high-level appointments of openly gay and lesbian people, like Roberta Achtenberg (assistant secretary for HUD) or Nan Hunter (director of the civil rights office at the Department of Health and Human Services) coexist with the administration's failure to lift the military ban. The White House has been unable to derail or unwilling to lobby against antigay congressional amendments. The President and Vice President have invited select (usually moneyed) gay and lesbian people to social functions and meetings, but they have not used their offices as a platform from which to condemn homophobia and prejudice based on sexual orientation.

When religious right leaders of the nineties place some of the blame on those who represented them in the eighties, their language echoes the criticism some gay radicals make of our Washington-based gay and lesbian leaders. In 1990, Paul Weyrich said that the right had been handicapped by leaders who were "ill-equipped, too 'nice' to engage effectively in hardball negotiations and politicking." He criticized what he termed a "ghetto mentality" that was easily appeased by their "being able to get in even the back door of the White House. They didn't want to do anything to jeopardize that [access]." To protect its individual or institutional standing with a supposedly gay-friendly White House, the Washington-based gay leadership takes too cozy a view of the Clinton administration. As a result, the gay and lesbian agenda at the national level is stalled. Our leaders' apparent appeasement, with White House invitations and photo-ops, contributes to the widening political cynicism among gay and lesbian people.

Gay and lesbian political leaders are obsessed with the Washington infrastructure. But the world inside the Beltway is not the world in which most of our people live. To the gay man fired from a local school or Cracker Barrel restaurant, it matters little how many parties wealthy gay people attend at the White House or the vice presidential mansion. Even what Newt Gingrich does and says on gay and lesbian rights matters far less than what our neighbors in the streets do or think about gay and lesbian equality. By focusing on Washington to the exclusion of Main Street, gay leaders are holding the gay and lesbian future hostage to relatively short-sighted, often personal, agendas.

Another reason that New Right activism floundered in the late seventies and early eighties was that it lacked a strong, coordinated structure. The movement was internally divided over organizational turf, theological differences, and the need for central coordination. Throughout the eighties, the right consciously addressed these weaknesses in several ways. The Council for National Policy was established in 1981 to coordinate Christian Right projects. It seems to function as an informal policy-setting board, comprising the heads of right-wing organizations, who meet, plan, and coordinate national campaigns. To bridge theological splits, the Coalition on Revival was launched in 1982 by Jay Grimstead. The ADL describes it as a "think tank and evangelical networking agency" whose goal is to "bridge theological differences in order to foster a conservative Christian regeneration of American culture—notably by means of political action." The researcher Fred Clarkson terms its mission an attempt to create a "trans-denominational theology," and has detailed the connection of prominent Christian Right leaders to this effort. More recently, Christian leaders reached out to Catholic conservatives, establishing an alliance that contributed to the defeat of the pro-gay Rainbow Curriculum in New York City.

Without a doubt, the best instrument for the Christian Right's national organizing efforts proved to be Pat Robertson's 1988 campaign. Presidential elections provided a similar boost to the even more conservative fringe represented by Pat Buchanan. If Robertson succeeded in creating a national political network by running for President, why couldn't a gay or lesbian candidate mount an independent run for the Democratic nomination—someone like the lesbian Democrat Virginia Apuzzo, for example? At a minimum, such a run would stimulate the development of a new national political network of activists, a network that would strengthen the gay rights movement in the long term. The sad fact that there is no place even to raise and discuss such a notion suggests that we need to establish some sort of National Gay and Lesbian Coordinating Council—our own Council for National Policy. Such a body, made up of representatives from national and state groups, would have the mission and the ability to set priorities and an overall course for our rights movement. Since even minimal coordination is difficult, given the decentralized nature of gay and lesbian politics, the

Coordinating Council would vastly help our movement's strategic planning. But there are huge obstacles to the implementation of this suggestion, obstacles such as the lack of trust among existing gay organizations and between our leaders and the constituents they represent. I believe that the gay rights movement must make serious and concrete efforts to bridge its ideological divisions. We need our own Coalition on Revival, but I'd call it the Coalition for Survival. Perhaps we could secure a commitment from different factions (from Log Cabin Republicans to Lesbian Avengers, from people of color organizations to the gay parents groups) in the movement to open up genuine dialogue with one another. At a minimum, we might spark constructive conversation about our political differences. At best, we could strengthen our overall political movement by working in concert.

To this end, we must start by ending the long-standing and unnecessary antagonism between so-called campaign professionals and the grassroots activists. For example, in March 1994, when I attended a retreat organized by the Human Rights Campaign Fund, I learned of an impressive array of current polling and research data about voter opinion. The consultants and activists with campaign experience repeatedly stressed that the object in elections is not to change the world, not to organize, but simply to win a simple majority vote. The media packages that the gay movement creates, they argued, have to be developed with this political "fact of life" in mind. Later at the same retreat, representative Barney Frank and his sister Anne Lewis, the astute political consultant, advised us that the gay and lesbian movement was at an impasse on Capitol Hill because we lacked the ability to generate and coordinate constituent support for our federal agenda. To my mind, these two messages represent mirror images of the same problem: we have still not recognized grassroots organizing as the critical missing component in the power of the gay and lesbian movement. Organizing means the kind of work the Christian Right has done to energize thousands of concerned and motivated people. We have those thousands of potential political workers, but they do not know how to get involved or where to direct their energies. If our anti-right campaigns consist only of fundraising, mail operations, and media campaigns aimed at defending ourselves from attack, what have we done to challenge the power of the right? Not much.

A consequence of *not* doing the organizing work, of not seeing the campaign against the right as a long-term battle but merely an electoral skirmish, can be seen in the Oregon experience. After the No on 9

Campaign mounted a huge effort, the statewide antigay measure was defeated by voters in 1992, but months after the vote the antigay Oregon Citizens' Alliance was back. It launched a county-by-county offensive to enact another version of the defeated Measure 9. By the end of 1994, the OCA had passed it in fifteen Oregon counties, was planning to put another measure to statewide vote in 1995, and even had plans to carry out its antigay initiatives into 1996. The No on 9 structure did not see itself as a vehicle to build gay political power in the state. Indeed, during the campaign, there was considerable tension between grassroots gay and lesbian activists and the No on 9 Campaign leadership. This led to a dissipation of effort in several unofficial (noncampaign sponsored) organizing initiatives, ranging from the 150-mile Walk for Love and Justice, which gained lots of media attention, to the Rural Organizing Project, which tried to organize in twenty counties, to the People of Faith Against Bigotry Coalition of religious leaders. If all these efforts had been coordinated and integrated by the No on 9 Campaign, if we had seen that campaign as a way to create a lasting, progressive statewide network, we could have turned that favorable vote into the building block it should have been, instead of the anomaly it now seems.

Instead of establishing think tanks or long-range projects whose mission is to study the right and devise strategies to counter its influence, we focus on the short-term strategies of litigation, the defensive electoral campaign, and so-called positive images media campaigns. Litigation by the Lambda Legal Defense and Education Fund has been the most effective strategy our movement has employed against the right. Successful cases have challenged antigay ballot initiatives before and after a vote. But as two leading litigators in this field concluded, "The fact that every court to consider these antigay initiatives has found them unconstitutional has not stemmed their spread around the country."

The defensive campaign and the positive images campaign are seen as separate efforts serving two different purposes. They should be seen as an integrated plan; a strong defense does not score without a strong offense. Unless we put forth positive messages to offset the distortions of the right, we will not win elections. The tendency to see these as two unrelated strategies results in a fragmentation of effort.

The defensive campaign itself has been the source of needless splintering among us. Since the Briggs Initiative, in 1978, gay organizations fighting the right have split between those favoring grassroots organizing, including door-to-door outreach, and those favoring media advertising. Each side believes its strategy carried the day in Oregon, and our loss in Colorado has been blamed by analysts on the lack of a strong grassroots educational effort. Could it be that both sides are right to claim credit, that traditional organizing techniques, education, and media messages do, together, produce victory? The focus of our work in opposition to the right's supremacist politics must of necessity be both short- and long-term. For two decades, we have fought the right issue by issue, campaign initiative by campaign initiative. Given the emergencies the right constantly imposes on us, we will need to maintain (indeed, improve) that short-term response. Yet ultimately to reverse the right's corruption of American democracy and pluralism, our political movement must evolve and embrace long-term strategies for achieving justice. Our campaigns must recognize that most opponents of the right mince their words and sugar-coat their appraisal, out of fear of reaction. The history and actual practice of the American right wing, religious and secular, reveals that it is a deeply totalitarian movement— out for control and for political, spiritual, and cultural supremacy.

CHAPTER ELEVEN

LEADERSHIP CONUNDRUMS

I ask you, where are my heroes?
Where are my saints?

—*Luis Alfaro*

Paradoxically, at this moment of great lesbian and gay visibility, we recognize and empower fewer and fewer people as our political leaders. Indeed, despite the high level of activism evident across the country and the vast talent within our organizations, the conventional wisdom among gay and lesbian people is that our movement confronts a leadership crisis. Our disregard for the political leaders we have and our cynicism about leadership in general are evidence of this crisis. We validate gay and lesbian cultural figures but disparage political activists. Cultural icons are our heroes, but gay leaders who work in gay institutions (be they AIDS service groups, youth projects, community centers, or legal and political groups) are often vilified. The few political leaders who do get community notice are the handful whom the gay and straight media promote, for a variety of bizarre or predictable reasons: some because they are flamboyant and make good copy, others simply because they hold office.

As if to confirm this conventional wisdom, our national movement in the past two years has undergone a dramatic transition in leadership. Searches for executive directors have been conducted by many of our leading lesbian, gay, and AIDS organizations: the Human Rights Campaign Fund, the ACLU Lesbian and Gay Rights Project, the Latino Lesbian and Gay Organization, the National Gay and Lesbian Task Force, the AIDS Action Council, Gay Men's Health Crisis, AIDS Project Los Angeles, and the Gay and Lesbian Alliance Against Defamation, to name just a few. Outgoing executive directors uniformly cite exhaustion, frustration with the expectations of the community and the lack of resources for the work, and a desire for more balance and peace in their lives. While incoming directors are greeted with indifference or skepticism, staff members leave in droves for many of the same reasons, but add disillusionment with the political judgement of leaders.

The leadership turnover in AIDS organizations is especially troubling at this critical juncture. In September 1994, Dan Bross, the executive director of the AIDS Action Council, the leading national lobby for AIDS service organizations, announced his resignation, citing "exhaustion" as a primary reason. In March 1995, the well-liked new director of Gay Men's Health Crisis, Jeff Richardson, abruptly quit; the rumor was that he was fed up with fighting with a micromanaging board. Leadership in the AIDS activist movement has also suffered in the past two years, during which a friendlier administration no longer provided a unifying target for our activism. People who worked well together in the late eighties to pass large national AIDS bills, like the Ryan White AIDS Care Act, ultimately fought bitterly to control the distribution of money. Tom Sheridan, a former lobbyist at the AIDS Action Council, started his own for-profit lobbying firm, and actively recruited large AIDS service organizations as clients, further undermining the united front that the service groups had presented since the start of the epidemic. Infighting grew among AIDS activists over the priority of research and treatment above AIDS prevention, on the need for minority and women's funding and the still unmet needs of gay men, and on the very formula by which federal funds were to be made available to local communities under the Ryan White bill. ACT UP chapters struggled to stay afloat. Many, like the Orange County ACT UP chapter, devolved into a group of one, which prompted arch-homophobe Lou Sheldon to quip to the *LA Times*, "I've watched that leadership in the last fourteen years come and go. Lou Sheldon is still here with traditional values."

Theories to explain the gay and lesbian leadership crisis abound.

Some say that because we are such a young movement, too few gay people have earned the credibility, built a constituency, or developed the moral authority to be regarded as genuine leaders. Others attribute the crisis to our internalized self-hatred. Others say our unwillingness to follow the leaders who do arise stems from the gap between the community's racial and gender diversity and our leaders' general lack of it. Yet others describe the crisis as a problem of ideology: leaders are too left wing for some, too right wing for others, and thus unacceptable to the mythic gay masses.

Lesbian feminist leaders and critics have long argued that our movement's leadership is too male-dominated and too invested in tradi-tional hierarchical styles of leadership. Lesbian feminism, in fact, is known for its invention of more inclusive and participatory styles of decision-making, which sometimes worked and more often frustrated the process. In lesbian groups, consensus is favored over majority vote, with the input of all people valued equally and great time spent ensuring adequate representation; leadership itself has, for many years, been seen as a dirty, patriarchal word. This strand of movement politics reached an absurd pinnacle in 1991. After three years of a grassroots and pains-takingly inclusive planning process, the National Lesbian Conference, held in Atlanta in April 1991, unraveled at the eleventh hour as the organizing committee split into factions. I still do not know what the real issues were but the consequence of the disagreement was a disaster for the conference. Three thousand lesbians arrived in Atlanta to find no conference program (the organizers had disagreed on how to print it), a chaotic schedule and agenda, and a conference coordinator who had simply left town. The NLC resembled a four-day camp-out of lesbians rather than the focused political conference it was intended to be. To this day, no lesbian leaders have taken responsibility for the waste that conference represented.

Conservative critics believe existing gay and lesbian leadership to be too leftist, out of touch with, and ineffectual on behalf of, "most" gay people. Implicitly, and sometimes explicitly, they argue that the new wave of conservative leadership represents the best hope for "most" gay and lesbian people because it is solely focused on matters queer, and therefore less bogged down by considerations of gender or racial inclu-sion. This neoconservative critique rests on the flawed assumption that the unmeasurable and unpolled majority of gay and lesbian people share conservative values. The voyeuristic relationship many gay neocons have had with the gay movement partly discredits this assessment. Until the

1990s, gay conservatives watched gay and lesbian politics from the sidelines. Their criticism that the gay movement is anticonservative is rapidly becoming a poor cover for the problems they themselves face as they try to organize an enormously diverse community. Their problems are quite similar to those once faced by liberal and radical leaders.

Direct-action activists in ACT UP, Queer Nation, and Lesbian Avengers have criticized the "mainstream" gay rights leadership as bureaucratic, assimilated, or compromised. Increasingly, in the 1990s, this direct-action wing has imploded in part over its refusal to recognize hierarchical leadership. ACT UP chapters in major cities like New York, San Francisco, and Boston have splintered. Some have formed AIDS-treatment–focused groups, while others engage in broader multi-issue activism. Supporters of the former strategy accuse the latter of betraying the "true" spirit of AIDS activism; the latter accuse the former of betraying the "true" spirit of gay and lesbian liberation. ACT UP and QN did represent a potentially revolutionary concept of leadership. Each functioned as a loosely knit body of the whole; the group existed wherever there was a meeting. The leaders were those members who attended. Such a structure was vital and empowering; ACT UP made political participation feel important because it put decision-making power in the hands of the people who were present. Yet ACT UP also functioned in ways that undermined gay political leadership—internally and in the broader movement.

ACT UP members devalued and disrespected existing gay leadership when they argued that theirs was the *only* effective strategy in AIDS activism. The claim grew out of the defensive reaction of the direct-action movement to attacks by conservative and more traditionally oriented political activists. Traditional activists felt far from friendly to ACT UP. In Washington I was treated with great suspicion and anger for supporting direct-action strategies. The traditional activists believed their strategy was paramount; ACT UP believed its strategy was the most effective! But both claims of superiority actually discredited the leadership of both sides. So, when ACT UP dissed the valuable work of AIDS activist lawyers, political leaders, doctors, and service providers in a variety of AIDS political fights, it adversely affected our movement's strength. By the same token, when conservatives derided ACT UP as merely the "politics of anger," they misrepresented the power that direct action allowed our movement to exert in the late eighties. Neither side deserved sole credit for advancing AIDS policy matters. The loud voice of ACT UP helped, as did the timbre of quieter leaders, like lawyer Jay Lipner and lobbyists Derek Hodel, Mike Isbell, and Dr. Mathilde Krim.

Direct-action activists also undermined our faith in leadership with what has become known as "horizontal hostility" toward mainstream gay and lesbian leaders. Even today, those involved in direct action often speak disparagingly of mainstream leaders, and actively discredit others with whom they disagree. Political arguments with ACT UP or QN on strategy frequently became personal attacks. In 1991, when members of Queer Nation disagreed with San Francisco supervisor Roberta Achtenberg on a gay rights issue, some individuals wheatpasted signs in Achtenberg's neighborhood and in front of her house, attacking, some say threatening, her personally. When Mayor Dinkins appointed an African-American man, Woodrow Myers, to head the city's Health Department, ACT UP members protested, citing as unacceptable some of the positions Myers had taken as health commissioner in Indiana. The appointment divided the gay community racially, as black gay leaders like Ron Johnson of the Minority Task Force on AIDS were told by straight black leaders to choose their blackness or gayness. Interestingly, ACT UP attacked gay leaders who defended the Myers appointment as traitors and Uncle Toms.

Like the attacks aimed at Bill and Hillary Clinton by the far right, personal attacks inside the gay movement function to discredit the authority of our leaders. The veracity of attacks on President Clinton seems to matter less than the relentless manner in which he has been criticized by Rush Limbaugh, Jerry Falwell, and others. Similarly, the attacks made by direct-action activists on the more mainstream gay leadership, calling it ineffective, corrupt, or spineless, have rarely been assessed for their truth or falsehood: the fact that the charges were raised at all was what stuck. Such ridicule undermines the confidence gay people feel in our leaders and institutions.

The gay mainstream, for its part, remains divided in its views on lesbian and gay leadership. The people I term "gay elitists" insist that what the community needs most is powerful people wielding power. ANGLE and HRCF embody this philosophy. The boards of gay and lesbian nonprofits are filled with people who hold this elite-centered view of political leadership. They tend to stress access to power, money, and media visibility over qualities like moral principle, accountability, and personal integrity. Elitists often fault the community for the lack of stronger leaders, pointing to the closet and internal conflict. It is ironic that the most elitist members of the gay mainstream are those who most loudly decry "horizontal hostility," since these same individuals quickly devalue the leadership of people who disagree with them politically or come from different class or educational backgrounds. They harbor disdain for the activists we do have, claiming that the closet hurts us because the "best" people are in it. In contrast, I maintain the best people in the movement are those who are out.

Another strand of the gay and lesbian mainstream are individuals engaged in electoral politics. These populists see gay and lesbian leadership in traditional, political terms: as a matter of constituency-building, accountability, and political power organized in traditional ways. In their view, the failure of political leadership is a result of our inability to organize into an effective political constituency. If we were better organized, they argue, leaders would be at once more clearly empowered and more accountable to a constituency.

A third segment comprises the staff members and directors of gay and lesbian organizations. They are the most criticized and least recognized for their abilities. A common expression used to deride these heads is "so-called leaders" or "self-appointed leaders." Labeling them self-appointed is like calling managing directors of corporations self-appointed; it is aimless and demeaning. As senior employees of nonprofits, lesbian and gay organization heads are at once the most capable of broad political leadership and the most constrained from exercising it. They are capable by virtue of their position: they have a constituency in their members, a platform in their role, access to the media, and the most accurate information about gay and lesbian rights. But they are often constrained from exercising their leadership by one dominating fact: fear. The heads of gay organizations rarely take strong, public leadership roles, because they are afraid of alienating potential supporters, core constituents, government funders, or even staff members. Instead, they often function as business managers, leading quietly and internally, avoiding public conflict, and not saying or doing controversial things. Managing an organization well can indeed be a form of effective leadership, but it is not the same as the visionary and public leadership any social change movement needs. We place impossible pressure on the heads of gay organizations when we expect them both to manage well and to lead forcefully in the political arena; running an organization differs from providing vision, courageous insight, and guidance to a broader community. Rarely can one person do both equally well. Yet even more rarely are the jobs divided into two parts.

Definition

To understand the queer leadership crisis requires tackling difficult questions: what constitutes it, what makes gay people so suspicious of it, how do we undermine it, and what we can do to foster more of it. Our definition of political leadership is central to any discussion, and as I interviewed gay and lesbian activists in 1993 and 1994, I found that most assessed gay and lesbian political leadership as being absent, misguided, hapless, or irrelevant. Yet nearly everyone I spoke with expressed a longing for effective political leadership, and all expressed common rationales for why our movement's leadership seemed so weak. Some expressed their desire for leadership as a desire for courage, others as a desire for vision, and still others as a desire for unity, common purpose, and empowerment. All acknowledged that their view of leadership was tinged by their own experience as activists; each had been personally attacked for exercising leadership and felt shaken by the experience.

Richard Burns, the executive director of the New York City Lesbian and Gay Community Services Center, expressed his desire for a motivational leader, as Ginny Apuzzo had been in the early eighties, someone who could reach a wide spectrum of people. "What I personally long for is a speaker who will inspire me and the gay men and lesbians around me to share a vision, a common vision, and to feel empowered and hopeful and clear on how to work together toward the achievement of that vision. We're looking for that speaker, that writer who touches and resonates with all of us, who enfranchises us in having a sense of movement and being in a movement."

Long-time AIDS activist Larry Kramer, who has been a vehement and exacting critic of gay and lesbian leadership, expressed his frustration in a 1992 *Advocate* article: "[O]ur own forces—our openly gay elected officials, our advocacy groups in Washington, our political organizations around the country, ACT UP and other AIDS advocacy and activist organizations—are demoralized, exhausted, burned-out, bureaucratized beyond effectiveness, second-rate, inadequate, useless, hateful, and/or dead. I do not see one gay or lesbian leader *anywhere* . . . that I feel is capable of leading us anywhere but farther down the toilet." When we spoke in 1994, I mentioned several people who ran gay organizations whom I identified as leaders. Kramer responded, "I don't look upon those people as leaders. I look upon them as employees of an organization." Kramer's critical anger at leadership is, like so much of what he raises in our movement, based on reality and over- stated. Not every gay or lesbian leader can be characterized as inade- quate or useless. Perhaps Kramer thinks so because they are not doing what he believes they should. Or perhaps he believes that better leaders exist in other movements. The problem is that such disregard for gay leadership precludes hard-working gay activists from being recognized and respected as our leaders. Indeed, this kind of disrespect surfaced when the planning committee of the March on Washington refused to invite Kramer as a speaker. I objected to the decision and asked them to reconsider, because he represented a unique voice in the AIDS move- ment, but I was told that people believed Kramer didn't stand for the march's platform—in other words, they disagreed with his politics. In the end, Kramer did speak at the march, but only because Torie Osborn —supported by Robin Tyler and Kate Clinton—brought him up to the stage.

A central problem with gay and lesbian leadership is definitional: What do we think constitutes a political leader? In every interview on gay leadership I have read or done, a question posed is why we have produced no leader of the stature of Dr. Martin Luther King, Jr. In asking this, are we really saying that unless we find the exceptional qualities that distinguished Dr. King, we will not recognize any gay or lesbian person as a leader? The vision, compassion, integrity, and moral principle that one finds in admirable leaders like Dr. King, Malcolm X, Gloria Steinem, and Ella Baker are not easily duplicated. Further, find- ing such exceptional leaders in our movement may be less important than defining the qualities of leadership we admire and want to foster.

To some extent our problem with defining leadership comes from our confusion about the difference between media celebrities, role mod- els, heroes, and political leaders. Media visibility today accords people the kind of automatic respect and credibility that used to take people years to earn. One can instantly collect a constituency for nearly any political viewpoint—simply by broadcasting it. Does visibility make a leader? I think not. We ought to look deeper than media stature to the authenticity of the people claiming to represent us as leaders. Do they have a constituency? To whom are they accountable? Who funds their work? Perhaps I am old-fashioned in my desire for political leadership that is tied to a particular constituency; perhaps I favor institutional leadership over individual leadership because I find the former to be more principled and more clearly accountable. The bottom line is that political leadership of a diverse people must in some way go deeper, be better coordinated, and rely on principles that are bigger than merely promoting the names and careers of individuals.

For example, while the personal courage and integrity of military veterans like Greta Cammermeyer and Perry Watkins inspire us, actual leadership on the issue of ending military discrimination comes from very different people; namely, the far less known Michelle Benecke and Dixon Osborn of the Servicemembers Legal Defense Network and the lawyers at Lambda Legal Defense and Education Fund. Despite their essential work, these individuals are not widely acknowledged as leaders because they appear less frequently in the media. Similarly, while every gay, lesbian, bisexual, or transgendered person can proudly recite the names of music and film celebrities who are gay or lesbian, few can list the people who lead the political fight, behind the spotlight, to advance and promote gay and lesbian equality in these industries.

A variation of the media-created leader is the famous role model as movement leader. When people come out, they are often expected to speak on behalf of a movement with which they may have little contact. I think we must question this practice, which our own press perpetuates as much as the straight media. In my view, not every gay person who comes out has the capacity, skill, or willingness to be a leader in the political movement. Some, like the gay conservative Marvin Liebman, have done an excellent job in developing a leadership role. Others, like the lesbian gadfly Camille Paglia, have exploited their visibility to promote themselves, making pronouncements on a movement they know nothing about. Still others, like Martina Navratilova, have the integrity to acknowledge their position as role models, speak their mind on gay rights, and present themselves as the vital cultural leaders they are rather than as political spokespersons.

To a large extent, the perception that our movement has a leadership problem comes from the definitions and ideals of leadership to which we subscribe. In *Certain Trumpets: The Call of Leaders,* Garry Wills compared the styles of dozens of cultural, literary, political, and artistic figures to determine what makes an effective leader. He suggests that Americans define political leadership as a choice between two "unacceptable alternatives—the leader who dictates to others, and the one who truckles to them. To Wills, these models ignore two critical ingredients needed in an effective political leader: shared goals and willing followers. He adds, "[The goal] is the reason for the existence of the other two [the leader and the follower]. It is also the equalizer between leaders and followers. The followers do not submit to the person of the leader. They join him or her in pursuit of the goal." Wills goes on to define a leader, in pragmatic terms, as "one who mobilizes others toward a goal shared by leaders and followers."

When I asked a number of people their views on leadership in our movement, they were divided. Very few identified leadership as simply as Wills had done. Some, for example, like the talented writer and lesbian feminist activist Susie Bright, expressed a desire for great and visionary leadership. Noting that she had gone to the 1993 March on Washington wanting to hear the "I Have a Dream" speech, Bright expressed her disappointment at the recycled rhetoric. "[W]e saw a couple of the pop celebrities who have nothing to say. I wanted leadership. I'm waiting for a kind of articulation and spokesmanship and leadership on national as well as local levels that can put out a voice that both addresses some kind of lowest common denominator issues, but also offers some strategies and some analysis and some vision that is cutting edge, that breaks through, that makes the other side shut up for a second, that makes us feel like—yeah, that's right! Somebody that can get across a justice message."

A comparable, but very different, desire for inclusive, representative leadership was expressed by activists like Ruth Finkelstein, former director of public policy at Gay Men's Health Crisis, who was as bleak and blunt about gay leadership as Larry Kramer. "I don't have any leaders. I don't see anyone articulating a vision that I could subscribe to. Nor do I see a process of articulating a vision that I can participate in and then subscribe to. It's not that someone's articulating a vision and I'm left out. As far as individuals, there's nobody I would follow around the corner, let alone [allow] to design a movement. As for gay organizations, I'm not a member of any of them."

To Maxine Wolfe, who co-founded Lesbian Avengers, helped do grassroots fundraising to buy a building for the Lesbian Herstory Archives, and organized for many years with ACT UP–New York, the question of leadership was fraught with egotism, elitism and gender, race and class bias. Wolfe wanted accessible, democratic models of leadership that empower people by giving them a role in decision-making, but she rejected the idea of representative leadership. "I'm perfectly willing to speak from my experience and about my experience and about my point of view. But I will never, ever say that I speak for a community. I think that that's nonsensical. I think that is a false kind of leadership."

While some activists argued that gay leaders were not democratic enough in their actions, others said we were too democratic in our desires. The black gay activist Charles Stewart, who works as legislative counsel to California state senator Diane Watkins, and who served in the early 1980s as the first co-chair of the national Black and White Men Together, found the leadership of the 1993 march completely out of touch with the mainstream of the gay community. To Stewart, the march's agenda "was too diffuse and not part of a focused strategy to accomplish specific measurable ends. That would have been okay if our leadership didn't seem to be deceiving themselves about it. With people you are leading, there's a mutual responsibility for candor . . . and I don't think candor existed. I felt that the march was amorphous in its objectives, just as our movement is at this point."

To my question of why he thought so few people were involved in the movement, Stewart posed another question. For whom does the movement exist? The purpose of a movement, Stewart replied, is "to identify and forward the legitimate objectives of its constituency." Stewart said that gay and lesbian leaders fail because they see the movement as more important than the people they represent. Perhaps few people are involved with the movement because most are actually happy with their lives just the way they are: "If the constituency tells you 'I'm happy,' and you're not happy with their saying that, you need to do some serious re-examining of your needs, not the movement's needs."

Assessing the leadership conundrum from an entirely different perspective, the New York State powerbroker Jeff Soref offered me some tough criticisms of gay and lesbian leadership. In his view, we are unwilling to follow the people who are qualified to lead our communities. Soref felt that the March on Washington's failure to feature nationally recognized leaders as speakers sent "a message the we don't have identifiable leaders, or the people we think are leaders are not our leaders. Ultimately, it's destructive. It's tearing down our own leadership in front of the whole country. We're saying, 'No. Larry Kramer, for whatever reason, doesn't represent us. And Tim Sweeney doesn't represent us. And Tom Stoddard doesn't represent us.' The fact is, whether we like it or not, these are the people who are seasoned, who have

negotiated, who have a record of success. We're still in the first generation. And, gradually, over time you develop leadership. Well, we're sort
of in a simultaneous process of not developing future leadership fast
enough and tearing down existing leaders."

Each of these comments reflects a different view of ideal leadership.
Some of us long for the Periclean perception of the "great man" (or
woman), the superior leader who stands out, above the crowd, whom we
can all admire. This longing underlies our respect for good orators and
visionary speakers and writers. Curiously, such leadership flourishes in
our movement today, among political writers and artists in all fields, but
the movement has backed away from featuring the work of these political artists. For example, at the First March on Washington, in 1979, the
political poets Audre Lorde and Pat Parker provided two of the most
lyrical and powerful messages on the stage. The Second National
March, in 1987, featured national political leaders like Cesar Chavez,
Ginny Apuzzo, and Jesse Jackson to deliver that same message, and the
most recent march attempted to present racial and gender diversity on
one hand and largely apolitical "entertainment" (with a few exceptions)
on the other. Somewhere along the way, we lost the benefit of the vision
of the political writers who encouraged us in the last two marches.

Other activists long principally for the democratic or representative
leader, one who listens to what we want, responds to our concerns, and
is accountable to us for his or her actions. This desire for representative
leadership is very deep and genuinely felt. The most frequent complaint
leveled at gay groups is that they are not representative. In response to
years of being disregarded and rendered invisible, gay people are extremely sensitive to being listened to. Our desire for a leadership that
listens to our will explains the anger that erupts when gay and lesbian
leaders do things or take positions with which rank-and-file activists do
not agree.

The strange reality of gay and lesbian leadership is that, while we
have lots of individual leaders aspiring to be heroic and lots of organizational leaders operating in the representative mold, we have few who
"mobilize others toward a goal shared by leaders and followers." If we
were to ask the average lesbian and gay people on a city street to name
gay people whom they regard as their political leaders, I predict more
would mention openly gay entertainment or sports figures or gay media
celebrities than political activists. Names and accomplishments of artists, cultural figures, and media celebrities are far more likely to be

known in our communities than the names of gay or lesbian politicians, political thinkers, litigators, strategists, or even the heads of our community organizations.

A problem often encountered by leaders who try to mobilize the community toward a shared goal is the lack of an agenda agreed on by the gay and lesbian constituency. Actually, those active in the movement are clearer about such an agenda than the mass of gay people who are not involved. Gay activists tend to see that several major issues, such as nondiscrimination laws, antiviolence efforts, family recognition, repeal of criminal laws, and the goal of visibility, unify the movement, but those who are not active see them as disparate items unlinked by the common thread of homophobia. Or they see homophobia as a problem residing in the more intractable institutions of religion and heterosexual family, and question the efficacy of a movement that does not confront either. Thus, when gay leaders try to marshal support for marriage- or sodomy-law repeal or AIDS policy, they encounter opposition from those who charge that another issue is the more important one. This happened in the military fight. Rather than uniting behind the effort to overturn this form of government discrimination, gay people argued about whether it was the right goal. Our division undermined our leadership and ultimately helped our enemies.

Without shared agreement about our movement's goals, our leaders will remain vulnerable to charges of pursuing "their personal" agenda instead of "our" agenda. Ironically, gay politics is very much about personal agendas. We seek individual liberation (a process we begin by coming out). At the same time, we seek the opportunity to exert our influence on the world as openly gay people. While we must be exacting and expect a great deal from our leaders, no person, short of a messiah, can satisfy the multitude of desires of our diverse communities. Many disagreements about leadership stem from our unwillingness to acknowledge that, in a hugely diverse movement, others will express political views or champion goals with which we disagree.

I often feel uneasy about our conversations on political leadership because they propose models with which I disagree. Defining leadership in heroic or visionary or traditional democratic terms is too limiting. While I find myself agreeing with aspects of these classical definitions, I disagree with their implicit assumption that leadership is something innate; that leaders are born that way.

To a large extent, our yearning for political leadership mystifies a process that has a fairly material and concrete reality: leaders are not born; they are made. Some individuals, like the millionaires who populate the Senate and mainstream politics at every level, become leaders by virtue of their access to money. Others, like Bill Clinton, become political leaders by their skillful exercise of networks and contacts. Some leaders, like Nelson Mandela, have admirable qualities of strength, wisdom, and integrity, which inspire loyalty and earn a following. Other leaders, like Mahatma Gandhi, open our hearts to the moral values they challenge us to strive for. Leadership is more often than not a by-product of a fairly specific set of experiences and opportunities. The mystery is not why so few people exercise it, but why so many people fail to see the exercise of political leadership as a responsibility.

My experience of leadership convinces me of its material basis. I have been afforded the ability and the opportunity to exercise many kinds of leadership in the gay and lesbian movement. At different times, I have led as a street activist engaged in direct-action protests, an organizational head, a board member, and as a cultural figure benefiting from the visibility accorded those on whom the media spotlight shines. My ability to lead politically is itself a product of my privileged education and the middle-class background from which I came. I went to an Ivy League school, which, as my parents often told me is, in America, tantamount to entering a private club, a network accessing the elite who run the country. I pursued graduate work and gained a law degree, thereby enhancing my marketability with a skill, and benefiting from another nationwide network—of the lawyers, politicians, and journalists who understand how the system works and how it can be manipulated to achieve certain ends. Further, I was raised, from the time I was eight, in a small town in upstate New York by Indian immigrant parents who taught me to believe the empowering clichés of middle-class entitlement: if I worked hard, lived by the rules, was disciplined, and showed initiative and talent, I could achieve anything I wanted.

The opportunities I have been given to lead were partly those which arise "naturally" from being in the schools and cultural environments where I lived. A liberal arts college education in the 1970s, when campuses were in the throes of feminism, the tail end of the peace movement, a divestment movement, and a student power movement, led me into student activism. Student activism led me beyond college walls, to community organizing, which took me to Boston and a public interest–oriented law school. Law school and activism pointed me toward mainstream politics, Washington, D.C., and the ACLU. Nonprofit work led me to consider a full-time job in the gay movement at a time when jobs

there were scarce. That work gave me experience as a national organizer, and the visibility I gained from that experience brought me to this
privileged place of writing a book. While my ability or competence at
each juncture certainly moved me on to the next step, as I review this
progression to "national leadership" I feel the hand of material things
far more than the impetus of my "natural ability." More often than not,
my recognition as a leader had a material basis in the people I knew, the
places I had lived and worked, the actions I took, and the results I got.
When I consider the backgrounds of many other leaders, I see these
common threads of education, graduate school, propinquity to support
and professional networks, access to money, and other material things.

There is little about leadership that is mystical or particularly heroic; the drama and heroism come in its exercise rather than from some
inherent quality. In fact, I believe that the way we regard leadership—as
a force outside our daily lives, as a superimposed set of visions or oratory
or direction—is counterproductive to the kind of political leadership
gay people need as we approach the twenty-first century. Characterizing political leadership solely in terms of "the vision thing" or the
admirable qualities of individual people keeps us from accepting the
responsibility to exercise some political leadership on our own behalf.

The kind of political leadership our movement needs into the next
millennium embodies several elements: consciousness of, and responsibility for, one's role as a leader, courage, honesty, a commitment to
inclusion, and a willingness to be held accountable for one's actions. In
some political leaders, one element outshines another. Some leaders
have more integrity than others, (like Representative Gerry Studds
(D-MA) versus Steve Gunderson (R-WI)); some are ruthless and unaccountable, (like Jesse Helms (R-NC)); others lack adequate consciousness of their power and duty as a leader like former House Speaker Tom
Foley. The many shades of each of these qualities suggest why it is so
rare to find leaders like Martin Luther King and Malcolm X and Gloria
Steinem, who embody them all. Among gay and lesbian political leaders who consciously claim the mantle, I feel there have been some
critical failures of principle, vision, or integrity. So, for example, I have
trouble with the leadership of David Mixner because he claims to speak
on behalf of "the gay community" yet has no constituency to whom he
is accountable. Similarly, the board leadership of most organizations I
have worked with seems incapable of developing a clear vision of where
their organizations are headed, and how to achieve goals. Instead of

exercising vision, board members become involved in micromanage-ment and petty arguments about institutional policies. The antileader-ship stance of lesbian feminism, with which far too many lesbians of my generation came to political consciousness, inhibits us from emphati-cally claiming leadership in the gay movement.

My definition of leadership places the responsibility for its exercise on the shoulders of each of us. My lover argues that my faith in our individual capacity for seeing leadership as the acceptance of responsi-bility to act is actually a disguised form of *dharma,* the Hindu notion of moral civil and familial duties that each individual is bound, by tradition and cultural expectation, to perform. As a lapsed Hindu, I am surprised by that observation, but I am willing to concede that she is right. *Dharma* can be defined as our duty to exercise "right conduct" in accor-dance with a set of moral principles. Adapted to the idea of leadership, the concept gives shape to the practice gay people need to develop in order to sustain and exercise political leadership. I believe we must nurture in ourselves, and praise in each other, the notion of a duty to act in accordance with a set of moral principles. In this sense, leadership is returned to its individual sources as a responsibility and an opportunity in which each of us can participate. Our lives bear out the truth of this simple definition: leadership, defined in this sense of individual respon-sibility, is exercised by each person who comes out of the closet. The movement's task is to articulate our expectations for and from gay leadership, rather than to focus on the strengths and shortcomings of individual leaders.

SOURCES OF OUR AMBIVALENCE TOWARD LEADERSHIP

Our ambivalence toward accepting leadership is a mark of pride for many gay and lesbian people. To some extent, our skepticism mirrors that of the broader American body politic. Politicians have often proved themselves fickle and less than admirable. But gay people are defiantly individualistic—because we have been so self-made—and we love to see ourselves as iconoclasts. In this sense, we would do well to consider Wills's admonition that every leader needs followers to succeed. In addition to the psychological barriers we may have to following other gay people, gay and lesbian ambivalence toward political leadership stems from two historical experiences: the closet and the media's treatment of our leadership.

The ambivalent attitude toward leadership, like most things queer, is partly rooted in the closet. The persistence of the closet limits the emergence, effectiveness, visibility, and power of our leaders in several ways. First, and most simply, we have too few gay and lesbian leaders because so many of our people are in the closet; those who are in the movement's leadership are those who have come out far enough to risk visibility. Closeted gay people who fear the impact of disclosure on their jobs, community status, or families may become involved in gay political groups in limited ways, but until they come out, they cannot play strong leadership roles. The closet limits the leadership of the movement to a fraction of all possible queer peoples. Only those with the energy, willingness, self-acceptance, and resources to be publicly gay will end up serving. I often wonder how many qualified leaders remain in hiding, yet I firmly believe that the process of coming out confirms the potential each of us has to be a leader. People with outstanding leadership qualities must go through the painstaking process of accepting themselves, coming out to their family and colleagues, and reaching a level of self-confidence to accept the responsibility of leadership.

What's worse is that those in the closet don't always help their out-of-the closet brethren. Closeted people often distance themselves from gay and lesbian issues, lest such support "discredit" or "expose" them in the eyes of straights. So, for example, until he was outed in 1992, the Pentagon spokesman Pete Williams and his boss, Defense Secretary and presidential contender Dick Cheney, said nothing publicly on the government's military policy. Forced by the outing, both Williams and Cheney made statements indicating their disagreement with the military ban.

In addition, the closet physically limits the access of gay and lesbian leaders to their followers. If your constituency is mostly silent and closeted, how can you legitimately claim to represent any but the small fraction that is out? Survey after survey concludes that 3 percent to 5 percent of men self-identify as homosexual, and that .5 percent to 1.5 percent of women so identify. Even though everyone prefaces these statistics with the caveat that people underreport their membership in a status as stigmatized as homosexuality, straight politicians and antigay demagogues use these low numbers to minimize the need to address gay and lesbian issues at all. In addition, since gay and lesbian leaders have politicized only a fraction of these self-identified queers, the question of the gay leaders' constituency is a very real one. For which small fraction of a fraction of an out-gay and out-lesbian community do our leaders speak?

Some of our leaders emerge with their coming out; Greg Louganis did this, for example, when he came out at the 1994 Gay Games and again as HIV-positive in his autobiography. By exposing and fighting discrimination, some individuals become leaders by default; the shattering of their closet forces them to be politically active, and often thrusts them into leadership positions. This was the case with Gerry Studds, naval cadet Joe Steffan, Air Force Sergeant Tracey Thorne, baseball umpire Dave Pallone, and scores of others who have faced and fought back against discrimination. But neither the recesses of the closet nor its shattering, by whatever force of prejudice or will, can bring us leaders of uniform depth, integrity, and ability; some gay leaders are stronger and more inspiring than others.

We often speak of the closet as a metaphor for lack of self-acceptance and forget to think of it in terms of physical space, a physical barrier to the recognition of gays and lesbians and to their interaction with potential followers. The closet is as material a place of hiding as if it were a real box inside which we lived. The ghetto, the privatized gay and lesbian family circle, the gay or lesbian bar—each is a physical closet, outside of which millions do not acknowledge their queerness. The material reality of the closet has an inside and an outside. The most obvious of such inside spaces is the one we enter whenever we deny the truth about our queer lives. The rush we feel at large public events like the Gay Games, gay cultural events, or gay and lesbian pride rallies comes from the temporary shattering of closet space, from the rare, public experience of community, from the release from the isolation in which most of us still live. Another kind of inside space is the ghetto, a somewhat out space that nonetheless keeps gay people physically contained and isolated from one another. Still another inside space is what Ginny Apuzzo recently described as the "emotional closet," into which many have retreated because of the grief and trauma of dealing with AIDS.

The closet is a cultural construction, with gay and lesbian invisibility a cultural reality, enforced by silence or hostility in the media, in schools, churches, local government, civic associations, and the business world. Despite progress, homosexuality is not in the culturally mainstream; we are not openly integrated into the fabric of the life of the community, family, workplace, or culture. Even though hundreds of daily battles are waged by gay and lesbian and AIDS organizations in localities across America, the daily newspapers, local television, and radio shows rarely cover news about gay and lesbian lives. The homosexual orientation of newsmakers is rarely mentioned, but the heterosexual orientation is routinely cited ("So-and-so is married to . . ." or is "the father of four"). Coverage of gay and lesbian lives is rarely seen as something to be integrated into coverage of the community at large. Cultural invisibility limits the power of gay and lesbian leaders; we are quoted only on gay-oriented articles, on those occasions when the straight media decide to cover the story. And if we are not quoted, we may as well not exist in the eyes of closeted gay and lesbian people.

Moreover, cultural invisibility keeps the effective work of strong local leaders from their constituents. We hear the names of gay leaders most when there is a scandal or political crisis, but rarely when they do a good job or achieve the daily victory of keeping our movement on track. One seldom reads profiles of gay and lesbian political leaders, infrequently reads accurate analyses of the budgets, goals, and accomplishments of gay organizations, and hardly ever finds a historic context given for the problems faced by gay leaders and organizations. Certainly scandal or conflict among leaders ought to be reported, but so should the more common truth that the gay and lesbian movement has come this far on the strength of hundreds of amazing, talented, political activists, exercising leadership in a variety of fields.

In addition, the emphasis that our political movement places on cultural visibility and media coverage has produced at least two unwelcome side effects: media action and coverage are seen as equivalent to substantive action and leadership; and the media celebrity displaces the genuine political leader. The decline of ACT UP and direct action began, in my view, the instant that concern about media coverage of actions displaced the political calculus of right or wrong. Actions were conceived for their headline-grabbing potential rather than for the beneficial effect they would have on the cause of AIDS activism or gay and lesbian freedom. One example of such an action was the Saint Patrick's Cathedral demonstration launched by ACT UP–New York in 1989, in which service was disrupted, and one Catholic participant, Tom Keane, actually stepped on the communion wafer he received. To participants like Ann Northrop and to ACT UP supporters like the media-savvy Larry Kramer, the action against Cardinal John O'Connor's AIDSphobic policies represented all that was the best about ACT UP: courageous leadership, targeting the real enemies and calling them out, proving that it had the power to disrupt in serious ways. But to gay and lesbian Catholics, ACT UP's action represented a desecration of what is sacred; to the public, it was an example of scary mob action. To me, the action was a grim statement of our helplessness in the face of the real enemies: organized religion in general and Catholicism in particular. What ACT UP gained in national notice, it lost in the erosion of its own base within the gay movement. The media coverage was worth it in the short run but irrelevant in the long run.

The confusion of media celebrity with legitimate political leadership poses a continuing problem. How are we to evaluate people who function as leaders in public? Is anyone who creates an organizational letterhead and makes a statement to the press to be treated as a community leader? One cannot imagine another group for whom the mere visibility of a member in the media would confer instant credibility— but for gay people, silenced so long, media coverage is hungrily watched as a sign of power and authority. In fact, the ranks of so-called gay and lesbian leaders are littered with individuals whose main claim to the mantle of leadership is that they are routinely quoted in the press as authorities on gay and lesbian issues. Such media celebrity is false leadership—unaccountable, ego-driven, and antithetical to the voices of more credible, less polarizing (and therefore less media-promoted) leaders.

HORIZONTAL HOSTILITY

Bullying behavior has yet to be challenged by most established gay and lesbian leaders. Richard Burns gave me a candid assessment of the detrimental impact of bullying behavior on his work. "When I think of individuals who have staked out a role for themselves as really mean-spirited people who just work, seemingly full time, to hurt other people, I don't quite understand it. I think, honestly, it's about their own personal unhappiness and this is a way for them to get attention. It disheartens me. My own response is to just stay away from them. And part of my response, I realize, is to stay out of the papers. The more visible you are, the bigger a target you are, and I can do my work and accomplish my political organizing goals without the glory of the press. But will I survive longer because I won't be such an obvious target for potshots from crazy people? I'm not really comfortable with that response. I think we're picked off one by one, and there's real hesitancy by other people to rally around the one who's been picked off, because you think, okay, you're going to be next. It's almost . . . it's cowardly."

Burns's honesty exposes another truth about our leadership crisis: that we have talented leaders who are held back, put down, and throttled by hypercritical and vicious personal attacks. As chronicled in the gay and lesbian press, movement history is replete with examples of such bitter episodes. As a lesbian leader, I experienced my share of both criticism and attacks, but I distinguish between the two. Criticism of my leadership—of decisions I made, policies NGLTF issued, projects we undertook—was something I welcomed and tried to respond to specifically and fairly each time. I answered hundreds of letters from members, spoke to hundreds of reporters in the gay and lesbian press, and argued politics with scores of people of every political persuasion. Criticism of my tenure came from the left and the right within the gay community. Criticism of political leadership is essential if our leaders are to be accountable to constituents. When NGLTF's board opposed the Gulf War and I drafted the statement, I regarded the criticism we received as constructive (if heated!). NGLTF invited several prominent critics to address the board directly with their concerns.

But attacks are different from political criticism. Attacks are personal, venal, distorted misstatements or half truths. These stung me, and I still shudder to remember them. I was called a "traitor" for withdrawing my involvement in an ACT UP action in which I had mistakenly agreed to participate. I was denounced as someone who should be impeached for treason for not demonstrating with ACT UP in the snowy South Dakota primary of 1992. I've been called an Uncle Tom, antimale, antiwhite, too radical because I engaged in direct action, a sell-out because I met with a GOP leader, too assimilationist because I worked in a traditional political organization, a Stalinist, an anarcho-syndicalist, someone who destroyed NGLTF, un-American, utopian, authoritarian, self-appointed, self-elected, a "so-called leader," stupid, naïve, not sufficiently hard-working, too narrowly focused, and much more. Michael Petrelis disrupted a joint NGLTF–HRCF press conference on the November 1992 elections by screaming at me that, among other things, I was a false leader of the gay community. "How many times have you been arrested for gay and lesbian demonstrations, Urvashi?" he yelled. "Why do you get arrested for abortion rights demonstrations and not gay rights demonstrations?"

Some personal attacks continued after I announced my departure from NGLTF. In an article about my resignation, the Chicago-based journalist Rex Wockner wrote "Vaid to Resign, Activists Pleased," an article in which he quoted only people who had been critical of my leadership, and suggested that I had undermined and weakened NGLTF in my six and a half years on staff. Since I left, conservative columnists like Paul Varnell, Bruce Bawer, and Stephen Miller have continued to attack me personally, even though they have never spoken with me, worked with me, or talked to many of the people I have worked with. Their main purpose now seems to be to revise my place in movement history, a labor whose motives I cannot fathom.

My experience as a leader is not unique. Nearly every one of my colleagues in leadership positions in gay, lesbian, and AIDS organizations has been subjected to similar epithets, columns, and attacks. Gay and lesbian people do not often bring constructive criticism to our leaders; we'd rather go for the jugular. The more successful our leaders become, the more personal and vicious are our attacks on them. For this reason, as the late gay activist Steve Endean said in 1992, "Attacks from other lesbians and gays were much more painful than any I've suffered from homophobes—and far more debilitating."

For years the movement has debated why these attacks take place. One theory dominates all other explanations: it is internalized hatred or self-loathing that leads us to be harsh and unforgiving toward our own. To this widely held view, I'd like to suggest two other factors: the lack of a tradition of critical debate within the gay and lesbian movement, and the lack of structures to hold gay and lesbian leaders accountable to their constituents.

In a 1992 article on the subject of gay and lesbian leadership, the *Advocate* described the problem of internalized homophobia in this way: "The history of the gay and lesbian movement is permeated with controversies that have rocked our organizations and our press with scandals that have caused our leaders to resign in rage and haste. Activist after activist has walked away from a national or local group—or from gay and lesbian community work altogether—claiming that she or he was no longer able to tolerate the intense scrutiny and cutting criticism directed at the more visible members of our community. More than a few have made apocalyptic predictions about the chances for success of a movement that insists on 'Eating Our Own.' " A number of leaders who were interviewed characterized the problem as "oppression sickness," "cannibalistic frenzy," the crab mentality, fear of success, and ambivalence toward leadership.

The theory goes that all gay people are raised with great shame and self-loathing about being homosexual. The lack of self-esteem and the fundamental sense of inferiority bear strange, sometimes poisonous, fruit, which leads us to devalue the leadership and accomplishments of other gay and lesbian people. Our criticism always seems to degenerate into personal attacks. We pounce on our leaders harshly if they fail us in any way. Gay and lesbian papers are so full of attacks and derision about leadership that many of our people shun leadership roles. In effect, we rapidly destroy the leaders we have. People active in movement work during the fifties, sixties, seventies, or even the eighties are rarely involved in gay and lesbian activism today, and the revolving doors to staff positions in gay and lesbian organizations illustrate the prevalence of burn-out.

I believe internalized homophobia may indeed lead gay people to be too harsh on their leaders, but I have long felt that this self-loathing has been blamed too readily. While the term may explain the venom with which some of us criticize our leaders, I submit that a fair amount of our antileadership bias stems from simpler sources: unresolved personality conflicts, often represented in a long history of personal dislike between the critic and the leader; unchecked opportunism and self-promotion on the part of some leaders; and the obsession with self-preservation, what I call essential cowardice, of the entrenched and institutionalized political leaders. In my experience, personality-driven reactions—envy, jealousy, resentment, dislike, distrust—and political disagreements— radical-conservative splits, racial differences, misogyny—are the main sources for much of the criticism leveled against gay and lesbian leaders. But in a community of people with a short history, few channels for national communication, a young press, and a poor tradition of political debate, the personal or political reasons for such attacks rarely get exposed.

Underlying a majority of these attacks on our leadership is some personal animus between the attacked and the critic. In countless projects or organizing campaigns, I have encountered resistance from someone unwilling to work with someone else in the community for reasons as varied and as individual as people themselves. But because we are unable to set aside our personal dislikes for the greater good, we fail to build effective community organizations. A good organizer, like NGLTF's Sue Hyde or Suzanne Pharr or Tim Sweeney, can get warring factions to work out their differences. But too often, a local organization or project falls apart over personality conflicts. When such tension appears in the gay and lesbian press, the reports often exacerbate the hostility felt by the parties involved, and a personal grudge becomes a major community obstacle.

Similarly, when critics on the left, right, and center of gay politics question the authority or competence of "mainstream" gay organizational leaders, I think that they do so with quite personal agendas. I think most of Michael Petrelis's attacks on gay and lesbian leaders, for example, stem from his resentment and anger at not being respected as one. Marvin Liebman, Rich Tafel, and other conservative gay leaders' criticisms arise from their frustration at not being respected by liberal and left gay activists, who have made up the rank-and-file of gay political activism since the 1950s. Wayne Turner, Steven Michael, and other direct-action leaders often set up the gay and lesbian establishment as the enemy in order to legitimate themselves as the alternative—even when the difference between the gay alternative and the gay establishment is a matter of style rather than substance. The cynical stance toward gay and lesbian leadership taken by progressives like Michael Bronski and other leftists serves as a self-fulfilling prophecy: the inevitable human fallibility of gay and lesbian leaders underscores their view that our desire for leadership is itself foolish.

Personal agendas also lie under the persistent lament "Where is our Martin Luther King?" In the fall of 1993, a *Boston Globe* reporter named Dan Golden, preparing a profile on David Mixner, asked me to comment on whether Mixner was in fact regarded by the gay community as a leader on the order of Dr. King. When I expressed surprise at the question, the reporter said he had gotten the impression from Mixner that he considered himself a leader of that order, an impression that Golden wrote into his story.

Finally, I find it frustrating when gay and lesbian leaders themselves refuse to point out the personal or political differences that underlie an attack on their leadership. We too often resort to the rationale of "horizontal hostility" to explain why we are criticized. Invariably, a gay leader under attack attempts to deflect, and not to exacerbate, the criticism. But all criticism of leaders does not originate from self-hatred. It may also stem from the leaders' poor judgment, lack of accountability, or aloofness.

Accountability of leadership will come when we are more able and willing to criticize ourselves and each other publicly, without personally

demonizing or negating each other. We shy away from such public
questioning because we say we do not want to air our dirty laundry in
public. Yet surely there is a difference between our questioning each
other's decisions and the heavy-handed carping that questions our fundamental integrity. Instead of calling each other Uncle Toms when we
disagree politically, what if we simply disagreed. The principal means of
holding leadership accountable is the voice of other leaders. The silence
of gay and lesbian leaders about each other's decisions or political issues
not only stifles debate; it promotes innuendo and back-stabbing. Indeed, speaking out—respectfully and forcefully—would diminish the
disproportionate power that a handful of gay columnists and a handful
of gay misanthropes wield in the gay and lesbian press.

NEW DIRECTIONS

As we look toward the next few years, none of us should pretend that
we will survive without strong, visionary, and supported political leadership. I have argued that such leadership exists within our movement,
often at the local level. The time has come for us to make a new
compact between gay leaders and gay followers. We must catch ourselves when we senselessly deride and bash gay leadership. We must
more consciously examine our impulse to be critical and angry at each
other when we merely disagree about the direction of our movement.
Our new compact must be based on respect and something I can only
call trust. We have wonderful leaders—inside and outside the organizations—who deserve and have earned our respect. Think of the hard-
working staff members at gay community centers and health clinics, the
volunteers who run gay business guilds and professional groups, the
teachers who are coming out in large numbers and joining the Gay,
Lesbian and Straight Teacher Network (GLSTN) to speak out against
homophobia.

Our new compact depends on a reciprocal commitment of trust on
the part of followers and accountability on the part of leaders. The
enforcement of the compact depends on our public willingness to tell
the truth. What if we each start with the local leaders we know, as if
with a clean slate, trusting them and affirming them as duly appointed
representatives? What if we support them and reach out to assist them?
If they fail us, then let us challenge their actions. But what if we refuse

to demonize them or diminish their validity as leaders? What if, in short, we agree to behave as fairly and ethically toward each other as we expect straight society to behave toward us?

The other side of this compact involves a greater willingness on the part of leaders—organizational and individual—to refrain from making irresponsible statements and to check their egos at the door. Any political position invites criticism and scrutiny. We leaders cannot be so thin-skinned as to characterize every criticism as an attack. When it is an attack, or is painfully personal, we must find the courage to speak about it directly. The fears that organizational leaders have—of alienating a constituency or a funding source—are less important than the reality that silence on matters of principle may let the allow falsehoods be perpetuated. So, for example, when leaders are attacked for doing "nothing" on a particular issue (a common refrain from a handful of media-savvy critics), we must take to task the media that report this lie, instead of being silent and allowing the charge to stand.

Finally, for all our talk about leadership, the movement invests virtually no money or time in the development and cultivation of new generations of leaders. There are no training programs, few formal internships for student leaders, few, if any, mentoring sessions, and only a handful of skills-building conferences. The vacuum leaves each generation of gay people on its own, deprived of formal engagement with its predecessors.

Each generation of queers then rediscovers (and re-creates) the same organizational and political problems confronted by earlier generations. As a changing crop of activists finds its voice, identities, and solutions to the fairly consistent problems of organization, funding, and politics, our movement advances slowly. We have a movement rich in history but poor in continuity; prolific in activity but endangered by burn-out; enriched by powerful individual leaders but impoverished by their inability to sustain their leadership over the long haul. My warning to the movement—and the communities of people who make up our movement—is that until we consciously develop, nurture, and promote queer leadership in concrete ways, our complaints will serve as prophecies: we will experience again and again the problems we face now.

There is no magical formula for leadership, and my view focuses less on the politics or ideologies of individuals than on their ethics. The people whom I regard as powerful queer leaders have a high degree of personal integrity, vision, moral courage, and eloquence, which I respect, regardless of their political viewpoints. The late Steve Endean, a hard-working liberal activist, was a leader I held in high esteem even when I disagreed with him. Another leader whom I admire was for many years Endean's nemesis: Ginny Apuzzo, whose eloquence made her one of the best national spokespersons that the gay movement has ever had. Apuzzo had a very different kind of leadership style and voice, but she gave her constituency the same fierce loyalty and honesty that Endean offered. A leader of a different mold is the radical black lesbian-feminist writer and organizer Barbara Smith, one of the pioneers of multi-issue politics in the gay and lesbian movement. Her effort to push the largely white gay and feminist movements to incorporate antiracism into their work stands as a tremendous example of courageous leadership, and helped pave the way for my own leadership role. The hard-working organizer Richard Burns, head of the NYC Lesbian and Gay Community Services Center, is another kind of leader: an institution builder, who makes his contribution quietly, by securing a vital, accessible, and diverse home for the lesbian and gay communities of New York. A leader who would describe herself as opposed to the conventional idea of leadership is Maxine Wolfe, who actually rejects the label of leader and believes in nonhierarchical, collective organizing, though her contribution to every project in which she worked is that of a person with broad vision.

To recall the words of Luis Alfaro, I have found my leadership heroes. None of them are saints. But I don't expect them to be.

CHAPTER TWELVE

THERE ARE THINGS TO DO

We need to open our eyes and look about us. We need to stare at the naked misery of our people, at the gullied land and gullied culture, until our imaginations begin to see what we have done to all our people and ourselves by not acting. Yes . . . there are things to be done.

—Lillian Smith, "There Are Things to Do"

As we approach the twenty-first century, what is our vision of the future of gay, lesbian, and queer people? What remains to be done? Throughout the book, I have argued that seeking political mainstreaming has yielded for gay and lesbian people a state I characterize as virtual equality. While it represents great progress over the profound denial and silence that surrounded gay and lesbian existence before the modern gay rights movement evolved, we must question whether it should be the ultimate goal for our movement or merely a marker along a longer road to fuller human dignity and freedom. There is an urgent need for many more people, with very different ideological viewpoints, to re-examine our movement and suggest the kinds of action needed to overcome the formidable obstacles in our path. A movement may become stale and irrelevant when changes in social conditions render it unnecessary or require adaptations that it resists. The unrelenting stigmatization of homosexuality allows the gay movement to avoid the first pitfall, but not the second.

THE VISION THING OR WHAT ARE WE FOR?

On the level of vision, several fundamental questions confront us. Are we a movement for civil rights, defined in the traditional ways, or are we a movement for social justice and liberation? What are the moral values and principles that guide us, as a movement and as gay people, in our political work?

Over the past decades, we have, when asked what the gay and lesbian political movement stands for, indicated these goals: cultural visibility, political representation, and civil rights. They have yet to be fully achieved. Until every gay and lesbian person is out of the closet, the visibility we now experience will resemble the distorted image of a fun-house mirror, blowing up certain segments of our broader communities out of proportion to their real size, and rendering others invisible. Anecdotal experience and poll after poll suggest that not even half of all gay and lesbian people are living openly gay lives. To change this fundamental consequence and cause of gay oppression remains a priority of our movement, and a personal commitment that, I believe, we must make on a far deeper, indeed moral, level.

Another truth about gay and lesbian visibility that bears repeating is its dependence on public opinion. While there is no sliding back for those of us who are out of the closet, the objective truth is that the cultural clout we wield will ebb and flow as it has over the past twenty-five years. If an antigay administration is elected in 1996, there is every reason to fear that gay issues will slide lower in political priority and cultural visibility. Even today, the antigay vote is very strong, causing our political representatives to backslide or waffle on support for gay and lesbian equality. This negative force is exerted as much in the sphere of culture as it is in politics. In 1995, despite the broad cultural visibility of gay and lesbian people, very few out-gay performers are allowed on television or in film. Those who do make it are often asked to compromise their identities and their politics.

The pursuit of political representation has been the major achievement and focus of the mainstream gay rights movement. Whether Democrat or Republican or Independent, we have exercised our right to political participation and have begun minimally to be heard by our elected officials. As I have recounted, this is not a victory we should take lightly, nor one whose current status can leave us feeling complacent. Yet the flaw in the strategy of mainstreaming is its confusion of access to power with power itself. Real power is represented by votes and the ability to win a goal or defeat our opponents. This is a power we muster in rare local battles but have failed to exert thus far on the national level. Political power must indeed be a focus for a movement centered on rights and liberation; without the power to exercise our political freedom, we will not be able to defend ourselves. For this reason, we must remain vigilant and wary of the efforts by the right to circumscribe our political freedom and citizenship—as it attempts to do in the antigay ballot measures. In addition, I confess to watching with great dread the Supreme Court's hearing of future important gay rights cases. Colorado's Amendment 2 will be argued in the autumn and illustrates the fragility of the political access that gay men and lesbians have won: decades of hard work can be erased in one decision, as, sadly, they have been by the Court in its recent civil rights decisions involving race and gender.

The question of whether we see ourselves as a civil rights movement or a broader movement for liberation is also more pressing than it has ever been, affecting what we see as the agenda of our movement. After tracing the long history of this tension, I believe that the question cannot be resolved one way or the other. We need a rights-oriented movement, but we have to recognize the limits of a civil rights–based strategy. While this may sound like equivocation to some, it is our reality. Further, it is futile to try to enforce unity among our people when we have such different ideologies. A more productive way for us to move beyond the dialectic of liberation and legitimation is to acknowledge that neither "side" is wrong, and support each other where we can.

My call is for a new understanding among gay people and for more debate among all political sides in our movement. This seems so basic as to need no restating, but our vitriol toward each other suggests we do not fully recognize that there are leftists, rightists, conservatives, liberals, and moderates within our movement. Further, a new tolerance for political diversity would allow us to argue with each other passionately (as we must), but not to bludgeon each other into accepting our point of view. I am as guilty of argument by demonization as my detractors are, a fault (in my case) of legal training and an adversarial mentality! If we can in fact enter into a new relationship of political debate, then we may well render irrelevant one of our most annoying and time-consuming arguments: what constitutes a "genuinely" gay or lesbian issue. The answer lies not in proving who is more authentically gay and who is not, but in accepting that our ideology, race, class, and gender affect our answer. I will never be convinced that racial and gender issues belong in some "other" movement; they are fused in my body with my lesbianism, and I reject single identity–based politics. Yet I recognize that I may never convince someone who wants such a movement that multiracial or multi-issue political work is valuable. Engaging in this fruitless argument prevents gay people from debating the more vital question of what more we can each do to eliminate sexual-orientation prejudice.

To this end, I have long argued that there is a basic political agenda on which the vast majority of gay, lesbian, bisexual, and supportive straight people can agree, and a larger set of issues around which we may part company. The narrow gay and lesbian agenda bears repeating again and again, not only because the right wing dramatically distorts it, but because our own racial and gender divisions prevent us from acknowledging what we have in common. There is nothing terribly special about this agenda; it embraces the aspirations of virtually every American, and its pursuit constitutes the work of nearly all gay and lesbian organizations. We seek, in short, full civil equality, defined as:

1. the right to live and work free from discrimination based on sexual orientation, to be evaluated on merit, not by our sexuality, to be free of unfair discrimination by our own government;

2. the right of freedom from violence and harassment directed at us because of who we are;

3. the right to privacy, defined as sexual autonomy and control over our sexual and reproductive lives without criminal sanction or the dictate of government;

4. the right to family, defined in the legalization of gay marriage and gay relationships, the elimination of unfair discrimination against our capacity to be parents;

5. the right to health care, defined as nondiscriminatory access to care and the receipt of services, and a nondiscriminatory response to health problems disproportionately faced by our people (such as AIDS, breast cancer, and other gay health issues); and

6. the right to live in peace as openly gay, lesbian, bisexual, or transgender people.

The gay rights agenda is just. Yet whenever they can, our detractors distort this basic truth by terming our pursuit of equal treatment a quest for "special rights." The future requires us to be extremely clear about

our goals and to challenge the misinformation of antigay forces wherever they air their views—in our churches, in our workplaces, our school
systems, and the media. We must counter the lies with the truth that
(a) discrimination based on sexual orientation exists and is massive;
(b) the prejudice we face stems from a discomfort with us as sexual
people, a discomfort that people must confront in themselves, and not
turn into social policy; (3) prejudice based on human difference is
wrong and immoral; (4) democracies value freedom and difference,
while totalitarian societies require conformity and extreme forms of
control over the individual; and (5) as the gay rights pioneer Frank
Kameny has said for nearly thirty years, "gay is good" and morally equal
to straight.

To our detractors, these goals are yet another sign that the civil
rights apparatus is out of control. If we let people with this sexual
behavior call themselves a bona fide minority, they huff, what other
"perverts" will seek civil rights? Our squeamish liberal allies would
grant us "civil rights" but would reject our claim that we are morally
equivalent to straight people in every way; the resistance to gay and
lesbian marriage shows this. Indeed, the irony of these clear goals and
the gay agenda for justice is that none speaks directly to the heart of the
fear and loathing we face: to the so-called moral question.

The moral resistance to homosexual equality is the most troubling.
For good reason, morality is something we have shied away from. Many
crimes and injustices have been committed against us in the name of
God and virtue. But these perversions of moral values should not deflect
us from upholding the morality, ethics, and spiritual values we hold as
gay and lesbian people. Nor should they deter us from the difficult task
of challenging any doubt of our moral character. As we do so, we must
resist the tendency to demonize those who feel we are immoral; many
genuinely believe that their religious traditions and value systems require them to reach this conclusion. There is a great body of work that
questions and challenges such an interpretation of the Judeo-Christian
tradition. I refer readers, for example, to the work of the late John
Boswell, John McNeil, Mary Hunt, Andrew Sullivan, Malcolm Boyd,
and Mary Daly, to name just a handful of thinkers dealing with homosexuality and traditional religion. I also cite again the critical political
work done by faith-based gay activists, like Unitarian Universalist
Church leader Meg Riley, Christian activist Mel White, Rabbi Sharon
Kleinbaum and many others in the reform and conservative Jewish
movements, black gay ministers Renée McCoy, Zachary Taylor, and

Carl Bean, Metropolitan Community Church leaders like the Reverend Troy Perry, and a large number of straight and gay ministers of every faith and denomination. All of these people can refute, from inside, the very structure so often cited to justify intolerance toward gay and lesbian people.

Morality is a practical tool that helps us negotiate between what is right and what is wrong, between goodness and evil. It may adopt the pose of divinity, but its operation is also quite secular. The condemnation of gay people by certain religions as immoral does not make us so. The amazing truth is that, despite the hostility of traditional religion, the rejection by our families, the shame and stigma that we all must overcome to accept our true natures, gay and lesbian people are a profoundly moral people. Sadly, because we are stigmatized by the moralism of traditional religion, we have been handicapped as a movement from developing a shared moral framework. What are the values and ethics we stand for? What world do we fight so hard to create? As we live through the despair of AIDS, cancer, violence, racism, sexism, prejudice, and as we face the threat of fascism, what spiritual vision sustains us? What do we believe is right or wrong?

Theoretically, our moral project lies in the postulation of principles that help us define the queer role in the human community. In a sense, it is the old Mattachine question of what queer people are "for"—what we stand for and represent. In another sense, the question implicates the moral values we cherish: what are our ethics, our principles? Are they the same as the heterosexist frameworks we came from? This is a project that artists and thinkers as different as Walt Whitman and Harry Hay, Adrienne Rich and Tony Kushner, Audre Lorde and Leo Bersani, Cindy Patton and Elias Farajaje Jones have all engaged in their work. In the provocative anthology *Gay Spirit*, edited by the thoughtful LA-based writer Mark Thompson, Harry Hay writes that the founders of the Mattachine Society started their work by posing these questions to themselves: "Who are we gay people? Where do we come from, in history and in anthropology, and where have we been? What are we for?" "What are we for" is the central question facing the queer movement as we approach the next century. Implicating our goals, tactics, and moral vision, Hay questions what we seek materially as well as what vision we offer the broader society.

Hay theorizes that gay and lesbian folk represent nothing less than a separate species, a conclusion similar to the one drawn by Michel Foucault when he distinguished between sodomy as a behavior and the homosexual as a state of being—or, as he explicitly put it, "a species." Hay states that queer people differ from straights in their consciousness. Ours is subject-subject consciousness, what Leo Bersani calls the pursuit of sameness, while the hetero model is subject-object, the requirement of difference. "On our small planet, it is . . . glaringly clear that the traditional hetero male-dominated subject-object consciousness is bankrupt worldwide to the point of becoming lethal. A new consciousness must surface to replace it, and I propose that we gay folk . . . must now prepare to emerge from the shadows of history because we are a species variant with a particular characteristic adaptation in consciousness whose time has come!"

Hay claims that gay and lesbian consciousness offers straights a "window" through which their own patriarchal order can be seen. We represent another way to behave, another moral code by which to live, and we can, in Hay's mind, move humankind to another level of social development. He terms this new consciousness one of "supplementarity," not "complementarity," of equality and mutual respect, not dominance and subordination, of love and support, not opposition and competition. He cautions that subject-subject consciousness between queers is a potentiality, not a given. Many of us reproduce hetero ways of being in our lives, and we least live up to our queer potential when we pursue assimilation as our goal. Hay implies but never explicitly characterizes this subject-subject consciousness as one in which heterosexuals can also partake. The argument he makes easily allows for this possibility.

While I do not regard queer people as a "species," I find Hay's ideas about queer consciousness provocative and brave. His argument against assimilation asks us to question the morality of the status quo. Queer moral vision—our view of what is right and what wrong—necessarily arises from our particular experience of injustice. We are outcasts of the dominant society, outsiders to the mainstream. Does this outsider consciousness afford gay people some insight into prejudice, discrimination, violence, hatred, and evil as it has granted such insight to women and people of color? I think it does. Our experience of marginalization is central to our capacity to be moral as individuals and as a political movement.

Living with prejudice does not inevitably make us more virtuous; like straight outsiders to the mainstream, gay people still do horrible and immoral things. Look at Roy Cohn and J. Edgar Hoover. But I believe our outsider experience can make us conscious of the hypocrisy in what we are taught is moral. It offers us a chance to question and interpret anew the concepts of virtue, morality, and faith. As we have seen in our lives, being queer gives us a chance to re-invent family, friendship, and community.

My modest contribution to the debate on moral terms is to remind gay activists that our commitment to justice and equality has a moral dimension that may intersect with our religious traditions but must also be seen as separate from them. These moral commitments, which are implicit in our movement, need to be made explicit as our movement pursues genuine equality. My personal desire for a set of moral principles to sustain and guide our movement has both pragmatic and spiritual components. I think such moral grounding will help us bridge identity-based differences and communicate better with each other and with straight America. And I long for a greater degree of integration between the moral values that drive me individually and the morality governing the movement in which I work.

What principles define gay and lesbian morality? I see them as a commitment to honesty, demonstrated by the experience of coming out; a commitment to community, or a love that surpasses the definition of family and relationship we inherited from the heterosexual norm; and a commitment to joy, expressed in our affirmation of pleasure, both sexual and nonsexual.

Coming out is a defining experience for all gay people, whether we begin the process or resist it, whether we do it partially or pursue it relentlessly. Yet the moral nature of the process is rarely presented as such by our movement. Because it is about truth, coming out is an act of goodness, integrity, and is a precondition for any gay person wishing to live a moral life. One may be virtuous in one's daily life and one may observe religious tradition faithfully; these are commonly recognized forms of moral practice. I suggest that being out of the closet may best be defined as a moral act because it moves us closer toward truth and away from falsehood, toward virtue, away from hypocrisy.

Being in the closet, therefore, ought to be viewed as immoral behavior. Sometimes immoral behavior is necessary—to preserve one's life, one may have to fight and take another. So, staying in the closet for a small number of us may be essential if we are to avoid physical harm. But unless there is such compelling justification, I urge the movement to adopt a new ethic toward the closet, characterizing it as intrinsically evil. Yet while I champion the elevation of coming out to a moral imperative, I affirm my discomfort with outing as an act of force; I view it as ethically and morally indefensible.

Another moral principle, I suggest, is the shared gay and lesbian commitment to the creation of community. Such a commitment arises from the human desire for connection, from the nature of the identity-based politics we have followed for the last forty years, and from the painful experience of rejection by our families. The desire for connection is a human desire, not merely a gay one. Gay and lesbian communities bind us in a common humanity—whether we come together to solve problems, like AIDS, or to share support or to celebrate. Identity-based organizing is what enabled these communities to take form and resulted in their relative insularity from the broader straight world. Gay spaces and networks often co-exist in close proximity to straight ones but are unacknowledged or strangely made invisible. For example, in Washington the Hung Jury, one of the longest-running lesbian bars, used to be a straight businessman's hangout by day and dyke bar by night. The men and women who patronized the bar at lunch hour had no awareness of the lives of the lesbians who danced there at night.

The ambivalence many of our families feel toward our sexuality produces one beneficial side effect: it leads us to deeper friendships and a reliance on one another. As a result, for most gay people friends function as family and gay community has a special meaning to all of us. We take care of each other when we are sick, show up in a crisis, lend each other money, help each other raise children, run small businesses, and do the hundreds of things that heterosexuals rely on their families to perform. In a sense, many gay people who enjoy good relationships with their families of origin have more support than heterosexuals: we can count on our traditional *and* nontraditional families. Here at least, homophobia has resulted in something beneficial: friendships coexist alongside our families of origin.

This network of relationships draws its strength from our ability to feel whole or, as Eric Rofes and Suzanne Pharr term it, "authentic." The gay and lesbian experience of forming community represents a desire for authentic relationships. It involves what Pharr calls a "moral imperative," which arises in response to conditions of injustice we face. Pharr observes, "In the United States, great numbers of people feel confused about cultural change, about violence and economic insecurity, and they are often dispirited and overwhelmed. Sunk into a commodity- and consumer-based culture, alienated within the workplace

where corporations have tossed them around in the downsizing necessary to fill corporate greed, they feel increasingly objectified and alienated from themselves and one another . . . It is here where the potential for evil—the spiritual, emotional, mental or physical enslavement or
destruction of others for one's own gains—begins." Pharr characterizes
the appeal of the right as stemming from the idea of unity that it offers
to a people longing for connection. She urges progressive people to offer
our own moral vision of why we engage in social justice work: "because
we believe every person counts, has human dignity, deserves respect,
equality and justice. This morality is the basis of our vision, and when
we do our best vision-based organizing (as opposed to response-based
or expediency-based), all our work flows from this basic belief."

To see the work of building community as a moral imperative lends
a special urgency to our support for those groups which foster community. Health clinics, churches and synagogues, community centers,
ASOs, are all part of the fabric of our community. Such institutions also
counter the illogical and incorrect notion that because gay people exist
outside the realm of the traditional family, we have no traditions or
families of our own. Indeed, many critics point out that gay and lesbian
people broaden the definition of family and offer new models for human relationships that are not predicated on rigid gender roles. Our
experience with AIDS certainly bears out the integrity of our concern
for one another. The point is not so much to convince straight America
that we are just like them—I do not believe that all of "us" are—but to
look at the ways gay people have created families and note their moral
equivalence to heterosexual families.

With the greatest enthusiasm, I suggest we embrace the very
threatening principle of joy. The poet Audre Lorde once said that
sexuality stems from a deep wellspring of joy. Gay people are by definition, and in my experience, joyous people. We have found a way to turn
everything into a celebration; in our lives, dancing resembles a sacred
act. The day after the candlelight vigil to mourn Harvey Milk, San
Francisco's community threw a huge party in his remembrance. Our gay
pride celebrations resemble festivals and fairs more than political events.
Generating excitement for parties, dances, masques, and other joyous
celebrations is easier than arousing it for letter writing, voter registration, or political action. We should not look at this as a sign of moral
weakness, as our enemies and the more self-hating among us do; we
should consider this gay impulse toward pleasure to be a central part of
the gay and lesbian character. The disdain of some gay activists toward

what Michael Bronski has termed "the pleasure impulse" reflects our adoption of straight morality's condescending attitude toward pleasure, joy, and desire. Heterosexual morality is predicated on the suppression of joy or, more accurately, on its control by religion: there are appropriate places to feel ecstasy (religious enlightenment and marriage), and all other arenas are wrong. Pleasure is seen as a force to be controlled and contained, not harnessed and enjoyed. But in gay life, pleasure serves a very different role. We do not fear it; we embrace it, ritualize it, and are transformed by its power.

These principles offer a starting point for a discussion of the moral foundations of gay and lesbian life as we approach the new century. Each of us expands them by our own religious and moral values. And that is perfectly appropriate. For example, some more left-leaning political activists may believe, as Jim Wallis argues in *The Soul of Politics:*

> We need to articulate clearly the essential moral character of the many crises we confront, the connections between them, and the choices we must make . . . We start by subjecting all projects, initiatives, decisions, and policies to new criteria: whether they make justice more possible for all of us and especially for those on the bottom; whether they allow us to live in more harmony with the earth; and whether they increase the participation of all people in decision making. In other words, we must learn to judge our social and economic choices by whether they empower the powerless, protect the earth, and foster true democracy.

More conservative-leaning gay people will likely find solace in the work of James Q. Wilson and Stephen Carter, whose books argue that religion provides universal moral definitions for all human behavior. Meanwhile, some atheists among our community may reject outright my formulation of a need for moral vision. That is their prerogative.

Finally, I'd like to suggest that the most productive moral project on which we could embark would be to define an ethical code of conduct toward each other as movement activists. I myself bristle at the idea of any moralizing that silences debate and vigorous criticism; this is not what I propose. In this context, ethics refer to shared principles or values that would guide our conduct inside the movement, values that would be widely debated and to which movement activists would voluntarily subscribe. My desire for such principles stems from my growing awareness of the vicious, untrue, and personal form that political discourse takes in our culture—broadly and within the gay community. A central principle I submit for debate is the commitment to nonviolent methods of discourse with each other and with our enemies. Such a commitment would require a close examination of the behavior of those who shout down speakers, push and shove people with whom they disagree, punch and hit each other in anger; it would question demonstrations that foment violent intrusion on another's physical being. Over the years, I have witnessed activists engaged in what I can only describe as violence—behavior rooted in force, malice, or the need to bully and dominate the other. Stifling debate, as was done to Secretary Louis Sullivan in San Francisco, hurts us all and betrays a movement whose ethical commitment is to honesty and nonviolence.

Other examples of personal intimidation I have seen by a handful of gay male activists are neither excusable nor based on principle. Moreover, I lament the sense of danger that prevents those who have experienced such harassment from challenging it publicly. Specifically, the actions of Michael Petrelis come to mind. In 1990, Petrelis became famous for throwing a drink in the face of the then-closeted gay congressman Steve Gunderson, when he saw him in a gay bar. (According to Internet conversations, Petrelis did so again in late 1994.) In May 1992, at an HRCF Leadership Conference in Washington, Petrelis screamed that the group was not doing enough and that he wished he had a machine gun so that he could kill all the people there. On the night before the March on Washington on April 24, 1993, Petrelis arrived at a Lambda Legal Defense and Education Fund cocktail party and punched the gay lawyer and Lambda director Kevin Cathcart in the stomach.

Nor is Petrelis an isolated example. Larry Bush wrote in the *Advocate* about the targeting of the home and neighborhood of Roberta Achtenberg by Queer Nation activists who disagreed with her politically. I think such behavior must be called out publicly and subjected to rigorous questioning. If we cannot commit ourselves to ethical behavior toward each other, then I genuinely question our ability as a movement to survive the polarization and internal factionalism we now face.

Further, I think we must debate our commitment to nonviolent civil disobedience itself. For the most part, and at our best, direct-action proponents have been disciplined, and have maintained the tradition of nonviolent civil disobedience adapted from the Gandhian struggle for Indian independence by Dr. King and the black civil rights movement. We have conducted excellent training in the philosophy and principles of nonviolence, developed handbooks and manuals, and organized our protests to make them symbolic challenges to the unjust laws we strive to change. The 1987 Civil Disobedience Action at the U.S. Supreme Court, the 1988 ACT UP protest at the FDA, and scores of local ACT UP and Lesbian Avenger demonstrations around the country illustrate how deeply committed we are to nonviolent direct action.

But also present in our movement today is the expedient tendency to promote direct action for the sake of media attention, to go for the headline and damn the moral consequences. Several members of ACT UP–New York whom I interviewed mentioned the group's demonstration at Saint Patrick's Cathedral as a turning point in the group's history. While David Barr and Peter Staley remembered the event unfavorably, Larry Kramer and Ann Northrop regarded the action as one that advanced the stature of ACT UP. Barr said:

> I think there was a turning point [in ACT UP] with the church action. There was conversation on the floor about that action before it happened, and after, in the analysis of the action by the group. At that point, ACT UP's desire to do the demo the way they wanted to do it, because that's what they liked, overrode how this message was going to be perceived. Tom's [Keane] act [of throwing the wafer on the floor] was one of the purest acts of civil disobedience. Here was this Catholic choirboy, his act was a very personal statement. But in the larger political context and what the group was supposed to be doing, it wasn't just the act, but the whole approach to the action [which] caused problems. The goal became more about personal expression and less about change.

This desecration of what many people believe is sacred was an act that critics were right to challenge—not because Keane or ACT UP was wrong to demonstrate at the church, but because of the lack of moral integrity of the action itself. Is that principle—that we cherish no one else's religion—what we stand for? Knowing Keane and many of the participants of ACT UP, I know the answer is an emphatic no. Yet what is it in our righteous anger that obscures from us the truth that the end does not justify the means? As Dr. Martin Luther King once wrote, "[Nonviolent resistance] makes it possible for the individual to secure moral means through moral ends . . . this is where nonviolent resistance breaks with communism and with all of those systems which argue that the end justifies the means, because we realize that the end is preexistent in the means. In the long run of history, destructive means cannot bring about constructive ends."

There are scores of incidents in which movement activists, struggling against the immoral realities of government negligence and cultural prejudice, have themselves resorted to violent means. Sometimes the goal has been symbolic, as when direct-action participants in Colorado entered a cemetery and placed signs and symbols on gravestones to protest government inaction on AIDS while we died. Two protestors were charged with federal crimes, and an activist from Chicago whom I respect a great deal, Debbie Gould, asked me for support in defending these persons. Gould argued that their act was a political protest and the government's prosecution was an infringement on direct action. While I agreed that government sanctions against political protest are something we must always suspect, I argued that the action itself was troubling, for it violated others' notions of the sacred. How did this action differ from the desecration of cemeteries by neo-Nazi skinheads? As two veteran activists, grounded in a feminist ethics of mutual respect, Gould and I were able to discuss, disagree, and part without acrimony. I believe some actions are not morally justifiable if our shared value is nonviolence. Of course I do not decry self-defense when one is violently attacked, but the idea of nonviolence, as developed in the black civil rights movement, has great integrity and is a principle that a morally centered gay and lesbian movement ought to debate and, I hope, affirm.

MOVEMENT RESTRUCTURING

On the structural level, the problems we confront require nothing less than a thorough reconstruction of gay and lesbian politics; we have to change the ways we now operate in order to work more effectively. Here are some guiding principles and several of their practical consequences. Among the questions are local versus national organizing (which leads me to emphasize infrastructure rather than superstructure); interaction with straight society (which results in my arguing for a move out of the ghetto and a new relationship to government); and greater accessibility of the movement and its institutions.

I believe that our recent political history is dispositive: we need to spend far more energy and money on statewide gay and lesbian organizations and local political units than on national ones. This is not to say we must entirely abandon the national realm; rather, that we must link it more directly with local strategies and actions. The base of any political movement is where people live, work, congregate, and make family —a reality as true for gay and lesbian as for our straight supporters. One political impact of the closet has been that we short-circuited the process of building a base from the ground up, instead creating national organizations essentially unconnected to local ones. This national superstructure is a disaster and must be modified.

Here are just four of the countless possibilities for infrastructure development within our movement:

1. Federate the state gay and lesbian movement. We need to create a federation that would unify existing state organizations into a national whole. Either HRCF or NGLTF could undertake such a project, but if they choose not to, then the state agencies ought to come together on their own, as gay health clinics and community centers have, to form a federation. Such a national organization would better mobilize voters to support gay rights, coordinate their actions, and leverage gay power. Related to this, we must commit ourselves to strengthening our state groups. For example, the Massachusetts Gay-Lesbian Political Caucus is a statewide lobby; it has no staff, no office, and no ongoing profile in the local media. This could easily be changed if we contributed dues to our statewide groups to pay for staff. The staff would then organize the local queer communities so that we could act on pro-gay and antigay legislation and media coverage, or engage in political activity—such as voter registration, voter education, and public forums on gay rights issues. Strengthening the movement at the state level pays quick dividends in the state legislature and in local power where we live.

2. Organize inside each state. Existing state organizations could gain great strength by tightening their connections to local activists and organizations, clubs, and social networks. Each local organization should turn over its mailing list to the existing state groups to bolster their bases. Considerations of turf must be suspended for a commitment to movement building. Again, using the example of Massachusetts, there are scores of strong local groups of every stripe, from business associations to social clubs, yet I venture that most of them have no relationship whatsoever to the statewide Gay Political Caucus.

3. Create a national communications network to be in touch with and train gay and lesbian activists. New communications technology offers us a way to connect political organizations in an efficient way.

The network of my dreams is a national organization linking as many state and local gay activists as possible, via computer, modem, and satellite-communication technology.

4. We must establish more think tanks. We cannot devise policy solutions to the problems that confront us unless some thinkers dream them up. The academic movement is completely unlinked to the political movement, and think tanks could help make a connection. More research into nearly every aspect of queer life is needed so that we can determine and pursue our shared goals. Currently two major think tanks are gearing up, the new Institute for Gay and Lesbian Strategic Studies (IGLASS) and the NGLTF Policy Institute. These are great beginnings, and there is plenty of room for more. The right musters dozens of think tanks to generate ideas and shape their cultural and political debate. If we wish to stop reacting and start going on the offensive, such activism is essential.

Another fundamental matter we need to debate is our relationship with straight society in general and with the government in particular. Consideration of straight-gay relationships implicates our largely unquestioned separatism as a people and a movement. During a panel discussion, the activist Sandy Lowe suggested that the gay movement struggles over whether it wants to cohere to a larger community, take our part in the world, or remain on its own. The relationship we wish to have with straight culture is yet to be resolved. Should it be one of integration, assimilation, opposition, rejection, or transformation? Must it be one of the above? Can it be all of the above? Or should it be none of the above? My personal answer lies in my assumption that our movement seeks the maximum freedom possible, not the compromised minimum. We seek to be gay or lesbian not merely in the shelter of the ghetto or in the "privacy" of the bedroom or in the confines of a more spacious closet. Rather, through our movement, we seek to expand the possibility of gay and lesbian people living open and unstigmatized lives, making our contributions in the world wherever we find ourselves. Some may argue, as Leo Bersani does, that such a dispersed presence is in fact the pursuit of gay absence. Others, like the thoughtful journalist Masha Gessen, have cautioned me that ghettos are as much places of shelter as they are places that confine us.

My feeling about the gay and lesbian ghetto is that it is not a destination but a point of departure or origin. Queerness gives me a base from which I enter the world; it does not limit me to things or matters gay or lesbian, just as my South Asian identity does not limit me to organizing only on matters Indian. I wish for our movement a commitment to leave the ghetto, to be interventionist in the political, cultural, and spiritual life of our world.

Related to this desire for a new relationship with the broader culture is the new relationship we seek with government. In each era of our movement, we have articulated a slightly different view of the role we see the government playing in our lives and the political role we see ourselves playing. Yet, because of our short history, each of these different views of queer politics is manifested today. For example, Mattachine-era activists faced red-baiting, government persecution, and charges of being morally inferior and therefore disqualified for full integration into society. These pre-Stonewall activists sought to restrain the power of the police state over our lives. They saw their political work principally as the building of gay and lesbian self-esteem. The work of uncovering our self-hatred and reconstructing whole selves remains a huge piece of each queer person's battle.

In another era, post-Stonewall activists were influenced by feminism, connected the personal to the political, and posited that coming out and making homosexual and bisexual people visible in every aspect of social life would transform both us and society at large. Our principal demand of government was that it stop harassing us, treat us fairly, and leave us alone. Living our lives openly and honestly became part of doing political work. Today, this philosophy still thrives in gay and lesbian communities across the nation. Political organizations fight government harassment; gay people demand the right to be left alone; coming out remains a top individual and movementwide priority; and visibility remains our most effective weapon.

AIDS activism served at once to organize us politically and to level a new set of demands on government; from insisting that government get out of our lives, we turned to government for help in saving our lives. Paradoxically, government was the obstacle (a bureaucracy that moved too slowly, a tool of the antigay right) and salvation (the institution that had the duty and resources to help us in this crisis). We demanded our fair share of government services; and through the funding we secured, we began to build a social service movement that dramatically increased gay and lesbian cohesion and visibility in local communities. Today, government responsiveness to gay and lesbian constituents is a mixed blessing. Such support allows us to combat violence, fund youth service programs, and gain health care services, but it leaves us dependent in frightening ways on an institution that still refuses to recognize our full equality.

Currently, we are locked in ideological warfare about our movement's view of the role of government. So, gay conservatives at the Log Cabin Republican Club assert that they agree with the "less government, lower taxes" refrain of the straight conservatives who run Congress. At the same time, Log Cabin states that its top legislative priority for 1995 is to secure full funding of the Ryan White AIDS Care act, a program that epitomizes the New Deal federalism they criticize. It's not clear how gay Republican leaders (or their conservative gay Independent and Democratic counterparts) resolve the dilemma of being for less government and making sure that gay people still get as big (or bigger) of a share of the pie. At the other extreme are queer liberals unable to articulate any position on the state's role in serving people. So much of what we seek as a community requires the involvement of government, whether it is for attention to problems like antigay violence, for recognition of gay marriage, for a cure for AIDS, or for tolerance and education as we work to change entrenched attitudes. Yet much of what we have gained derives from our engagement of the private, market-based economic culture of our nation: workplace non-discrimination policies, domestic partner benefits, widespread recognition as competent employees and responsible citizens. These and other differences have yet to be debated vigorously among us. Ideological polarization should not obviate the conversation we still need to have.

My view is that both "devolution" (moving programs and power from the federal to the state level) and privatization (shifting responsibility for services from public agencies to private enterprises) are dangerous for queer people. The fundamental issue is control and disparate treatment. Because gay, lesbian, bisexual, and transgendered people, and our allies, are not well organized at the state level (despite the existence of more than a dozen statewide gay and lesbian organizations), we will not have adequate say in the way our tax dollars are spent by state legislatures and local political bodies. With the devolution of political power, we can expect a nation dotted with homophobic territories, no-fly zones, in which gay and lesbian people are not welcome and are, indeed, singled out for discriminatory treatment. Twenty-three states maintain laws criminalizing same-sex sexual behavior (sodomy laws); five enforce such laws only against homosexual people. Meanwhile, new laws stigmatizing queer people are passed as the devolution of civil rights continues. Utah's legislature, for example, recently passed a law banning gay marriage in the state and refusing to recognize marriage laws of other states that do validate same-sex marriage.

While the impact of the new federalism is not clear, the effort to shrink federal control over many social programs (education, welfare, health, even law enforcement) may on its surface have little effect on gay people, who have so few federally recognized rights. But in fact such defederalization would require gay and lesbian activists to adapt in several ways. First, a restriction of federal lawmaking will attenuate the way we leverage the political clout of communities with a high density of gay and lesbian voters to benefit less organized or lower-population communities. The Ryan White bill is an example of such leveraging. It was passed in 1990 as a result of the lobbying efforts of AIDS Action Council, a group funded by several of the largest AIDS service organizations in the country, and was headed at the time by the talented Jean McGuire. The bill made funds available for AIDS-related care to the cities hardest hit by AIDS and constructed careful formulas for making funds available to racial minority communities. The clout of the big-city groups actually benefited a number of smaller communities as well. If federal programs such as Ryan White are gutted, and funds made available to states only under discretionary block grants, the site of political action will shift to the gubernatorial and state legislative level. We must ready ourselves for this change by moving away from our focus on national politics and strengthening our movement locally.

Another reason the new conservative federalism requires us to reconsider our political strategy is its treatment of civil rights. In *The Color of Gender*, the political scientist Zillah Eisenstein summarizes how the Reagan-Bush–dominated Supreme Court gutted civil rights laws: "Racial discrimination has now been narrowed to mean only specifically factually proven discriminatory action against an individual. The understanding of race as a structural element of society has been replaced with a view of disparate individuals. The ability to use racial categories to address prior discrimination has been destroyed: there are no categories as such—hence, no institutional discrimination. Even the recognition of race as a category unfairly distinguishes the person of color from a white person." The process of rolling back federally guaranteed civil rights is today well established. Since 1977, when the Supreme Court decided *Baake*, the backlash to civil rights has become a carefully coordinated assault. States, not the federal government, will create "new" civil rights. The current battle in California to restrict government services to immigrants, illegal or legal, and to ban affirmative action represents the right's recognition of this fundamental shift.

But the civil rights movement has not recognized the implications of the shift. The black movement, women's movement, and the gay and lesbian movement continue to concentrate on the national level, acting as if the groundswell from the right can be countered nationally. None of our movements works to build strategic electoral majorities for civil rights in state and local political districts. I believe that if racist bills were introduced in the state legislatures of the South, they would pass with the same ease that antigay and anti-abortion bills currently pass. In the context of this displacement of civil rights from the national level to the state level, how much sense does it make for the gay movement to keep the federal Employment Non-Discrimination Act (ENDA) as its top legislative priority, rather than invest its resources into building grassroots electoral power? In my view, ENDA serves a symbolic purpose—to publicize the problem of employment discrimination—but it will not pass in a climate so hostile to federal civil rights. Perhaps we should consider enacting state versions of ENDA first, since more comprehensive gay and lesbian rights bills have repeatedly failed.

One more effect of the conservative wave on gay and lesbian people is the right's move to privatize many of the state's functions while bolstering the state's police power over individual rights. Cloaked in the appealing mantra of lower taxes, the right is playing a fascinating shell game: our tax dollars now go to support private, for-profit companies that provide the same services. The argument is that they do so more efficiently, and if they don't, a competitor will arise who will: the market replaces the public square. Two questions arise with this privatized model of government: the first has to do with the public's control over the private enterprises, and the second has to do with the assumption that private is better than public in most situations. In the first instance, the power of the voter (and the meaning of democratic government itself) is further eroded. Rather than requiring government to organize and deliver certain services to its people, we now elect public officials who use our money to award contracts to private companies. This enhances the power of the middleman—the politician—while reducing the power of the buyer—the taxpayer. The related assumption, that the private sector is always better than the public sector, is as much a myth as the converse. In the savings-and-loan debacle of the last two decades, for instance, the public has been forced to bail out the private sector because profiteers ran amuck, without adequate regulation. Privatization of education, prisons, police departments, fire departments, and other essential government services poses enormous complications—in accountability, oversight, and control—that are rarely discussed either within the gay and lesbian movement or in the mainstream media.

What impact would such privatization have on our people? How, for example, would privately run schools deal with the Rainbow Curriculum? Will such schools be more or less susceptible than public schools have been to pressure from lobbies like the American Family Association and the Christian Coalition? Will they follow the lead of the corporate sector where nondiscrimination is practiced (Levi Strauss, Apple Computer), or will they pursue discrimination as some have done (Cracker Barrel)? We simply don't know. Our movement must study the situation before it jumps on a bandwagon and must prepare for whatever outcome appears.

A final challenge regarding our movement's structure relates to the accessibility and accountability of our institutions. Politics is still seen by too many of us as a dirty word or a distant concern, better handled by others. To change this view requires a commitment to greater democracy by gay and lesbian political institutions themselves. Many organizations today are inaccessible and elitist, in part because they are not structured around chapters, in which people can participate in their communities. It is no coincidence that chapter-based groups like ACT UP, GLAAD, and Lesbian Avengers are among those which enjoy the broadest participation. The major national gay and AIDS organizations have been asked repeatedly to launch chapter programs, and I renew that call.

A more fundamental problem comes from the class-based elitism of our organizations. There is undeniable truth that the average gay person feels that his or her membership is not welcome unless it is accompanied by lots of money. This myth needs to be countered by the political groups. In fact, membership is affordable to anyone who wants to join. The base rate of some groups is $10 a year, and the policy of most gay institutions is not to reject people from membership for their inability to pay. The aura of elitism comes from the overrepresentation of wealthy and professional people in our organizations as Board and staff members. To a large extent, the problem is endemic to nonprofit organizations. This structural, and some may argue necessary, elitism speaks volumes about the inability of the left to be anything more than an armchair critic of class. If we are committed to broadening the political involvement of working-class and poorer gay people, the class biases of

$250 events must be offset with something more affordable—or free. Indeed, many people may argue that this is the way of the world, and that, as with every other movement, gay liberation will remain the province of the middle to professional classes. If it does, its potential for success will also be limited. History shows that being middle class or wealthy does not protect any group from persecution. As economic conditions deteriorate for many middle-class people—a large number of whom are gay or lesbian—a movement that does not speak to their concerns abandons them to the religious conservatives, much as the left abandoned moral issues to the right in the 1970s.

PROJECTS FOR A TRULY EQUAL FUTURE

Lastly, the question of individual action remains—for us and for every movement for social change, the most pressing and most accessible one. As the courageous Southern writer Lillian Smith wrote in 1942, when she urged white Southerners to take action on racism, "It is now a matter of good and decent people having the *will*. Yes, it is true: in times of peace and ease, customs change slowly. But in times of strain and stress customs change quickly . . . Things are happening; things are going to continue to happen. We can sputter and break a blood vessel or we can roll up our sleeves and get to work to make them happen smoothly and harmoniously, The choice is ours only in *what we do about it;* not in the changes themselves" (emphasis in original).

I end this book by being extremely specific. These projects reflect my view that vision is sharpest in its practice, grounded by a moral framework. Throughout, I have offered theoretical choices in order to overcome the impasse we face in certain areas, be it financing, structure, leadership, racial and gender division, or specific issues like AIDS. Now, I want to suggest projects for individuals interested in gay organizing. The notion of not ending with a globalizing conclusion, but with a practical list of activities, stems from my own frustration in reading books that end in rhetoric or in ideas that are so impractically big that they boggle the mind. Some of my own ideas may strike people as equally impractical: Who will fund them, who will oversee them? But I believe most of the ideas can be carried out within the existing framework of our movement, by motivated individuals taking action with others wherever they live. The projects offer a partial, and by no means complete, blueprint for queer activism over the next few years. It is a modest proposal, inspired by a buoyant, unshakable sense of hope in the future of social justice. It's a list of work still to be done, much of which I am confident has already begun, and will in fact be completed long after my lifetime. Organizing involves imagined solutions, ideas for bringing people together, strategies for making change, means of connecting and empowering people, and efforts to build stronger organizations or invent new projects to make the world safer and friendlier toward our people. Only a fraction of queer organizing ideas are achieved. But in the thrill of generating ideas and strategies lies the transformative power and potential of community organizing.

SUGGESTIONS FOR THE ANTIPOLITICAL

My premise is that many gay and lesbian people remain unaware how easy it is to be "political" (which I define as being passionate about ideas, policies, and social justice), nor do they consider how political they already are, much less how much fun it might be to link up with other political persons. My suggestions call for exploration, open-mindedness, and commitment.

1. Start a discussion group with friends or acquaintances. Do it for one year. Read and discuss magazine articles, books about gay and lesbian history, or identify hot topics that interest you and create a list of films, videos, music, or articles on them and then discuss. All political change begins locally—with you and your consciousness.

2. Use the phone, computer, and gay and lesbian press to discover the groups in your area—urban, rural, or suburban. Explore them, whether you get involved or not, whether you are out of the closet or not. At least find out what is out there. Notice what you think is missing. Ask the people involved in projects that interest you what they do. Tell them what interests you. Explore groups you are not necessarily interested in at first glance (like a bowling league or a direct-action group). Push yourself to learn about your community institutions outside the bars and consider volunteering for them.

3. Make sure you are registered to vote. Find out what groups in your area, if any, tell queer voters what candidates are friendly; get on their mailing lists. Find out who all your elected officials are; write down each one's name, address, phone and fax numbers next to the

phone at home. This is easy to do. Use your phone book; call the League of Women Voters; call the gay national groups. You will be ready to respond when you get mad about an issue. You will have handy all the stuff you need!

4. Make a commitment to join at least two gay or lesbian political groups—one local and one national. Attend at least two gay- and lesbian-friendly events this year. They could be your local pride rally, a concert by Sweet Honey in the Rock or Melissa Etheridge, a play, a speech by a political activist, a meeting of a local political group, or a regional or national gay political conference. Join at least *two* groups and attend at least two events, and I guarantee you it will double the clout of your local, state, and national political movement.

5. Make it a point to read at least one local and at least one national gay or lesbian publication on a regular basis, like: *The Advocate* (Los Angeles), *Out* (New York), *Poz* (New York), *Washington Blade* (D.C.). If you don't like print, you can look into other kinds of media to keep up with current queer affairs, like Network Q, a monthly video magazine, or local cable TV shows, like Dyke TV and Gay Cable Network.

6. Visit your local gay and lesbian or feminist and alternative bookstore at least once this year, if you have not, and twice if you have! Just drop by and check it out; you will be amazed at the networks and resources you will find. Check out the following mail-order businesses if you live in a rural area: Lambda Rising (D.C.), Giovanni's Room (Philadelphia), A Different Light (San Francisco, New York, Los Angeles), or Ladyslipper Distribution (Durham, North Carolina).

7. Stop collaborating! Come out of the closet in more and more aspects of your life, unless you feel your life is threatened if you do so. You know all the arguments. Please do it for yourself. And do it for our future. National Coming Out Day (based at HRCF in Washington) provides great resources for you to engage in this act of moral courage and visionary resistance! Come on; it's a lot of fun out here, and we need you when the going gets tough and when it gets fabulous.

8. Be open-minded and practice tolerance when it comes to your gay and lesbian brothers and sisters. Try to understand and appreciate that political diversity means we will not agree with each other at all times. Try to appreciate that racial diversity means that gay people of color exist and are affected by any curtailment of services or programs based on racial prejudice. Struggle means that we will attempt to communicate even when we disagree. Don't fall prey to the politics of meanness!

9. Change your attitude toward gay and lesbian politics. Make a commitment—to yourself—that you will see yourself as a political person. This may call for a shift in attitude, in stance. If you care at all about any gay or lesbian person, about being queer yourself, about the institutions and community organizations in your town—declare yourself! Don't be afraid! Take responsibility.

SUGGESTIONS FOR THE ALREADY POLITICAL

This list is aimed at those who are toiling away in the movement, the millions of folk who march in Pride celebrations each year, the hundreds of thousands who came to the 1994 Stonewall 25 March, the 1993 March on Washington, and the millions of us touched by the loss from AIDS of someone we cared about.

1. Create a discussion group. I think this is essential for veteran activists to revitalize themselves. We need connection, a space to talk about ideas and our work as activists. It may be another monthly meeting, but it is one that will nourish you directly. The group can get together to share personally, talk about issues, read an article and book, and talk or invite a speaker to lead a discussion. Keep it small and simple.

2. Focus and streamline your commitments. Many activists I know find themselves overcommitted and overwhelmed. Cut back! We need each other in the movement for the long haul; don't burn out trying to do it all. We sometimes fail to cut back because we fear no one else will pick up the slack, but often we are being grandiose, denying opportunities to others who want to get involved by assuming that they are not qualified, too green, or not informed enough. Although most of us feel that no one can do as good a job as we can, we need to let others get involved, and if we are more realistic about our time commitments, we will be more effective.

3. Mentor local activists. Make yourself available to sponsor at least two people in the coming year. Teach them the skills and the history you know. This is not a dating game; it is a way to develop leadership and pass it on.

4. Mend one fence per year! Many veteran gay and lesbian organizers I know are angry at someone (or many ones) in their communities. This personal warfare inhibits the development of a stronger

movement, because people refuse to work together, sabotage the work
of folk they don't like, and much more. Don't fall into that trap. If each
of us swallowed pride, self-will, and righteousness and mended fences
with one colleague—I mean really, not just superficially—imagine how
much stronger the local movements would be!

5. Reach out to our allies. Find out what allied organizations are up
to in your community. In particular, check out the work of your local
NOW chapter, NAACP chapter, NARAL chapter, ACLU office,
ADL, and religious denominations that are supportive of gay and lesbian people. We have allies. We are not alone. But we need to find and
know each other.

6. Make explicit your commitment to opposing racial and gender-
and class-based injustice. Although political differences may prevent
some people from taking this step, I pose it nevertheless for a large
number of people who I know harbor these commitments in their
hearts. The importance of being explicit is something each of us who
has fought against silence can appreciate; silent support for antiracism
or antisexist policies is not enough. We must acknowledge that many
gay and lesbian people are equally committed to opposing racism, sexism, economic injustice, and sexual-orientation prejudice.

7. Work statewide. Get involved with your existing state gay and
lesbian organization. Many states have such networks; few are staffed;
all need more involvement. If there are no state groups, network with
activists across the state to form one. If there is more than one, work
with the group closest to your heart. We need strong, staffed, nonparti-
san gay and lesbian and bi and trans political groups in every single state
capital in this country. There is a full plate of work to be done in state
legislatures, from media education, to fighting antigay laws, to curriculum work in schools, to funding for projects that we care about.

8. Live out everywhere you go. Make sure you are out in more and
more aspects of your life. Coming out never ceases. Don't give in to
complacency; they don't know until you tell them. Tell your family,
especially the younger nieces, nephews, and others *before* they adopt
prejudicial attitudes!

9. Communicate as much as you confront. The key to our future lies
in communication with our neighbors, colleagues, friends, and communities. We have to speak up about what we face as gay people. Don't
hide it; talk about it.

10. Join one national and one local group as a dues-paying member.

Even veteran activists are often not card-carrying members of our political organizations, national or state.

11. Don't despair, no matter what. Every action you take, every step you take, contributes to the possibility of gay and lesbian freedom. We need faith to guide us through the bleak times and the times when justice prevails.

SOME BIG IDEAS FOR THE BRAVE

A handful of us may want to tackle some of the bigger challenges facing our movement. They require resources, experience, and contacts.

1. Create a direct-communication movement. Our old direct-action movement needs to be revitalized and reborn as something we might christen a direct-communication movement. People reaching out to other people is the most important new grassroots tactic we can implement. We have become locked into seeing political change solely in dualistic terms—either we protest or we appease; either we confront or we assimilate. Engaging in communication does not mean one or the other. Such projects move beyond the dualistic notion of us and them and strive to break down barriers to communication and understanding.

For example, when the Colorado measure passed in 1992, a number of queer activists proposed to Colorado activists that, instead of a boycott movement, we engage in a "come out to Colorado" campaign. We proposed the establishment of a sister city program between Colorado cities and gay communities in cities around the nation. Activists from the sister city would work with Colorado-based folk to plan a "good works" campaign: we would come in and pick up litter, build shelters, volunteer at soup kitchens, teach in literacy programs—in short, come out to Colorado and display the kind of citizenship that gay and lesbian people believe in and are capable of. Instead of boycotting, our goal would be to flood the state media with pro-gay and pro-lesbian stories, and reach out and educate straight Coloradans about how wrong their vote was. This kind of campaign has never really been attempted.

In 1994, a small project was launched in Missouri by the Progressive Student Leadership Exchange. Organizer Gary Schiff, from Minneapolis, organized a six-week summer program to bring students and young activists from Minnesota down to Missouri to work against antigay and antilesbian initiatives. Missouri Freedom Summer was modeled directly on the civil rights movement's Freedom Summer. The project worked so well that the Progressive Student Leadership Exchange is planning such efforts in Maine and other states facing antigay referenda.

2. National media campaigns. Since the people with money in our communities have not decided that this kind of queer visibility is vital, movement activists must continue the guerrilla PR tactics we have perfected over the past twenty-five years. Sadly, too few media campaigns aimed at improving AIDS or gay news coverage ever reach the airwaves. We cannot let up just because the straight press has accepted some of us. Educational messages conveyed through the straight media are vital to expanding understanding of our issues and lives.

Specifically, I think we need news-focused campaigns aimed at ensuring fair and accurate local media coverage. This is a project that interested activists can quickly participate in under the auspices of GLAAD. Another kind of media activism we need is the creation of useful videos, audio tapes, and other materials to communicate the truth of gay and lesbian lives to straight America. We still lack an effective tape that authoritatively responds to the propaganda put out by the right.

3. Better ways to mobilize and motivate our families. The good work that PFLAG does is largely disconnected from the queer political movement—mostly because of our failure to take our parents and families seriously as our allies. The National AIDS Memorial Quilt is a perfect example of an underutilized network of supporters. Why are all of those volunteers, families, and friends—literally millions touched by losing someone with AIDS in their close circle of family—not organized into a powerful AIDS lobby? I recognize our families' need to grieve a loss in a way that heals, yet many remain frustrated by their desire for greater political action on the issue, long after the tears have dried. That frustration could be channeled into making the political effort on AIDS more effective, as the Family AIDS Network attempts to do and as Mothers' Voices Against AIDS has done.

4. The common movement. Because many activists are now talking about the need to work across the lines of identity-based politics, the time is right for us to negotiate a common movement for social justice. Among those embarking on the process are the Center for Democratic Renewal in Atlanta, the network known as Southerners on New Ground (SONG), broad national civil liberties groups like the

ACLU and People for the American Way, scores of small grassroots activist projects and campaigns, like the New Party, the National Alliance of Organizers, and intellectuals like bell hooks, Cornel West, and June Jordan. What is still missing is an umbrella organization to enable local activists to participate in a national process of movement building —in short, a progressive equivalent to the Christian Coalition. The Rainbow Coalition has not yet managed to do such organizing, tied as it is to the personal goals of its founder, Jesse Jackson, but it has the potential. Gay and lesbian activists who share the dream of a common movement must find each other at the myriad political gay conferences we attend and launch a campaign to reach out and connect to nongay folk who harbor a similar vision.

NOTES

1. VIRTUAL EQUALITY

P. 1 W. H. Auden, "Leap Before You Look," *Collected Poems*, ed. by Edward Mendelson (New York: Vintage, 1991), p. 313. The quote from Nicholas Negroponte is from *Wired Magazine*, vol. 1, no. 6, 1993.

P. 3 Chandler Burr, "Newt Gingrich speaks out," *Washington Blade*, November 25, 1994, vol. 25, no. 48, p. 1.

P. 5 Suzanne Pharr, *Homophobia: A Weapon of Sexism* (New York: Chardon Press, 1988).

Virtual Nondiscrimination

P. 6 Tim McFeeley, Speech at Boston Human Rights Campaign Fund Dinner, Nov. 5, 1994, attended by author.

P. 7 An extensive assessment of the nature of antigay and lesbian discrimination exceeds the scope of this chapter. Several recent books present such comprehensive information. See, for example, Michael Nava and Robert Dawidoff, *Created Equal: Why Gay Rights Matter to Americans* (New York: St. Martin's Press, 1994); Richard Mohr, *Toward A More Perfect Union: Why Straight America Must Stand Up for Gay Rights* (Boston: Beacon Press, 1994); Tom Stoddard, *The Rights of Gay People*, (ACLU–Bantam, 1992).

P. 8 Lou Chibarro, Jr., "Rhode Island is odds-on favorite to pass rights law," *Washington Blade*, March 17, 1995, vol. 26, no. 11, p. 1.

P. 8 Lou Chibarro, Jr., "In the states few anti-gay bills surface," *Washington Blade*, March 10, 1995, vol. 26, no. 10, p. 24. Two weeks after this listing came out, the Montana State Legislature debated and passed a bill that would have required people convicted of sodomy to register their whereabouts with the state for the rest of their lives. The bill was reconsidered and revoked, two days after its passage, because of a general outcry.

P. 8 *Ibid.*, pp. 24–25. For information on the Montana bill and its eventual repeal, contact NGLTF Public Information Department, telephone (202) 332-6483.

P. 8 In a 6–1 decision rendered on Oct. 11, 1994, the Colorado State Supreme Court upheld a lower trial court's ruling that Colorado's antigay Amendment 2 was unconstitutional. See *New York Times*, October 12, 1994, p. A1.

P. 10 In testimony submitted on behalf of the Leadership Conference on Civil Rights to the U.S. Senate Committee on Labor and Human Resources, Georgetown University Law Professor Chai R. Feldblum summarized some data from complaints filed with state human rights commissions. Feldblum noted, for example, that in Massachusetts since the state antidiscrimination law passed in 1989, more than 330 complaints alleging sexual orientation discrimination have been filed with the Massachusetts Commission Against Discrimination; of these, 256 alleged employment discrimination. In New Jersey, 72 complaints were filed from 1982–1994; 25 of these alleged employment discrimination. In Connecticut, 50 complaints of employment related discrimination have been filed from 1991–1993. In Minnesota, 14 complaints have been filed since the law took effect in August 1993; 10 of these alleged employment discrimination. See "Statement of Chai R. Feldblum, Associate Professor of Law, Georgetown University Law Center in Support of S. 2238, The Employment

Non-Discrimination Act of 1994," July 29, 1994 (Leadership Conference on Civil Rights, 1629 K Street NW, Suite 1010, Washington DC 20006).

P. 10 The data provided in this chapter are based on a variety of publications by the National Gay and Lesbian Task Force, 1734 14th Street NW, Washington, DC 20009. Publications used for this chapter include: the *Anti-Gay/Lesbian Violence, Victimization and Harassment,* an annual report published since 1986; the *NGLTF Domestic Partnership Organizing Manual* (1992); the *Lesbian, Gay, Bisexual Civil Rights Protections in the U.S.* (Feb. 1994); *Report Summarizing Employment Discrimination Surveys* (1991). See also, Lambda Legal Defense & Education Fund, "Summary of States, Cities, & Counties Which Prohibit Discrimination Based on Sexual Orientation," UDEF, 666 Broadway, New York, NY 10012 (212)995-8585.

For a complete list of progay corporate policies, please contact the NGLTF Workplace Project at 2320 17th Street NW, Washington, DC 20009, telephone (202) 332-6483. Additional resources in this area are: Daniel B. Baker, Sean O'Brien Strub, Bill Henning, *Cracking the Corporate Closet* (NY: Harper Business, 1995).

P. 11 See *Boston Globe,* December 1, 1994.

P. 11 Peter Finn & Taylor McNeil, *The Response of the Criminal Justice System To Bias Crime: An Exploratory Review,* Submitted to National Institute of Justice, US Dept of Justice, 1987.

P. 11 Credit for the Hate Crimes Act has been taken by a lot of gay and lesbian leaders, but, in truth, such credit belongs to a small number of gay and straight people. The two gay people most responsible for this federal victory are Kevin Berrill and his then-colleague Peri Jude Radecic, the chief NGLTF lobbyist on the Hate Crime issue from 1988 to 1992. The straight allies who helped pass this bill were the Anti-Defamation League (especially Michael Liebermann), the ACLU Legislative Office (especially Diane Rust Tierney), the NAACP Legislative Office, the People for the American Way, and the legislative offices of Senator Paul Simon (D-IL), Congressman John Conyers (D-MI), and Representative Barney Frank (D-MA). Scores of local anti-violence activists from around the country also contributed by lobbying, writing letters and pushing their members of congress.

P. 12 Cindy Loose, "206 Anti-Gay Actions Cited in '94 Report on Violence," *Washington Post,* March 8, 1995.

P. 12 Criminal Justice Information Services, Uniform Crime Reports, "Hate Crime —1993," U.S. Department of Justice, June 1994, p. 1.

P. 12 For a list of antiviolence projects and reports they have released, contact, NGLTF Anti-Violence Project, telephone (202) 332-6483.

P. 12 Kevin Berrill, *Anti-Gay Violence, Victimization and Harassment in the United States, 1991,* p. 14 (NGLTF: Washington, DC).

P. 14 See, for example, Nan D. Hunter, "Life After Hardwick," 27 *Harvard Civil Rights Civil Liberties Law Review* 531 (1992).

P. 14 A notable national exception was the groundbreaking organizing done by Sue Hyde, who staffed a project to repeal sodomy laws at the National Gay and Lesbian Task Force (NGLTF) from 1986 to 1991. Hyde trained local and state activists in Southern states on sodomy law repeal and helped organize several statewide gay and lesbian organizations (including the hard-working Virginians for Justice and the Silver State Gay and Lesbian Task Force in Nevada).

P. 16 See Nancy Polikoff, "Lesbian and Gay Parenting: What's at Stake," *Gay Community News,* Fall 1993, p. 3.

P. 17 For further information, readers should contact the Gay and Lesbian and Straight and Teacher Network (GLSTN), headquartered in New York City.

P. 17 See Randy Shilts, *The Mayor of Castro Street* (New York: St. Martin's Press, 1982). See also essay by Barbara Gittings entitled "The Homosexual and the Church," printed in *The Same Sex: An Appraisal of Homosexuality,* Ralph W. Welge, ed. (Philadelphia: Pilgrim Press, 1969).

P. 18 For an extensive discussion of the Catholic Church's treatment of gay people, see the following: John McNeil, *The Church and the Homosexual* (Boston: Beacon Press,

1987); John McNeil, *Freedom, Glorious Freedom* (Boston: Beacon Press, 1994); Andrew Sullivan, "Alone Again," *The New Republic,* 1994; "Are God's Loving Words Meant for the Ears of Heterosexuals Only?" *National Catholic Reporter,* September 2, 1994. See also John Kennedy, "Episcopal Bishops Divided Over Sexuality," *Christianity Today,* February 1995; "Homosexuality Debate Strains American Baptist Churches of USA," *The Christian Century,* July 27, 1994, vol. 111, no. 21, p. 714 (1); "The Plight of the Presbyterians," *The Christian Century,* June 1, 1994, vol. 111, no. 18, p. 565 (2); "The Welcoming Denomination Faces Down Homophobia," *The World: The Journal of the Unitarian Universalist Association,* July–Aug. 1994.

Virtual Equality and Public Opinion

P. 19 Susan G. Hibbard, "The Right Response: A Survey of Voters' Attitudes on Gay-Related Questions," published by the National Gay and Lesbian Task Force Policy Institute, 2320 17th Street N.W., Washington, DC 20009, telephone (202) 332-6483 (March 17, 1994), p. 15.

P. 20 See Hibbard, p. 6; see also J. Davis and T. Smith. *General Social Surveys, 1972–1984.* (Chicago: NORC, 1984); E. Dejowski, "Public Endorsement of Restrictions on Three Aspects of Free Speech Expression by Homosexuals: Socio-demographic and trends analysis," *Journal of Homosexuality,* 23(4), 1–18.

P. 20 See polls by ABC, August 1987; *Los Angeles Times,* August 1987; Roper, August 1985; reported in Greg Herek, "Stigma, prejudice and violence against lesbians and gay men," in *Homosexuality: Research Implications for Public Policy,* J. Gonsiorek and J. Weinrich, eds. (Newbury Park, CA: Sage Publications, 1991), pp. 60–80. For polls from the 1990s, see, Hibbard (1994), cited above; Hart and Teeter Research Companies, NBC News, and the *Wall Street Journal,* June 1993; Gallup-CNN and *USA Today,* Aug. 1993.

P. 20 D. Moore, "Public Polarized on Gay Issue," *The Gallup Poll Monthly,* no. 331, (April 1993), pp. 30–33. In an unpublished paper entitled "AIDS and Homophobia: A Review of the Literature," researcher Greg Herek cites a number of earlier surveys in which opposition to the legalization of same-sex behavior ranged from 43 percent in 1977 to as high as 55 percent in 1986. (Herek, unpublished paper, 1994, p. 9).

P. 20 Hibbard, *supra,* p. 8.

P. 20 *Ibid.,* Table II: Equal Rights in Terms of Job Opportunities, p. 18.

P. 21 *Ibid.*

P. 21 At the beginning of 1994, antigay ballot initiatives were broached in 14 states and cities. Five of these petition drives gathered enough signatures to make the November 1994 ballot: in Oregon, Idaho, and Alachua County, Florida. While the statewide antigay ballot measure failed in Oregon (53 percent to 47 percent), two counties in the state passed antigay laws (Grants Pass and Lake County). In Idaho, the antigay measure lost by fewer than 3000 votes (out of 406,265 cast). And in Alachua County, Florida, two separate ballot measures passed: one repealed an existing local ordinance that banned discrimination (by 57 percent of the vote), and the other passed a new law forbidding passage of any gay rights bills in the future (by 59 percent). See Lisa Keen, "Initiatives in Oregon, Idaho appear defeated," *Washington Blade,* vol. 25, no. 46, Nov. 11, 1994, pp. A1, A33.

P. 22 Herek, G. M. (1984), "Beyond Homophobia: A social psychological perspective on attitudes toward lesbians and gay men." *Journal of Homosexuality,* 10(1/2), 1–21. Herek, G. M. (1995), "Psychological heterosexism in the United States." In A. R. D'Augelli and C. J. Patterson, eds., *Lesbian, Gay, and Bisexual Identities Across the Lifespan: Psychological Perspectives* (New York: Oxford University Press, 1995). Herek, G. M., and Capitanio, J. P. (1995), "Black Heterosexuals' Attitudes Toward Lesbians and Gay Men in the United States" *The Journal of Sex Research,* vol. 32 no. 2, pp. 95–105. A list of citations is available from the author of this book.

P. 23 Herek, *supra,* pp. 18–22.
P. 27 Hibbard, *supra,* p. 9.

Virtual Equality and the Closet

P. 28 Samuel S. Janus and Cynthia L. Janus, *The Janus Report on Sexual Behavior* (New York: John Wiley & Sons, 1993), p. 69.
P. 28 *Ibid.,* p. 4, pp. 69–70.
P. 28 Margaret L. Usdansky, "Study Fuels Homosexuality Debate," *USA Today,* Aug. 17, 1994, p. 8A.
P. 28 Joannie M. Schrof and Betsy Wagner, "Sex in America," *U.S. News & World Report,* October 17, 1994, pp. 74–81.
P. 29 See *Bi Any Other Name: Bisexual People Speak Out,* Loraine Hutchins and Lani Kahimanu, eds. (Boston: Alyson, 1991).
P. 29 *Ibid.,* p. 76.
P. 32 See Michelangelo Signorile, *Queer in America* (New York: Anchor Books, 1994); Larry Gross, *Contested Closets: The Politics and Ethics of Outing* (Minneapolis: University of Minnesota Press, 1993); Richard Mohr, *Gay Ideas: Outing and Other Controversies* (Boston: Beacon Press, 1992).

2. LEGITIMATION, LIBERATION, AND HISTORY

P. 35 David Wojnarowicz, *Close to the Knives: A Memoir of Disintegration* (New York: Vintage, 1991), p. 144.
P. 35 Lou Chibarro, Jr., "Log Cabin: GOP Takeover Was 'Best Thing for Gay Movement,'" *Washington Blade,* vol. 25, no. 49, December 2, 1994, p. 14.
P. 37 John D'Emilio, *Sexual Politics, Sexual Communities: The Making of a Homosexual Minority in the United States* (Chicago: University of Chicago Press, 1983), p. 110.
P. 38 Bruce Bawer, *A Place at the Table* (New York: Simon & Schuster, 1993), p. 56.
P. 38 Adrienne Rich, "Compulsory Heterosexuality and Lesbian Existence," in *Powers of Desire: The Politics of Sexuality,* Ann Snitow, Christine Stansell, and Sharon Thompson, eds. (New York: Monthly Review Press, 1983), pp. 177–205.
P. 38 This point is also emphasized by the scholar Margaret Cruikshank, in her helpful overview, *The Gay and Lesbian Liberation Movement* (New York: Routledge, 1992).

Pre–World War II Era

P. 39 See George Chauncey, *Gay New York: Gender, Urban Culture and the Making of the Gay Male World, 1890–1940* (New York: Basic Books, 1994), p. 100, quoting Jonathan Ned Katz, "The Invention of Heterosexuality," *Socialist Review* 20 (January–March 1990), pp. 7–34. Chauncey's book challenges the notion that "nineteenth-century medical discourse constructed the 'homosexual' as a personality type, and that the appearance of the homosexual in medical discourse should be taken as indicative of or synonymous with the homosexual's appearance in the culture as a whole" (pp. 26–27).
P. 39 Elaine Showalter, *Sexual Anarchy: Gender and Culture at the Fin de Siècle* (New York: Penguin Books, 1990), pp. 3–4.
P. 39 Michael Bronski, *Culture Clash: The Making of Gay Sensibility* (Boston: South End Press, 1984), pp. 58–64.
P. 39 See, generally, Barry Adam, *The Making of a Gay and Lesbian Movement,* (Boston: Twayne Publishers, 1987), pp. 17, 24, 50; Cruikshank, *supra.,* p. 5. See, also,

John Lauritsen and David Thorstad, *The Early Homosexual Rights Movement, 1864–1935* (New York: Times Change Press, 1974); James Steakley, *The Homosexual Emancipation Movement in Germany* (New York: Arno, 1975); Hans Georg Stumke and Rudi Finkler, *Rosa Winkel, Rosa Listen* (Hamburg: Rowholt, 1981).

P. 40 See, generally, Adam, *supra*, pp. 17, 24, 50; Cruikshank, *supra*, p. 5.

P. 40 Dr. Klaus Mueller, interview in *The Advocate*, May 4, 1993. A firsthand account of one gay man's experience in a Nazi concentration camp was written by Heinz Heger, in a book called *The Men with the Pink Triangle*, trans. by David Fernbach (Boston, Alyson Publications, 1980).

P. 40 An account of the Chicago Society for Human Rights written by Henry Gerber in the 1950s is published in Jonathan Katz's *Gay American History: Lesbians and Gay Men in the USA* (New York: Avon, 1978), pp. 581–591.

P. 40 Jonathan Ned Katz, ed., *Gay American History: Lesbians and Gay Men in the U.S.A.*, (New York: Avon Books, 1976), pp. 581–597, about the Chicago Society for Human Rights.

P. 41 Barry Adam, *supra*, p. 67.

P. 41 George Chauncey, *Gay New York: Gender, Urban Culture, and the Making of the Gay Male World, 1890–1940*.

P. 41 *Ibid.*, p. 47.

P. 41 *Ibid.*, p. 48.

P. 42 *Ibid.*, p. 101.

P. 42 Elizabeth Kennedy and Madeline Davis, *Boots of Leather, Slippers of Gold: The History of a Lesbian Community* (New York: Routledge, 1993), p. 6.

P. 42 *Ibid.*, p. 384.

P. 43 Chauncey, *supra*, p. 105.

P. 43 *Ibid.*, pp. 105–106.

P. 43 *Ibid.*, p. 106.

P. 43 This summary does not do justice to Chauncey's nuanced treatment of these developments. See in particular his introduction and chap. 4, especially pp. 111–127. See also, Jonathan Ned Katz, *The Invention of Heterosexuality* (NY: Dutton, 1995).

P. 45 Peter Frieberg, "Poll: 1 in 3 Gays Voted for the GOP," *Washington Blade*, November 25, 1994, vol. 25, no. 48, p. 25.

P. 45 Stuart Timmons, "Managed Scare: Why Are Leaders of the Gay Community Trying to Defeat the Single-Payer Health Initiative?" *L.A. Village View*, Oct. 21–27, 1994, p. 32.

P. 45 *Ibid.*, pp. 32–34, 46–48.

P. 45 *Ibid.*, p. 33.

P. 46 *Ibid.*, p. 48.

P. 46 Kennedy and Davis, *supra*, p. 386.

The Post–World War II Movement

P. 47 Allan Bérubé, *Coming Out Under Fire: The History of Lesbians and Gay Men in World War Two* (New York: Free Press, 1990).

P. 47 *Ibid.*, for VBA reference, see p. 249; for quotation, see p. 271.

P. 48 *Ibid.*, p. 249.

P. 48 John D'Emilio, *supra*, see chap. 3.

P. 49 Jonathan Katz, *supra*, p. 620.

P. 49 *Oxford Dictionary of English Etymology*, edited by C. T. Onions (Oxford, England: Oxford University Press, 1966), p. 561.

P. 49 D'Emilio, *supra*, p. 67.

P. 49 Shilts, *The Times of Harvey Milk*, p. 26.

P. 49 Toby Marotta, *The Politics of Homosexuality* (Boston: Houghton Mifflin, 1981), p. 9.

P. 50   Harry Hay, interview reprinted in *Gay American History,* Katz, ed., pp. 621–622.

P. 50   D'Emilio, *supra,* pp. 67–72.

P. 50   Del Martin and Phyllis Lyon, *Lesbian/Woman* (San Francisco: Bantam, 1972); see also John D'Emilio, *supra,* pp. 92–107.

P. 50   See D'Emilio, *supra,* pp. 196–209; Toby Marotta, *supra,* pp. 22–47; Martin Duberman, *Stonewall* (New York: Dutton, 1993), pp. 100–117; Barry Adam, *supra,* pp. 64–74.

P. 51   D'Emilio, *supra,* pp. 58–59; p. 61; p. 62; Eric Marcus, *Making History,* interview with Chuck Rowland, pp. 26–36.

P. 51   Lou Chibarro, Jr., "Log Cabin: GOP takeover was 'best thing for Gay movement,'" *Washington Blade,* Dec. 2, 1994, p. 14.

P. 51   See, for example, Chris Bull, "Paras Is Burning," *The Advocate,* January 9, 1995; Michelangelo Signorile, "Earth to Planet Beltway," *OUT,* Dec.–Jan. 1995; Bob Roehr, *In Newsweekly,* December 9, 1994.

P. 51   Duberman, *supra,* p. 77.

P. 53   Katz, *supra,* pp. 627–631; see also, D'Emilio, *supra,* pp. 76–81.

P. 53   *Ibid.,* p. 631.

P. 54   D'Emilio, *supra,* pp. 79, 81.

P. 54   *Ibid.,* p. 79.

P. 54   Katz, *supra,* p. 631.

P. 54   Bawer, *supra,* p. 51.

Stonewall and the Birth of Gay and Lesbian Liberation

P. 55   Duberman, *supra;* Donn Teal, *The Gay Militants* (New York: Stein & Day, 1971); Marotta, *supra,* D'Emilio, *supra,* pp. 220–240; Cruikshank, pp. 69–77.

P. 55   Randy Shilts, *The Mayor of Castro Street,* pp. 56–57.

P. 55   Teal, *supra,* p. 24.

P. 56   For a history of SNCC, see *In Struggle.* For a history of SDS, see Kirkpatrick Sale, *SDS.*

P. 56   See Alice Echols, *Daring to Be Bad: A History of Radical Feminism, 1968–1975* (Minneapolis: University of Minnesota Press, 1989); Robin Morgan, *Going Too Far* (New York: Vintage, 1978); *Sisterhood Is Powerful* (New York: Vintage, 1970).

P. 56   The manifesto is reprinted in *Out of the Closets: Voices Of Gay Liberation,* Karla Jay and Allen Young, eds. (New York: Douglass Books/Quick Fox, 1970), pp. 330–345.

P. 57   Gay conservatives today dismiss this post-Stonewall generation of leaders as hopelessly orthodox, far too liberal, and unwilling to share power with succeeding generations of leaders. Their critique is more self-serving than truthful. Rich Tafel of the Log Cabin Club wrongly dismisses this post-Stonewall generation as "the first generation of gay leaders," but the Mattachine militants preceded the gay people who emerged in the 1970s by nearly twenty years. Tafel's comments also ignore the wealth of talent represented in this generation.

Among the leaders who shaped the gay, lesbian, and emerging feminist movements in this post-Stonewall period were: Rita Mae Brown, the lesbian-feminist writer and organizer; Ron Gold, Frank Kameny, Barbara Gittings, Nath Rockhill, Jeffrey Carples and Howard Brown, who founded the National Gay Task Force in 1973; Michael Seltzer, Roz Richter, the late Margot Karle, and others who started the Lambda Legal Defense and Education Fund in 1973; Virginia Apuzzo and black-lesbian organizer Betty Powell, both of whom helped build the National Gay Task Force and the Fund for Human Dignity; black gay leaders like Brandy Moore, Gilberto Gerald, Angela Bowen, Mel Boozer, and Joyce Hunter, who pioneered involvement in the mixed gay movement and helped build an autonomous black movement as

Notes

well; Jean O'Leary, Bruce Voeller, the late Jim Foster, David Goodstein, David Roth-
enberg and other early mainstream political activists.

The late Marty Robinson, Jim Owles, Arthur Bell, and others like Arnie Kantro-
witz, Arthur Evans, and others who helped found GAA; the late Craig Rodwell, who
helped nationalize the commemoration of Stonewall each June; Los Angeles lesbian
feminist leaders Diane Abbitt and Roberta Bennett, who in the 1990s founded the
ANGLE (Access Network for Gay and Lesbian Equality); and the late Leonard
Matlovich, army captain and gay rights pioneer.

Black lesbian feminist leaders Barbara Smith and Audre Lorde who co-founded
Kitchen Table Women of Color Press; veteran organizer Suzanne Pharr, who worked
in the domestic violence movement and now leads the fight against the Christian
Right; Midwestern organizers Rhonda Rivera (Ohio), Debbie Law and Kris
Kliendienst (Missouri), the late Steve Endean (Minneapolis), who founded the Gay
Rights National Lobby (GRNL); organizers Steve Ault, Pat Norman, A. Billy Jones,
Nicole Ramirez-Murray, and Leslie Cagan, who helped make the 1979 and 1987
marches a reality; long-time movement leader Eric Rofes, who started out as a staff
member of the movement publication *Gay Community News* and made huge contribu-
tions as a writer and leader in the gay and AIDS movement; lesbian organizers Carmen
Vazquez; New York City Lesbian and Gay Community Services Center Director
Richard Burns; Lambda Legal Defense and Education Fund Director Kevin Cathcart;
Boston writers Mitzel and Michael Bronski, Charley Shively, and Amy Hoffman;
lesbian sexpert Susie Bright; cultural pioneers Bernice Johnson Reagon and Amy
Horowitz, who founded Roadwork, a multiracial women's cultural foundation; Judy
Dlugacz and the artists at Olivia Records, who launched a lesbian-feminist record
company in 1976; and thousands of others who founded and built the gay and lesbian
organizations of the 1970s.

P. 59 Histories of the GLF's founding and split can be found in: Donn Teal's *The
Gay Militants*, chaps. 5, 7, 8; Duberman's *Stonewall*, pp. 219–233; Marotta's *The
Politics of Homosexuality*, chaps. 4, 6, 8; Laud Humphreys, *Out of the Closets* (Engle-
wood Cliffs, NJ: Prentice-Hall, 1972); Sidney Abbott and Barbara Love, *Sappho Was a
Right-On Woman* (New York: Stein and Day, 1972).

P. 59 Teal, *supra*, p. 50.

P. 59 *Ibid.*, p. 51.

P. 60 *Ibid.*, pp. 126–128.

P. 62 Ronald Bayer, *Homosexuality and American Psychiatry* (Princeton: Princeton
Univ. Press, 1987).

P. 62 Randy Shilts, *Conduct Unbecoming: Gays and Lesbians in the United States
Military* (New York: St. Martin's Press, 1993).

Post-Stonewall Gay and Lesbian Cultural Politics

P. 65 See, for example, Larry Kramer, *Faggots* (New York: Plume, 1987); John
Rechy, *The Sexual Outlaw* (New York: Grove, 1990); Edmund White, *States of Desire*
(New York: Plume, 1983); Michael Bronski's essays on sexual liberation in *Gay Com-
munity News;* Alice Echols, *Daring to Be Bad: Radical Feminism in America 1967–1975*
(Minneapolis: University of Minnesota Press, 1989); see also Shane Phelan, *Identity
Politics: Lesbian Feminism and the Limits of Community* (Philadelphia: Temple Univer-
sity Press, 1989). Frank Browning, *Culture of Desire* (New York: Crown Books, 1994).

P. 68 Interview with Virginia Apuzzo, July 8, 1993, New York City, pp. 16–17.

3. AIDS AND TRANSFORMATION

P. 69 "Newt Set Strategy for Religious Right—10 Years Ago," *Freedom Writer,* Feb. 1995, p. 2 (Institute for First Amendment Studies, P.O. Box 589, Great Barrington, MA 02130). Newt Gingrich was the closing keynote speaker at a conference sponsored by the now-defunct American Coalition for Traditional Values (ACTV). The conference was called "How to Win an Election" and was held in Washington DC, October 15–17, 1985.

P. 71 Among the nationally known activists who have come out of the GCN staff are journalists Chris Bull, Liz Galst, Michael Bronski, Chris Guilfoy; writers Neil Miller, Cindy Patton, Amy Hoffman, Warren Blumenfeld; activists Richard Burns, Kevin Cathcart, Sue Hyde, Eric Rofes, Wickie Stamps, Chris Witke, Jennie McNight, Harry Seng, and me. Many accomplished gay and lesbian writers, scholars, and artists contribute regularly to GCN: Sarah Schulman, Peg Byron, Peg Cruikshank, Barbara Smith, Stephen MacCauley, John Preston, Kate Rushin, Andrea Loewenstein, Bob Nelson, David France, John Zeh, Jennifer Camper, Dorothy Allison, Jewelle Gomez, Cheryl Clarke, John Mitzel, and Scott Tucker. And then there are the GCN-ers who died: Mel Horne and David Brill were murdered; Ian Johnson killed himself; Bob Andrews, David Stryker, Mike Riegle, John Preston, Sioung Huat, Craig Harris, Jim Ryan, Greg Howe, Tim Grant, Porter Mortell, Reg Taylor, Raymond Hopkins, died of AIDS-related illness.

P. 73 Jeffrey Schmalz, "Whatever Happened to AIDS?" *New York Times Magazine,* November 28, 1993; Darrell Yates Rist, "The Deadly Cost of an Obsession," *The Nation,* February 13, 1989.

Mainstream Access and the Degaying of AIDS

P. 76 Eric Rofes, *OutLook* magazine, pp. 13–14.

Visibility and Desexualization

P. 80 Notable among this early AIDS reporting is the work of gay community journalists like Anne Christine D'Adesky, Tim Kingston of *Bay Times;* Neenyah Ostrom, Ann Giudici Fettner and Chuck Ortleb in the *New York Native;* the work of writers Cindy Patton, Simon Watney, Chris Guilfoy, John Preston; the AIDS columns of treatment activists like John James, Marty Delaney, Project Inform, ACT UP, Mark Harrington and others from Treatment Action Group (TAG).

P. 81 Greg Herek, *AIDS and Stigma: A Review of the Scientific Literature,* unpublished paper, p. 22.

P. 82 I am particularly aware of AIDS and gay media visibility because I served as the public information director of NGLTF from 1986 to 1989, at the height of the media interest in these issues in the 1980s.

Early AIDS-media activism was conducted by some little-known or remembered pioneers. I think it is important to name names. Ron Najman, the former director of media for the National Gay Task Force (NGTF), which had not changed its name at that time, played a major role in securing TV news coverage of AIDS; the late film historian and ACT UP member Vito Russo was an early media spokesman; Larry Kramer harassed the straight press about its coverage for years before ACT UP was founded; former CBS "This Morning" producer and lesbian organizer Ann Northrop and gay reporter Randy Shilts pushed from inside the news industry; former NGTF Executive Directors Ginny Apuzzo and Jeff Levi who became two effective national spokespersons; and ACT UP national media pioneers Michelangelo Signorile, David Corkery, Avram Finkelstein (who co-created the Silence = Death logo), Peter Staley, Chip Duckett, Mark Kostopolous, as well as the scores of local media coordinators of

ACT UP chapters who helped organize the national demonstrations held in the late 1980s.

Others influential in winning media coverage on AIDS include gay rights attorney Tom Stoddard; former GMHC staffers Tim Sweeney and Lori Behrman; AMFAR founders Mathilde Krim, Mervyn Silverman, and Elizabeth Taylor; West Coast media advocates like Holly Smith, Paul Boneberg (of Mobilization Against AIDS), Cleve Jones (founder of the Names Project), Jean O'Leary, Leonard Graff, and Ben Schatz (all formerly of National Gay Rights Advocates); public relations experts Steve Rabin, Bob Rafsky, and Robert Bray; Washington insiders like congressional staffers Tim Westmoreland and Michael Iskowitz.

Finally, a handful of AIDS reporters in the straight press made invaluable contributions (even as some of them were severely criticized by ACT UP for the inadequacy of their coverage): Marlene Cimons *(Los Angeles Times);* Phil Boffey, Gina Kolata, Dr. Lawrence Altman, Bruce Lambert, Robert Pear, Nicholas Wade *(New York Times);* Sandra Boodman, Michael Spector, and Phil Hilts *(Washington Post);* Laurie Garrett and B. J. Colen (Newsday); George Strait (ABC); Bob Bazell (NBC); Susan Spencer (CBS).

A book on gay and lesbian issues in the media is forthcoming from Washington DC-based writer Ed Alwood. Others who have written about the straight media and AIDS, gay and lesbian coverage include: Michelangelo Signorile, *Queer in America* (New York: Anchor Books, 1994); Larry Kramer, *Reports from the Holocaust* (New York: St. Martin's Press, 1989); Craig J. Davidson and Michael G. Valentini, "Cultural Advocacy: A Non-Legal Approach to Fighting Defamation of Lesbians and Gays," *Law and Sexuality: A Review of Lesbians & Gay Legal Issues,* vol. 2 (1992), pp. 103–130; American Society of Newspaper Editors, *Alternatives: Gays and Lesbians in the Newsroom* (1990); Simon Watney, *Policing Desire: Pornography, AIDS and the Media* (1987); Randy Shilts, *And the Band Played On* (NY: St. Martin's Press, 1987), pp. 575–582 in particular; Edwin Diamond and Elyse Kroll, "Unsafe Sex and Unsafe Journalism," *Lear's* magazine, July–August 1988; A. J. Baker, "The Portrayal of AIDS in the Media: An Analysis of Articles in the *New York Times,*" in *The Social Dimensions of AIDS: Methods and Theory,* Douglas A. Feldman and Thomas Johnson, eds. (1986).

P. 83 Dr. Gregory Herek and Dr. Jeanine Gogan, "AIDS and Stigma: A Review of the Scientific Literature," November 29, 1994, p. 14. This unpublished paper was prepared for the Public Media Center and the Ford Foundation.

P. 84 See, for example, Ronald Bayer's *Private Lives, Public Consequences* (New Brunswick, NJ: Rutgers Univ. Press, 1991), which documents some otherwise untraced political history, but takes too dualistic and simplistic a view of the actual conflict confronting gay and lesbian advocates in the early years of AIDS.

P. 84 Greg Herek, "AIDS and Stigma: A Review of The Scientific Literature," p. 25, cited the following published study: Greg M. Herek, "The HIV epidemic and public attitudes toward lesbians and gay men," in M. P. Levine, P. Nardi, and J. Gagnon, eds., *The Impact of the HIV Epidemic on the Lesbian and Gay Community* (Chicago: University of Chicago Press, 1995).

P. 84 Greg Herek and J. P. Capitanio, "Public Reactions to AIDS in the United States: A Second Decade of Stigma," *American Journal of Public Health,* pp. 83, 574–577.

Decoupling AIDS from Systemic Reform

P. 87 See Ronald Bayer's *Homosexuality And American Psychiatry* (Princeton, NJ: Princeton University Press, 1987).

P. 88 Interview with Ruth Finkelstein, July 8, 1993, pp. 22–24.

P. 88 See, for example, Kramer's letter to GMHC dated February 4, 1987, reprinted in Larry Kramer, *Reports from the Holocaust: The Making of An AIDS Activist* (New York: St. Martin's Press, 1989).

P. 90   Interview with Rodger McFarlane, p. 4.
P. 91   Larry Kramer has written about this and discussed the founding of GMHC in interviews. See, for example, *Reports from the Holocaust.* Several activists I interviewed also made this observation: Rodger McFarlane, Stanley Newman, and Michael Seltzer.
P. 92   Victor Zonana, "Survivor's Syndrome: AIDS Takes Toll on Ones Left Behind," *Los Angeles Times,* May 6, 1989, p. 1+.
P. 92   Interview with Vic Basile, July 15, 1993, p. 22.

The Direct-Action Strategy and Its Decline

P. 94   For a text of this speech and an account of the founding of ACT UP, see Larry Kramer's *Reports from the Holocaust,* pp. 127–139.
P. 95   Interview with Peter Staley, June 23, 1993, pp. 5–6.
P. 96   Interview with Maxine Wolfe, pp. 62–63.
P. 97   Interview with David Barr, July 1993, pp. 7–8.
P. 97   Interview with David Barr, p. 49.
P. 98   *Ibid.,* p. 14.
P. 100   Michelangelo Signorile, *Queer in America* (New York: Anchor Books, 1994).
P. 104   Ruth Schwartz, "New Alliances, Strange Bedfellows: Lesbians, Gay Men and AIDS," *Sisters, Sexperts, and Queers: Beyond the Lesbian Nation,* Arlene Stein, ed. (New York: Plume Books, 1993), p. 239.

4. THE PREVAILING STRATEGY

P. 107   Frankel was reputed to have remarked at a staff meeting that the gay and lesbian community was the last group of people this society felt it was acceptable to reject. Meanwhile, Sulzberger appeared at gay functions, like a 1992 reception hosted by the Lesbian and Gay Journalists Association and *The Advocate* during the Democratic Convention in New York City.
P. 108   See, generally, Randy Shilts, *The Times of Harvey Milk* (New York: St. Martin's Press, 1983).

Mainstream Politics and a Gay Mainstream

P. 109   This early history is recounted by Randy Shilts in *The Mayor of Castro Street* and *Conduct Unbecoming,* by John D'Emilio in *Sexual Politics, Sexual Communities,* and by Eric Marcus in *Making History.* See John D'Emilio's *Sexual Politics, Sexual Communities,* pp. 186–192, for a summary of the forces that helped build the West Coast movement. See Eric Marcus's *Making History,* pp. 140–145. See Randy Shilts, *The Mayor of Castro Street,* pp. 57–65, for a brief history of the San Francisco political movement's development out of police crackdowns on the city's gay bars. See also *Conduct Unbecoming,* pp. 166–175, for a report on gay activist Jim Foster's speech at the Democratic Convention.
P. 109   D'Emilio, *supra,* p. 191.
P. 109   Shilts, *The Mayor of Castro Street,* p. 63.
P. 109   *Ibid.*
P. 110   Shilts, *Conduct Unbecoming,* p. 166.
P. 110   *Ibid.,* pp. 169–170.
P. 111   *Doe* v. *Commonwealth's Attorney,* certiorari denied (1975).
P. 111   Shilts, *Conduct Unbecoming,* pp. 274–275.
P. 112   *Ibid.,* p. 370. Shilts reports that Department of Defense figures showed that the armed forces fired 937 enlisted persons for homosexuality in 1975, 1296 in 1976,

and 1442 in 1977 (p. 295). "According to Defense Department figures, the four services ejected 1966 enlisted personnel for homosexuality in fiscal year 1980, more than twice the number discharged five years earlier. Gay discharges *increased* during the Carter Administration; in fact, the last year of this Democratic presidency saw more such separations than at any time since the McCarthy era" (p. 356).

P. 113 Cal. Proposition 6, Section 3(b)(2) (1978).

P. 114 E. J. Dionne, *Why Americans Hate Politics* (New York: Simon & Schuster, Touchstone Edition, 1992), p. 139.

P. 115 Shilts, *Conduct Unbecoming*, p. 348.

P. 115 *Ibid.*, p. 369.

P. 115 *Ibid.*, p. 367–368.

P. 115 Shilts, *Conduct Unbecoming*, p. 369.

P. 116 *Ibid.*, p. 346.

P. 116 See, for example, Matthew Moen's analysis of what happened to the Christian right's legislative agenda in the first six years of Reagan, in *The Christian Right and Congress* (University of Alabama Press, 1988).

P. 116 Shilts, *Id.*, p. 454.

P. 116 *Ibid.*

P. 117 *Ibid.*, p. 455.

P. 119 Anecdote told to author by Tim McFeeley.

P. 121 See "NGLTF 1988 Presidential Questionnaire and Position Paper," September 1987; "NGLTF 1988 Presidential Candidate Survey—Results," two-page chart, Spring 1988; telephone Interview with Mary Matalin, March 30, 1994.

P. 122 This was the term used recently by Capital Area Log Cabin Club chairman Carl E. Schmid II in a letter to the Editor, published in the *Washington Blade*, January 27, 1995, p. 35.

P. 122 See "Buchanan Buster," *Task Force Report* (Winter-Spring 1992), p. 1. Newsletter of the National Gay and Lesbian Task Force.

P. 124 Letter from eight members of Congress to President George Bush, February 24, 1992, protesting Mosbacher meeting with NGLTF, in author's possession and also available from NGLTF.

P. 124 Reaction to the meeting was reported in the conservative daily paper the *Washington Times*.

P. 127 See Daniel Golden, "Mixner's Moment," *Boston Globe Magazine*, June 6, 1993, p. 14+.

Legal Mainstreaming and Queer Status

P. 130 Among the lawyers who taught such courses in the early 1980s were some of the pioneers of our legal rights movement: San Francisco lawyers Donna Hitchens, Roberta Achtenberg, Mary Dunlap, and Matt Coles; Ohio State law professor Rhonda Rivera, and New York Law School professor Art Leonard; Washington-based lawyers Nancy Polikoff, Susan Silber, and Jane Dolkart; New York–based lawyers Abby Rubenfeld, Tom Stoddard, Roz Richter, and Nan Hunter; Boston attorneys John Ward, Cindy Rizzo, David Lund, and Katherine Triantafillou.

P. 130 See, for example, *The Rights of Gay People*, Tom Stoddard, ed. (New York: Bantam, 1992); *Sexual Orientation and the Law*, Roberta Achtenberg, ed. (Clark Boardman Publishers 1990); *Lesbians, Gay Men, and the Law*, William Rubenstein, ed. (New York: New Press, 1993).

Two scholarly journals dedicated to the field are the independently published *Journal of Homosexuality*, which features a wide range of original scholarly research, and a publication out of Tulane University School of Law called *Law and Sexuality: A Review of Lesbian and Gay Legal Issues*. In addition, a number of major law reviews have devoted special issues to gay and lesbian rights; a complete list can be obtained from a search of legal indexes. The National Gay and Lesbian Bar Association sponsors panels at the annual meeting of the American Bar Association, and hosts a semiannual conference called the Lavender Law Conference. Examples of local and regional bar associations include the San Francisco–based BAILIF (Bay Area Lawyers for Individual Freedom), the Massachusetts Lesbian and Gay Bar Association, the Los Angeles Lawyers for Human Rights, and GAYLAW (Gay and Lesbian Lawyers of Washington).

P. 131   See, for example, Nan D. Hunter, Sherryl E. Michaelson, Thomas B. Stoddard, *The Rights of Lesbians and Gay Men: The Basic ACLU Guide to a Gay Person's Rights* (Carbondale, Il: Southern Illinois University Press, 1992); Roberta Achtenberg, *supra; AIDS Agenda: Emerging Issues in Civil Rights,* Nan D. Hunter and William Rubenstein, eds. (New York: New Press, 1992).

See also *Lesbian and Gay Law Notes,* edited monthly by Professor Arthur Leonard, New York Law School. For pending litigation, see the dockets and publications of the Lambda Legal Defense and Education Fund, telephone (202) 995-8585; and the ACLU Lesbian and Gay Rights and AIDS Projects, telephone (212) 944-9800.

P. 131   See, for example, *Stoumen* v. *Reilly,* 234 P. 2d 969 (Cal. 1951), overturning the suspension of a liquor license to a gay bar; Mattachine's lawsuit against the LA police brought by founder Dale Jennings and described by D'Emilio in *Sexual Politics, Sexual Communities,* pp. 70–71; and the lawsuits brought in 1954–1958 by the publication *One, One, Inc.* v. *Olsen,* 355 U.S. 371 (1958), per curiam decision by U.S. Supreme Court overturning lower court decisions finding the magazine obscene.

P. 131   See D'Emilio, *supra,* pp. 112, 144–148. For a list of current sodomy statutes and penalties associated with them, contact NGLTF, Washington, DC.

P. 132   See, generally, Patricia Cain, "Litigating for Lesbian and Gay Rights: A Legal History," 79 *Virginia Law Review* 1551 (October 1993); and Nancy Polikoff, *Gay Community News* (Fall 1993).

P. 132   Arizona Rev. Stat. Ann. Section 15–716(C) (1992); Alabama Code Section 16-40A-2(a)(8) (1992).

P. 132   See D'Emilio, *supra,* p. 112, 211–214.

P. 135   David Cole and William Eskridge, Jr., "From Hand-Holding to Sodomy: First Amendment Protection of Homosexual Conduct," 29 *Harvard Civil Rights–Civil Liberties Law Review* no. 2 (Summer 1994), p. 322. See also an article by Nan D. Hunter, "Life After Hardwick," 27 *Harv. Civ. Rights Civil Liberties Review* 531 (1992). (need to get citation).

P. 135   Nan D. Hunter, "Identity, Speech & Equality," 79 *Virginia Law Review* 1695 (Oct. 1993), at 1717.

P. 135   *Ibid.,* at 1717.

P. 136   Their argument is contained in 29 *Harvard Civil Rights–Civil Liberties Law Review* no. 2 (Summer 1994).

P. 136   See Janet Halley, "Reasoning About Sodomy: Act and Identity In and After *Bowers* v. *Hardwick,* 79 *Virginia Law Review* no. 7 (October 1993) at 1721–1780; see also Patricia Cain, "Litigating For Lesbian and Gay Rights: A Legal History," 79 *Virginia Law Review* no. 7 (Oct. 1993) at 1551–1643.

P. 136   "Senate Loudly Debates Gay Ban," *New York Times,* May 8, 1993, p. A9.

P. 137   Hunter, "Identity, Speech, and Equality," *supra,* p. 1718.

The Legislation of Civil Rights

P. 140   See a very interesting article by Anna Marie Smith, "Resisting the Erasure of Lesbian Sexuality: A Challenge for Queer Activism," in *Modern Homosexualities: Fragments of Lesbian and Gay Experience,* Ken Plummer, ed. (New York: Routledge, 1992).

P. 141   See Vatican Letter on Homosexuality, 1986.

P. 143   National Institutes of Justice, 1987.

P. 144   Kevin Berrill, "Countering Anti-Gay Violence Through Legislation," (Washington, DC: NGLTF Policy Institute, 1992), p. 18.

P. 144   *Ibid.*
P. 144   *Ibid.*, p. 19.

5. THE MAINSTREAM RESPONSE

P. 148   Norman O. Brown, *Love's Body* (New York: Vintage Books, 1966), p. 32.
P. 148   Eric Schmitt, "Judge Overturns Pentagon Policy on Homosexuals," *New York Times*, March 31, 1995, p. A1.
P. 149   Jeffrey Schmalz, "Homosexuals Wake to See a Referendum: It's on Them," *New York Times*, January 31, 1993.

Why the Military Policy?

P. 152   Allan Bérubé, *Coming Out Under Fire: A History of Lesbians and Gay Men in World War II* (New York: Free Press, 1990); Randy Shilts, *Conduct Unbecoming: Gays and Lesbians in the U.S. Military.*
P. 152   Shilts, *supra*, p. 15.
P. 152   *Ibid.*, pp. 16–17.
P. 152   Department of Defense Directive 1332.12.
P. 155   Shilts's book details the stories of some of the women caught up in this witch hunt. See his Index, p. 778, under "Parris Island Marine Corps Recruit Training Depot, purge of lesbians," for the citations to the overall story of this purge.
P. 157   *Ibid.*, p. 640.
P. 160   Katharine Q. Seelye, "Gingrich Is Seeking to Restore Gay Ban in Military Services," *New York Times*, April 4, 1995, p. A1.
P. 161   Fred Barnes, "Major Dud," *The New Republic*, Feb. 15, 1993.
P. 161   *Ibid.* Barnes took the quotation from *Putting America First*, p. 64.
P. 162   Interview with Rebecca Hensler, San Francisco, July 22, 1993.
P. 163   Fred Barnes, "Clinton and the Interest Groups," *The New Republic*, April 27, 1992.
P. 163   As an aside, it should be noted that many activists argue that the movement made a big mistake in 1993 by not focusing on an executive order to reform the grant of security clearances rather than on the military policy. They are right. The treatment of gay people as security risks—and therefore our prohibition from employment in a range of jobs—runs parallel to and intersects with the history of the ban on openly gay and lesbian service. Shilts and other writers have noted the irony that one of the people most responsible for the classification of gay men and women as security risks, former FBI director J. Edgar Hoover, was himself widely known to be gay. In his first hundred days as President, Dwight Eisenhower signed into law Executive Order 10450, citing "sexual perversion" as an appropriate basis for rejecting or terminating the employment of federal workers. These classifications in turn fueled the antigay witch hunts conducted throughout the 1950s and led to the classifying of gay people with subversives, communists, and other "un-American" persons. But the history of security clearance law began to change in the early 1960s, as a result of the combined agitation of gay activist Frank Kameney and the litigation that resulted in a series of cases (beginning with *Norton v. Macy)*, which declared that sexual orientation per se was no basis for denying a security clearance. In most federal agencies, the per se denial of essential security clearances stopped by the mid-1970s, but in key agencies like the CIA and FBI, and throughout the military, such high-level classifications were routinely denied to employees discovered to be gay or lesbian.
          Drafts of executive orders ensuring nondiscrimination in the ward of security clearances had been prepared by Jeffrey Levi in 1987 and 1989; a behind-the-scenes

lobbying campaign to enact these changes began during the 1988 election year and continued through 1989, supported from inside the Bush administration by moderate Republicans. In the 1992 campaign, the security clearance issue got lost in the more dramatic issue of military reform.

P. 166 Fred Barnes, "Major Dud," *The New Republic,* Feb. 13, 1993.

P. 167 Tim McFeeley, "Operation 'Lift the Ban': The Military Freedom Project or 'Where Was HRCF?'" Memorandum to HRCF Board of Directors and Board of Governors, Feb. 11, 1993, given to author by McFeeley.

P. 168 Interview with Chai Feldblum, Feb. 24, 1994, pp. 10–13.

P. 168 Details are obtained from news reports and interviews with journalists and activists, including Chai Feldblum, Tom Stoddard, Chandler Burr, and Tim McFeeley; also see McFeeley memorandum, p. 4.

P. 169 Based on interview with Chai Feldblum, *supra.*

Where Does This Leave Us?

P. 174 "The Politics of Homosexuality: A New Case for a New Beginning," *The New Republic,* May 10, 1993, p. 37.

P. 175 *Ibid.,* p. 36.

P. 176 See Department of Defense News Release, December 22, 1993, announcing new policy, entitled "Secretary Aspin Releases New Regulations on Homosexual Conduct in the Armed Forces"; "New Policy Is Business as Usual for Military," by Michelle M. Benecke, *Washington Blade,* March 25, 1994, p. 37. See also Randy Shilts, *Conduct Unbecoming.*

P. 176 Eve Kosofsky Sedgwick, *Between Men: English Literature and Male Homosocial Desire* (New York: Columbia University Press, 1985).

P. 177 Sullivan, *supra.,* May 10, 1993, p. 36.

6: BEYOND RIGHTS AND MAINSTREAMING

P. 178 Interview with Grace Paley, *Paris Review,* vol. 34, no. 124, Fall 1992, p. 196.

The Civil Rights Framework

P. 183 See Chandler Burr, *Washington Blade,* vol. 25, no. 48, Nov. 25, 1994, p. 1+.

P. 183 Data are from the voting record of Newt Gingrich since 1978, obtained from Cathy Woolard at the Human Rights Campaign Fund, Washington, DC.

P. 184 Interview With Tim McFeeley, Sept. 6, 1993, p. 162.

P. 184 *Ibid.,* pp. 160–161.

P. 184 *New York Times,* "Many Gay and Lesbian Groups Want Big March to Back Clinton," April 18, 1993.

P. 184 See, for example, Neff Hudson, "How Effective Is 'Don't Ask, Don't Tell,'" *Air Force Times,* June 6, 1994. ("In 1993, 682 service members were discharged for homosexuality compared to 708 the previous year and 949 in 1991"); "Few Benefit From New Military Policy on Gays," *Los Angeles Times,* February 6, 1995.

P. 184 See Eric Schmitt, "Judge Overturns Pentagon Policy on Homosexuals," *New York Times,* March 31, 1995, p. A1.

P. 185 Polling data gathered by Celinda Lake indicate that the first hurdle gay rights supporters must overcome with the public is the notion that gay people do not have full civil rights. The average American does not believe that. (Data presented at March 4–6, 1994, retreat attended by author.)

P. 186 Interview with Virginia Apuzzo, July 8, 1993, New York City, pp. 26, 30.

P. 187 See *Boston Globe*, April 6, 1995, p. A8.

P. 187 See Richard Herrnstein and Charles Murray, *The Bell Curve* (New York: Free Press, 1994).

P. 187 For further discussion of the difference between the black and gay experience in the military, see, for example, an article by John Sibley Butler, "Homosexuals and the Military Establishment," *Society*, Nov.–Dec. 1993, vol. 31, no. 1.

P. 188 Richard Goldstein, "From Here to Equality," *Village Voice*, April 27, 1993, p. 22.

P. 188 Lena Williams, "Blacks Reject Gay Rights Fight as Equal to Theirs," *New York Times*, June 28, 1993, p. A1, at A18.

P. 188 Mellman, Lake, and Lazarus, "Summary of African-American Views of Gay Rights," Memorandum to the Human Rights Campaign Fund, May 9, 1994, pp. 1–2.

P. 189 Lena Williams, *supra*.

P. 189 *Ibid.*

P. 189 Henry Louis Gates, Jr., "Blacklash?," *The New Yorker*, May 17, 1993, pp. 42–44.

P. 190 *Ibid.*, p. 43.

Civil Rights Language and the Sexual Impasse

P. 194 Lisa Duggan and Nan D. Hunter, *Sex Wars: Sexual Dissent and Political Culture* (New York: Routledge, 1995), pp. 7–9.

Assimilation or Freedom

P. 204 Patrick J. Kiger, "The Gay Republican," *Gentleman's Quarterly*, Jan. 1994, p. 82.

P. 205 Memorandum from Richard Goldstein to author, 1993.

7: POLITICS AND POWER

P. 210 June Jordan, *Technical Difficulties* (Boston: Beacon Press, 1993), p. 197.

P. 210 Transcript of CBS Reports, "Gay Power, Gay Politics," as broadcast on Saturday, April 26, 1980, 10:00–11:00 P.M., EST, p. 5 and p. 9. Available from the National Museum and Archive of Lesbian & Gay History, New York City Lesbian and Gay Community Services Center, 208 W. 13th Street, New York, New York 10011.

Our Definition of Power

P. 213 Interview with Vic Basile, July 15, 1993, p. 22.

P. 221 Strub made the statement in a panel presentation at a gay and lesbian leadership retreat I attended on March 5–6, 1994. The retreat was sponsored by the Human Rights Campaign Fund and was held in Dedham, MA.

P. 223 See, e.g., Randy Shilts, *The Mayor of Castro Street, supra*, in which he recounts the tensions between these men.

P. 232 Interview with Tim McFeeley, Sept. 6, 1993, p. 25.

Liberation and Its Discontents

P. 232 See *Newsweek,* Feb. 1995.
P. 232 Vatican Letter on Homosexuality, Sept. 1986.
P. 233 Jean Bethke Elshtain, *Democracy on Trial* (New York: Basic Books, 1995), p. 38.
P. 233 *Ibid.,* pp. 54–55.

Synthesis, Politics, and Genuine Power

P. 237 bell hooks, *Feminist Theory: From Margin to Center* (Boston: South End Press, 1984), p. 91.

8: MONEY AND THE MOVEMENT

P. 238 Patti Smith Group, "Free Money," from the *Horses* album, Arista Records, 1975.
P. 239 Tony Kushner, *Angels in America: Millennium Approaches* (Theatre Communications Group, 1993), p. 45.
P. 241 Some of Signorile's columns are reprinted in Larry Gross's excellent book on outing, *Contested Closets: The Politics and Ethics of Outing* (Minneapolis: University of Minnesota Press, 1993).

The Economy of Queerness

P. 245 Jeffrey Escoffier, Opening Remarks, "Homo/Economics Conference," CUNY Center for Lesbian and Gay Studies, New York, May 1994.
P. 248 See *Boston Globe,* March 8, 1995.

Myths and Realities of Gay and Lesbian Wealth

P. 249 Martha T. Moore, "Courting the Gay Market," *USA Today,* April 23, 1993, p. 1B.
P. 250 *Ibid.,* p. 2B.
P. 250 *Ibid.*
P. 250 Liz Galst, "Reel Hate: Right-Wing Tape Pits Gays Against Blacks," *One in Ten: The Publication for Gay and Lesbian Readers,* Supplement to *The Boston Phoenix,* Oct. 1993, p. 10.
P. 250 Information based on interviews with NGLTF and CMS lobbyists.
P. 250 Jeremiah Films, "Gay Rights, Special Rights: Inside the Gay Agenda," Summer 1993, distributed by the Traditional Values Coalition, 100 S. Anaheim Boulevard, Suite 350, Anaheim, CA 92805, telephone (714) 520-0300.
P. 251 Galst, *One in Ten* supplement p. 11.
P. 251 The *Wall Street Journal* article cited in the videotape was never documented, but research by economist and University of Maryland professor Lee Badgett places it in the July 18, 1991, issue in an article about how gays are "a dream market." See pamphlet by Lee Badgett, "The Economic Status of Lesbians and Gay Men," National Organization of Gay and Lesbian Scientific and Technical Professionals and the Lesbian/Gay/Bisexual Policy Research Network, 1994.

P. 252 Jeremiah Films, "Gay Rights/Special Rights: Inside the Gay Agenda," distributed by the Traditional Values Coalition.
P. 252 Amy Gluckman and Betsy Reed, "The Gay Marketing Moment: Leaving Diversity in the Dust," *dollars and sense*, Nov.–Dec. 1993, pp. 16–19, 34–35, at p. 17.
P. 252 Badgett, *supra.*
P. 252 H. G. Bissinger, "The Killing Trail," *Vanity Fair*, Feb. 1995, p. 80+.
P. 253 *Ibid.,* p. 88.
P. 253 *Ibid.,* p. 143.
P. 253 Lee Badgett, *supra.*
P. 253 *Ibid.*
P. 254 *Ibid.* The pamphlet compares readership/marketing data from the Simmons Market Research Bureau surveys and the Bureau of Census publications.
P. 254 Gluckman and Reed, *supra,* p. 19.
P. 254 Stuart Elliott, "A Sharper View of Gay Consumers," *New York Times,* June 9, 1994, p. D1.
P. 254 *Ibid.,* at p. D19.
P. 255 Professor M. V. Lee Badgett, "Economic Evidence of Sexual Orientation Discrimination," unpublished paper, Nov. 1993 (School of Public Affairs, University of Maryland, College Park, Maryland 20742).
P. 255 Gluckman and Reed, *supra,* p. 18.
PP. 255–56 *Ibid.,* pp. 19, 34–35. The article by Jonathan Rausch is "Beyond Oppression," *The New Republic*, May 1993.
P. 259 Peter Freiberg, "Poll: 1 in 3 Gays Voted for the GOP," *Washington Blade*, column 26, no. 48, Nov. 25, 1994, p.1 at 25.
P. 259 Mark Miller, "The Newt Era: Is It Good for the Gays?", *Out* magazine, March 1995, p. 61.

Myths and Realities of Funding the Movement

P. 261 Kristina Campbell, "Gingrich Confirms He'll Hold GI Hearing About Gay Issues," *Washington Blade*, vol. 26, no. 3, Jan. 20, 1995, p. 1+, at p. 27.
P. 262 Consider the names: Human Rights Campaign Fund, Lambda Legal Defense and Education Fund, Triangle Institute, Pride Foundation (Seattle), Heritage of Pride (New York), Empire State Pride Agenda (New York), Dignity, Integrity, Lutherans Concerned, Fund for Human Dignity (now defunct). A notable example of a previously closeted organization that has came out fully in 1994 and changed its name is the prestigious gay doctors' group that went from being the American Association of Physicians for Human Rights (AAPHR) to the Gay and Lesbian Medical Association.
P. 264 Information based on conversation with Tim McFeeley, March 7, 1995.
P. 267 Sean Strub, panel presentation on "The Market and the Future of Community," at the Homo/Economics Conference, sponsored by the Center for Lesbian and Gay Studies, City University of New York, May 10, 1994.

Political Impact of Economic Realities

P. 271 Interview with Jeff Soref, June 23, 1993, p. 14.
P. 271 *Ibid.,* p. 20.
P. 272 *Ibid.,* pp. 61–62.
P. 273 *Ibid.,* pp. 65–69.

9: DIVIDED WE STAND

P. 274 Quotation from Antonio Gramsci, *Prison Notebooks*, cited from Nadine Gordimer, *The Essential Gesture: Writings, Politics & Places* (New York: Penguin Books, 1988), p. 263.

Understanding Intersectional Politics

P. 279 Remarks by Urvashi Vaid at Symposium on "Stonewall at 25 . . . And Beyond," sponsored and taped by the *Harvard Civil Liberties/Civil Rights Law Review*, Harvard Law School, April 9, 1994.

P. 282 Charlotte Bunch, "Making Common Cause: Diversity and Coalitions," in *Passionate Politics: Feminist Theory in Action, Essays 1968–1986* (New York: St. Martin's Press, 1987), p. 153.

P. 282 *Ibid.*, pp. 154–156, 156.

P. 282 Notes of Ivy Young to manuscript, 1994.

P. 284 Mandy Carter expressed this frustration at a retreat on the religious right that she and I attended in Nov. 1994.

Strategies: Multiculturalism and Coalitions

P. 286 Suzanne Pharr, "Multi-Issue Politics," *Transformation*, v. 9 no. 1, Jan/Feb 1994, p. 2.

P. 286 *Ibid.*

P. 287 *Ibid,* p. 101.

P. 291 The National Coalition Against Domestic Violence used to receive more than $800,000 in federal funds. It was dependent on that income for its survival. In 1985, the Reagan Justice Department, under Ed Meese, began to dyke-bait the organization by questioning the presence of lesbians on its board. The ensuing internal splits caused by the threatened loss of funds resulted in the fracturing of NCADV and in its eventual collapse. This story is recounted by the lesbian organizer Suzanne Pharr, who served as co-chair of the NCADV board during that period.

P. 296 Barbara Smith, "Where's the Revolution?" *The Nation*, July 5, 1993, p. 14.

P. 297 See, for example, Andrew Sullivan, "The Politics of Homosexuality," *The New Republic*, May 10, 1993.

10: THE SUPREMACIST RIGHT

P. 307 Anti-Defamation League, *The Religious Right: The Assault on Tolerance and Pluralism in America* (New York: ADL Publications, 1994), p. 30.

P. 307 *Ibid.*, p. 40.

P. 308 *Ibid.*, p. 4. Randall Terry is quoted from an article in the *Fort Wayne News Sentinel*.

P. 308 Ralph Reed, "Conservative Coalition Holds Firm," *Wall Street Journal,* Feb. 13, 1995.

P. 309 *Ibid.*

P. 310 Sara Diamond, *Spiritual Warfare: The Politics of the Christian Right* (Boston: South End Press, 1988). Diamond has also written extensively on the right in *Z* magazine, and other progressive publications. Political Research Associates is located in Cambridge MA, telephone: (617) 661-9313. The Center for Democratic Renewal is located in Atlanta GA, telephone: (404) 221-0025. The Institute for First Amendment Studies is in Great Barrington MA, telephone: (413) 274-3786. The Data Center is in Oakland CA, telephone: (510) 835-4692.

Background of the Supremacist Right

P. 310   Sidney Blumenthal, "Christian Soldiers," *The New Yorker*, July 18, 1994, p. 35.

P. 311   See, generally, Sara Diamond, *supra*, and in particular, pp. 45–81, 54. See also Matthew C. Moen, *The Christian Right and Congress* (Tuscaloosa: University of Alabama Press, 1989), pp. 9–31.

P. 311   Diamond, *supra*, p. 60.

P. 311   ADL, *The Religious Right*, p. 92.

P. 311   *Ibid.*, pp. 93–94.

P. 312   *Ibid.*, pp. 94–97.

P. 312   Howard Fineman, "The Warrior," *Newsweek*, Jan. 9, 1995, p. 33.

P. 312   See Matthew C. Moen, *The Christian Right and Congress*, chaps. 3–7.

P. 312   ADL, *The Religious Right*, p. 93, quoting from a January 26, 1984, *New York Times* op-ed piece by Weyrich entitled, "Beware, Reagan's Vulnerable."

P. 313   ADL, *The Religious Right*, p. 65.

P. 313   *Ibid.*, p. 17.

P. 313   Diamond, *Spiritual Warfare*, p. 72.

P. 313   *Ibid.*, p. 73.

P. 314   *Ibid.*, p. 80.

P. 314   Garry Wills, *Under God: Religion and American Politics* (New York: Simon & Schuster, 1990), p. 267.

P. 314   *Ibid.*, p. 183. Wills takes this phrase from a biography of Robertson by Jeffrey K. Hadden and Anson Shupe, *Televangelism: Power and Politics in God's Frontier* (New York: Henry Holt, 1988), p. 189.

P. 314   Pat Robertson, *The Turning Tide: The Fall of Liberalism and the Rise of Common Sense* (Dallas: World Publishing 1993), p. 61.

P. 314   ADL, *The Religious Right*, pp. 69–70.

P. 315   *Ibid.*, p. 27.

P. 315   Blumenthal, *The New Yorker*, July 18, 1994, p. 37.

P. 315   Pat Robertson, *The Turning Tide*, p. 63. Robertson explains the so-called 15 percent solution on pp. 62–65.

P. 315   Craig Goldin, "The 15 Per Cent Solution: How the Christian Right Is Building from Below to Take Over from Above," *Village Voice*, April 6, 1993, p. 19.

P. 316   Todd S. Purdum, "A Conversation with Mario Cuomo, Ann Richards, and Lowell Weicker," *New York Times Magazine*, March 20, 1995, p. 38.

P. 316   Ralph Reed, Jr., "Casting a Wider Net—Religious Conservatives Move Beyond Abortion and Homosexuality," *Policy Review* (Heritage Foundation), Summer 1993.

P. 317   Adam Meyerson, "Manna 2 Society: The Growing Conservatism of Black America," *Policy Review*, Spring 1994, p. 5.

P. 317   *Ibid.*, pp. 4–5.

P. 317   Deborah Toler, "Black Conservatives, Part I and II," *The Public Eye*, Sept. 1993 and Dec. 1993 (Cambridge, MA: Political Research Associates, 1993), Part I, p. 2.

P. 318   *Culture Watch*, August 1993, item #163, p. 3.

P. 318   ADL, *The Religious Right*, p. 38.

P. 318   *Ibid.*, pp. 38–39.

P. 318   *Ibid.*, p. 6.

P. 319   *Ibid.*, p. 4.

P. 319   Garry Wills, *supra*, p. 25.

P. 319   *Stars in The Constitutional Constellation: Federal and State Constitutional Provisions on Church and State*, annotated and edited by Steven K. Green and Regina

Reaves Hayden (Americans United Research Foundation, 900 Silver Spring Avenue, Silver Springs, MD, 20910, 1993), p. ii.

P. 319 *Ibid.*, p. iii.

P. 320 An invaluable resource to activists in this area is a fact sheet, published by the Institute for First Amendment Studies in Massachusetts, that refutes point by point the leading Christian arguments on the separation of church and state. The institute also distributes three useful documents: Rob Boston, *Why the Religious Right Is Wrong about Separation of Church and State* (Prometheus Books); *Stars in the Constitutional Constellation, supra;* and a videotape called "America's Constitutional Heritage" (ACLU Video). Institute for First Amendment Studies, P.O. Box 589, Great Barrington, MA 01230, telephone: (413) 274-3786.

Antigay Campaigns of the Right

P. 320 Jeffrey Weeks, *Sexuality and Its Discontents* (London and New York: Routledge, 1985), pp. 32, 44.

P. 321 Focus on the Family, "In Defense of a Little Virginity," advertisement in the *Boston Globe,* July 18, 1994, p. 7.

P. 321 See, for example, the amendments attached to the appropriations bill for the National Endowment for the Arts (NEA) since 1989. An instance occurred in Cobb County, Georgia, in 1994, when the Cobb County Commission withdrew funding for a local arts institution because it sponsored a play with gay and AIDS themes.

P. 321 See Dr. Jean Hardisty, "Constructing Homophobia: Colorado's Right-Wing Attack on Homosexuals," *The Public Eye,* March 1993 (Political Research Associates, 678 Massachusetts Avenue, Cambridge, MA 02139).

P. 322 In 1994, the Christian Right circulated petitions to place anti-gay ballot measures in nine states: Arizona, Iowa, Idaho, Washington, Ohio, Maine, Missouri, Florida, and Oregon. They secured enough signatures to put two statewide measures in play in November 1994. In addition, Christian activists mounted local campaigns to challenge city council and county commission laws in a number of cities and counties; at least two were voted on that month, in Alachua County, Florida, and Oberlin, Ohio. For the most recent rundown of antigay ballot campaigns, contact Karen Bullock-Jordan at the NGLTF Fight the Right Project, telephone: (202) 332-6483.

P. 322 Dr. Jean Hardisty, supra, p. 2.

P. 323 Randy Shilts, *The Mayor of Castro Street,* pp. 238–250.

P. 323 The count of antigay ballot measures always shifts as new ones are introduced. The National Gay and Lesbian Task Force Fight the Right Project maintains a list called "The Record on Gay-Related Referenda Questions." My conclusion is based on the NGLTF list available as of the end of 1994.

P. 323 The Supreme Court of Colorado's decision is *Evans* v. *Romer,* 854 P. 2d 1270 (Colo. 1993). The lawsuit was filed on November 12, 1992. Following an evidentiary hearing, a preliminary injunction was granted by the Denver District Court on January 15, 1993. Defendants appealed to the Colorado Supreme Court. On July 16, 1993, the Colorado Supreme Court upheld the award of the preliminary injunction. The case was tried on its merits in 1994, and decided for the plaintiffs.

P. 323 Ellen Debenport, "Governor Candidate: 'I Don't Know Gays, I Wouldn't Hire Any,'" *Miami Herald,* June 17, 1994, p. 1A.

P. 324 Suzanne Pharr, "How Wrong Can the Right Be?: Pedophilia and the Endangerment of Children," *Transformation,* May/June 1993, vol. 8, issue 3, p. 1.

P. 324 *Ibid.,* p. 5.

P. 325 Hardisty, "Constructing Homophobia," p. 3.

P. 325 Gene Antonio, *The AIDS Cover-Up* (San Francisco: Ignatius Press, 1986); Bill Dannemeyer, *Shadow Over the Land: Homosexuality In America* (San Francisco: Ignatius Press, 1989); Michael Fumento, *The Myth of Heterosexual AIDS* (Washington: Regnery Gateway, 1993).

P. 325   Mark E. Pietrzyk, "Queer Science: Paul Cameron, Professional Sham," *The New Republic,* Oct. 3, 1994.

P. 326   *Ibid.*

P. 326   GLMA, *The Silent Crisis, supra,* p. 17.

P. 326   See, for example, Jim Kinsella, *Covering the Plague;* Randy Shilts, *And the Band Played On* pp. 320–324; Larry Kramer, *Reports from the Holocaust;* Laurie Garrett, *The Coming Plague.*

P. 327   Shilts, *And the Band Played On,* pp. 347, 352.

P. 328   See the National Gay and Lesbian Task Force's list of Gay-Related Referenda Questions.

P. 330   Jane S. Schacter, "The Gay Civil Rights Debate in the States: Decoding the Discourse of Equivalents," 29 *Harvard Civil Rights/Civil Liberties Review* 2, Summer 1994, pp. 283–317, 285.

P. 330   Suzanne Pharr, "Eliminating Civil Rights," p. 2.

P. 330   *Ibid.,* p. 291.

P. 331   Tim Kingston, *supra,* p. 5.

P. 331   Pharr, *supra,* p. 286.

P. 331   Schacter, pp. 296–297, 296.

P. 331   Data presented by Celinda Lake at workshop attended by author. HRCF Leadership Retreat, March 4–5, 1994, Dedham, MA.

P. 331   Suzanne Pharr, "Racist Politics and Homophobia," p. 2.

P. 332   Randy Shilts, *Conduct Unbecoming,* p. 298.

P. 332   *Ibid.,* p. 303.

P. 333   Tim Kingston, "Blueprint for Hate: Contents of Secret Colorado Anti-Gay Election Kit Revealed," *San Francisco Bay Times,* May 19, 1994, p. 5.

P. 333   Jane Schacter, "The Gay Civil Rights Debate in the States," p. 294.

Our Response, Our Future

P. 336   Arendt, p. 323. Hannah Arendt, *The Origins of Totalitarianism* (Cleveland: World Publishing Co., 1966).

P. 337   *Christianity Today,* March 1995.

P. 337   Ralph Reed, "Conservative Coalition Holds Firm," *The Wall Street Journal,* Feb. 13, 1995.

P. 337   Arendt, *supra,* 346.

P. 338   *Ibid.,* p. 361.

P. 338   *Ibid.,* p. 367.

P. 339   John Weir, "In God's Country," *Details,* May 1994.

P. 339   Figures are taken from the 1993 edition of *Challenging the Christian Right: An Activist's Handbook,* by Fred Clarkson and Skipp Porteous (Great Barrington, MA: Institute for First Amendment Studies). The figures change annually. Other leading groups on the Christian Right include Free Congress Research Foundation, Family Research Council, National Association of Christian Educators, Operation Rescue, Traditional Values Coalition, Eagle Forum, the Report, Rutherford Institute.

P. 340   Suzanne Pharr, "The Christian Right: A Threat to Democracy," pp. 2–3. This is a publication of the Women's Project in Little Rock, Arkansas, and it has collected as a monograph several articles by Pharr published in past issues of the magazine. Contact Women's Project, 2224 Main Street, Little Rock, Arkansas 72206.

P. 341   ADL Report, p. 69.

P. 342   Sara Diamond, *supra,* p. 107.

P. 342   ADL Report, *The Religious Right,* p. 127.

P. 342   See Fred Clarkson, "HardCOR," an article on the Coalition on Revival, *Church and State,* Jan. 1991, reprinted in *Challenging the Christian Right: The Activist's Handbook.*

P. 344   For a useful overview, see John F. Niblock, "Anti-Gay Initiatives: A Call for

Heightened Judicial Scrutiny," *UCLA Law Review*, vol. 41, no. 1 (Oct. 1993) pp. 153–198. See also decisions in the following court cases: *Equality Foundation of Greater Cincinnati* v. *City of Cincinnati*, 838 F. Supp. 1235 (S.D. Ohio 1993); *Evans* v. *Romer*, 854 P.2d 1270 (Sup Ct. Colorado 1993); *Citizens for Responsible Behavior* v. *City of Riverside*, 1 Cal.App.4th 1013, 2 Cal. Rptr. 2nd 648 (Cal. App. 1991); *Jester* v. *City of Concord*, No. C91–05455 (Cal. Sup. Ct., Nov. 16, 1992).

P. 344 Mary Newcombe and Suzanne Goldberg, "Anti-Lesbian and -Gay Right-Wing Initiatives: A Strategy for Response," *The Guild Practitioner* (National Lawyers Guild), vol. 50, no. 3 (Summer 1993), p. 94.

11: LEADERSHIP CONUNDRUMS

P. 346 Luis Alfaro is a gay Latino poet and performance artist from Los Angeles. This quotation is from his solo performance, *downtown*.

P. 347 Aras van Hertum, "AIDS Action Council's Dan Bross resigns," *Washington Blade*, Sept. 2, 1994, p. 1+, at p. 35.

P. 347 Debbie Kong, "Ranks of ACT UP Members in O.C. Dwindle to Just 1," *LA Times/Orange County Edition*, Feb. 6, 1995.

P. 348 Among these critics I include myself, activists like Barbara Smith, Paula Ettlebrick, Kathy Acey, and writers like Adrienne Rich, Donna Minkowitz, Julia Penelope.

P. 348 These critics include Bruce Bawer, Marvin Liebman, and the writers Paul Varnell, Stephen Miller, and Rich Tafel.

P. 349 These include people as diverse as Michael Petrelis, Luke Sissyfag, Margaret Cantrell, Ann Northrop, Maxine Wolfe, Wayne Turner, Sandra Johnson, and Sarah Schulman.

P. 350 Larry Bush, "San Francisco's Nightmare: Anti-Gay Gays Take Charge," *New York Native*, Dec. 7, 1992, pp. 18–19.

P. 350 Johnson recounted a specific incident involving a prominent, straight black leader at the Gay and Lesbian Leadership Retreat I attended in Laguna Beach in 1990. He discussed his anger and pain at being asked to divide loyalties he considered indivisible.

P. 351 These include elected and appointed officials, like Barney Frank, Gerry Studds, Sherry Harris, Harry Britt, Ken Reeves, Carole Migden, Marjorie Hill, Karen Clark, Allen Spear, Ginny Apuzzo.

Definition

P. 352 Author interview with Richard Burns, Sept. 1, 1993, Provincetown, MA, p. 63.

P. 352 Larry Kramer, "Why We Are Failing," *The Advocate*, Aug. 13, 1992, p. 39.

P. 353 Interview with Larry Kramer, June 24, 1994, p. 66.

P. 354 Garry Wills, "What Is Political Leadership?" *The Atlantic Monthly*, April 1994, pp. 63–80, 64; see also Garry Wills, *Certain Trumpets: The Call of Leaders* (New York: Simon & Schuster, 1994).

P. 355 Wills, *The Atlantic Monthly*, p. 70.

P. 355 Author's interview with Susie Bright, July 19, 1993, San Francisco, pp. 33, 36.

P. 355 Author interview with Ruth Finkelstein, July 8, 1993, New York City, pp. 66–67.

PP. 355–56 Author interview with Maxine Wolfe, July 6, 1993, New York City, p. 79.

P. 356 Author interview with Charles Stewart, July 28, 1993, Los Angeles, p. 2.
P. 356 *Ibid.*, p. 21.
P. 356 Author interview with Jeff Soref, June 23, 1993, New York City, pp. 17–18.
P. 357 See *Webster's New World Dictionary*, second college edition (William Collins Publishing, 1979).

Sources of Our Ambivalence toward Leadership

P. 363 GLMA, *The Silent Crisis, supra*, p. 70.
P. 364 For an extensive discussion of these media realities, see Michelangelo Signorile, *Queer in America*.
P. 364 While exceptional stories may appear in many of the weekly papers in the gay and lesbian press, and certainly in the gay monthly and bimonthly magazines, they are not the rule. On a consistent basis, the gay press that tries to report on the movement and its leadership includes *The Washington Blade*, San Francisco's *Bay Area Reporter* and *Bay Times*, Chicago's *Windy City Times*, Boston's *In Newsweekly*, and Denver's *Out Front*.

Horizontal Hostility

P. 365 A notable exception to this is the opening plenary speech by Eric Rofes, given on July 22, 1993, at the National Lesbian and Gay Health Conference in Houston. The speech was entitled, "Roots of Horizontal Hostility in the Lesbian and Gay Community," and analyzed how the experience of being terrorized by bullies while growing up affects gay men psychologically. An excerpted version of the speech was published in *Gay Community News*, Spring 1994.
P. 365 Author interview with Richard Burns, Sept. 1, 1993, pp. 54–55.
P. 367 Robin Stevens, "Eating Our Own," *The Advocate*, Aug. 13, 1992, p. 36.
P. 367 *Ibid.*, pp. 33–41.
P. 369 Dan Golden, "Mixner's Moment," *Boston Globe*, June 6, 1993.

12: THERE ARE THINGS TO DO

P. 373 The title and quotation are from an essay calling on white Southerners to take action about racial inequality. The essay, written in 1942–1943 by the white Southern writer Lillian Smith, was brought to my attention by Minnie Bruce Pratt. Lillian Smith, "There Are Things to Do," in *From the Mountain*, White and Sugg, eds. (Memphis: Memphis State University Press, 1972), p. 117.

The Vision Thing or What Are We For?

P. 378 *Ibid.*, p. 281.
P. 379 Harry Hay, "A Separate People Whose Time Has Come," in *Gay Spirit: Myth and Meaning*, Mark Thompson, ed. (New York: St. Martin's Press, 1987), p. 280.
P. 381 Larry Gross, *Contested Closets: The Politics and Ethics of Outing* (Minneapolis: University of Minnesota Press, 1994). Gross provides an excellent and comprehensive discussion and collects many original gay and lesbian press texts of the debate over outing. Michelangelo Signorile, *Queer in America* (New York: Anchor Books, 1994). Signorile is the best known and most eloquent proponent of outing. Richard Mohr, *Gay Ideas: Outing and Other Controversies* (Boston: Beacon Press, 1992). Mohr is an

original thinker whose insight and moral grounding make him a thoughtful correspondent on outing and other moral dilemmas.

P. 381 Suzanne Pharr, "A Moral Imperative," *supra.*, p. 5.

P. 381 *Ibid.*, p. 2.

P. 382 *Ibid.*, p. 3.

P. 382 See, for example, John D'Emilio, "Capitalism and Gay Identity," in *Powers of Desire;* William N. Eskridge, Jr., "A History of Sam Sex Marriage," 79 *Virginia Law Review* no. 7 (Oct. 1993), pp. 1419–1511; Nan D. Hunter, "Marriage, Law and Gender: A Feminist Inquiry," 1 *Law & Sexuality* 9 (1991); Barry D. Adam, "Sex and Caring Among Men: Impacts of AIDS on Gay People," *Modern Homosexualities*, Ken Plummer, ed. (New York: Routledge, 1992), pp. 175–183.

P. 382 This is something I think Phyllis Burke does in her book *Family Values* (New York: Random House, 1992).

P. 383 This is the title of a book by Bronski to be published by St. Martin's Press.

P. 383 Alicia C. Shepard, "Challenging the Moral and Political Values of a Troubled America," *San Jose Mercury News*, Nov. 11, 1994, quoting Jim Wallis and quoting from his book, *The Soul of Politics* (New York: Knopf, 1994).

P. 383 See James Q. Wilson, *The Moral Sense* (NY: The Free Press, 1993); Stephen Carter, *The Culture of Disbelief* (Yale University Press, 1993).

P. 384 Profile of Michael Petrelis, *The Advocate,* 1993.

P. 384 Based on conversation with HRCF director Tim McFeeley, who was present when this happened, as were more than 150 people.

P. 384 Based on conversation with Kevin Cathcart on that same night. Kevin came to the hotel where I was staying and described the incident, which had taken place in front of several Lambda board members and donors.

P. 384 Larry Bush, "San Francisco's Nightmare: Anti-Gay Gays Take Charge," *New York Native*, Dec. 7, 1992, pp. 18–19.

P. 385 Interview with David Barr, July 9, 1993, pp. 16–17.

P. 385 Martin Luther King, Jr., "The American Dream," *The Essential Writings and Speeches of Martin Luther King, Jr.*, James Washington, ed. (San Francisco: Harper San Francisco, 1986), p. 214.

P. 386 Panel discussion at the New School for Social Research, Sandy Lowe, Richard Goldstein, and Urvashi Vaid, June 24, 1993.

Movement Restructuring

P. 388 See Leo Bersani, *Homos* (Cambridge: Harvard University Press, 1995).

P. 389 Former NGLTF directors Ginny Apuzzo and Jeffrey Levi spoke out often about the distinction between the gay and lesbian movement's pre-AIDS and post-AIDS stance toward government. See, for example, Levi's speech to the National Press Club, October 9, 1987 (C-SPAN).

P. 391 An interesting footnote to this came in 1994, during the legislative battle to re-authorize the bill for another four years. An unsuccessful effort was brought by Midwestern activists to rewrite the formula by which the Ryan White Act allocated funds to different communities. Rather than the funding being linked to the incidence of AIDS in different communities, these activists pressed for an equal distribution of funds to all states. The effort failed but divided the AIDS lobbying community in Washington.

P. 391 Zillah R. Eisenstein, *The Color of Gender: Reimagining Democracy* (Berkeley: University of California Press, 1994), p. 53.

P. 391 *Ibid.*, pp. 129–130.

INDEX

ABOUT THE AUTHOR

Urvashi Vaid is a community organizer and attorney whose involvement in the gay and lesbian movement spans fifteen years. From 1986 to 1992, she served as Public Information Director and Executive Director of the National Gay and Lesbian Task Force. In 1994, Vaid was named one of *Time* magazine's "Fifty for the Future," a list of America's most promising leaders age forty and under.

Printed in the United States
by Baker & Taylor Publisher Services